Piping System Fundamentals

The Complete Guide to Gaining a Clear Picture of Your Piping System

SECOND EDITION U.S.

Ray T. Hardee, P.E. & Jeffrey L. Sines

ESI PRESS ■ Engineered Software Inc.
4529 Intelco Loop SE ■ Lacey, WA 98503
360-412-0702 ■ ESIPRESS.COM

Piping System Fundamentals:

The Complete Guide to Gaining a Clear Picture of Your Piping System

U.S. Edition

Engineered Software, Inc. can be found on the web at: www.eng-software.com

Ordering Information

For related titles, additional copies, and support materials visit www.ESILearning.com or call 800.786.8545

Notice of rights

Engineered Software, Inc.
4529 Intelco Loop SE
Lacey, WA 98503
800.786.8545
360.412.0702
360.412.0672 FAX

LIMITATION OF LIABILITY

First Edition ISBN: 978-0-918601-10-0
Second Edition ISBN: 978-0-918601-12-4
PSF-V0312

Printed and bound in the United States of America.

Contents

About the Authors

Ray T. Hardee, P.E.
CEO & Chief Engineer of Engineered Software, Inc.

One of the principal founders of Engineered Software, Ray Hardee is also co-owner and Chief Engineer. Starting in 1982, Hardee was chiefly responsible for engineering and sales for Engineered Software. Prior to establishing Engineered Software, Hardee had over 13 years in the power generation industry. Hardee graduated with Honors from the United States Merchant Marine Academy in Kings Point, NY. Upon graduation, Hardee became an officer in the U.S. Naval Nuclear Power program and qualified submarines. After the Navy, Hardee worked for Ebasco Services and was involved in the start-up and test group where he would perform the pre-operational tests for both nuclear and fossil power plants. Hardee has contributed dozens of articles and papers to various magazines and standards publications and has given over a thousand presentations on fluid piping around the world.

Jeffrey L. Sines
Engineering Training Lead with Engineered Software, Inc.

Currently the Engineering Training Lead, Jeff Sines has also been an instructor and support engineer for Engineered Software products since joining the company in 2008. Sines began his career as an electrician in the U.S. Navy Nuclear Power Program in 1986. He was selected for the Enlisted Commissioning Program and earned his Bachelor's of Science degree in Mechanical Engineering from the University of Texas in Austin. Following commissioning and completion of additional nuclear power training, he served as reactor mechanical division officer and Chemistry and Radiological Controls Assistant aboard a nuclear-powered cruiser. After nine years in the Navy, Sines worked for 11 years at Weyerhaeuser as a production supervisor, operations training coordinator, and power house engineer at a specialty pulp mill. He worked closely with operators, maintenance technicians, and staff engineers to troubleshoot and repair system problems, meet production goals, and implement numerous modernization projects.

Foreword

by Ray T. Hardee

In 2007, as a member of a Hydraulic Institute committee developing a book on *Optimizing Pumping Systems*, I was asked to write a chapter on pump and system interaction. This effort was initiated because of the committee's concern about the general lack of understanding about pumped system operation. During that same period, I was asked by the Crane Company to conduct a half-day course at a refinery in Louisiana on how the *Crane Technical Paper 410, Flow of Fluids Through Valves, Fittings, and Pipe* could be used in an operating plant.

After completing the sections for the Hydraulic Institute's publication and the course for the Crane Company, I realized that the material would be an excellent starting point for a book about piping system fundamentals. The focus of the first edition was to demonstrate the value of gaining a clear picture of the operation of the total piping system by building upon the interrelationship between the various elements that make up the system. In addition, I focused on the need to understand how various items of equipment should be operated to reduce operating, maintenance, and capital costs.

After completing the first edition of *Piping System Fundamentals: The Complete Guide to Gaining a Clear Picture of Your Piping System* in 2008, I developed a two-day companion training course with the same name. I originally anticipated the course attendees would be recent college graduates or engineers with limited experience. After two other engineers at Engineered Software and I taught around 75 courses totaling around 2,000 attendees, we discovered that many of the attendees were engineers with 5 to 15 years of experience seeking a good refresher on the fundamentals. The customer mix included engineers at design firms, owners/operators of industrial plants, and process equipment sales representatives who needed to gain a better understanding of the total system. One of the benefits of having such a diverse group of attendees is their ability to share their specialized knowledge of piping systems with others in the course and with their instructors.

After reviewing feedback from the attendees, in 2011 the course content underwent a major revision to better meet the needs and expectations of our customers to include content we didn't originally cover and remove content that didn't add as much value. Due to the extent of the course changes it was decided at that time we needed to come out with a second edition of *Piping System Fundamentals*. As Engineered Software's Training Lead, Jeffrey Sines, had been instrumental in the major revision to the training course, I determined that the second edition of the book would be greatly enhanced by utilizing his skills as a co-author on this release. His research, writing and real-world engineering knowledge were invaluable in developing this book.

The objective of the second edition was to help people involved with industrial piping systems gain a better understanding enabling them to increase plant safety and reliability while reducing operating, maintenance, and capital costs. In this second edition, more emphasis has been placed on understanding the flow of energy within the piping system and giving the reader the ability to quantify that energy in terms of various engineering units enabling them to calculate the financial cost of that energy.

More emphasis has also been placed on building the foundation of knowledge needed to understand the total piping system by providing clear definitions for common terminology, engineering units, and the physical laws that govern the flow of fluid in a piping system.

With this in mind, three key topics have been added to the book or greatly expanded since the first edition.

- Considering tanks and vessels provide a key piece of information about the piping system, namely a boundary condition defining the total energy state of the fluid in the tank, they warranted a much more in-depth treatment. In the first edition, tanks and vessels were briefly mentioned in the "Piping System Components" chapter. We have since dedicated a full chapter on tanks and vessels.
- Secondly, piping systems exist to carry out processes that alter the properties of the working fluid. To emphasize the importance of this, a high level look at various types of processes are discussed in a new chapter, along with the unique equipment designed to carry out these processes. This chapter now includes some material originally located in the "Piping System Components" chapter in the first edition. Now a full chapter titled "Processes and Process Equipment" has been added.
- Finally, because it is important to measure and control the processes that occur in the piping system, a high-level look at the role of process measurement and controls is examined. The "Flow Meter" chapter from the first edition was pulled into this chapter, but more types of flow meters are now covered along with instruments used to measure fluid pressure, temperature, and tank level. Major elements in a process control loop are discussed including the PID controller, the importance of tuning a control loop, and various types of control methods.

Common pieces of equipment found in a piping system are described in detail throughout the book, including the function of the equipment, the theory of operation, how it should be properly operated to reduce operating cost and maintenance cost, how to troubleshoot operating problems with the equipment, and what information is required to be an educated consumer.

Each chapter has been greatly expanded to include additional key equations, concepts, and images to support the discussion in the text of the chapter. For example, the chapter on pumps now includes an equation to calculate the total head of a pump, better cutaway images to explain the theory of how a pump works, concepts such as the importance of running the pump within a reasonable range of the BEP, and what things can be done to stop a pump from cavitating. A concise equation is presented to calculate the cost of the power that is being added to the fluid by the pump and calculations are done to determine if a variable speed drive is economically feasible compared to flow control with a control valve.

A separate chapter on valves and fittings was written to allow additional discussion on the application of different types of valves, how their hydraulic resistance can be characterized, and what contributes to the amount of head loss across the fitting. Equations are presented to calculate the cost of head loss and compare energy and power consumption of various types.

The control valve chapter has been expanded to provide more discussion of the purpose and role of the components of a control valve, how the trim affects the valve's characteristic curve, and how valves are classified by leak tightness and pressure and temperature considerations. More attention is given to cavitation and choking in a control valve and the considerations for sizing and selecting control valves. Lastly, examples are given to demonstrate the use of the control valve equations to size a valve, calculate the pressure drop and head loss across the valve, calculate the cost of the head loss, and determine flow rate through a control valve.

The chapter entitled "Total System" has been expanded to describe the operation of single path open systems, branching systems, single loop closed systems, and multiple loop closed systems. The siphon effect is explored in more depth, including understanding what would cause a siphon, when would this be advantageous or undesirable, and what can be done to alleviate the siphon effect. Understanding the performance of a branching system is covered in more detail, along with new equations given for calculating static head in a system. Considerable time is spent in developing visualization techniques to provide a clear picture of the energy addition and consumption in different types of systems. In addition to more discussion on the use of the pump and system resistance curves, another method is presented that shows the graph of the total fluid energy state as a function of the distance traveled in the piping system, which provides a clear picture of how more complicated systems with multiple destinations can be evaluated.

Finally, a key addition to this second edition is the application of the system knowledge to develop troubleshooting techniques. These techniques can be applied to recognize abnormal operating conditions and evaluate if the condition is understandable considering the hydraulic performance of all the components in the system. The troubleshooting technique then methodically narrows down the root cause to explain what is being seen in the actual system. This section has a tremendous amount of value to those who operate, maintain, supervise, or are in any capacity responsible for troubleshooting problems affecting the production rate and bottom line of companies with piping systems in their facilities.

The second edition incorporates over 90 additional pages of information, charts, graphs, and images providing a comprehensive view of the interaction for the various components found in industrial pumped systems. We've also included a CD at the back of this book that contains a PIPE-FLO Professional demo program and 36 demo files that support various calculations shown in this book. If there is a PIPE-FLO demo file associated with an image or example exercise, the following symbols are used to reference the demo file: **PF** ⓢ

Ultimately, the second edition of *Piping System Fundamentals* should provide tools and knowledge to better understand system operation and how to troubleshoot problems in a piping system.

Acknowledgements

Writing a book is a daunting task that requires the efforts, knowledge, and skills of many people. We'd like to thank all of the individuals who contributed to this second edition.

First and foremost, we would like to thank the customers and training attendees who provided feedback and professed the need for a comprehensive book about piping systems. Without their suggestions and willingness to share their examples, this book might not have had three new chapters.

Special thanks go to Natalie Jensen, the Marketing Manager for Engineered Software. Without her assistance with the use of the InDesign software this project would have taken much longer to complete. In addition, she spent many hours obtaining permissions to use the images in the book, which greatly enhances the ability to convey key concepts.

There were several engineers at Engineered Software who contributed to the success of this book as well. George Stephens, Roy Lightle, Jesse Bahr, Christy Bermensolo, Buck Jones, and Chris Luzik contributed knowledge and time to review various sections of the book to ensure technical accuracy as well as correct misspellings and grammatical errors.

This edition was also reviewed by several engineers outside of Engineered Software. Special thanks go to the following:

- Mike Pemberton, Manager of Energy Performance Services for ITT (Goulds)
- Mike Volk, owner of Volk & Associates and noted pump system author, trainer and consultant
- Tom Angle, Vice President of Engineering for Hidrostal AG (a Swiss-based pump manufacturer)
- Greg Case, owner of PD^3 (Pump Design, Development & Diagnostics)
- Hans Vogelesang, owner of Pump Support in the Netherlands and noted pump trainer and consultant
- Gunnar Hovstadius, PhD, US Department of Energy consultant and owner of Hovstadius Consulting

Finally, we'd like to thank all the companies who have given permission for the use of their images in both the first and second editions. Without their images this book would surely miss it's mark.

While the authors bear sole responsibility for the content and any possible innacuracies, this book expounds on the principles of understanding energy flow through a piping system, and quantifying it in order to design piping systems more efficienctly. We hope this book clarifies why total system understanding is important, and how it can be used to improve future system designs.

Jeffrey L. Sines
March 2012

Chapter One

Introduction

Chapter 1: Introduction

A piping system consists of tanks, pumps, valves, and components connected together by pipelines to deliver a fluid at a specific flow rate and/or pressure in order to transport mass and energy to perform work or make a product. The piping system may also contain a variety of instrumentation and controls to regulate the processes that are occuring within the boundaries of the piping system.

The configuration, working fluid, and purpose of the piping system will vary depending on the application, but there are fundamental concepts, principles, and mathematical relationships that apply across industries and disciplines. Piping systems meet the needs of a variety of applications including:

- Industrial and commercial heating & cooling applications
- Process piping systems in chemical plants and refineries
- HVAC chilled water systems and hydronic heating systems
- Municipal water supply, irrigation, and dewatering applications
- Pharmaceutical process systems
- Ultra pure water systems used in pharmaceutical and integrated chip manufacturing
- Marine and shipboard applications
- Waste collection and treatment systems

Most textbooks on fluid dynamics limit the study of piping systems by isolating the various items in the system and evaluating them individually. For example, one learns how to calculate the energy of a fluid anywhere in the system using the Bernoulli equation and how to determine the head loss in a fully charged pipe with a Newtonian fluid, but little effort goes into learning what happens when multiple pipelines are connected. The study of pumps is often limited to how the impeller imparts kinetic energy to the fluid and how the casing converts the energy of the fluid to potential energy, but may not cover Net Positive Suction Head and what can be done about a cavitating pump.

After entering the work force, we continue to look at the piping system as a collection of the various parts. We talk to a valve vendor when we have a problem with a control valve, a pump vendor for pump problems, and an instrument vendor when there are control issues. However, seldom is there a vendor to call when there is a problem with the overall piping system that affects its operation. As a result, we are typically left to our own devices to gain a clear understanding of how the total piping system operates.

The objective of this book is to provide piping system practitioners (engineers, designers, maintenance supervisors, and plant operators) with the fundamentals of how the total piping system operates. Our approach is to look at the big picture of what elements are in the system, focus in on each element to provide a basic understanding of how each works, and then gain an understanding of how the elements operate together as a whole.

It is not our objective to overwhelm the reader with complex mathematical formulas or to derive the equations involved in describing system operation. However, many devices in a piping system have a well-defined mathematical relationship that can best be described with an equation or using a graph. We will present these in such a way that one can gain an understanding of the hydraulic performance of the various devices and what is happening in the overall piping system.

In addition to using equations and graphs, and because good communication is critical to any operation, we will also be concise and consistent with the language and nomenclature we use in this book. Appendix A is the nomenclature for the terminology that is used in the equations, along with the units associated with the terms. Appendix B is a glossary that provides clear definitions for key terms used throughout the book.

The Value of a Clear Picture

Once a piping system is designed and built, it is turned over to the operators to operate and the maintenance crews to maintain. Support personnel such as supervisors, process engineers, environmental engineers, maintenance foremen, and training coordinators provide knowledge and resources to those directly responsible for the daily operation and maintenance of the piping system. The more knowledge each of these groups of personnel have about the system and how it works, the more reliably the system will be operated, resulting in increased worker safety, improved product quality with a reduction in variability, and reduced environmental emissions.

To see the piping system clearly, the system boundaries must be defined, including where the system begins and ends, what devices are installed in the system, and how all the devices in the system are configured. For complex systems, it is often useful to break the system into more manageable sub-systems and understand how the boundary conditions in the sub-system are affected by operation in the rest of the system.

Clear Picture of System Operations

A clear picture of the total piping system provides a better understanding of the "normal" operating conditions of the system, including the expected ranges of flow rates, pressures, temperatures, tank levels, and other system parameters. It involves more than just knowing the values of these parameters, but also understanding why and how they change at different operating conditions.

The clear picture also includes understanding the function and expected hydraulic performance of the individual devices installed in the system. Equipment performance is typically characterized by how the pressure (or head) changes with the flow rate through the device.

Understanding system operation also includes knowing what processes are occurring in the piping system, and how these processes are measured and controlled. A key aspect to this is knowing the relevant physical laws that apply to the system and how the working fluid properties change and affect the system operation.

Clear Picture For Troubleshooting

Because a piping system is a collection of devices interconnected with pipelines, a problem manifested in a component in one part of the system may have its root cause in another part of the system. This makes it difficult to troubleshoot problems in a complex piping system.

A clear picture not only provides a better understanding of the "normal" operating conditions of the system, it also helps to identify abnormal conditions and to quickly troubleshoot the system when an operational problem is encountered.

Clear Picture of System Energy Consumption and Costs

Transporting the working fluid requires the addition of energy to the fluid to overcome the energy losses that occur in every device in the piping system. Energy loss occurs due to friction, noise, and vibration and shows up as inefficiencies in the motor and pump, and as head loss in the pipelines, valves, fittings, and other components.

There are various forms of energy throughout the piping system. The energy source may be AC or DC electricity that turns a motor, chemical energy in a fuel that drives a combustion engine, or thermal energy in steam that drives a turbine. The output of the driver is mechanical energy in the form of a rotating shaft, which is then converted by a pump into hydraulic energy in the fluid in the form of pressure, velocity, and elevation head.

Of course, energy costs money. The more energy loss there is in the system, the more energy has to be added to deliver the working fluid to the end users at their required flow rate and pressure. In addition, the energy loss causes wear and tear on the piping system components, so the more energy loss in the system the higher the maintenance costs will be. For the engineers who design the system, one goal is to reduce the amount of energy required to transport the working fluid to the end users. For the team looking to optimize a piping system, their goal is to reduce the energy losses in the system so that the energy addition (and operating and maintenance costs) can be reduced.

Elements of a Piping System

A piping system is made up of a variety of items or elements that are connected together, as shown in a typical single path open system in Figure 1-1. This system consists of a supply tank that is open to atmosphere, a supply pump, a component such as a heat exchanger, and a pressurized product tank. It also contains various types of instrumentation and controls such as level, temperature, flow, and pressure measurements; as well as flow and temperature meters, controllers, and control valves. All of these individual devices are connected by pipelines, valves, and fittings to transport the working fluid throughout the system. The performance of each device in the system affects the operation of the other devices in the system.

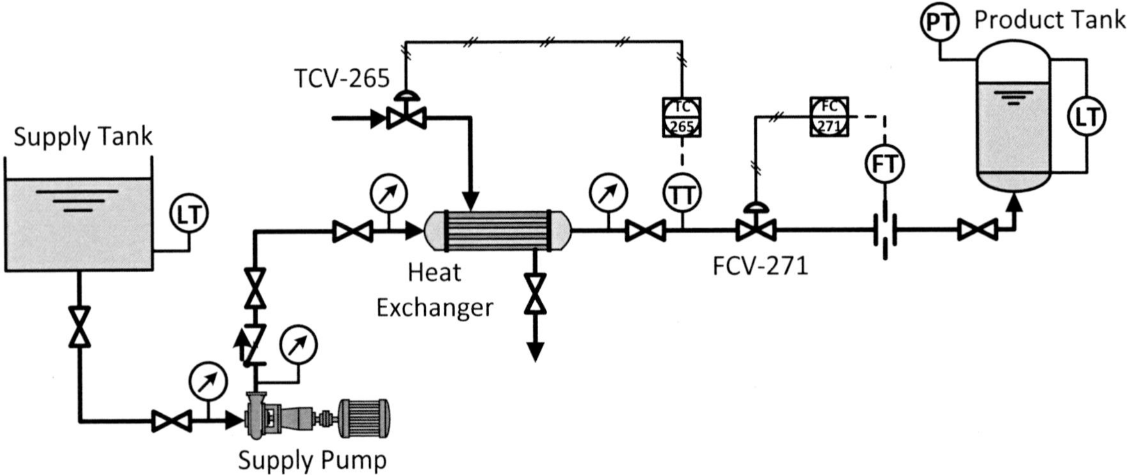

Figure 1-1. Typical single path open piping system.

There are several processes occuring in this system such as heat and mass transfer. These processes are governed by physical laws that have been well-established by scientists and engineers throughout history. For example, the conservation of mass and energy apply throughout the piping system, as well as the application of Pascal's Law to the pressure distribution in the system.

This piping system can be considered a sub-system of a much larger system that may exist at a facility. What's not shown is the system that transfers fluid to the supply tank, the distribution of the fluid from the product tank, or the piping system for the heating or cooling fluid on the shell side of the heat exchanger. This shows the importance of dividing complex systems into more manageable sub-systems at well-defined boundaries.

To have a clear picture of how this system operates, we need to have knowledge about the process or system demand, how each device operates, what is happening in each device, and how that affects the fluid properties. We also need to understand how those properties are changed by the processes in the system, and how the properties affect the hydraulic performance of the interconnected devices.

Every piping system has unique operating characteristics depending on how the system is configured. Figure 1-2 shows a typical single path closed loop system that can be found in many heating or cooling applications in various industries. This system contains a lot of the common devices we may see in an open system such as tanks, pumps, heat exchangers, instrumentation, pipelines, valves and fittings.

Of course, in many industries the piping systems are not limited to single path open or closed loop systems. There are many multiple path open branching systems and multiple path closed loop systems depending on the particular application of the system. Each system has unique operating characteristics that provide challenges when trying to understand how they operate and how to troubleshoot problems in the system.

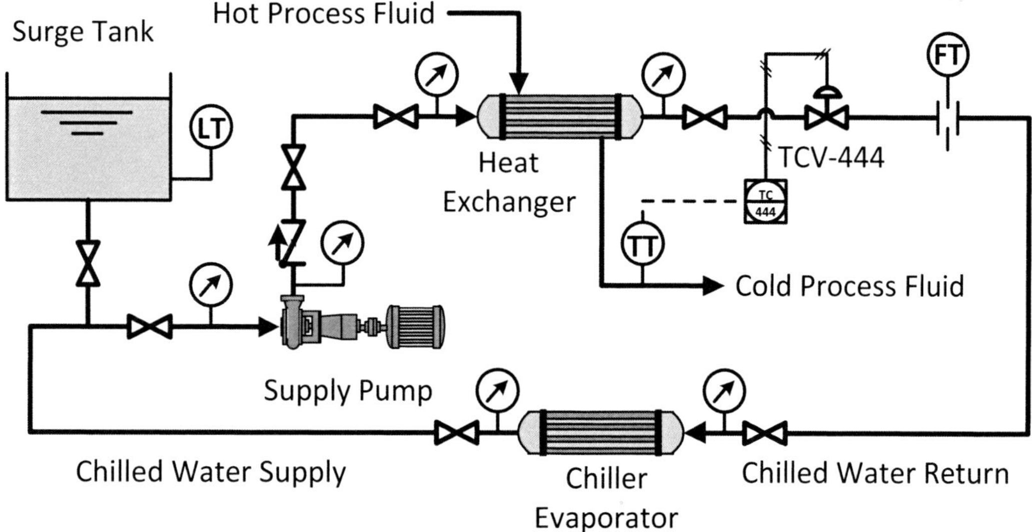

Figure 1-2. Typical single path closed loop piping system used to control the temperature of a chilled process fluid.

The key to understanding any piping system is to gain an insight into the operation of the individual elements, then to look at the entire piping system to see how the individual parts work together.

This book is divided into chapters to explore each element that makes up a piping system, then looks at the total system to see how the individual parts work together. It concludes by demonstrating how understanding the normal operation of a system can be used to effectively troubleshoot abnormal conditions caused by various problems that can occur in different devices.

Terminology, Units, and Physical Laws

Before we look at the individual elements of a piping system, we want to establish a solid foundation for the terminology, nomenclature, units, fluid properties, and basic mathematical relationships that are used throughout this book. Key physical laws that govern how the system operates will also be discussed.

Tanks and Vessels

Tanks and vessels play an important role in establishing the boundary conditions for a piping system and provide a location for dividing complex systems into smaller, more manageable systems for analysis.

Pumps

Pumps are unique devices in a piping system in that they add hydraulic energy to the working fluid of the system. Pumps come in two types, kinetic (dynamic) and positive displacement. Since the majority of piping systems employ centrifugal pumps, the most common kinetic type, they will be our focus when looking at pumps.

Pipelines

Pipelines are the building block of every piping system. They contain the working fluid and connect the various elements in the piping system together. Pipelines are a source of energy loss due to friction between the internal pipe walls and the working fluid. Pipelines are generally thought of as circular conduits, but can be other shapes such as rectangular duct, annular piping, or open channels.

Valves and Fittings

Valves and fittings are also a source of energy loss from the fluid, but play a key role by connecting pipelines, isolating equipment, redirecting flow, or preventing reverse flow.

Control Valves

Control valves are variable resistance devices placed in a piping system to regulate a system parameter such as the fluid pressure, flow rate, temperature, etc. They control the amount of energy dissipated across them by varying the shape and size of the flow passage.

Process Measurements and Controls

Key system properties such as pressure, flow, and tank level, or fluid properties such as temperature, pH, or conductivity, must be measured and controlled to ensure the requirements of the end users are met. There are various devices to measure these properties and various methods to control them.

Processes and Process Equipment

The piping system exists to perform a process on the working fluid to achieve an objective, whether it is to transfer energy, perform work, or transform raw materials into an intermediate or final product. Processes include various mechanisms for heat transfer, the transfer of mass or energy, or momentum transfer. Unique equipment such as heat exchangers, filters, washers, and absorption or cooling towers are designed to carry out these processes.

The Total System

In the Total System chapter, we will use the information presented in the previous chapters to obtain an overall system approach to understanding the operation of the piping system. Using smaller systems, key concepts will be presented to help understand the operation of larger, more complex open and closed loop systems. Two methods to visualize the energy addition and consumption in the system will be discussed. We will also look at how to troubleshoot a piping system given normal and abnormal operating conditions.

Understanding Energy Consumption and Cost

Three case studies will be presented to demonstrate how to minimize operating, maintenance, and capital costs.

Chapter Two

Terminology, Units, and Physical Laws

This chapter reviews the terminology, units, and physical laws used throughout the rest of the book. It also presents key mathematical relationships and equations that are universally applicable to a wide range of fluids and piping systems. This may be a review for many but provides a solid foundation for the terminology, nomenclature, units, and concepts used in the rest of the chapters. A fluid dynamics class is not a prerequisite for understanding this next section. Many college level fluids classes spend the majority of time deriving equations and include a fair amount of calculus. In this piping system fundamentals book, we will not derive equations, but instead focus on understanding what the variables in the equations tell us about the operation of the piping system.

Fluid Properties

Mass and Weight

Mass (m) is a measure of the amount of matter in a given volume of fluid and has units of pounds mass (lbm). Weight, in units of pounds force (lb or lbf) is the force exerted by a fluid due to its mass and the gravitational force acting on it. Mass and weight are often used interchangeably, but the distinction should not be over-looked. The weight of a given mass of fluid is given by Equation 2-1, which is Newton's second law.

$$Weight = \frac{mg}{g_c}$$ *Equation 2-1*

where: $g = 32.2 \frac{ft}{sec^2}$ and $g_c = 32.2 \frac{lbm \cdot ft}{lbf \cdot sec^2}$ on earth

The constant g_c is a dimensional constant used to allow Newton's second law to be used with the English system of units. By substituting g and g_c into Equation 2-1, it is easy to see that 1 lbm weighs 1 lbf on earth, which is why the terms are used interchangeably.

Density

Density is a measure of how closely the atoms or molecules of a substance are to each other and can be expressed in terms of a fluid's mass or weight. Weight density (ρ) is the weight of a substance per unit volume, in units of pounds per cubic foot (lb/ft^3).

$$\rho = \frac{Weight}{Volume}$$ *Equation 2-2*

Specific Gravity

Specific gravity (SG) is a relative measure of the weight density of a fluid compared to water and is unitless. For liquids, the specific gravity is the ratio of the fluid's weight density at a specified temperature to that of water at 60 °F (62.37 lb/ft^3). For gases, the specific gravity is the ratio of the molecular weight of the gas to that of air at standard conditions of 14.7 psia and 60 °F.

$$SG = \frac{\rho_{liquid}}{\rho_{water}}$$ *Equation 2-3*

Specific Volume

Specific Volume ($\bar{V}$) is a measure of the amount of volume occupied by a given weight of fluid and has units of cubic feet per pound (ft^3/lb). It is the reciprocal of the weight density and is typically used to describe gases since the density of a gas is a very small number.

$$\bar{V} = \frac{V}{m} = \frac{1}{\rho}$$ *Equation 2-4*

Viscosity

Viscosity is a measure of a fluid's ability to flow and varies widely depending on the fluid's temperature. As temperature increases, the viscosity decreases for liquids but increases for gases. Pressure has only a very small effect on the viscosity of liquids and ideal gases and can be neglected, but the effect of pressure on the viscosity of steam is much greater and should be taken into account. For vapors other than steam, the data for the pressure effect on viscosity is incomplete and sometimes contradictory and is often neglected because of the lack of adequate data.

Viscosity can be expressed as an absolute or kinematic viscosity. Absolute viscosity (μ) is a measure of a fluid's resistance to internal deformation or shear when acted upon by an external force. There are many units for absolute viscosity in both US and metric units, but one unit that is universally used by the Crane Technical Paper No. 410 and the majority of fluids textbooks (even with US units) is the centipoise (cP), which will be used throughout this book.

- Bunker C fuel oil is highly viscous, in the range of 100 - 1000 cP
- Water has a medium viscosity, in the range of 0.2 - 1.9 cP
- Gases and steam have a low viscosity, in the range of 0.007 - 0.05 cP

Kinematic viscosity (ν) is the ratio of the absolute viscosity to the mass density and represents a fluid's ability to flow when only acted upon by gravitational forces. The unit for kinematic viscosity is the stoke (St), with the relationship between the two viscosity units given in Equation 2-5.

$$\nu = \frac{\mu}{SG}$$ *Equation 2-5*

Vapor Pressure

Vapor pressure (P_{vp}) is the pressure at which a liquid at a given temperature changes phase to a gas. Vapor pressure is typically tabulated in units of pounds per square inch absolute (psia) in most fluid property references. The vapor pressure of a liquid is a function of the liquid and its temperature. As the temperature increases, the vapor pressure increases.

To better understand vapor pressure, consider an enclosed liquid at rest. When the liquid evaporates, vapor molecules escape from the liquid's surface and enter the space above the surface. When this space becomes saturated, any additional vapor molecules will cause some of the vapor to condense and drop back into the liquid. Equilibrium is reached when the rate of evaporation from the liquid equals the rate of condensation from the vapor. The pressure exerted by the vapor molecules on the surface is the liquid's vapor pressure. When the pressure above the fluid drops below the vapor pressure, vapor bubbles form in the liquid and boiling occurs.

Vapor pressure is also refered to as the fluid's saturation pressure.

Flow Rate Terms and Units

The flow of fluid in a pipe can be described in several ways: by its volumetric flow rate, its mass flow rate, or its average fluid velocity as shown in Figure 2-1.

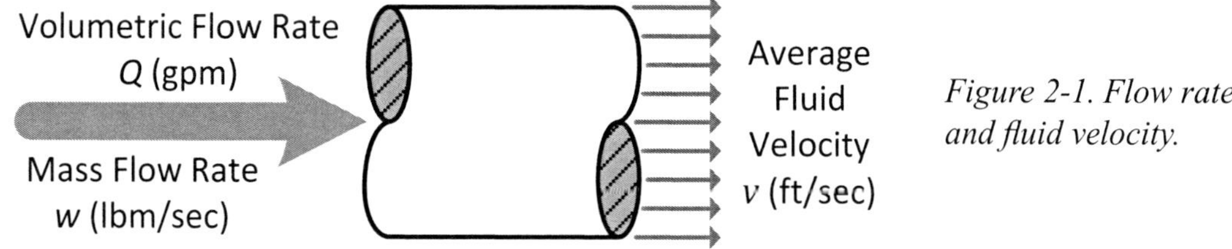

Figure 2-1. Flow rate and fluid velocity.

Volumetric Flow Rate

The volumetric flow rate is the volume of fluid passing through a plane per unit time. The nomenclature for volumetric flow rate is Q when expressed in US units of gallons per minute (gpm) or q when expressed in units of cubic feet per second (ft^3/sec). Other common units used are cubic feet per minute, gallons per day, and barrels per day. Volumetric flow rate is obtained by multiplying the flow area (A, in feet squared) times the average fluid velocity (v, in feet/sec), as shown in Equation 2-6.

$$q = Av \qquad \textit{Equation 2-6}$$

The conversion of volumetric flow rate in ft³/sec to gpm is given in Equation 2-7, using 1 minute = 60 seconds and 1 ft³ = 7.48052 gallons.

$$Q = 448.8\, q \qquad \textit{Equation 2-7}$$

Mass Flow Rate

The mass flow rate is a measure of the amount of mass passing through a plane per unit time and can be calculated by multiplying the volumetric flow rate times the fluid density (ρ in lb/ft³), as shown in Equations 2-8 and 2-9, depending on the units used. Mass flow rate w is in units of pounds per second (lb/sec) or W in pounds per hour (lb/hr).

$$w = \rho q \qquad \textit{Equation 2-8}$$

$$W = 8.021\, \rho\, Q \qquad \textit{Equation 2-9}$$

Fluid Velocity

The average fluid velocity (ft/sec) for flow in circular piping can be calculated knowing the flow rate in gpm and the inside pipe diameter (d in inches) using Equation 2-10.

$$v = 0.4085 \frac{Q}{d^2} \qquad \textit{Equation 2-10}$$

Fluid Energy

Pressure

Pressure (P) is a measure of the amount of force acting on a surface per unit area and is typically expressed in units of pounds per square inch (psi). Pressure can also be expressed in terms of the height of a column of mercury (inches Hg) or water (inches water column) that can be supported by the pressure, with the following equivalencies:

1 psi = 2.04 ″Hg = 27.6 ″wc = 2.31 feet of head

Absolute and Gage Pressure

Pressure is traditionally based on one of two datum-referenced values, absolute pressure or gage pressure, as shown in Figure 2-2. Absolute pressure (in units of *psia*) is referenced from a perfect vacuum, which is a volume that has no atoms or molecules of any substance. Although a perfect vacuum cannot be achieved on the surface of the earth, it serves as a convenient reference point for expressing values of pressure.

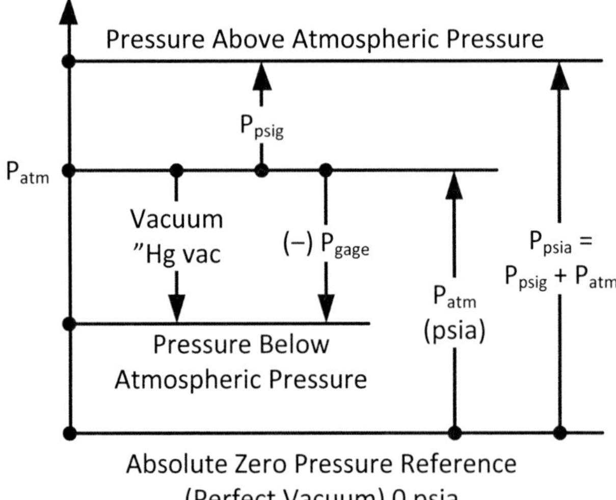

Figure 2-2. Graphical representation of pressure when referenced to absolute and atmospheric.

Gage pressure (in units of *psig*) uses the local atmospheric pressure as the datum reference. Atmospheric, or barometric, pressure varies with elevation and is the weight per unit area of a column of air at a given elevation. For example, at sea level the Standard Atmospheric Pressure is defined as 14.696 psia, whereas the local atmospheric pressure in Denver, Colorado, (about 5200 feet above sea level) is approximately 12.1 psia. Atmospheric pressure also varies by about +/- 0.5 psi with weather conditions.

Absolute and gage pressures are related by Equation 2-11.

$$P_{psia} = P_{psig} + P_{atm} \qquad \textit{Equation 2-11}$$

Vacuum

Vacuum is a value of pressure below the local atmospheric pressure and is usually expressed in inches of mercury for high vacuums and inches of water column for slight vacuums. Vacuum can also be expressed as a negative value of gage pressure. Figure 2-2 shows the relationship between absolute pressure, gage pressure, and a vacuum.

Total, Static, and Dynamic Pressure

Pressure can also be expressed as a total, static, or dynamic pressure as related in Equation 2-12.

$$P_{total} = P_{static} + P_{dynamic} \qquad \textit{Equation 2-12}$$

Static pressure is the pressure that most industrial pressure gages measure and is the pressure a fluid exerts on other molecules around it and to the pipe walls. It would be the pressure felt if moving along with the flow.

Dynamic pressure is an expression of all the fluid's kinetic energy, or velocity head, in units of pressure, and can be calculated with Equation 2-13 knowing the density in lb/ft^3, the average fluid velocity in ft/sec, and g = 32.2 ft/sec^2.

$$P_{dynamic} = \frac{\rho}{144} \cdot \frac{v^2}{2g} \qquad \textit{Equation 2-13}$$

The relationship between total, static, and dynamic pressures can also be seen in Figure 2-3 in which a pressure tap on the side of the pipe measures the static pressure and the pitot tube inserted into the flow stream measures the total pressure. The difference between the heights of columns of fluid represents the dynamic pressure.

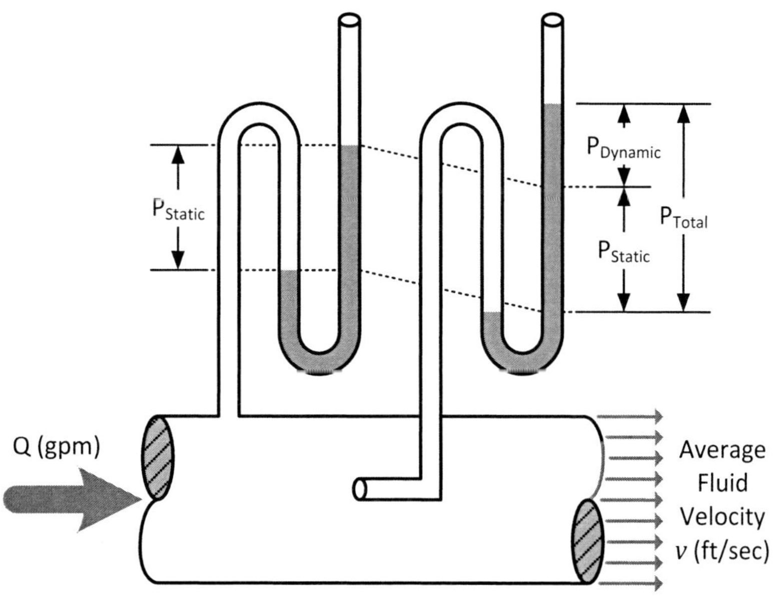

Figure 2-3. Total, static, and dynamic pressures.

Head and Hydraulic Energy

The term "head" is used to describe the energy content of a liquid per unit weight as referenced from a datum. Using Equation 2-14, with energy in units of foot • pounds and unit weight in pounds, it can be seen that head is expressed in units of feet of liquid.

$$Head = \frac{Energy}{Unit\ Weight} = \frac{ft \cdot lb}{lb} = ft \qquad \textit{Equation 2-14}$$

There are three forms of hydraulic energy in a fluid:

- Elevation head (Z) is the amount of energy a fluid has due to its vertical height above (or below) a reference datum plane. Elevations are commonly measured from sea level or the grade of a facility, but can be measured from any plane as long as the user is consistent when defining elevations in the piping system.
- Pressure head is the amount of energy a fluid has due to its static pressure and can be calculated using Equation 2-15 knowing the fluid's pressure and density (ρ in lb/ft^3).

$$Pressure\ Head = \frac{144\ P}{\rho} \qquad \textit{Equation 2-15}$$

- Velocity head is the amount of energy a fluid has due to its velocity. It can be calculated using Equation 2-16 with the fluid's velocity in feet per second and the gravitational constant, $g = 32.2$ ft/sec^2.

$$Velocity\ Head = \frac{v^2}{2g} \qquad \textit{Equation 2-16}$$

Hydraulic Grade and Static and Dynamic Head

The sum of the fluid's elevation and pressure head is called the static head, which is also called it's Hydraulic Grade. The velocity head is also refered to as the fluid's dynamic Head.

Pressure and Head Equivalencies

Pressure and head are equivalent ways to describe the fluid energy shown in Figure 2-4, it can be shown that:

$$H = \frac{144\ P}{\rho} \quad or \quad P = \frac{\rho\ H}{144} \qquad \textit{Equation 2-17}$$

Equation 2-17 can be expressed using specific gravity instead of the fluid density by substituting in the density of water at 60 °F = 63.37 lb/ft^3, resulting in Equation 2-18 as a commonly used form for the conversion between pressure and head.

$$H = \frac{2.31\ P}{SG} \quad or \quad P = \frac{H \times SG}{2.31} \qquad \textit{Equation 2-18}$$

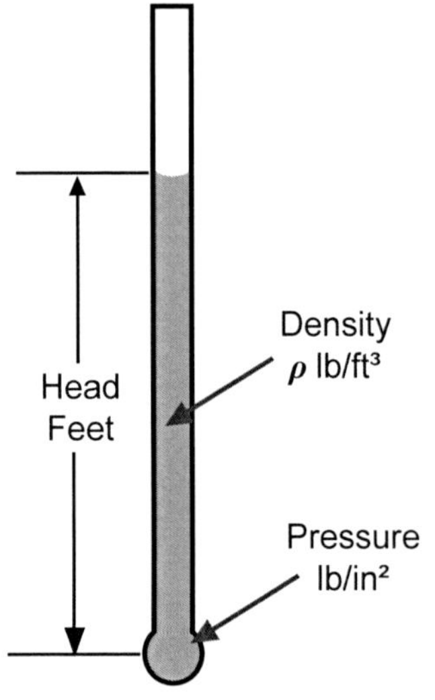

Figure 2-4. Pressure shown as an equivalent column of fluid at rest.

As shown in Equations 2-15 and 2-17, the pressure head of a fluid depends on its density. This means that the energy content at a given pressure will vary for different fluids. Consider the fluids in Figure 2-5, all at 100 psi. Notice that as the density of the fluid decreases, the hydraulic head of the fluid increases to maintain the same pressure.

For example, water at 60 °F with a density of 62.4 lb/ft^3 has a head of 230.8 feet at 100 psi, whereas water at 200° F has a lower density of 60.1 lb/ft^3 and a higher head of 239.6 feet. The energy content of the higher temperature water is greater than the energy content of the lower temperature water.

A typical gasoline with a lower density of 49.9 lb/ft^3 has a head of 288.6 feet, but 40% NaOH with a density of 92.0 lb/ft^3 has a head of 156.5 feet.

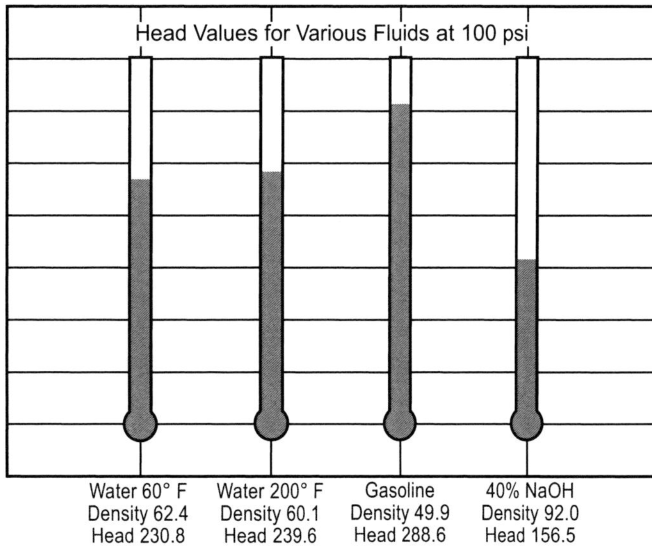

Figure 2-5. Values of head for various fluids at 100 psi.

Head Loss

As fluid flows through a pipeline, friction and changes in fluid momentum cause some of the hydraulic energy to be converted to non-recoverable energy in the form of heat, noise, and vibration. This energy loss, or head loss, is no longer capable of producing work.

Head loss (h_L) is measured in units of feet and is seen as a reduction in the static pressure of the fluid. It can be calculated using various methods that will be described later in Chapter 5 on pipelines. For horizontal pipelines with no elevation changes or changes in the pipe diameter, it can also be calculated using two pressure measurements and Equation 2-19.

$$h_L = \frac{144\, dP}{\rho} \qquad \textit{Equation 2-19}$$

Conversely, if the head loss is calculated, then the pressure drop or differential pressure resulting from the head loss can be determined using Equation 2-20.

$$dP = \frac{\rho\, h_L}{144} \qquad \textit{Equation 2-20}$$

Physical Laws that Govern Fluid Flow

In addition to having a good foundation for the terminology and units used in discussing fluid flow, it's also important to build a solid foundation for some of the key physical laws that apply to fluid flow in a piping system. This section is intended only to introduce these laws, not to go in-depth into the vast body of knowledge behind each of them.

Conservation of Mass

The conservation of mass states that the sum of the mass flow rates entering the system must equal the sum of the mass flow rates leaving the system, plus the amount of mass accumulated in the system over a given time period. This can be described mathematically using Equation 2-21.

$$\sum w_{in} = \sum w_{out} + \frac{\Delta mass}{\Delta time} \qquad \textit{Equation 2-21}$$

In a steady state system, there is no accumulation of mass in the system so the sum of the mass flow rate into the system equals the sum of the mass flow rate out of a system, as shown in Equation 2-22.

$$\sum w_{in} = \sum w_{out} \qquad \textit{Equation 2-22}$$

Conservation of mass plays a key role in analyzing a piping system and when evaluating tank level changes in non-steady state flow or transient conditions.

Conservation of Momentum

Momentum (p) is the product of a fluid's mass and its velocity as shown in Equation 2-23, but not only does it have a magnitude, it has direction as well. When a fluid flows through an elbow for example, the magnitude of the velocity may not change but its direction does. This generates a force on the pipe walls that creates vibration and energy loss from the fluid resulting in a pressure drop across the elbow.

$$p = mv \qquad \textit{Equation 2-23}$$

Conservation of Energy

The conservation of energy is an important physical law that applies to fluid flow in a piping system and one that helps explain what is happening throughout the system. In its simplist form, the conservation of energy states that energy can be neither created nor destroyed, only altered in form. There are many forms of energy in a fluid flowing through a piping system, including:

- Potential energy (*PE*) is the energy a fluid possesses due to its vertical position in a gravitational field. This is anaologous to the fluid's elevation head.
- Kinetic energy (*KE*) is the energy a fluid has due to its velocity which is the fluid's velocity head.
- Enthalpy (*H*) includes two forms of energy:
  - Internal energy (*U*) is due to the rotation, vibration, and interaction between molecules and atoms in the fluid. This includes the energy due to the fluid's temperature and chemical energy.
  - Flow energy (*PV*) is the amount of energy in the fluid due to the pressure of the fluid contained within a specific volume of the system. This is the fluid's static pressure head.
- Energy in transit including:
  - Heat ($\dot{Q}$) transferred into or out of the fluid per unit time.
  - Work ($\dot{W}$) added to the fluid or removed by the fluid per unit time.

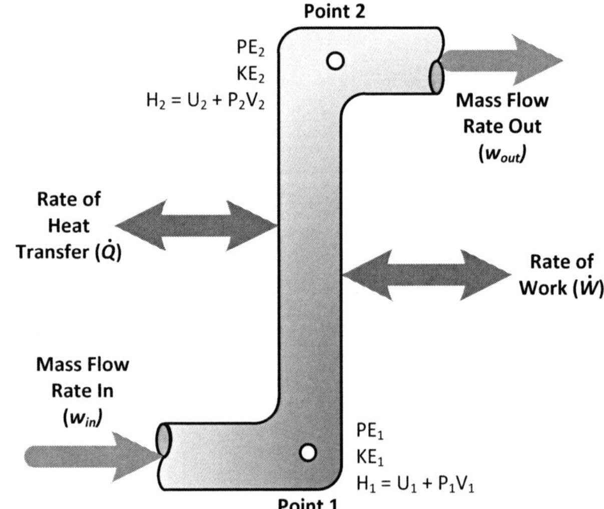

Figure 2-6. Conservation of energy in a piping segment.

Consider a segment of piping that changes elevation as shown in Figure 2-6. The fluid enters the pipe at Point 1 with a certain amount of potential, kinetic, internal, and flow energy. As the fluid moves up the pipe to Point 2, heat may be transfered into or out of the fluid and work may add energy to or remove it from the fluid. It leaves the pipe at Point 2 with a certain amount of potential, kinetic, internal, and flow energy.

The overall equation for the conservation of energy for this pipe segment is given by Equation 2-24 and further expanded in Equation 2-25 using the more familiar nomenclature.

Units of Energy and Power

$$U_1 + (PV)_1 + KE_1 + PE_1 = U_2 + (PV)_2 + KE_2 + PE_2 + \left(\dot{W} - \dot{Q}\right)$$ *Equation 2-24*

$$\left(U_1 + \frac{P_1}{\rho_1} + \frac{v_1^2}{2g} + z_1\right) = \left(U_2 + \frac{P_2}{\rho_2} + \frac{v_2^2}{2g} + z_2\right) + \left(\dot{W} - \dot{Q}\right)$$ *Equation 2-25*

When using the equation for the conservation of energy, it is important that the units for each term in Equation 2-25 are the same. It may be common to quantify various forms of energy using different energy units. For example, heat transfer is usually quantified using the British Thermal Unit (BTU) while the energy added to the fluid by a pump is quantified by the pump's Total Head in feet of fluid. The electrical energy added to a motor is quantified in kilowatt hours (kWh). Table 2-1 below provides convenient conversion factors for energy and power units.

Table 2-1. Energy and Power Conversion Factors

Units of Energy	*Units of Power*
1 ft-lb = 0.001285 Btu	1 ft-lb/sec = 4.626 Btu/hr = 0.001356 kW
1 Btu = 778.2 ft-lb	1 Btu/hr = 0.2162 ft-lb/sec = 0.0002931 kW
1 ft-lb = 3.766 x 10-7 kWh	1 kW = 3,412 Btu/hr = 737.6 ft-lb/sec
1 kWh = 2.655 x 106 ft-lb	1 hp = 550 ft-lb/sec
1 kWh = 3,412 Btu	1 kW = 0.7457 hp

Bernoulli Equation

The law of conservation of energy leads directly into the Bernoulli Equation, which describes perhaps one of the most important but readily forgotten concepts in the application of fluid flow through pipelines.

As described earlier in this chapter, the total hydraulic energy of a fluid consists of its elevation, pressure, and velocity head. The Bernoulli Equation given in Equation 2-26 is essentially the law of conservation of energy applied to steady state fluid flow in a pipeline, with Point 1 located in the system upstream from Point 2.

$$Z_1 + \frac{144\,P_1}{\rho} + \frac{v_1^2}{2g} = Z_2 + \frac{144\,P_2}{\rho} + \frac{v_2^2}{2g} + h_L$$ *Equation 2-26*

The head loss term in the Bernoulli Equation is the amount of non-recoverable energy lost from the fluid due to the friction between the pipe walls and the fluid molecules and due to the changes in the fluid momentum. This is energy lost in the form of heat, noise, and vibration.

Example 2-1 Applying Bernoulli for a Pipeline with No Flow

To help understand the conservation of energy and the application of the Bernoulli Equation, consider a pipeline containing 60 °F water with no fluid flow that changes elevation as shown in Figure 2-7.

Since there is no flow from Point 1 to Point 2, the fluid velocity is zero and therefore the velocity head is zero. Also, with no fluid flow, there is no friction between the fluid and pipe walls and no momentum changes so there is no head loss between the two points. With no velocity head or head loss, the total hydraulic energy at both points only consists of elevation and pressure head and the total energy at Point 1 is equal to the total energy at Point 2.

If clear tubing were connected to Points 1 and 2, the fluid would seek its own level and rise to the same height in both tubes. If the liquid height in both tubes reached 100 feet measured from some reference datum plane, Point 1 would have 25 feet of elevation head and 75 feet of pressure head. Point 2 would have 75 feet of elevation head and 25 feet of pressure head.

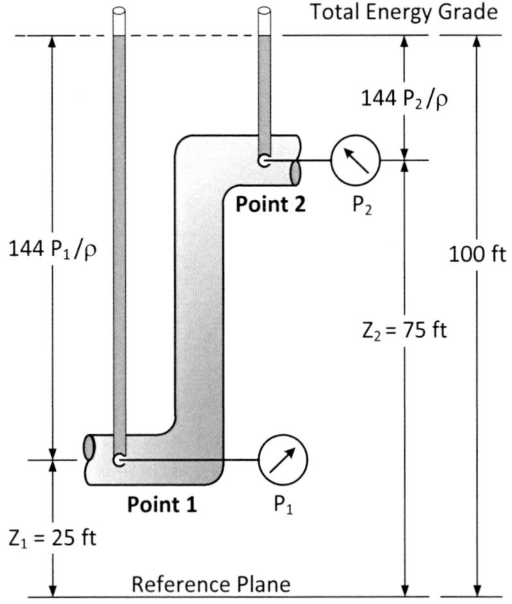

Figure 2-7. Pipeline with an elevation change and no fluid flow. **PFF**

If pressure gages were located at Points 1 and 2, how would the values of pressure compare?

Point 1 has 75 feet of pressure head:

$$P_1 = \frac{\rho\, H_1}{144} = \left(\frac{62.4\, lb}{ft^3}\right)\left(\frac{75\, ft}{}\right)\left(\frac{ft^2}{144\, in^2}\right) = 32.5\, psi$$

Point 2 has 25 feet of pressure head:

$$P_2 = \frac{\rho\, H_2}{144} = \left(\frac{62.4\, lb}{ft^3}\right)\left(\frac{25\, ft}{}\right)\left(\frac{ft^2}{144\, in^2}\right) = 10.8\, psi$$

If this pipeline was being followed in an operating plant and the pressure readings compared, one might think that there was flow from the higher pressure at Point 1 to the lower pressure at Point 2, but this is a common misconception. Fluid does not necessarily flow from a higher pressure to a lower pressure, but it does always flow from a point of *higher total energy* to a point of *lower total energy.*

This is an example of how the pressure head at Point 1 is converted into elevation head just by a change in the elevation of the pipeline.

Example 2-2 Applying the Bernoulli Equation in a Constant Diameter Pipeline with Flow and an Elevation Change

Now consider the flow of 368 gpm of 60 °F water in a 4" Schedule 40 pipeline (ID = 4.026") with the elevation change shown in Figure 2-8. The pressure gage at Point 1 reads 50 psig and the gage at Point 2 reads 26 psig.

Chapter 5 will cover how to calculate the amount of head loss between Points 1 and 2 using the pipeline and fluid properties, but the head loss can also be calculated using the Bernoulli Equation with the information that is known about this example.

The total energy, or Total Head (*TH*), at Points 1 and 2 can be calculated by adding the elevation, pressure, and velocity heads together at those points. The elevation heads are given, and the pressure gage readings can be used to calculate the pressure head at both points. Since the flow rate and inside pipe diameter are known, Equation 2-10 can be used to calculate the fluid velocity and Equation 2-16 can be used to calculate the velocity head. The difference between the total head at Point 1 and Point 2 will be the amount of head loss between those points.

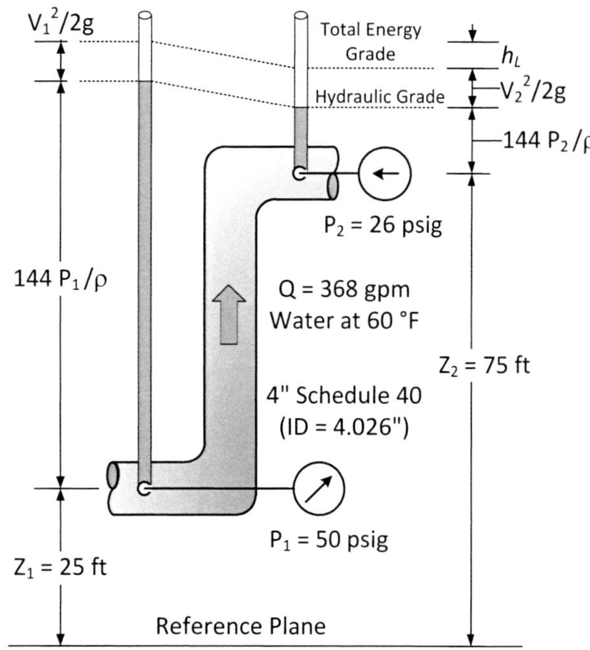

Figure 2-8. Applying the Bernoulli Equation in a pipeline with flow.

At Point 1:

$$Elevation\ Head = Z_1 = 25\ ft$$

$$Presure\ Head = \frac{144\ P_1}{\rho} = \frac{144\ (50\ psig)}{(62.4\ lb/ft^3)} = 115.4\ ft$$

$$v_1 = 0.4085\frac{Q}{d^2} = 0.4085\frac{(368\ gpm)}{(4.026)^2} = 9.27\ ft/sec$$

$$Velocity\ Head = \frac{v_1^2}{2g} = \frac{(9.27\ ft/sec)^2}{2(32.2\ ft/sec^2)} = 1.33\ ft$$

$$TH_1 = 25\ ft\ + 115.4\ ft + 1.33\ ft = 141.7\ ft$$

At Point 2:

$$Elevation\ Head = Z_2 = 75\ ft$$

$$Presure\ Head = \frac{144\ P_2}{\rho} = \frac{144\ (26\ psig)}{(62.4\ lb/ft^3)} = 60.0\ ft$$

$$v_1 = v_2 = 9.27\ ft/sec$$

$$Velocity\ Head = \frac{v_2^2}{2g} = \frac{(9.27\ ft/sec)^2}{2(32.2\ ft/sec^2)} = 1.33\ ft$$

$$TH_2 = 75\ ft + 60.0\ ft + 1.33\ ft = 136.3\ ft$$

$$h_L = TH_1 - TH_2 = 141.7\ ft - 136.3\ ft = 5.4\ ft$$

As can be seen in this example, the pressure drop is due to two factors: the change in elevation of the pipeline and the head loss caused by the flow of the water. The pressure drop due to the change in elevation can be calculated using Equation 2-17 and the pressure drop due to the head loss can be calculated using Equation 2-20.

$$dP_{elevation} = \frac{\rho\,\Delta Z}{144} = \frac{(62.4\,lb/ft^3)(75 - 25\,ft)}{144\;in^2/ft^2} = 21.7\,psi$$

$$dP_{head\ loss} = \frac{\rho\,h_L}{144} = \frac{(62.4\,lb/ft^3)(5.4\,ft)}{144\;in^2/ft^2} = 2.34\,psi$$

In this example, pressure decreases as the fluid flows up the pipeline, but if the flow was in the opposite direction, the pressure would increase. The elevation change can either add or subtract static pressure, but the head loss will always diminish the pressure. Whether the net effect is a pressure gain or a pressure loss will depend on the relative amounts of each.

Example 2-3 Applying the Bernoulli Equation in a Pipeline with a Diameter Change

In the previous example, if there is a pipe expansion from 4" to 6" just after the pressure gage at Point 2 as shown in Figure 2-9, what happens to the pressure and fluid velocity at the outlet of the expansion? The Bernoulli Equation can again be applied to understand what would be seen in a real world operating facility.

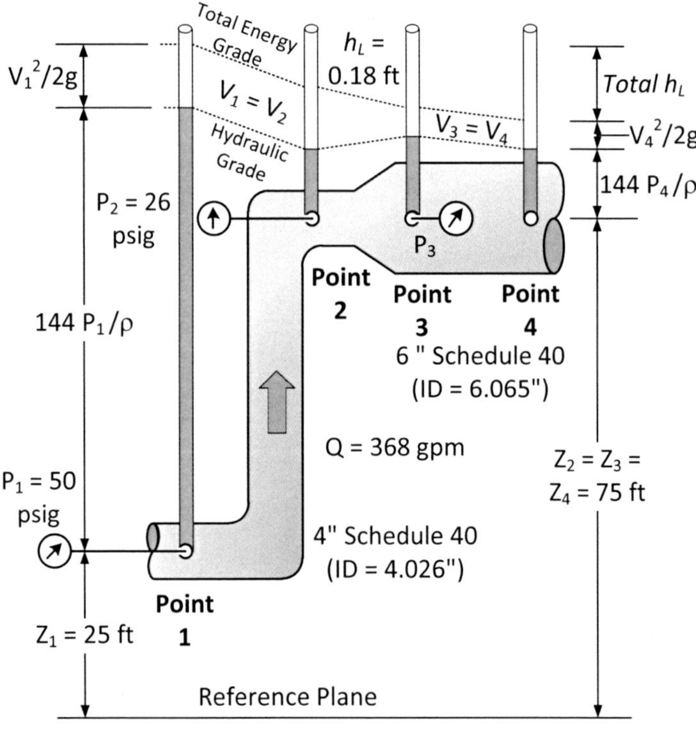

Figure 2-9. Applying the Bernoulli Equation for a change in pipe diameter.

Figure 2-9 shows some additional data that will be needed to determine the pressure at Point 3. The 6" Schedule 40 pipe has an inside diameter of 6.065" and the expansion itself creates 0.18 feet of head loss (the calculation for the head loss across a fitting will be discussed in Chapter 6).

Knowing the flow rate and the inside diameter at the outlet of the expansion, the fluid velocity in the 6" pipeline can be calculated using Equation 2-10 and the velocity head can be calculated using Equation 2-16.

The Bernoulli Equation, Equation 2-26, can then be re-arranged to calculate the pressure at Point 3.

The Total Head at Point 2 was previously calculated to be 136.3 feet.

At Point 3:

$$v_3 = 0.4085\frac{Q}{d^2} = 0.4085\frac{(368\ gpm)}{(6.065)^2} = 4.09\ ft/sec$$

$$TH_2 = Z_3 + \frac{144\ P_3}{\rho} + \frac{v_3^2}{2g} + h_L$$

$$P_3 = \frac{\rho}{144}\left(TH_2 - Z_3 - \frac{v_3^2}{2g} - h_L\right)$$

$$P_3 = \frac{62.4\ lb/ft^3}{144}\left(136.3ft - 75\ ft - \frac{(4.09\ ft/sec)^2}{2(32.2\ ft/sec^2)} - 0.18\ ft\right) = 26.4\ psig$$

The velocity decrease due to the increase in pipe size results in an increase in the static pressure according to the Bernoulli principle, but the head loss acts to reduce the static pressure. Whether the static pressure actually increases or decreases depends on the amount of head loss and whether the fluid velocity decreases (with a larger pipe diameter) or increases (with a reduction in pipe diameter) and by what amount.

A few other things to note about this example:

- The increase in static pressure results in an increase in the hydraulic grade (which is the sum of the elevation head and pressure head) as can be seen in the Hydraulic Grade line in Figure 2-9. The increase in hydraulic grade comes at the expense of the velocity head, but the total fluid energy is not changed because of this energy conversion.
- The total energy only decreases due to the head loss in the pipe expansion, which can be seen in the Total Energy Grade line in Figure 2-9.
- The slope of the Total Energy Grade line is steeper for the 4" Schedule 40 segment of piping from Point 1 to Point 2 compared to the 6" Schedule 40 segment of piping from Point 3 to Point 4. This is because head loss is a function of the fluid velocity squared, which will be discussed in Chapter 5.

The previous three examples show the importance of the Bernoulli Equation and the conservation of energy in a piping system. Elevation head can be converted into pressure head (or vice versa) and velocity head can be converted into pressure head (or vice versa). This is a key concept that should be kept in mind when working in operating plant or in a field that involves piping systems.

Solving the Bernoulli Equation for Pressure Drop

Many have probably heard the saying that fluid flows from high pressure to low pressure. If the Bernoulli Equation is re-arranged to solve for the differential pressure between two points in a system, as shown in Equation 2-27, it can be used to explain this common misunderstanding about fluid flow in a pipeline.

$$(P_2 - P_1) = \frac{\rho}{144}\left[(Z_1 - Z_2) + \left(\frac{v_1^2 - v_2^2}{2g}\right) - h_L\right] \qquad \textit{Equation 2-27}$$

Equation 2-27 shows that the pressure drop (P_2 - P_1) is due to three things: a change in the elevation, a change in fluid velocity, and head loss.

If the downstream elevation is higher than the upstream elevation, then the fluid's static pressure will drop as the fluid flows up to the higher elevation, representing a conversion of pressure head into elevation head. If the downstream elevation is lower than the upstream elevation, then the fluid's static pressure will rise as the fluid flows down to the lower elevation. This is a result of converting elevation head into pressure head.

Similarly, the downstream fluid velocity can be higher than the upstream velocity if the pipe gets smaller in diameter. The pressure head is converted into velocity head, resulting in a drop in the fluid's pressure. Likewise, a slower downstream fluid velocity results if the pipe size is increased, causing the fluid pressure to rise due to the velocity change.

Head loss will always act to reduce the fluid's static pressure because pressure head is converted into a non-recoverable form of hydraulic energy.

If the downstream pressure (P_2) is less than the upstream pressure (P_1), then the differential pressure will be negative, indicating a drop in the fluid's static pressure. If the downsteam pressure is greater than the upstream pressure, there will be a rise in the fluid pressure as it flows down the pipeline. The change in elevation and the change in velocity can either cause the static pressure to increase or to decrease. So the net effect, whether pressure increases or decreases, with depend on the magnitude of the change in elevation, fluid velocity, and the head loss. A more technically accurate way to decribe fluid flow is to say that fluid will flow from a region of higher total energy to a region of lower total energy.

Kirchhoff's Laws

Kirchhoff's Laws were originally used to describe the conservation of energy and charge in electrical circuits, but because there are many concepts in the study of fluid flow that are analogous to the study of electricity, Kirchhoff's Laws can be used to understand what is happening in a piping system. Kirchhoff's Laws are essentially the law of conservation of mass and conservation of energy that were presented earlier in this chapter, but when used together they can be applied to solve for flow rates and pressure drops in a steady state piping system in balance.

Kirchhoff's First Law

Kirchhoff's First Law is the conservation of mass at a junction in a piping system. The total mass flow rate into the junction plus the total mass flow rate out of the junction must equal zero. In other words, what goes in must equal what goes out since there is no accumulation of mass at a junction.

In order for Kirchhoff's Laws to work, a sign convention must be established and followed for the direction of flows into and out of the junction. One convention that can be used is that all flow going into a junction is negative and all flow leaving a junction is positive. The opposite convention can be used as long as the convention is adhered to throughout the analysis of the system.

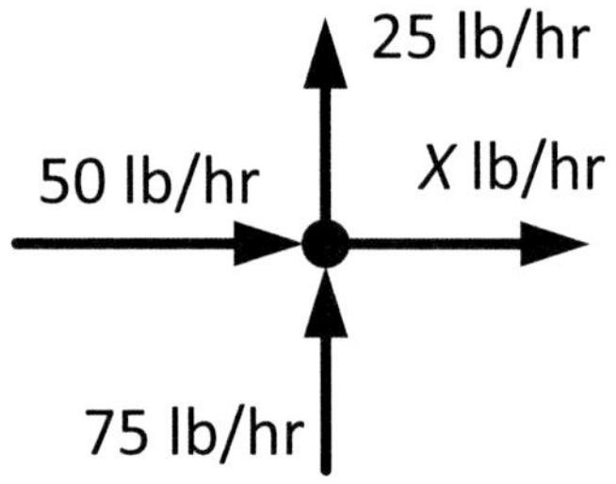

25 lb/hr
50 lb/hr
X lb/hr
75 lb/hr

Figure 2-10. Kirchhoff's first law is the conservation of mass at each junction.

As a simple example, consider the 4-way Tee in Figure 2-10 with two flows entering the tee and two flow leaving it.

If the flows are 50 lb/hr and 75 lb/hr entering and 25 lb/hr leaving, then the unknown value can be calculated using Kirchhoff's first law.

$$(-50\ lb/hr) + (-75\ lb/hr) + (25\ lb/hr) + (X\ lb/hr) = 0$$

$$X = 100\ lb/hr$$

Kirchhoff's Second Law

Kirchhoff's Second Law is the conservation of energy around each loop in a piping system. It states that the sum of the pressure drops and gains around a loop must equal zero. In other words, after completely tracing around a loop, all the pressure losses and gains must be accounted for. This includes pressure changes due to head loss, elevation changes, velocity changes, and any energy addition in the loop such as that which would occur at a pump, resulting in an increase in the pressure across the pump.

Just as with the first Kirchhoff law, the second law must also have a sign convention that is followed. This sign convention must take pressure drops and gains into account, but it must also take the flow direction into account.

For pipelines, valves, fittings, and other components with head loss, when tracing clockwise around the loop, if the flow is in the same direction, the pressure drop is positive. If the flow is counterclockwise, the pressure drop is negative. Also, to account for a change in elevation, if the elevation at the inlet is lower than the outlet, the pressure drop is positive.

For pumps, if the flow is in the direction of the convention, the pump's Total Head is negative, indicating that energy is added to the fluid at that point in the piping system.

Figure 2-11 is an example of using Kirchoff's 2nd Law as applied to the supply and return of chilled water to two heat exchangers with different flow rates in a system. The values of differential pressure were calculated based on the head loss across each device.

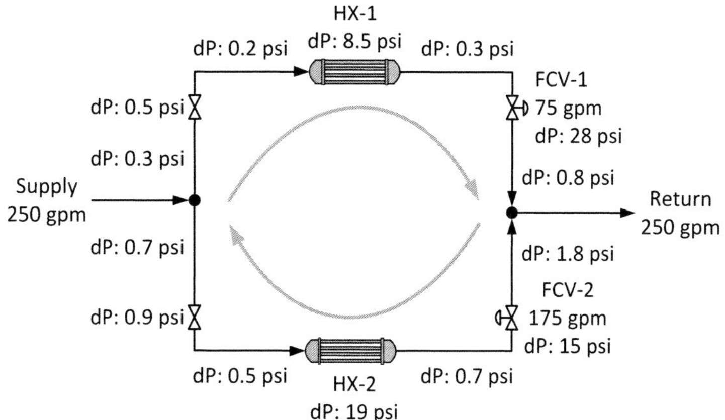

Figure 2-11. Kirchhoff's second law is the conservation of energy around each loop in a piping system. PF ⑤

Tracing a loop from the inlet junction around the upper heat exchanger (HX-1) and down through the lower heat exchanger (HX-2), the differential pressures are added for each pipeline, valve, heat exchanger, and control valve.

$$Upper\ Half\ of\ Loop:\ (0.3) + (0.5) + (0.2) + (8.5) + (0.3) + (28) + (0.8) +$$

$$Lower\ Half:\ (-1.8) + (-15) + (-0.7) + (-19) + (-0.5) + (-0.9) + (-0.7) = 0$$

Using the established sign convention, the pressure drops in the upper half of the loop are positive since the flow is in the same direction that the loop is being traced, which is clockwise around the loop. The pressure drops are negative for the devices in the lower half of the loop since the flow in the pipelines is opposite of the direction that the loop is being traced. Since all the pressure drops add up to zero, the system is in steady state balance.

These examples of Kirchhoff's Laws are simplified to present the concept, but the usefulness of Kirchhoff's Laws come when analyzing a complex piping system with numerous unknown flow rates.

Pascal's Law

Pascal's Law states that the pressure applied to the surface of an enclosed fluid is transmitted equally and undiminished in all directions throughout the fluid and to the walls of its container.

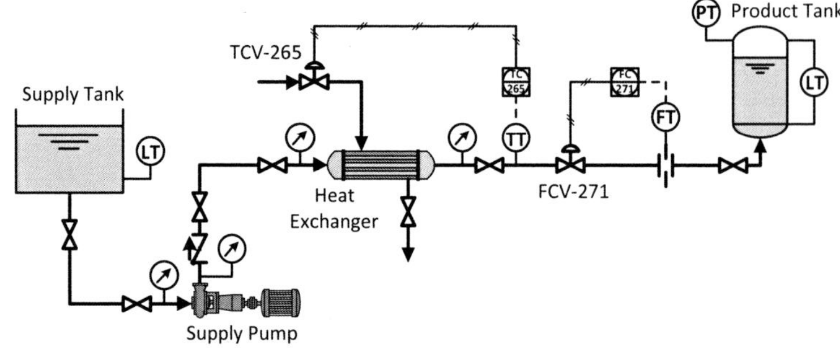

Figure 2-12. Pascal's Law applies to piping systems.

The application of Pascal's Law can be seen with the typical open piping system shown in Figure 2-12. The pressure created by the liquid level in the Supply Tank is felt at the bottom of the tank, at the pump suction, and throughout the system. If the level is increased, the pressure will increase at the pump suction, pump discharge, and at the control valve inlet by an amount equal to the pressure equivalent of the increased level (Equation 2-17). The system would have to respond in one of two ways:

1. If the flow control valve, FCV-271, is an automatically controlled valve as shown in Figure 2-12, the increased inlet pressure at the control valve would tend to increase the system flow rate, but the controller would throttle down the valve in order to maintain its setpoint. Chapter 8 on Process Measurement and Controls will further explore this system response.

2. If the valve was manually adjusted, the increased pressure due to the higher Supply Tank level would increase the system flow rate.

If the level or pressure of the Product Tank in Figure 2-12 were increased, this pressure increase would be felt not only on the system that the Product Tank supplies, but also back to the system that supplies liquid to it. The system in Figure 2-12 would respond in one of two ways:

1. If FCV-271 is an automatically controlled valve, the increased pressure at the valve outlet would require the valve to open more in order to maintain the controller set point. This will be further explained in Chapter 7 on control valves.

2. If the flow control valve is manually set, the increased pressure in the Product Tank would cause the flow rate in the system to decrease, the Supply Pump would operate further back on its pump curve, and the pump Total Head (and therefore differential pressure) would increase. Chapter 4 on pumps will explore this response in more depth.

Chapter Three

Tanks and Vessels

This chapter presents some of the key information to understand the role tanks and vessels play in a piping system. The focus of this chapter won't be on how to design or size a tank, but rather on the effect a tank has on the hydraulic operation of the piping system. It will also look at different types of tanks and what instrumentation may be installed to monitor and control key operating parameters. A key hydraulic aspect of tanks and vessels is that they establish the boundary conditions at connecting pipelines, and because of this they make a good place to divide complex systems into more manageable systems for evaluation.

Applications for Tanks and Vessels

The role a tank or vessel plays in the piping system depends on the application. In general, tanks and vessels store and supply fluid to the piping system. This fluid is a source of hydraulic energy to the piping system based on the level and pressure in the tank.

Storage tanks provide for long term storage of the system working fluid. Some tanks may be designated as "Day Tanks" which provide immediate and short-term use in a process.

Surge tanks provide room for the fluid during a transient in flow or production rate. For example, a large tank dividing two processes may be sized to provide additional capacity to allow one process to operate at a different rate in the event that a maintenance issue slows down the other process.

Figure 3-1. Typical tank farm used in many applications. (Photo courtesy of Tankconnection.com)

Thermal expansion tanks provide capacity for the working fluid to expand as its temperature increases during start-up or changes in operating conditions of the process. The thermal expansion tank also provides make-up fluid to the system as the fluid contracts when its temperature decreases.

Tanks also provide a convenient location for chemical addition or mixing and a place for recirculation or minimum flow lines to return fluid to the system.

Types of Tanks and Vessels

Tanks fall into two general categories, open tanks and closed tanks.

Open Tanks

Open tanks may be covered or uncovered, but the space above the surface of the liquid is exposed to atmospheric pressure and the tank is neither pressurized nor under a vacuum. Examples of open tanks include:

- Storage tanks
- Water towers (hydrophores)
- Cooling towers
- Sumps
- Reservoirs
- Barometric condensers
- Surge and expansions tanks
- Rail cars and tank trucks
- Oceans, lakes, and rivers
- Even the atmosphere itself can be considered a large tank!

Closed Tanks

Closed tanks are sealed and are either under pressure or under a vacuum. A tank with over 15 psig internal or external pressure is typically considered as a "pressure vessel" and are subject to more stringent design, construction, and inspection requirements.

Pressurized vessels include:

- Chemical reaction vessels
- Absorption towers
- Air receivers
- Surge Tanks
- Pressurizers
- Accumulators
- Condensate receivers
- De-aerator tanks
- Steam drums / mud drums
- Flash tanks

Tanks under a vacuum include:

- Condensers
- Absorption towers
- Boiler furnaces
- Chemical reaction vessels
- Evaporators

Key Hydraulic Measurements

There are several key measurements that are important in considering the hydraulic effect of a tank on the overall piping system. Figures 3-2 through 3-5 show these key measurements for various types of tanks and vessels.

Open Tank

Inlet

Atmospheric Pressure

Inlet Penetration Height

Liquid Level

LT

Level Transmitter

Bottom Elevation

Outlet

Datum Plane (0 ft)

Figure 3-2. Key hydraulic measurements of an open tank.

Pressurized Vessel

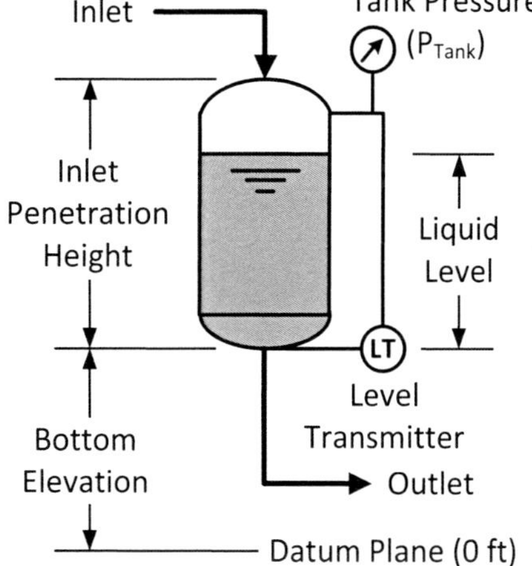

Figure 3-3. Key hydraulic measurements of a pressurized tank.

Bottom Elevation

The elevation of the bottom of the tank as measured from some reference datum plane helps establish the amount of hydraulic energy of the fluid in the tank. The reference datum plane can be any point as long as the same plane is used when taking elevation measurements for all the equipment in the system. Elevations can be measured from sea level, from the grade of the facility, from the keel of a ship, or from the lowest piece of equipment in the system.

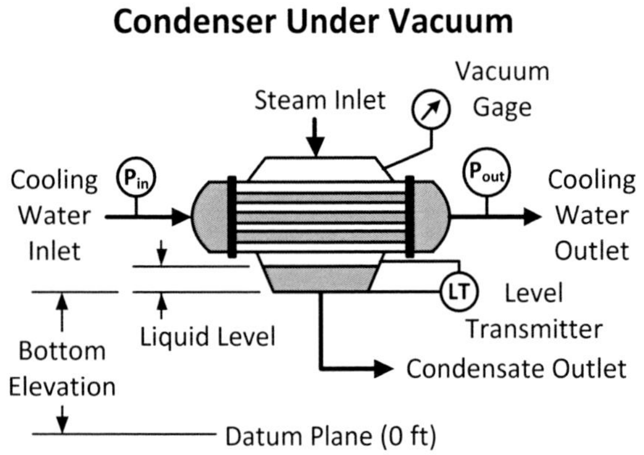

Figure 3-4. Key hydraulic measurements of a condenser under vacuum.

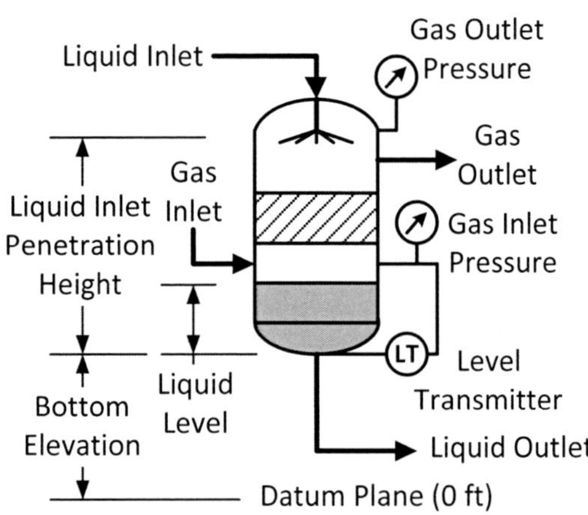

Figure 3-5. Key hydraulic measurements of a packed absorption tower.

Tank Liquid Level

The level of the liquid surface as measured from the bottom of the tank is a key hydraulic measurement. For the consistent use of units for the equations in this book, the liquid level is measured in units of feet from the bottom of the tank. In practical application, however, many level instruments are calibrated as a percentage of the maximum working height of the tank.

Tank Surface Pressure

The pressure on the surface of the liquid is also a key hydraulic measurement, typically measured in units of psig. An open tank is at 0 psig since it is exposed to the atmosphere, but a closed tank can have a pressure above or below the atmospheric pressure. A pressurized tank will have an internal surface pressure above atmospheric pressure and a (+) psig value, and a tank under vacuum will have a surface pressure below atmospheric pressure. Vacuum gages can be calibrated in various units, such as inches of mercury vacuum ("Hg vac) or inches of water column vacuum ("wc vac), but for consistency in this book, vacuum will be shown in units of negative gage pressure, or (–) psig.

Penetration Heights

The elevations of where the fluid discharges into the tank as measured from the bottom of the tank are also important hydraulic measurements. The height at which the fluid enters the tank will determine the pressure that is felt at the discharge, which makes the tank a good boundary condition to analyze the hydraulic performance of a piping system.

The pressure at the pipe penetration can be calculated using the pressure on the liquid surface, the height of liquid above the discharge, and the density of the fluid in the tank with Equation 3-1.

$$P_{penetration} = \frac{\rho H}{144} + P_{surface} \qquad \textit{Equation 3-1}$$

Consider a hypothetical tank that could be used to store gasoline (density = 47.0 lb/ft^3), 40% sodium hydroxide (density = 92.0 lb/ft^3), or water (density = 62.4 lb/ft^3), as shown in Figure 3-6. If the tank is open to atmosphere and has a 30 foot liquid level in it, the pressure measured at the bottom of the tank will be 9.8 psig if it contained gasoline, 19.2 psig if it had sodium hydroxide, and 13 psig if it had water.

If that same tank is pressurized to 10 psig as shown in Figure 3-7, the pressure at the bottom of the tank also increases by 10 psig, an application of Pascal's Law.

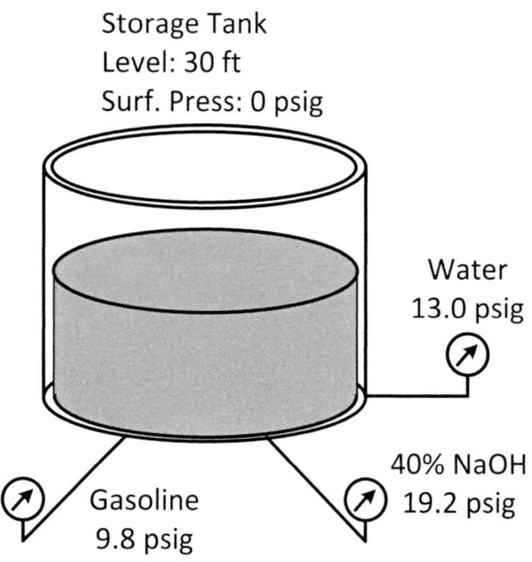

Figure 3-6. Pressures at the bottom of an open tank with 30 feet of water, 40% NaOH, or gasoline.

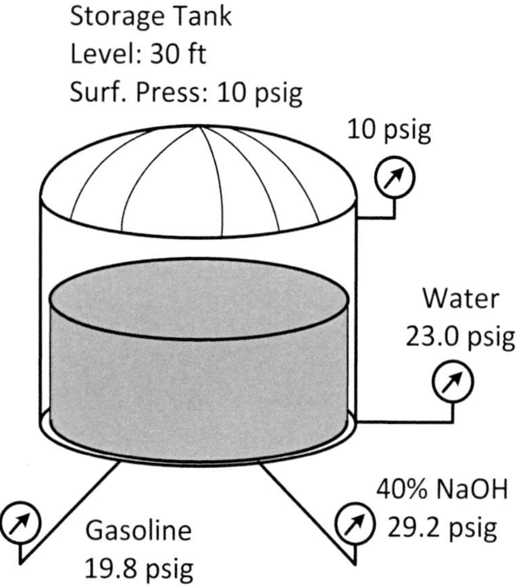

Figure 3-7. Pressures at the bottom of a tank pressurized to 10 psig with 30 feet of water, 40% NaOH, or gasoline.

The graph in Figure 3-8 shows that there is a linear relationship between the pressure felt at the penetration and the liquid level above the penetration, as indicated by the form of Equation 3-1. The slope of the line depends on the fluid density.

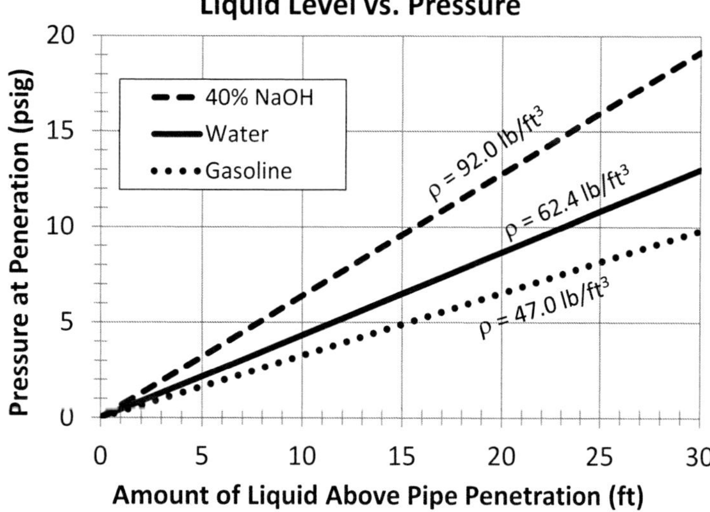

Figure 3-8. Graph of the pressures felt at a penetration given the height of the liquid level above the penetration, for 40% NaOH, water, or gasoline.

Other Key Tank Dimensions

Since tanks come in all shapes and sizes, other key dimensions will depend on the geometry of the tank. For the vertically mounted cylindrical tank shown in Figure 3-9, key dimensions include the tank height and the inside diameter.

These values are important in the calculation of the volume of the liquid in the tank and in understanding the dynamic response of the attached piping system. For example, the level of a tank with a larger volume will change more slowly than a tank with a smaller volume for a given mismatch between the flow rate entering and leaving the tank.

The calculation for the maximum total volume and the volume of the liquid in the tank will depend on the geometry of the tank. Perhaps the most common geometry for tanks and vessels is the vertical cylindrical tank shown in Figure 3-9. Equation 3-2 shows the maximum volume of the liquid in the tank, in gallons, is the cross-sectional area times the tank height, with the inside diameter, D, and the tank height in feet.

The volume of the liquid in the tank (in gallons) at any given level (in feet) is calculated with Equation 3-3. If the tank diameter is constant, then the volume of the tank is a linear function of the liquid level.

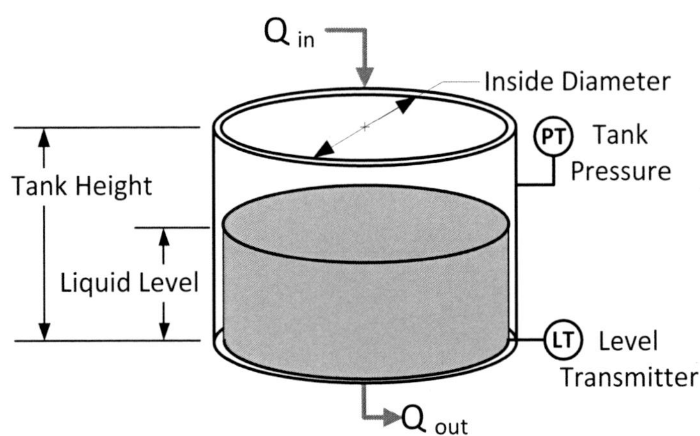

Figure 3-9. Other key tank dimensions.

$$\begin{matrix} Maximum \\ Volume \end{matrix} = \frac{\pi D^2}{4} \times \begin{pmatrix} Tank \\ Height \end{pmatrix} \times \frac{7.48\, gal}{ft^3} \quad \text{Equation 3-2}$$

$$\begin{matrix} Liquid \\ Volume \end{matrix} = \frac{\pi D^2}{4} \times \begin{pmatrix} Liquid \\ Level \end{pmatrix} \times \frac{7.48\, gal}{ft^3} \quad \text{Equation 3-3}$$

Another common geometry for tanks and vessels is a horizontally mounted cylindrical tank with flat heads as shown in Figure 3-10 with a low level and in Figure 3-11 with a high tank level. Because the cross-sectional area occupied by fluid in the tank is not constant with level, the calculation for the volume of the liquid at a given liquid level is more complicated.

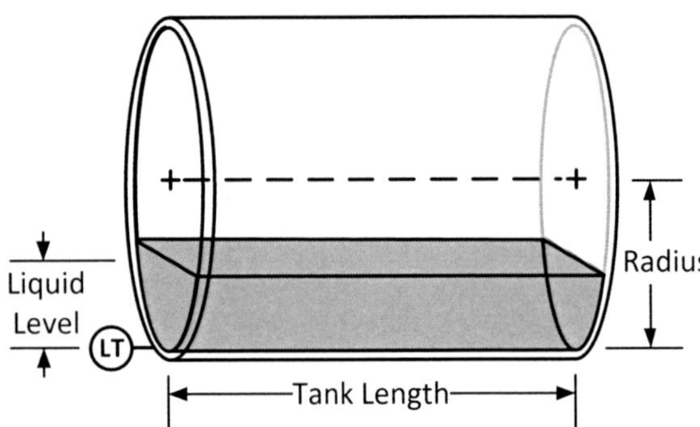

Figure 3-10. Horizontally mounted cylindrical tank with a low tank level.

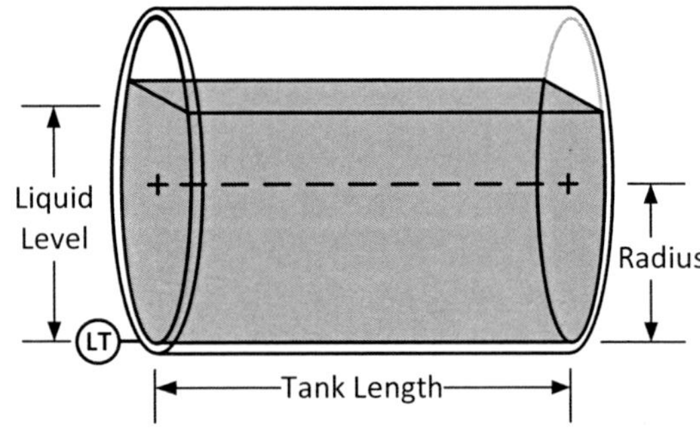

Figure 3-11 Horizontally mounted cylindrical tank with a high tank level.

Equation 3-4 can be used to convert the liquid level in feet to volume in gallons (with tank length and radius, r, in units of feet).

$$Volume = Length \times \left[\left(r^2 acos\left(\frac{r - Level}{r} \right) \right) - (r - Level)\sqrt{(2r \times Level) - (Level)^2} \right] \times \frac{7.48\, gal}{ft^3}$$

Equation 3-4

As can be seen in the graph in Figure 3-12, the volume of liquid in a horizontally mounted cylindrical tank is not a linear function of the tank level. This is important when filling a tank because the tank level increases quickly at the beginning and end of the filling procedure, which may result in over-flowing the tank if care is not taken.

The calculation for volume becomes much more complicated as the tank dimensions become more irregular. Tanks with spherical, ellipsoidal, or conical heads require complex fomulas to convert the level as measured at the bottom of the tank to a volume of fluid. For this reason, many facilities will have a "tank book" that tabulates the volume as a function of the tank's level.

From a hydraulic perspective, tank geometry does not affect the pressure at the pipeline penetrations of the tank. This pressure depends only on the height of the liquid level above the penetration, the fluid density, and the pressure on the liquid surface.

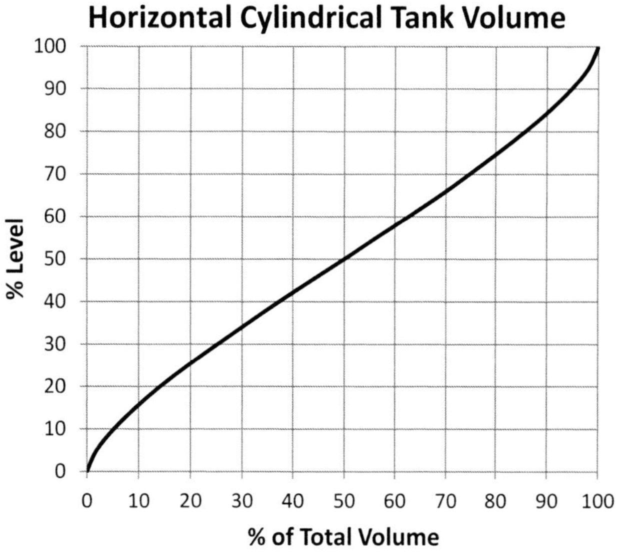

Horizontal Cylindrical Tank Volume

% Level: 0 10 20 30 40 50 60 70 80 90 100

% of Total Volume: 0 10 20 30 40 50 60 70 80 90 100

Figure 3-12. Graph of the volume of a horizontally mounted cylindrical tank with flat heads as a function of the tank level.

Tank Level Measurement

There are many methods to measure the liquid level in a tank and that number increases with the development of new technologies. Liquid level is perhaps the most difficult measurement to take. Many methods use the fluid density to calibrate the instrument and the density can change from startup to normal operation as the fluid temperature changes.

Tank level measurements fall into two general categories: direct measurement and indirect measurement. Direct measurement involves measuring the actual height of the liquid surface from the bottom of the tank, whereas indirect measurement uses some other property to derive the liquid level.

Direct measurement of tank level

A rudimentary and direct method to measure level is with the use of a scaled or notched dip-stick inserted into the tank. Although not suitable for continuous measurement and control, it is typically used for inventory control or to verify another measurement.

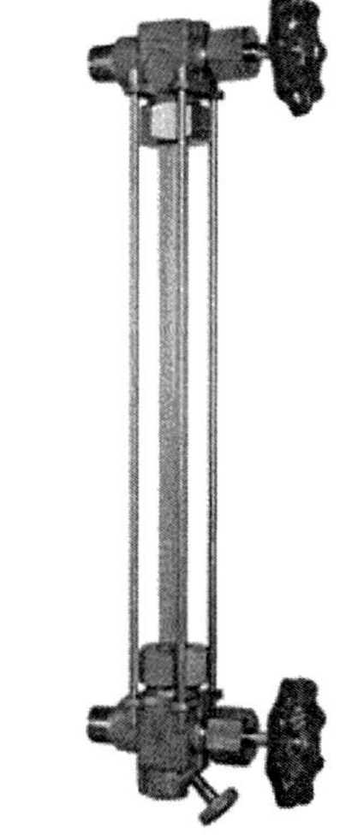

Model 446

Figure 3-13. Site glass used to measure tank level (photo courtesy of Johnernst.com).

A site glass is another common direct method to measure tank level. A site glass, such as the ones shown in Figure 3-13, is a clear plastic or glass tube mounted on the side of a tank with connections to the bottom of the tank and to the vapor space above the liquid level. As the level in the tank rises or falls, the liquid level in the site glass will change correspondingly. Site glasses can be used on open tanks or on high pressure vessels such as boiler steam drums.

A float gage, shown in Figure 3-14, is another direct method to measure the tank level. The float gage consists of a plastic or hollow metallic float attached to a counter-weight with a graduated stainless steel tape, a chain, or rope. The level in the tank can be read off the graduated tape, or if used in conjunction with a gage board, the location of the counter-weight measured against the graduated gage board will provide the tank level measurement.

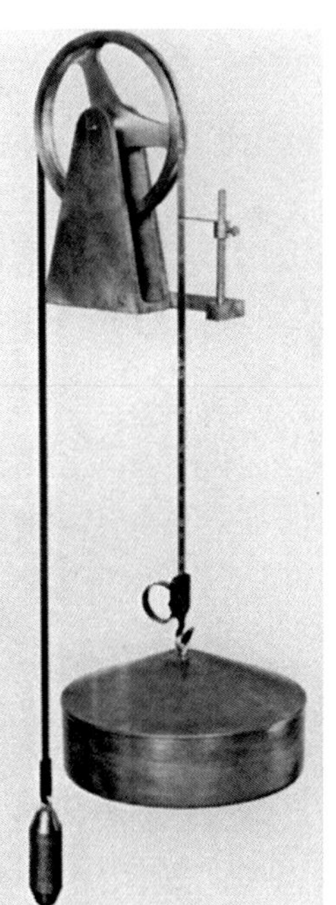

Figure 3-14. Float gage (courtesy of rickly.com).

Indirect measurement of tank level

The static pressure exerted by a fluid is a common method to indirectly derive the liquid level in a tank. Figure 3-15 shows an air bubbler, also called a surge tube, which consists of a tube that extends into the fluid to the minimum liquid level line. Air is supplied to the tube such that there is sufficient pressure to maintain a constant flow of air bubbles from the bottom of the tube when the tank is at its maximum level. As the level drops, the measured air pressure will decrease in direct proportion to the change in level.

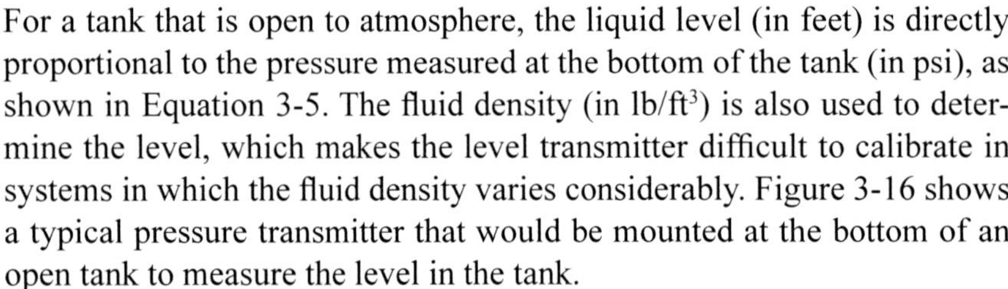

For a tank that is open to atmosphere, the liquid level (in feet) is directly proportional to the pressure measured at the bottom of the tank (in psi), as shown in Equation 3-5. The fluid density (in lb/ft^3) is also used to determine the level, which makes the level transmitter difficult to calibrate in systems in which the fluid density varies considerably. Figure 3-16 shows a typical pressure transmitter that would be mounted at the bottom of an open tank to measure the level in the tank.

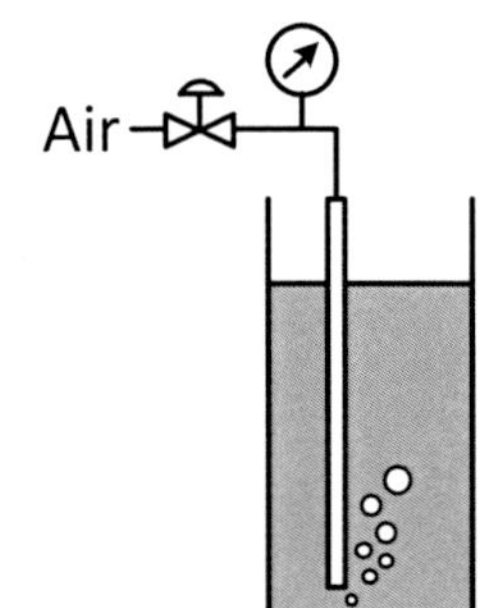

Figure 3-15. Air bubbler.

$$Liquid\ Level = \frac{144\ (P_{LT})}{\rho} \qquad \text{Equation 3-5}$$

Figure 3-16. Pressure transmitter used to measure the liquid level in an open tank (photo courtesy of Emerson.com).

For a closed pressurized tank (or a tank under vacuum), a differential pressure transmitter must be used to accurately determine the liquid level. The high side of the differential pressure transmitter is connected to the bottom of the tank and the low side is connected to the top of the tank above the liquid level. Figure 3-17 shows the connections for a typical differential pressure transmitter used to measure tank level for a pressurized tank or a tank under vacuum. Equation 3-6 can then be used to determine the level in feet of fluid (where P_{LT} is the pressure measured on the liquid side of the transmitter and P_{Tank} is the pressure measured in the vapor space at the top of the tank).

$$Liquid\ Level = \frac{144\ (P_{LT} - P_{Tank})}{\rho} \qquad \textit{Equation 3-6}$$

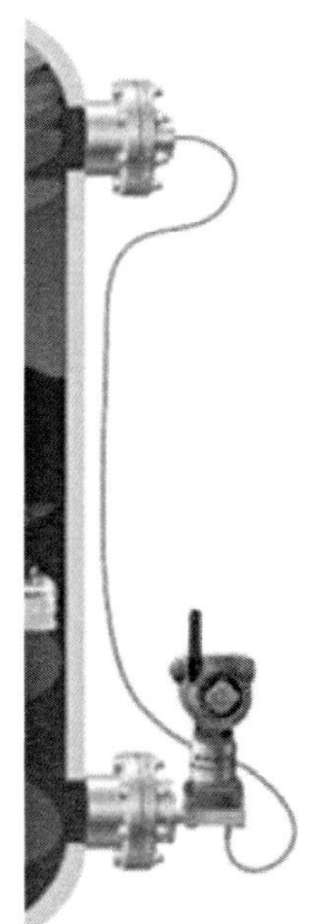

To calibrate the level transmitter in units of percent of maximum working level, Equation 3-7 can be used to display the level in percentages.

$$\%\ Level = 100\% \times \left(\frac{Liquid\ Level}{Tank\ Height}\right) \qquad \textit{Equation 3-7}$$

Figure 3-17. Differential pressure transmitter used to measure the liquid level in a pressurized tank (photo courtesy of Emerson.com).

For pressure vessels containing saturated liquids and vapors, such as a boiler steam drum, a condensing pot is often used to help mitigate level inaccuracies due to the thermodynamic effects of changing drum pressure. The condensing pot is connected to the vapor space of the steam drum and condenses any steam that reaches it, providing a constant head of liquid for the reference leg connected to the high side of the differential pressure transmitter, as shown in Figure 3-18. The sensing leg provides a variable pressure to the low side depending on the liquid level in the steam drum. Special care needs to be taken when calibrating the level transmitter, and for large industrial boilers, the level transmitter is often a part of a 2- or 3-element drum level control scheme.

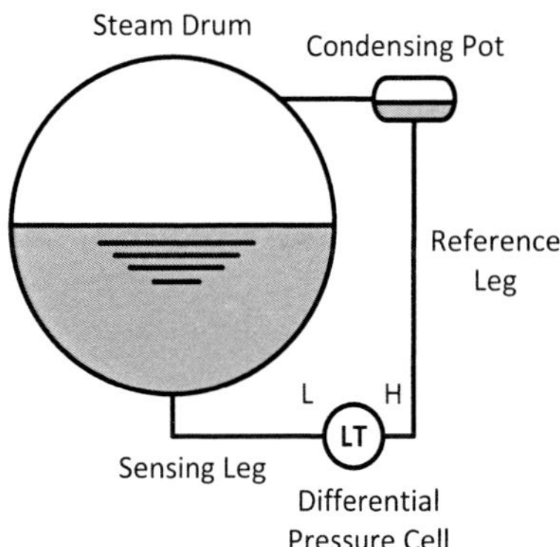

Figure 3-18. Boiler steam drum level measurement using a condensing pot and differential pressure transmitter.

Various indirect methods for level measurement use other properties of the fluids in the tank. These include weight, electrical capacitance, or electromagnetic conductivity. Still other methods utilize ultrasonics, infrared, microwave, laser, or nuclear radiation in their theory of operation to measure the level in the tank or vessel.

Controlling Tank Level

The level of a tank can be controlled by regulating the flow of liquid entering the tank or the flow leaving the tank, as shown in Figures 3-19 and 3-20. The level can be controlled manually by an operator who adjusts the fill valve or the outlet valve, or the level can be regulated using automatic controls. Various control methods will be discussed later in the "Process Measurement and Control" chapter of this book.

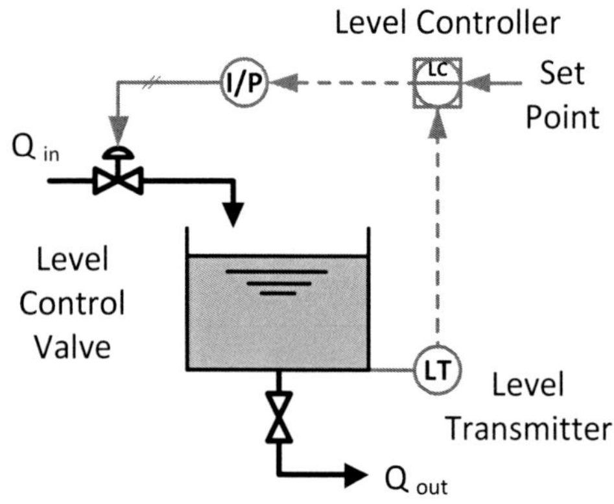

Figure 3-19. Tank level control by regulating the flow of liquid into the tank.

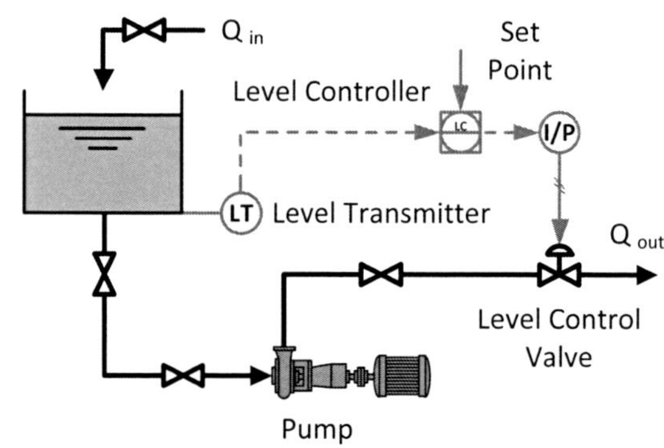

Figure 3-20. Tank level control by regulating the flow rate leaving the tank.

Changing Tank Levels

To understand how the tank level changes during a transient condition, the law of conservation of mass applies. It states that the sum of the mass flow rate into the tank equals the sum of the mass flow rates leaving the tank plus the change in the mass of the liquid in the tank over time, as shown in Equation 2-21 in Chapter 2. If the densities of all liquids entering and leaving the tank are the same, volumetric flow rates can be used, so the conservation of mass can be stated as the sum of volumetric flow rate into the tank (in gpm) equals the sum of the volumetric flow rates leaving the tank (in gpm) plus the change in tank volume (in gallons) over time (in minutes), shown mathematically in Equation 3-8:

$$\sum Q_{in} = \sum Q_{out} + \frac{\Delta Volume}{\Delta time}$$ *Equation 3-8*

For the vertically mounted cylindral tank shown previously in Figure 3-9, the volume of liquid in the tank is given in Equation 3-3. By re-arranging Equation 3-8 and incorporating Equation 3-3, the conservation of mass for this tank can be expressed in Equation 3-9:

$$\sum Q_{in} - \sum Q_{out} = \frac{Area \times \Delta Level \times \frac{7.48\ gal}{ft^3}}{\Delta time}$$ *Equation 3-9*

Further re-arranging gives Equation 3-10:

$$\frac{\Delta Level}{\Delta time} = \frac{(\sum Q_{in} - \sum Q_{out})}{\left(\frac{\pi D^2}{4} \times \frac{7.48\ gal}{ft^3}\right)}$$ *Equation 3-10*

Since the units of the variables in Equation 3-10 are consistant with the nomenclature that has been used throughout this book (Q in gpm, D in feet), the change in level per unit time is in feet per minute with the inclusion of the conversion factor of 7.48 gal/ft^3.

Equation 3-10 can be evaluated to determine several things about the dynamic response of the tank level. If the sum of the flow rate into the tank equals the sum of the flow rate leaving the tank, the tank level will remain constant, which is intuitively obvious. The change in level per unit time will be positive if the flow rate entering the tank is greater than the flow rate leaving the tank, in which case the level will increase. The change in level per unit time can be negative if the flow rate leaving the tank is greater than the flow rate entering the tank, in which case the level will be decreasing.

Also, how fast the level changes during transient conditions depends on the magnitude of the difference between the inlet and outlet flows of the tank. It also depends on the tank diameter and geometry: the larger the tank diameter, the slower the level will rise for a given mismatch between flow into and out of the tank.

System Response to Changing Tank Level

A changing tank level will have an impact on the rest of the piping system. Consider the system with an open tank of 60°F water with a level of 5 feet shown in Figure 3-21. It has a pump delivering 400 gpm to an end user. The 5 feet of level corresponds to 2.2 psig pressure at the bottom of the tank. The head loss in the suction piping is 1.7 feet, but combined with the elevation change, a net pressure gain occurs to give a pump inlet pressure of 3.6 psig. At 400 gpm, the pump produces 86.9 feet of total head, which corresponds to a pressure gain of 37.6 psig, giving a pump discharge pressure of 41.2 psig. Also, the piping system provides 41.7 feet of NPSHa to the pump (centrifugal pumps will be discussed in Chapter 4 and head loss calculations will be discussed in Chapter 5.)

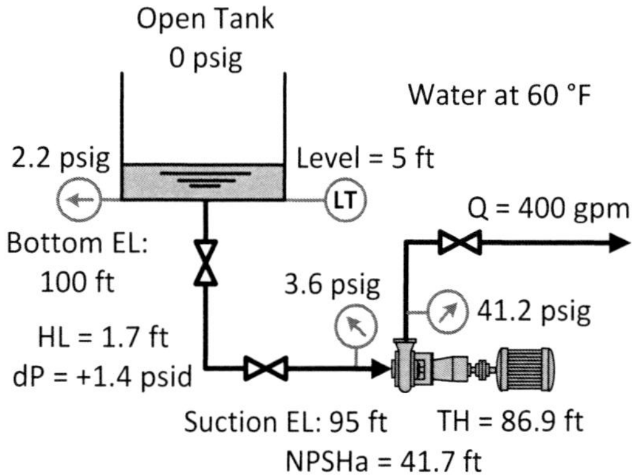

Figure 3-21. Piping system response with a 5 feet liquid level in a tank. PF

Now consider the system response to increasing the tank level to 15 feet as shown in Figure 3-22. Raising the tank level by 10 feet will increase the pressure at the bottom of the tank by 4.3 psig to 6.5 psig. The pump inlet pressure also increases by 4.3 psig to 7.9 psig. If the flow rate is maintained at 400 gpm, the pump Total Head stays the same, so the pump discharge pressure also increases by 4.3 psig to 45.5 psig. NPSHa increases by 10 feet as well.

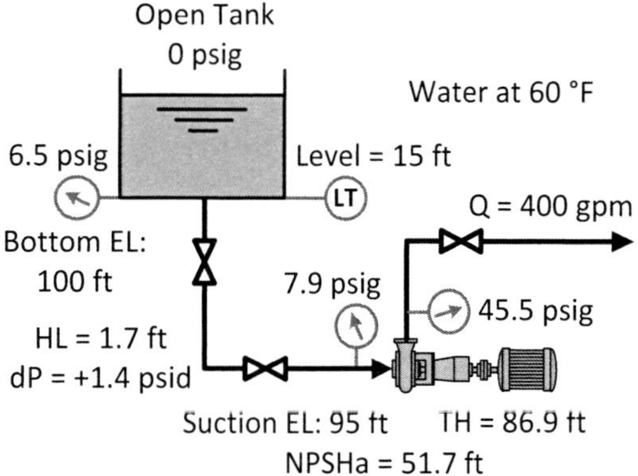

Figure 3-22. Piping system response with a 15 feet liquid level in a tank. PF

Check of Operational Understanding

Question: If the 400 gpm flow rate to the system is controlled by a control valve at the outlet of the pump, what has to happen to the valve position?

Answer: The valve will throttle down some since the inlet pressure of the valve also increased by 4.3 psig.

Operational Problems Involving Tank Level

A high tank level or low tank level can cause numerous problems with the operation of a piping system. Of course, high tank level can result in over flowing the tank. Depending on the contents of the tank and where the tank is located, this can result in just a nuisance and additional work to clean up the liquid, or it can be an extremely hazardous situation. Cold water can be easily cleaned up, but overflowing a sulfuric acid storage tank will require a hazmat response. In addition, overflowing the tank may result in damage to surrounding equipment and to the environment.

Operating a tank with the level too high can result in covering pipe penetrations located at the top of the tank. In the case of a pressurizer in a nuclear power plant, this would result in the loss of pressure control for the primary cooling loop. For a boiler steam drum, a high drum level could result in moisture carry-over and water droplets damaging the steam turbine.

Low tank level can result in pump cavitation, air entrainment into the pump suction, or vortex formation at the tank outlet which could cause additional problems with the pump. For a tank with a submerged heat exchanger, low level could result in exposing the heater tubes which could overheat the tube bundle.

Tank Surface Pressure

According to Pascal's Law, the pressure on the surface of the liquid in a tank is distributed equally and undiminished throughout the liquid and to the walls of its container. This has a significant impact on the hydraulic performance of the entire piping system.

There are several ways to measure the surface pressure of a tank. The bourdon tube pressure gage shown in Figure 3-23 is one of the most common methods to measure the pressure in a tank or pipeline locally.

A U-tube manometer shown in Figure 3-24 may be used for tanks with slight pressures or vacuums. Pressure transducers and pressure transmitters are also common methods of measuring the tank pressure. These will be discussed in the Process Measurement and Controls chapter.

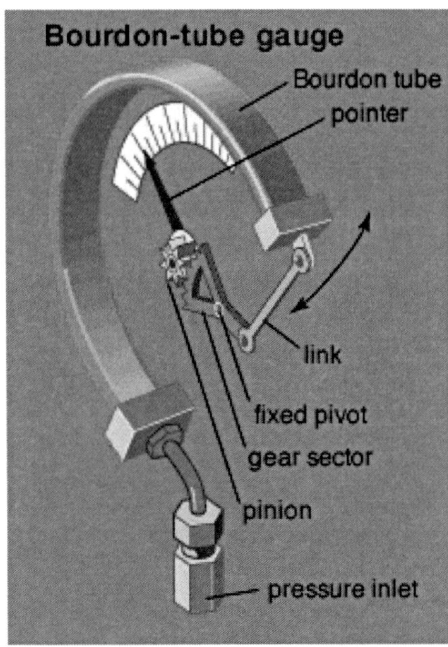

Figure 3-23. Bourdon tube pressure gage (courtesy of Encyclopaedia Britannica).

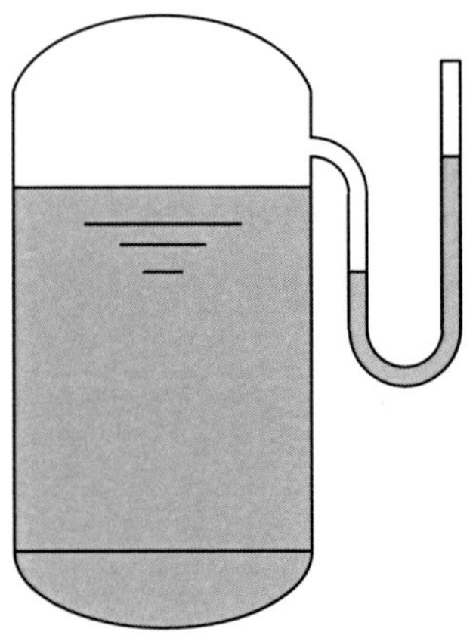

Figure 3-24. Manometer used to measure slight tank pressures or vacuum.

Controlling Tank Pressure

In many applications, the pressure of the tank must be controlled for process reasons, as a safety issue, or for some other purpose such as quality control or environmental regulations. There are a variety of methods to control the pressure (or vacuum) in a tank.

The pressure may be controlled by a flow rate going into a tank, for example using a nitrogen or air padding as shown in Figure 3-25.

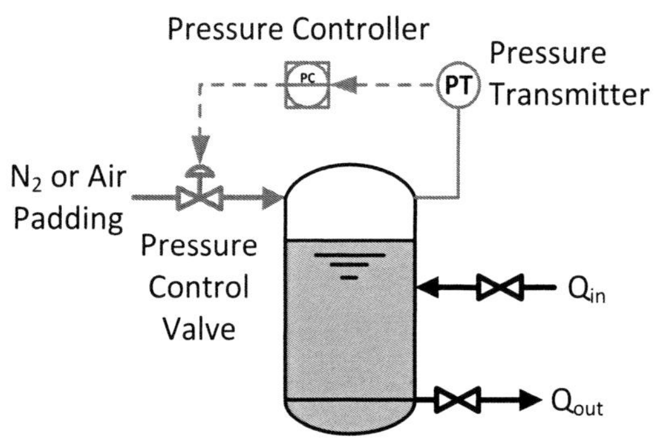

Figure 3-25. Tank pressure control using a nitrogen or air padding.

The flow of gases or vapors leaving the tank may also be used to control the tank pressure, as shown in Figure 3-26. Applications of this method of pressure control include a condensate flash tank or a digester vent gas pressure control in the pulp and paper industry or a waste water treatment facility.

Figure 3-27 shows the pressure control method used to maintain the pressure of the primary coolant loop in a pressurized water nuclear reactor. Pressure is controlled using a pressurizer, which is a staturated steam system. Heat input through an electric heater bundles increases the water temperature and therefore increases the saturated steam pressure, while spray from a cooler stream reduces the pressure when needed.

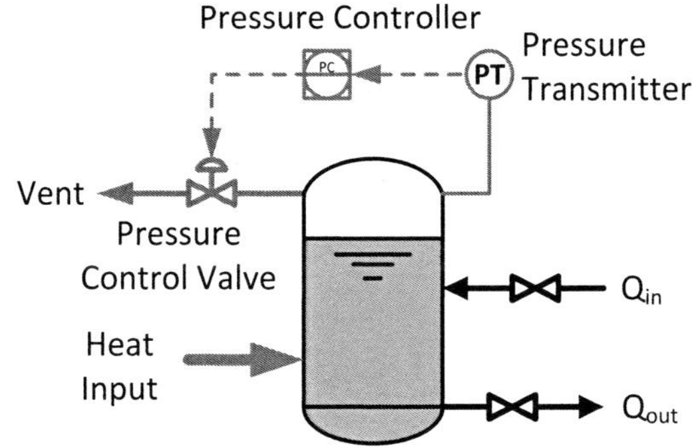

Figure 3-26. Tank pressure control by regulating the flow of vent gases leaving the vessel.

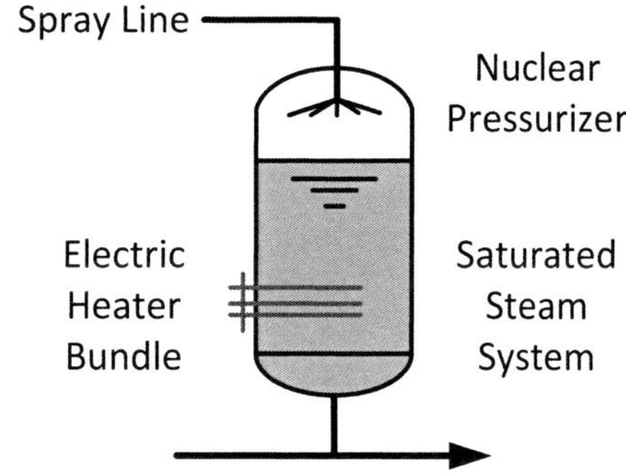

Figure 3-27. Pressure control method used in a pressurized water nuclear reactor primary loop.

System Response to Changing Tank Pressure

Pascal's Law can be used to understand how a piping system will respond to a change in the surface pressure in a tank. The pressures for the piping system shown in Figure 3-28 were determined with an open tank at 0 psig. This is the same system that was discussed in Figure 3-21.

Compare the pressure reading in Figure 3-28 to those in Figure 3-29, which shows the same piping system except that the tank is a closed tank pressurized to 25 psig.

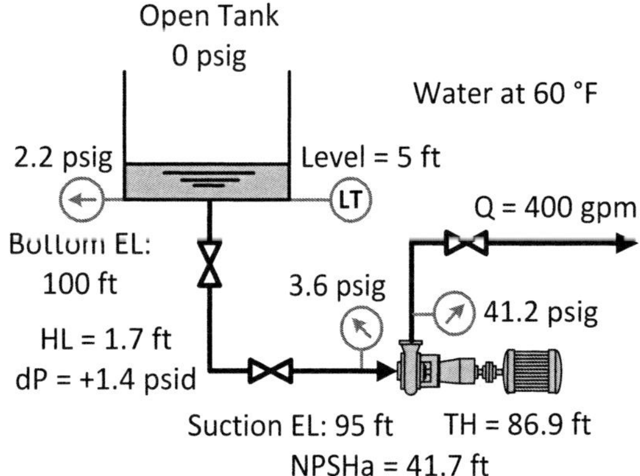

Figure 3-28. Piping system response with an open tank at 0 psig. PF

According to Pascal's Law, the additional 25 psig that is applied to the surface of the liquid in the tank is distributed to the rest of the piping system. The pressure at the bottom of the tank increases by 25 psig, the pump suction pressure increases by 25 psig, and because the pump produces the same amount of total head at 400 gpm flow rate, the pump discharge pressure also increases by 25 psig.

The NPSHa also increases by the equivalent head of 25 psig, or an additional 57.7 feet to 99.4 feet of NPSHa (again, this will be discussed in Chapter 4).

> **Check of Operational Understanding**
>
> *Question*: If the flow rate is controlled with a control valve downstream of the pump, what happens to the valve position to maintain the flow rate at 400 gpm?
>
> *Answer*: Because the pressure at the inlet of the valve also increases by 25 psig, the valve has to throttle down in order to maintain the desired flow rate through the system.

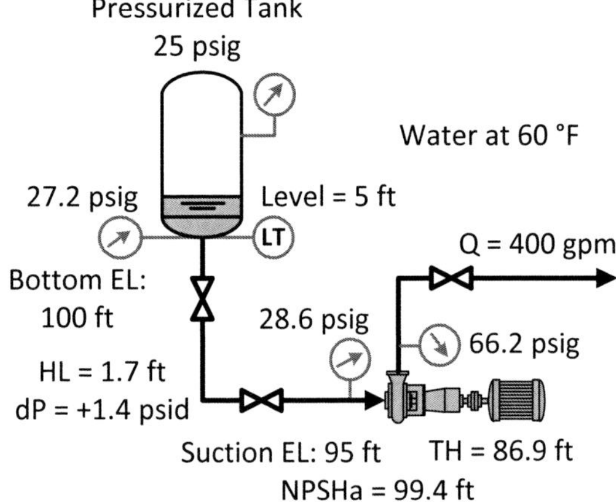

Figure 3-29. Piping system response with a tank pressurized to 25 psig. PF

Operational Problems Involving Tank Pressure

Tanks are designed and constructed to ensure the integrity of the vessel under normal operating conditions. These conditions include not only the volume and weight of the liquid in the tank, but also other conditions such as anticipated stresses due to thermal transients, pressure transients, wind, and earthquakes. A safety factor is incorporated in the sizing of the structure to allow for certain abnormal operations. Pressurized tanks are subject to more rigorous requirements than open tanks due to the higher energy state of pressurized fluids.

Pressurized tanks and vessels are built to withstand a design pressure. It is important to control the process to ensure that this pressure is not exceeded. Of course there are many things that can go wrong if a tank's pressure is not properly controlled.

Rupture discs, vacuum breakers, and pressure relief valves are installed to prevent catastrophic failure of a pressure vessel in the event of a pressure excursion.

Short of catastrophic failure, abnormal pressure conditions can cause addition problems. Depending on the application, high or low pressure can result in changes to chemical reaction rates if the reaction is dependent on pressure. In addition, if there is a crack or leak on the tank or leak-by of an isolation valve, abnormal pressures can increase the size of the crack and increase the leak rate.

Tank Temperature Measurements

If the fluid temperature is an important parameter for a process in which a tank is installed, the temperature of the fluid may be measured and controlled in or around the tank. The fluid temperature may be measured directly on the tank with a thermowell installed in the side of the tank, or the temperature may be measured in the fluid entering or leaving the tank.

Controlling Tank Temperatures

Tank temperature may be controlled using a variety of methods depending on the application. One method is to control the flow of hot and cold fluid into the tank as shown in Figure 3-30, or to control the temperature of the fluid using a heat exchanger before the fluid enters the tank. A tank may also contain a submerged heater in which the flow of steam or a hot liquid or cold liquid is controlled to maintain the temperature of the fluid in the tank, shown in Figure 3-31.

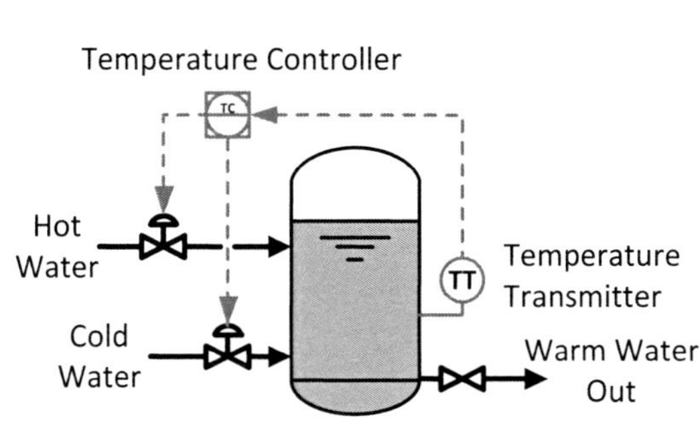

Figure 3-30. Controlling tank temperature by regulating the flow of hot and cold liquid entering the tank.

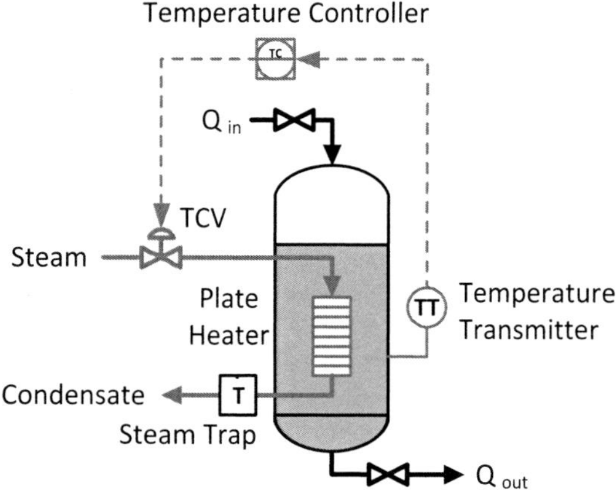

Figure 3-31. Controlling tank temperature with the control of steam flow to a submerged plate heater.

System Response to Changing Tank Temperature

The effect that a fluid's temperature has on the hydraulic performance of a piping system will be presented in the pumps and pipelines chapters, but because the fluid's temperature may be controlled at the tank, a discussion of the fluid properties impact on the system response is warranted here. Consider the piping system in Figure 3-32, which is the same system that was used to understand the effects of level and pressure changes in a piping system and shown in Figures 3-21 and 3-28.

The original system was pumping water at 60 °F, which has a vapor pressure of 0.26 psia, a viscosity of 1.1 cP, and a density of 62.4 lb/ft^3. Compare the head loss and pressure values in Figure 3-32 to those in Figure 3-33, which shows the same system except that the working fluid is water at 160 °F. Water at 160 °F has a vapor pressure of 4.75 psia, viscosity of 0.39 cP, and density of 61.0 lb/ft^3.

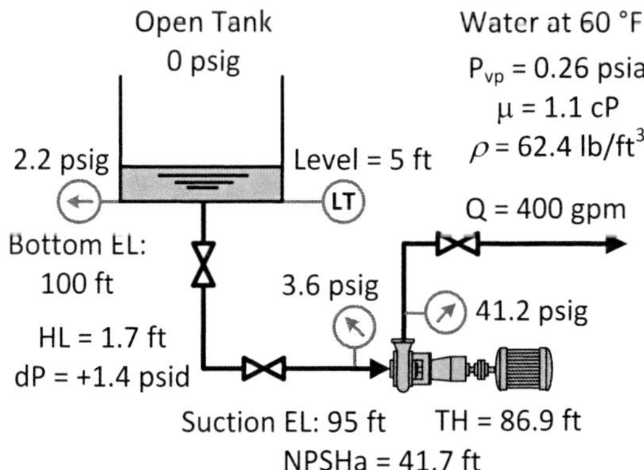

Figure 3-32. Piping system response when working fluid is water at 60 °F.

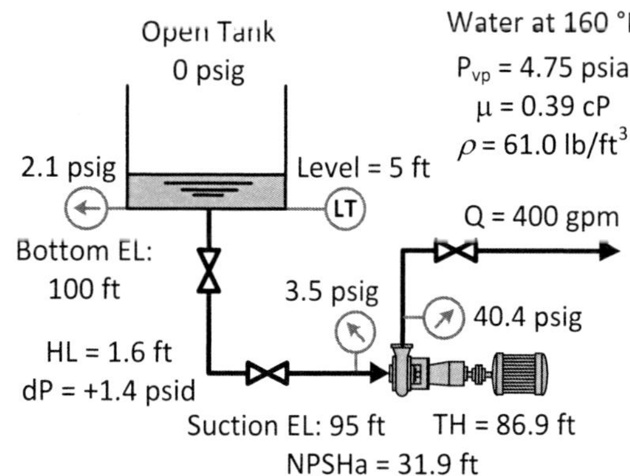

Figure 3-33. Piping system response when working fluid is water at 160 °F.

The reduced fluid density reduces the pressure at the bottom of the tank slightly from 2.2 psig to 2.1 psig. The change in density and viscosity reduces the head loss in the pump suction piping slightly, but not enough to change the pressure drop across the pipeline within the significant digits that are displayed. The net effect is a reduction of the fluid pressure at the pump suction by 0.1 psig.

For the same flow rate of 400 gpm, the pump Total Head stays the same at 86.9 ft, but since the fluid density decreased, the pressure gain across the pump decreases as well, which reduces the discharge pressure of the pump. The net effect is a reduction of the pump discharge pressure of 0.8 psig.

Depending on the accuracy and the range of the scale of the pressure gages, these changes may not even be detectable. However, a thorough analysis should be done when designing and evaluating the hydraulic performance of a piping system in which the fluid temperature, and therefore fluid properties, change significantly. The magnitude of the change in the fluid properties will vary depending on what the working fluid is and how much the fluid temperature changes.

The most significant change in the performance of the system is the reduction of the NPSHa for the pump. The increased fluid temperature results in a higher fluid vapor pressure, which reduces NPSHa from 41.7 feet to 31.9 feet. The effect this has on pump performance is discussed in the next chapter.

Operational Problems Involving Temperature

Several operational problems may result if the temperature of the fluid in a tank is not properly controlled. From a hydraulic perspective, the major problem that could occur with high fluid temperatures is cavitation occuring in a centrifugal pump due to the increased fluid vapor pressure. Also, if the tank is full, a small change in the fluid temperature will result in a large change in fluid pressure.

There are non-hydraulic effects that should be considered if the fluid temperature is not maintained at the appropriate value. If the tank is used in a process for controlling chemical reactions, the rate of the reaction may be increased or decreased depending on the nature of the reaction.

High temperatures could also result in high thermal stresses and the formation of cracking at the welds, which could lead to catastrophic failure of the tank.

Tank Penetrations

A tank may have many penetrations depending on the application and the fluid it contains. The tank will have connections for the fluid entering and leaving the tank. It may also have dedicated fill and drain lines. A vent line may also be installed to vent the vapor space during filling or to vent gases produced during normal operations. A separate chemical injection line may also penetrate the tank.

The tank may have safety and relief valves, vacuum breakers, loop seals, rupture discs, or other overpressure protection devices installed to ensure the maximum allowable pressure (or vacuum) is not exceeded.

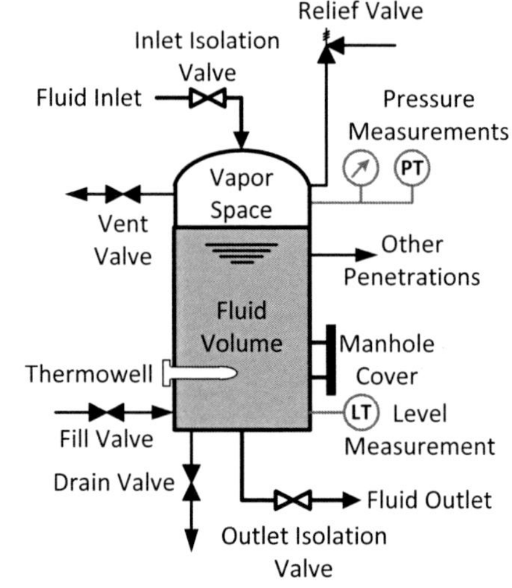

Figure 3-34. Typical penetrations found on tanks.

In most applications, there will also be penetrations for instrumentation such as level and pressure taps and thermowells for temperature measurement. Many will have a manhole for tank entry or other penetrations such as inspection site glasses.

Common Operating Procedures

There are many operating procedures involving tanks and vessels that should be documented by the company and followed by operations personnel. The extent to which each step is documented will depend on the application and whether the tank is a part of a hazardous process. Filling and draining a tank are common procedures, as well as venting and de-pressurizing the tank. There may be special precautions that need to be specified and adhered to when performing these tasks, depending on the fluid in the tank.

The tank may occasionally require entry by maintenance and operations personnel for repairs, inspection, or cleaning on a periodic basis. Tanks may be cleaned using steam, hydroblasting, or just washing the inside with a wash down hose. The tank may have to be entered to remove foreign material, especially after maintenance is completed. The tank may need to be inspected periodically, either by entering the tank for a visual inspection, or by another method such as measuring the wall thickness with ultrasonic testing or inspecting welds using X-RAYs.

Any time the tank has to be entered, the tank needs to be locked and tagged out of service using the company's lock out program. In addition, the tank may need to be tested for a toxic atmosphere using the company's Confined Space Entry procedures.

Abnormal Operations

A company should also have procedures for handling abnormal operations involving tanks and vessels. An operator may have to deal with a loss of level, pressure, or temperature control. Over-filling or emptying out a tank during normal operations may be encountered. The tank may over-pressurize resulting in the lifting of a safety relief valve, rupture disk, or vacuum breaker. The tank may collapse if it is not vented during drainage or cool down. A pluggage of the inlet or outlet pipe may cause operational problems that have to be resolved to return to normal operations.

A leak on the tank may just be a nuisance, or depending on the fluid, it may be extremely dangerous to personnel and surrounding equipment. It may also lead to a complete rupture of the tank. Responding to many of these abnormal operations may just be a matter of common sense, but depending on the severity of the problem, drastic action may need to be taken.

Over-Filling a Tank

A tank experiencing a level control problem may result in over-flowing the contents of the tank. The impact of over-filling the tank is going to depend on the nature of the fluid. The response to a spill of sulfuric acid or sodium hydroxide will be much more severe compared to a spill of cold water.

One of the first things that should be done is to notify others and warn them of the situation. A minor situation can become a major incident if the situation gets out of control due to a single person trying to contain a small spill.

The operator should stop the flow of fluid going into the tank and if possible increase the rate of controlled flow out of the tank. This may require shutting down the process or the entire plant.

The overflow will need to be cleaned up as well. Depending on the contents, personnel may need to don protective gear, contain the overflow, and direct it to a suitable waste disposal.

Tank Ruptures

A tank rupture may be one of the worst casualties that can happen with the operation of a tank. The catastrophic failure resulting from the rupture may result in injury and death, environmental damages and clean up costs, equipment and product loss, and a lengthy downtime to replace the tank.

Some immediate actions for a tank rupture include notifying others, shutting down systems that are pumping into the tank or adjacent systems, and evacuating plant employees, adjacent businesses, or the surrounding community.

Figures 3-35 and 3-36 show the results of an oil tank rupture in the port city of Dalian in China in July 2010 as the result of back pressure from an oil pipeline explosion. The tank contained a heavy crude oil that flowed into the port. Workers who fell into the heavy crude almost lost their lives. The financial cost of the incident included damaged equipment, lost production, and environment clean up costs.

Figure 3-35. Tank rupture due to an oil line explosion in Dalian, China, July 2010 (courtesy of Reuters).

Figure 3-36. Workers nearly lost their lives when they fell into the heavy crude from the ruptured tank (courtesy of Reuters).

Tank Failure Due to Excessive Vacuum

In addition to excessive internal pressure, a tank can fail due to extreme vacuum as well. Figures 3-37 and 3-38 show a rail car that had just been steamed out and still had hot steam inside when it started to rain. The cool rain caused the steam to condense. The volume occupied by water is much less the volume occupied by steam, so a vacuum was created inside the rail car.

Figure 3-37. Railcar being steam cleaned.

Figure 3-38. Collapse of railcar due to excessive vacuum as steam condensed.

The tank had a vent designed to release pressure, not vacuum. Also, since the tank was designed for internal pressure, it had no vacuum support rings. When the vacuum became high enough, the pressure stresses created by the vacuum completely collapsed the tank.

Chapter Four

Pumps

Pumps convert mechanical energy into hydraulic energy and add it to the working fluid in order to transport mass and energy throughout a piping system. There are two general categories of pumps used in piping systems: kinetic (centrifugal) and positive displacement pumps. This chapter will focus on the most common kinetic type used in the majority of industrial and commercial applications: the centrifugal pump.

How a Centrifugal Pump Works

A centrifugal pump can be viewed as an energy conversion device: it converts mechanical energy from a driver into hydraulic energy in the form of pressure and flow. Figure 4-1 shows a typical driver and pump, in this case the driver is an AC motor. However, the driver can be a DC motor, a diesel engine, a steam turbine, or some other driving mechanism such as a pneumatic actuator in the case of an air operated diaphragm pump.

Figure 4-1. Photo of typical motor and centrifugal pump (courtesy Crane Pumps & Systems).

The output of the driver is typically mechanical energy in the form of a rotating shaft. This mechanical energy from the driver is delivered to the pump shaft which is connected to the pump impeller, as shown in Figure 4-2. The centrifugal forces from the rotating impeller impart kinetic energy to the fluid which is then converted into potential energy in the form of higher fluid pressure at the discharge of the pump. This conversion of kinetic energy into potential energy occurs in the volute, or diffusing section of the pump.

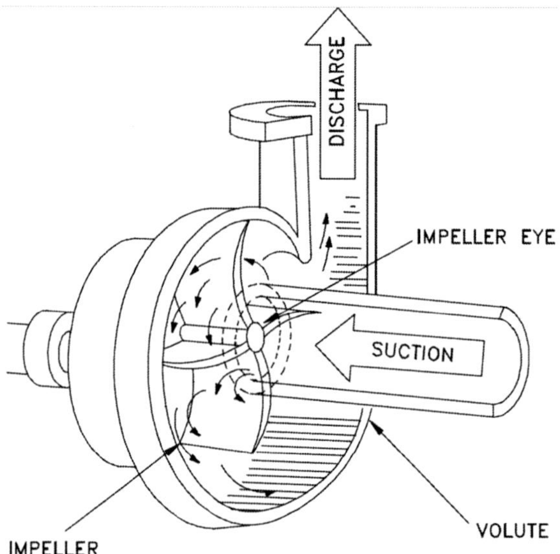

Figure 4-2. Cutaway drawing of an end suction pump showing fluid flow path (courtesy of U.S. Department of Energy).

Consider the flow path of a drop of liquid moving through the pump in Figure 4-2 and the generalized pressure and velocity profile shown in Figure 4-3. The liquid's pressure initially drops due to the head loss in the suction piping. The liquid enters the pump suction and proceeds to the eye of the rotating impeller. As the liquid approaches the eye, its pressure drops even more as its direction changes from axial flow to radial flow as it feels the centrifugal forces of the rotating impeller. The fluid velocity increases as it feels these centrifugal forces. The eye of the impeller is the lowest point of pressure in the pump.

The liquid is then accelerated by the impeller vanes due to the centrifugal forces, causing the fluid velocity to increase. Pressure also increases slightly due to the increasing cross-sectional area between the vanes. The fluid velocity increases until it reaches the impeller tips. The velocity is the greatest at the tips of the impeller vanes.

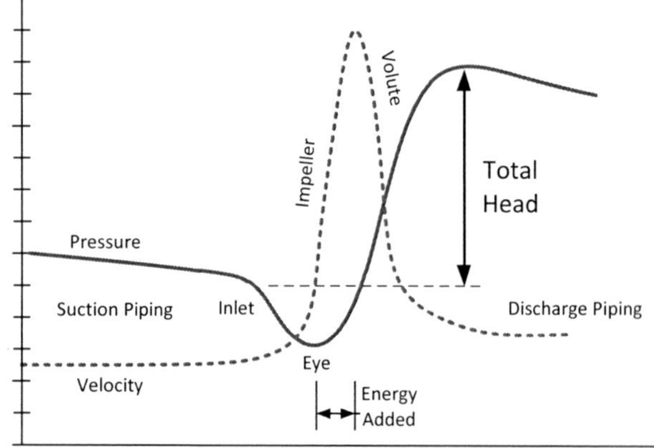

Figure 4-3. Pressure and velocity profile as a function of distance travelled through a pump.

The high velocity liquid then enters the volute, which has an increasing cross-sectional area around the circumference of the impeller. This increasing cross-sectional area causes the velocity to decrease and the pressure to increase in accordance with the Bernoulli Theorem. This is the conversion of kinetic energy into potential energy in the form of pressure.

The amount of energy that is added to the fluid per unit weight is called the "Total Head" (TH) of the pump. The pump manufacturer conducts performance test of their pumps to determine the Total Head of the pump at various flow rates and develops the pump performance curve for each line of pumps. These tests should be conducted in accordance with the ANSI/HI standards or equivalent international standards.

Equation 4-1 gives the complete equation for calculating the amount of total head based on the measured suction and discharge pressures, elevations of the pressure gages, and suction and discharge velocities.

$$TH = \frac{144}{\rho}\left(P_{discharge} - P_{suction}\right) + \frac{\left(v_{discharge}^2 - v_{suction}^2\right)}{2g} + \left(Z_{discharge} - Z_{suction}\right)$$

Equation 4-1

If the suction and discharge pipelines are the same diameter, the velocity head component of Equation 4-1 drops out, and if the elevations of the pressure gages are the same, the elevation head component drops out. Even when these conditions are not the case, the velocity head and elevation head components typically account for only a couple of feet of head, so Equation 4-2 can be used as a reasonable approximation for a pump's Total Head.

$$TH \cong \frac{144 dP_{pump}}{\rho}$$

Equation 4-2

Major Parts of a Centrifugal Pump

The major parts of a centrifugal pump can be seen in Figure 4-4 and include the pump shaft, bearings, seal, impeller, and the pump casing, which contains the pump suction and discharge and the volute (or diffusing section).

The pump shaft supports the impeller and transfers the mechanical energy from the driver to the pump impeller.

The bearings support the weight of the shaft and impeller, as well as absorbs the radial and axial forces acting on the impeller due to fluid flow through the pump.

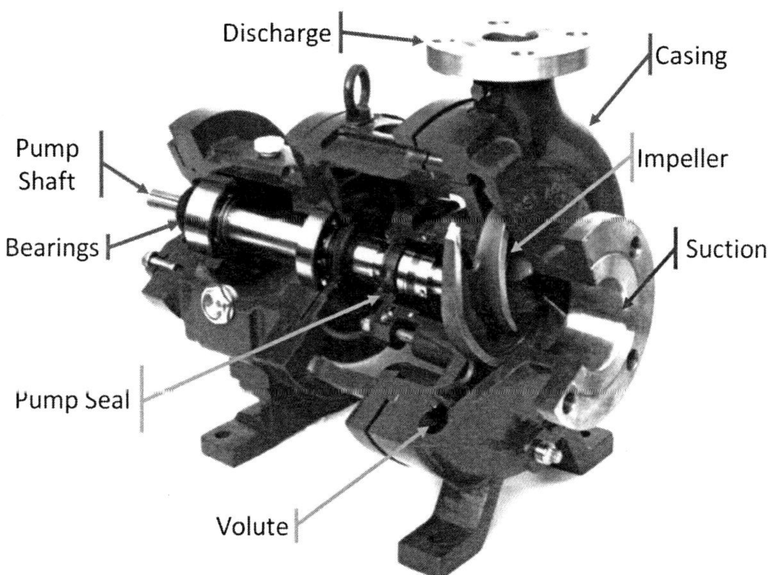

Figure 4-4. Major parts of a centrifugal pump (courtesy of Truflo Pumps).

A pump seal prevents excessive leakage from the pressurized casing to the outside of the pump (or prevents excessive air intake if the casing is at a vacuum). The seal can be a packing gland or a mechanical seal.

The impeller converts the mechanical energy of the rotating shaft into hydraulic energy in the form of velocity head by increasing the fluid velocity as it travels from the eye to the tip of the impeller vanes.

The pump casing contains the impeller and its shape forms the volute, which converts fluid velocity head into pressure head.

The pump suction directs the fluid flow to the eye of the impeller and the discharge provides a connection for the high pressure fluid to flow into the system piping.

Impeller Types

Centrifugal pump impellers can be an open, semi-open, or fully enclosed design, as shown in Figure 4-5. Open impellers consist only of vanes attached to a central hub. The semi-open impeller has a full or partial shroud that provides structural stability to the vanes. Open and semi-open impellers are considered a good choice for pumping liquids containing solids or stringy materials because they reduce the opportunity for solids in the liquid from becoming trapped as they pass through the impeller.

Figure 4-5. Open, semi-open, and fully enclosed impeller types (courtesy U.S Department of Energy).

Closed impellers have a shroud on the front and back side of the vanes to provide a very defined flow path through the impeller. Closed impellers are a good choice for pumping relatively clean, non-corrosive liquids, and for high temperature applications. These are used on most multi-stage pumps. However, a closed impeller is more expensive to manufacture than an open impeller.

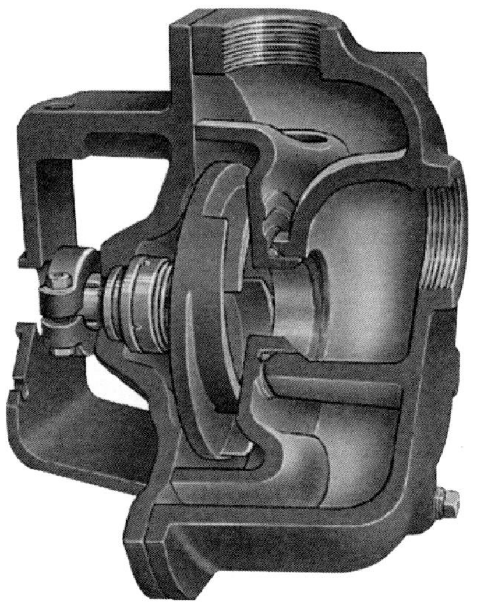

Figure 4-6. Cutaway diagram of a centrifugal pump with a semi-open impeller (courtesy Crane Pumps & Systems).

Another major difference between open and closed impellers is the way in which leakage occurs from the high pressure discharge to the low pressure suction side of the impeller. Because the rotating impeller is contained within a stationary casing, there must be some internal clearance between them, called the leakage joint.

Figure 4-6 shows a cutaway of a self-priming pump with a semi-open impeller. The leakage joint for the impeller is located between the front face of the impeller vanes and the pump casing. The tight clearance between the impeller and casing minimizes the amount of impeller leakage, or internal circulation within the pump. As this clearance opens up, the amount of internal circulation increases and the total head produced by the pump decreases.

For a pump with a closed impeller, such as the one shown in Figure 4-7, the leakage joint is between the wear ring and the rotating impeller. The wear ring is a soft metal cylindrical ring mounted in the pump casing located between the impeller and the pump casing. The wear ring is designed to wear in the event of contact with the rotating impeller or erosion. The close tolerance and length of the wear ring minimizes the amount of internal impeller leakage from the high pressure discharge back to the low pressure suction side of the impeller. As the wear ring wears, the clearance and the internal recirculation will increase, decreasing the total head at a given flow rate or decreasing the flow rate at a given head.

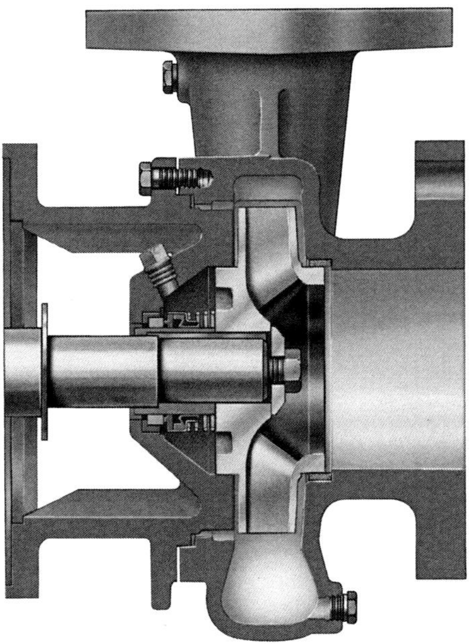

Figure 4-7. Cross-sectional diagram of a centrifugal pump with a closed impeller (courtesy Crane Pumps & Systems).

Closed impellers come in two types: single suction and double suction. In a single suction closed impeller such as the one shown in Figure 4-7, all the fluid enters the impeller from one side. This type of impeller is used on most centrifugal pumps. A double suction impeller is used on horizontal split case pumps or as the first stage in some multi-stage pumps. Figures 4-8 and 4-9 show the double suction impeller.

The axial thrust on the double suction impeller is more balanced because of the equal areas and pressure gradients on the suction and discharge portions of the impeller. The areas of the two suction sides of the impeller are equal or nearly equal, and the discharge of the pump is common to both sides.

On a single suction impeller, the suction side has much lower pressure than the discharge portion of the impeller, and the back side of the entire impeller is exposed to the higher discharge pressure, resulting in a larger axial thrust on the impeller and pump shaft.

Figure 4-8. Double-sided closed impeller (courtesy Crane Pumps & Systems).

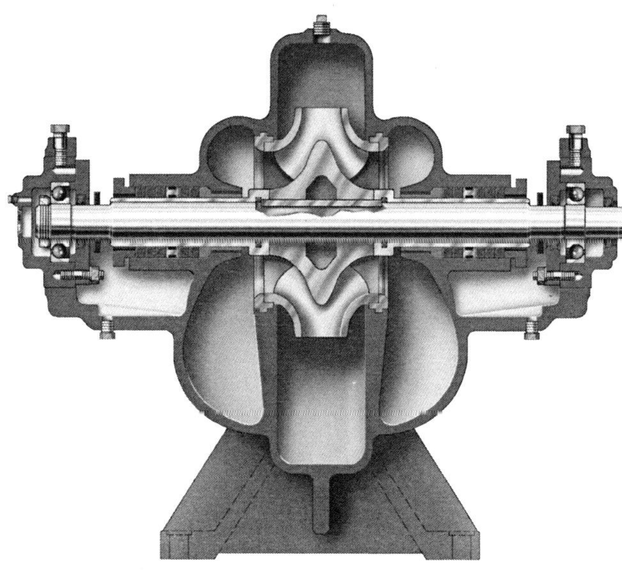

Figure 4-9. Double-sided closed impeller (courtesy Crane Pumps & Systems).

Pump Casings

Another difference among centrifugal pump designs is the method used to slow the fluid leaving the impeller and increase fluid pressure. This is accomplished by designing the pump casing as a single volute, double volute, or by using a diffuser.

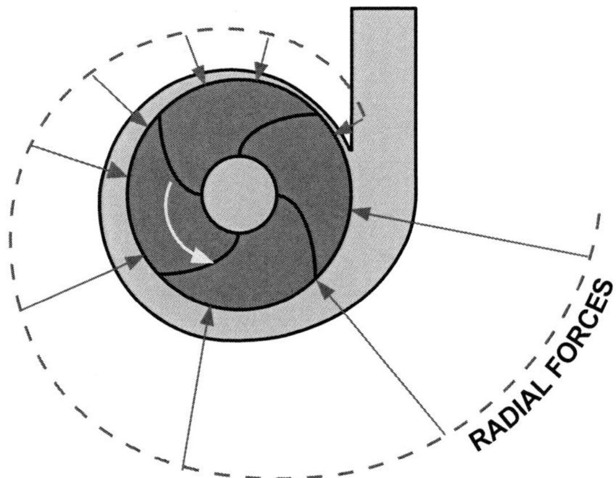

Figure 4-10. Cross section of a single volute pump showing the radial forces created by the pressure profile around the impeller.

Figure 4-10 shows a pump with a single volute. The volume of the volute increases moving counter-clockwise around the impeller from the discharge, causing the fluid velocity to decrease and the pressure to increase in accordance with the Bernoulli Theorem. The "cutwater" is the narrowest gap between the impeller and the casing where the fluid can either exit the pump discharge or recirculate around the volute. The increasing pressure profile around the impeller creates an increasing radial force as shown in Figure 4-10, with the lowest radial force just to the left of the cutwater and the highest radial force just to the right of the cutwater at the pump outlet. The net radial hydraulic force, combined with the weight of the impeller cantilevered on the pump shaft, creates a total radial force acting on the impeller that causes the shaft to deflect and the entire rotating assembly to vibrate. The greater the radial loads, the greater the vibration, and the more wear and tear on the pump bearings and seals.

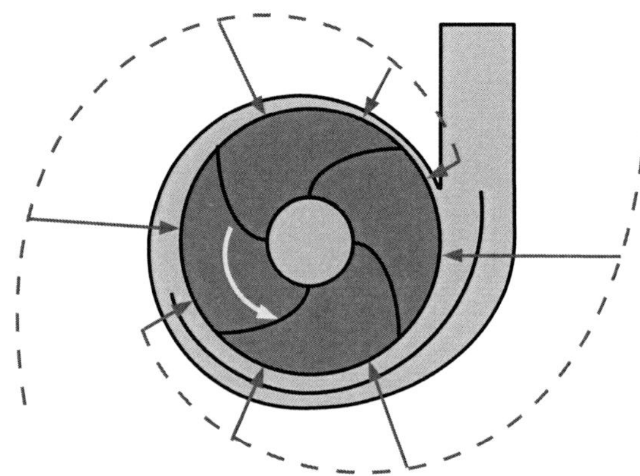

Figure 4-11. Cross section of a double volute pump showing the radial loads created by the pressure profile around the impeller.

The net radial loads can be reduced by using a double volute design such as the one shown in Figure 4-11. The double volute design has a divider plate cast in the volute to provide two flow paths on the lower half of the volute. This creates two cutwaters about 180 degrees apart. As a result, the radial loads caused by the hydraulic pressure profile around the volute is more balanced than with the single volute. Pumps with a double volute are more expensive to manufacture, and as a result, are typically used on larger centrifugal pumps to reduce the radial loads.

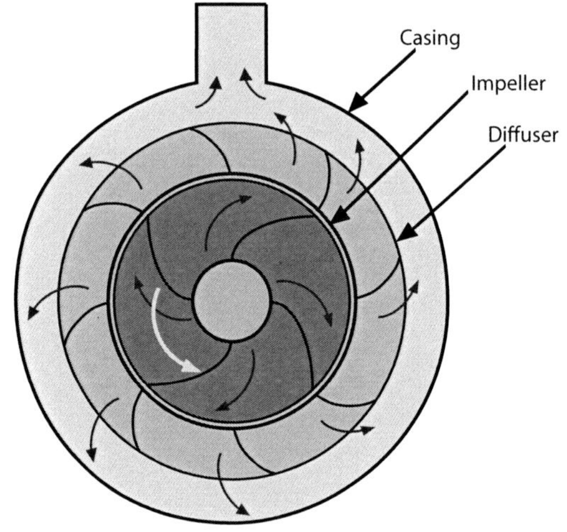

Figure 4-12. Cross-section a centrifugal pump with a diffuser.

A centrifugal pump with a diffuser shown in Figure 4-12 produces the smallest radial loads of all centrifugal pumps. As the high-velocity liquid leaves the impeller, it travels directly into a stationary diffuser with vanes that form passages of increasing cross-sectional area. As the liquid flows through the diffuser, the fluid slows down and the pressure increases.

Radial Loads and Pump Reliability

The pressure gradient around the impeller produces radial loads that are transferred to the shaft. These radial loads cause the shaft to deflect and the impeller to vibrate, increasing the loads on the pump bearings and seals. The larger the radial forces on the pump shaft, the greater the shaft deflection, the greater the vibration, and the greater the wear and tear on the pump's bearings and seal. This vibration also results in the loss of energy at the bearings and seal, causing the pump efficiency to decrease the farther the pump opertates to the right or left of the best efficiency point.

All centrifugal pump impellers are designed for a specific flow rate that corresponds to the pump's best efficiency point (BEP), which also corresponds to the location in which the radial loads on the impeller are at a minimum. Figure 4-13 shows typical radial loads produced by single volute, double volute, and diffuser casings all normalized to the BEP. The minimum radial loads for each design occurs at the pump's best efficiency point and increases the further the pump's operating point is from the best efficiency point. Diffuser type pumps typically have the lowest amount of radial loads while single volute casings have the greatest amount of radial loads.

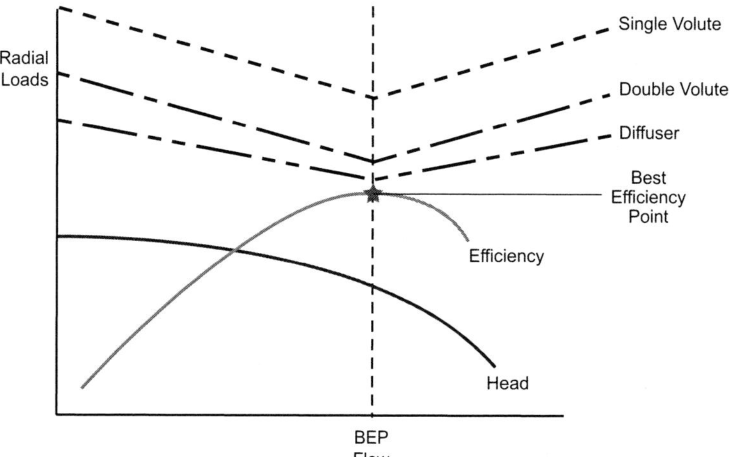

Figure 4-13. Relative radial loads for single volute, double volute, and diffuser casing designs normalized to the BEP.

Understanding these radial loads can help explain the reliability of the pump and the various problems that can occur. Barringer & Associates conducted a study of the reliability of centrifugal pumps and the various modes of failure in relation to where the pump operated with respect to the BEP. Figure 4-14 shows a bell-shaped reliability curve along with the pump curve. The reliability curve shows that the Mean Time Between Failure (MTBF) is the greatest when the pump is operated at its BEP. The MTBF decreases the farther the pump is operated to the right or the left of the BEP. Low bearing and seal life and cavitation are the main modes of failure when operated to the right of the BEP. Operating to the left of the BEP results in discharge and suction recirculation problems that cause

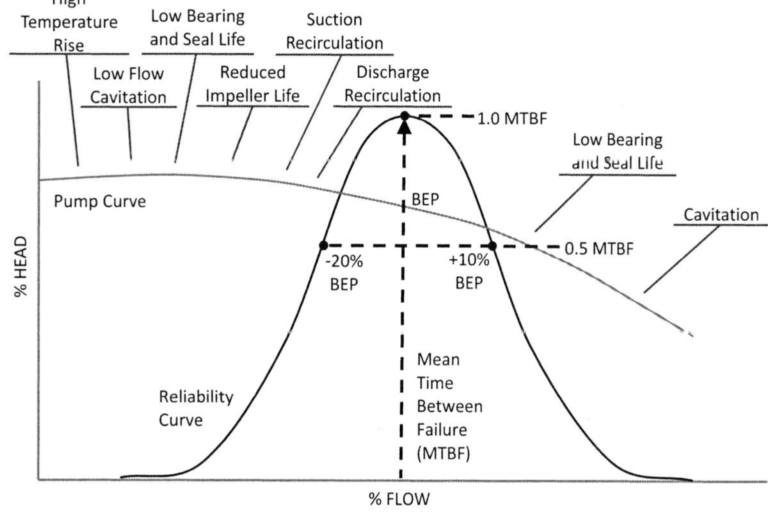

Figure 4-14. Reliability of a centrifugal pump in relation to where it operates with respect to the BEP. (Barringer & Associates)

pump failure; impeller, bearing, and seal failures when operated further to the left of the BEP; and low flow cavitation and high temperature rise failures when operated close to the shutoff point of the pump.

Pumps rarely operate at a single flow rate and are typically required to operate over a range of flows, so the best an engineer can do when sizing a pump for a given application is to select one that will operate within a reasonable area around the BEP or to design the system so that the pump(s) will operate within that range. The Hydraulics Institute provides recommendations for a reasonable operating range around the BEP based on the pump type, with typical values of 80-110% BEP and 70-120% BEP, based on pump design.

Pump Seals

Because the pump consists of a rotating shaft / impeller and a stationary casing that contains the working fluid, a sealing mechanism must be employed to keep the fluid from leaking out of the pump between the shaft and casing (or to keep air from entering the pump if the casing is at a vacuum). The stuffing box is the part of the casing where the shaft enters the pump and it contains the pump seal. The sealing mechanism can be either a packing gland or a mechanical seal.

Packing Glands

The traditional method of sealing a pump is with a packing gland, shown in Figure 4-15, which allows a minimal amount of leakage out of the seal. The packing gland consists of a bushing, several rings of packing, a lantern ring (optional), and a packing follower.

The bushing prevents the packing from being squeezed into the gap between the pump casing and the rotating shaft.

The packing is inserted into the stuffing box and consists of multiple rings of pliable braided fibers which can be made of a variety of materials with some lubricating property. Graphite impregnated braided packing is commonly used because the graphite reduces the friction between the rotating shaft and the stationary packing.

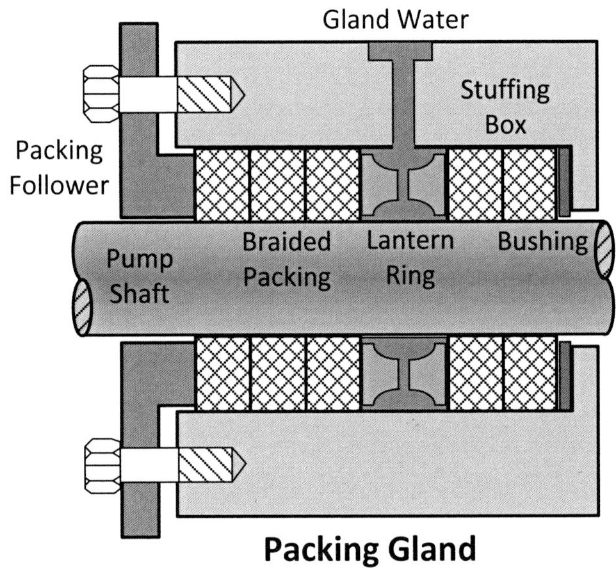

Figure 4-15. Cross-sectional diagram showing the various components of a packing gland.

A packing follower compresses the packing in the stuffing box. The rings of packing deform and fill in the gap in the stuffing box to minimize the leakage around the pump shaft. The packing gland must have a slight leakage, in the range of 1-2 drops a second, to keep the packing cool by removing the heat generated by the friction between shaft and packing. The packing follower will occasionally need to be adjusted and should be done equally one or two flats at a time on both bolts to prevent skewing the follower. When all the adjustment is taken up on the follower, the packing will need to be replaced or another ring of packing added.

A lantern ring may also be inserted between the rings of packing to allow sealing fluid to be injected into the packing gland, keeping it lubricated and cool. When a sealing fluid is supplied, it flows in both directions in the stuffing box; some leaks out of the seal to the atmosphere, some flows into the fluid inside the pump. If the fluid in the pump is clean, cool water, the sealing fluid is often supplied by the pump's discharge piping. External gland water is usually supplied under the following conditions:

- The pump's suction lift exceeds 15 feet
- The pump's discharge pressure is under 10 psig
- The pump's discharge temperature is greater than 250 °F
- Gritty fluid is being pumped
- There is a liquid other than water being pumped

Mechanical Seals

Mechanical seals are also used to keep the fluid leaking out of the pump at a minimum, but unlike packing glands, mechanical seals do not require leakage of the liquid to keep the sealing surface cool.

Mechanical seals are used when dealing with fluids other than water, or when seal leakage is undesirable. If installed properly, mechanical seals require less maintenance than packing glands.

Figure 4-16 shows a typical mechanical seal for a pump. The mechanical seal is designed to be installed in the pump's stuffing box so that the packing glands can be easily replaced by a mechanical seal.

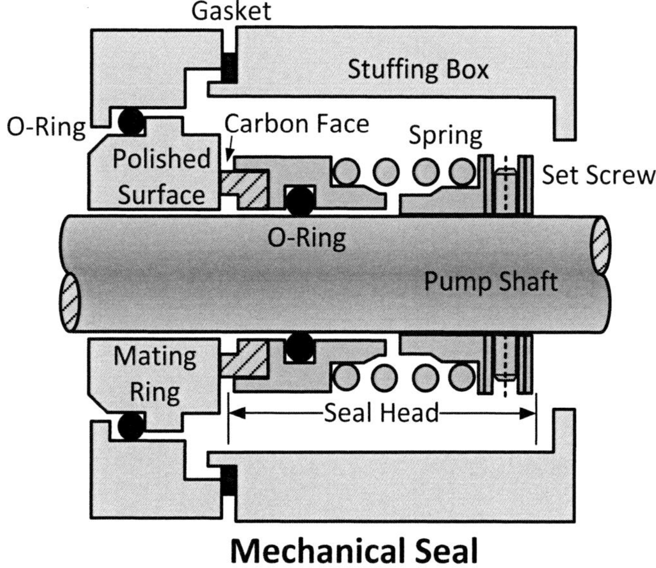

Figure 4-16. Cross-sectional diagram showing the various components of a mechanical seal.

The mechanical seal consists of a mating ring and a seal head that contact each other at a very highly polished sealing surface. The mating ring is the stationary part of the seal that is mounted to the pump casing. An O-ring and gasket provide the stationary seals between the mating ring and pump casing.

The seal head is the rotating part of the mechanical seal and is mounted to the shaft by means of a setscrew or rubber boot. The seal head consists of a set of springs that exert pressure on the primary carbon ring. The dynamic seal face is where the seal head and mating ring meet. Each of the surfaces on the dynamic seal face are highly machined and polished, providing an extremely small gap between the two elements that form the seal. A thin film of liquid from the pump is quickly vaporized by the heat that is generated at the contact point of the two polished surfaces. The miniscule amount of leakage that does occur is in the form of a vapor and can be measured in parts per million.

Double mechanical seals are used when no leakage of the pumped fluid can be tolerated, such as highly toxic liquid applications. Double mechanical seals incorporate an inboard and outboard seal with a chamber in between. This chamber can be filled with a gas or a barrier fluid to lubricate and cool the seals, and the pressure can be measured to provide an indication and alarm if the inboard seal fails. In the event of an inboard seal failure, the outboard seal provides leak protection until maintenance can be performed.

Mechanical seals are available in a wide variety of configurations in order to meet the specific needs of different challenging applications. A mechanical seal specialist should be contacted for challenging sealing applications.

Pump Drivers (Fixed vs. Variable Speed)

The pump driver supplies the energy to the rotating elements of the pump. Pump drivers can be an electric AC or DC motor, a steam turbine, an internal combustion engine, or a hydraulic turbine. The selection of the type of pump driver is based on available energy, cost, and preferences. The selection of the driver type is not covered here, but the vast majority of centrifugal pumps are driven by AC motors.

The drivers can either be fixed speed or variable speed drivers. With a fixed speed drive, the pump rotates at an essentially constant speed. To change the flow rate through the pump, valves in the piping system are throttled in order to increase or decrease head loss, thereby changing the flow rate. This method requires a minimal investment in equipment, but can be inefficient.

With a variable speed drive, the rotational speed of the pump varies based on the amount of flow rate needed for the application. This method requires the investment of a variable speed drive, but is more energy efficient. Flow control methods will be covered later in this book.

Pump Types

There are a variety of pump types to choose from for a given application. In addition to the cost of the pump, selecting a pump is a matter of meeting the hydraulic needs of the piping system, physical limitations, and company preferences. The pump selection process will be covered later in this chapter.

Basic Pump Configurations & Arrangements

The shape, size, speed, and design of the impeller and casing determine the operating characteristics of a pump. The design of the pump impeller and diffusing element is based on the intended use of the pump and the manufacturer's intended markets. Once a pump is selected, the major design elements cannot be changed by the user. The only changes that can be made to the pump are the impeller size, rotational speed, and leakage joint clearance which allow the user to make adjustments to better meet their pumping conditions.

Centrifugal pumps come in a variety of configurations based on the location of the bearings, design of the impeller, the number of stages, and application. Figure 4-17 is a chart listing the various configurations of centrifugal pumps.

The Hydraulic Institute Standard Centrifugal Pumps for Nomenclature and Definitions ANSI/HI 1.1-1.2 is an excellent reference describing the various pump configurations available. Additionally, on the Hydraulic Institute website (http://www.pumps.org) under the About Pumps tab is an excellent source of pump definitions and diagrams showing various pump configurations.

Centrifugal Pumps

Centrifugal pumps are the most common kinetic type that convert mechanical into hydraulic energy through centrifugal activity. They include overhung bearings, impeller between bearings, and regenerative turbine type pumps.

Overhung Pumps

Overhung pump impellers are mounted onto the end of the pump shaft, and the bearings are located at the other end. The impeller is cantilevered on the shaft, or "overhung" from its bearing supports. These pumps are either close or separately coupled.

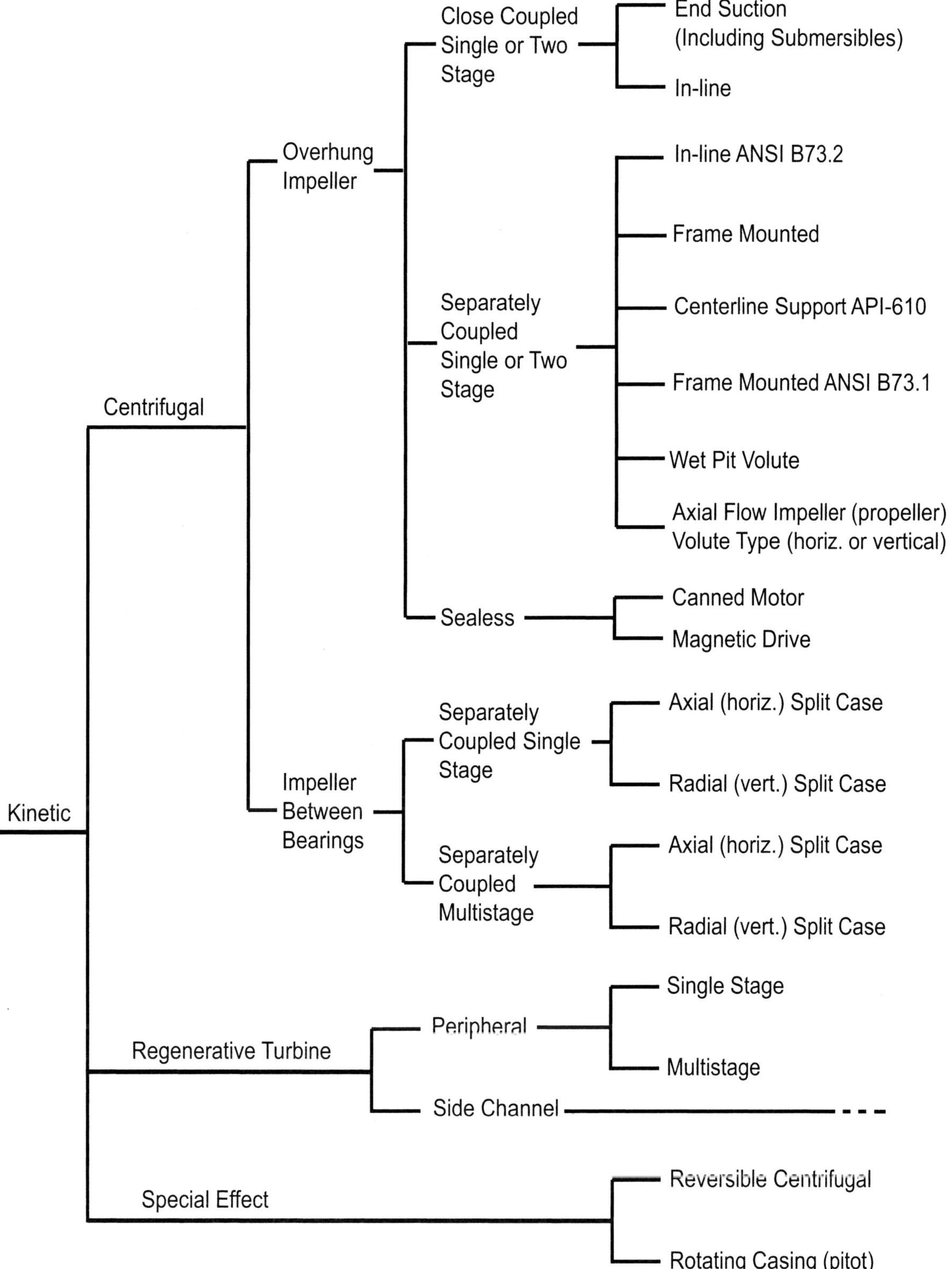

Figure 4-17 Classification of pumps based on construction and application, courtesy The Hydraulic Institute. Visit www.pumps.org for more information.

Close Coupled Pumps

A close coupled pump is one in which the impeller is mounted directly onto the driver shaft. Figure 4-18 shows a close-coupled centrifugal pump. With this type of design, the pump and motor share the same shaft, resulting in a pump that is less expensive to manufacture, but more difficult to maintain.

Figure 4-18. A typical close coupled pump (courtesy Crane Pumps & Systems).

Separately Coupled Pumps

A separately coupled pump is one in which the pump impeller is mounted onto a separate pump shaft supported by its own bearings. The driver is connected to the pump shaft by a coupling. Figure 4-19 shows a separately coupled centrifugal pump. In this application, the pump and motor are each mounted on a frame, and a coupling connects the motor shaft to the pump shaft. These pumps are typically more expensive than the close-coupled pumps and take up a bigger footprint in the plant, but they are easier to maintain.

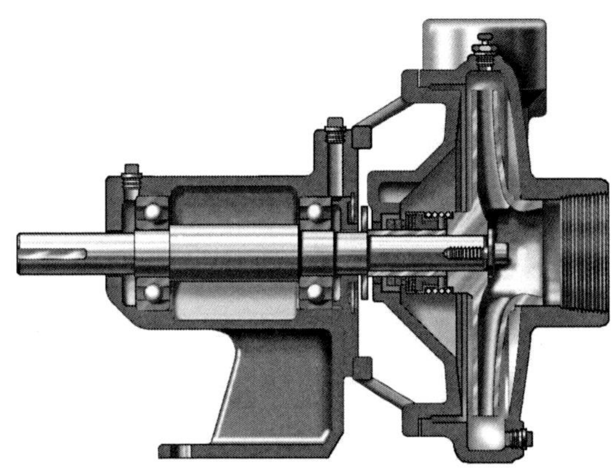

Figure 4-19. Cross-sectional drawing of a typical frame mounted separately coupled pump (courtesy Crane Pumps & Systems).

Sealless Pumps

A sealless pump does not employ a mechanical seal or packing gland to prevent the pumping liquid from escaping into the environment. In sealless pumps, the casing, rotor, shaft, and drive are encased in a pressure boundary, eliminating the possibility of leaking fluid along the pump shaft. Sealless pumps come in a canned rotor design or a magnetic drive pump. Figure 4-20 shows a sealless pump employing a canned rotor.

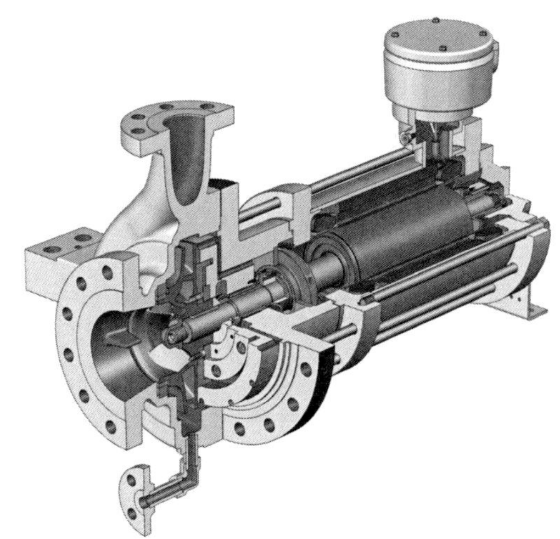

Figure 4-20. Typical sealless canned rotor pump (courtesy Sultzer Pumps Ltd. ©2008).

Impeller Between Bearings Pumps

For this type of centrifugal pump, the shaft and impeller are supported by bearings on each end of the shaft and the impeller is suspended between the bearings. This type of arrangement is typically used in horizontal split case pumps and has little axial loading. Figure 4-21 shows a horizontal split case pump with the impeller between the bearings.

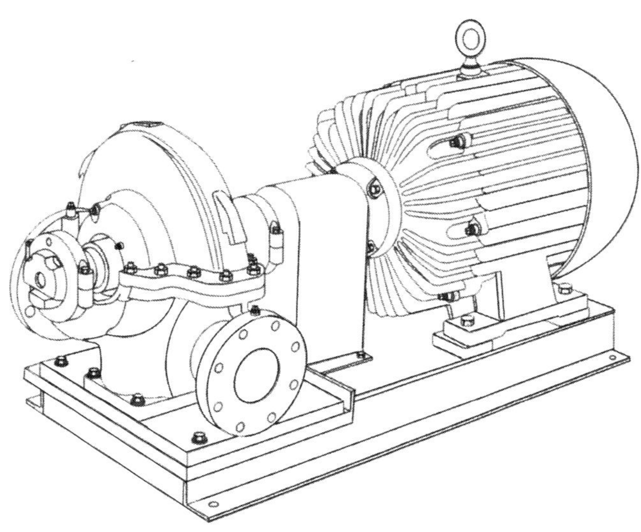

Figure 4-21. Typical horizontal split case pump (courtesy Crane Pumps & Systems).

Regenerative Turbine Pumps

A regenerative turbine such as the one shown in Figure 4-22 is a kinetic pump that produces a low flow rate and high head. This design uses peripheral or side channel vanes on the rotating impeller to impart energy to the pumped fluid. The liquid travels in a helical pattern through the impeller vanes, with the liquid pressure increasing through each passage.

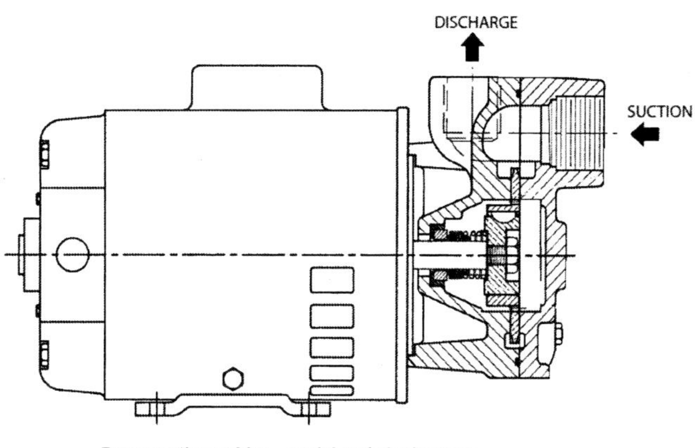

Figure 4-22. Typical regenerative turbine pump (courtesy The Hydraulic Institute).

Vertical Turbine Pumps

This type of kinetic pump, shown in Figure 4-23, is defined by the following:

- One or more bowls (stages).
- Radial flow, mixed flow, or axial flow impeller.
- The pumping element is in the fluid being pumped and is usually suspended by a column pipe that carries the liquid from the bowls to the discharge.

These pumps are available as either line shaft or submersible pumps. With a line shaft pump, the driver is on the surface and is connected to the pump by a line shaft. A submerged

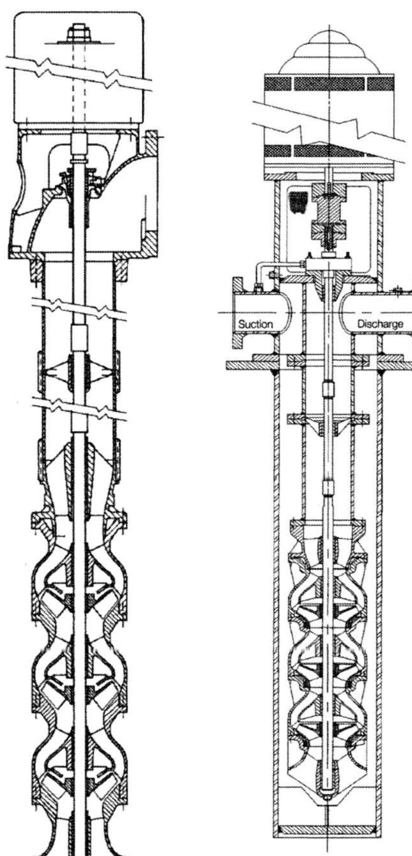

Figure 4-23. Typical vertical turbine pumps with multiple stages (courtesy The Hydraulic Institute).

pump has the motor connected directly to the pump and the pump and motor are submerged in the fluid being pumped.

Pump Selection Considerations

Selecting a pump for a particular application depends on the hydraulics of the system, the available space for the pump and driver, manufacturer preference, the properties of the fluid being pumped, the process conditions, the type of drive needed, and the desired total head and flow rate the pump must achieve. In addition, there must be sufficient net positive suction head available to prevent the pump from cavitating.

Pump selection is a multi-step, multidisciplinary process requiring a clear understanding of the piping system and how it will be operated. Detailed information on pump selection is not covered by this book. Pump manufacturers and their representatives can assist customers in selecting the best pump for their application.

Understanding the Pump Performance Curve

A key aspect of evaluating and selecting a pump is knowing the operating characteristics of the pump over the expected range of flow rates. The pump performance curve defines the hydraulic operation of the pump by plotting the amount of head the pump produces over its range of operating flow rates, as well as its efficiency, input power, and Net Positive Suction Head Required (NPSHr). The pump curve is needed to select a pump to fit the hydraulic requirements of the piping system. It is also used to monitor the "health" of the pump. If the pump is operating as designed, it must operate at a location on the curve based on the resistance of the system in which it is installed. In this respect, the pump curve can be used as a troubleshooting tool by occasionally checking measured performance against the manufacturer's curve.

Types of Curves

There are three types of pump curves supplied by manufacturers:

- the selection chart
- the published curve
- the certified curve

A selection chart shows the allowable operating range for the various pump sizes and speeds for a given manufacturer's pump type. The desired head and flow values are entered on the curve, and the pumps that overlap the design point are valid choices. Figure 4-24 is an example of a selection chart for a line of general-purpose end suction pumps. The head and flow on the hydraulic range chart may be graphed with a semi-log or log-log scale to display a wider range of flow and head values on a single chart.

The selection chart is very useful in developing a short list of pumps for consideration. For example, if you are looking for a pump running at 1800 rpm that could develop 100 ft. of head at 1000 gpm, the selection chart shows that the 5x6x11, 5x6x13.5, 6x8x11, 6x8x13.5 and possibly the 8x10x13.5 sized pumps have the design point within their range of operation.

> **NOTE:** *Many pump manufacturers describe a specific pump using a series of three numbers, consisting of the nominal size of the pump discharge, nominal size of the pump suction, and the maximum diameter of the pump impeller. For example, a 5x6x11 has a 5-inch discharge, 6-inch suction, and can have a maximum impeller diameter*

of eleven inches. A few manufacturers list the pump suction first, then the pump discharge, followed by the impeller diameter using an "x" or "-" (6x5-11). To avoid confusion, the pump discharge is always smaller than the suction. For example, a 5x6x11 from manufacturer A and a 6x5-11 from manufacturer B both have a 6-inch suction and a 5-inch discharge.

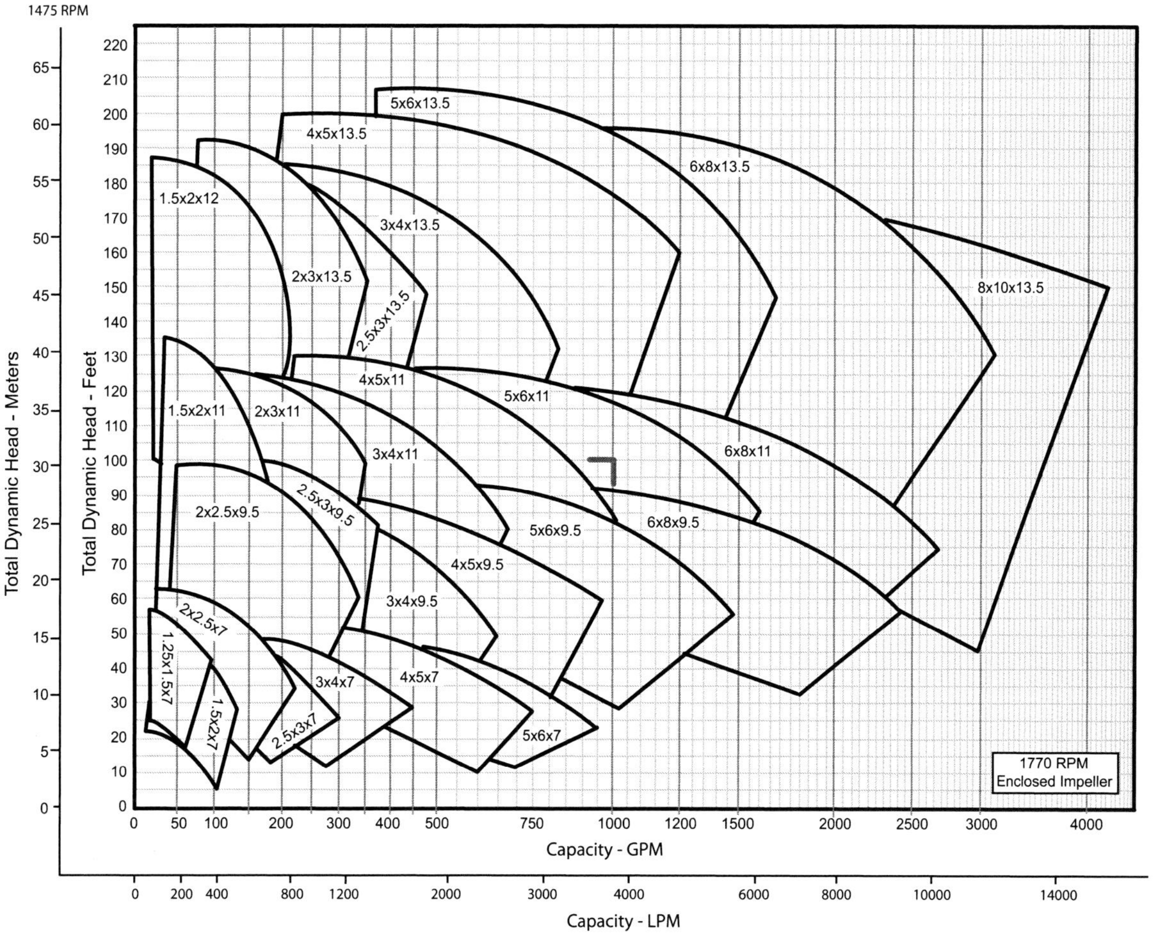

Figure 4-24. Typical selection chart for a line of centrifugal pumps.

Once a short list is developed, the manufacturer's published curve is referenced, which shows the pump performance based on an average of test data points for a given pump size and impeller diameter. Since pumps are specific to individual manufacturers, their performance varies slightly even when two identical pump sizes are compared.

Figure 4-25 is an example of a published curve for a 5x6x11 pump running at 1770 rpm. This type of curve is called an "iso - performance curve" because it shows the pump performance with constant efficiency lines for the range of impeller diameters for the same pump plotted on a single graph.

A tremendous amount of information can be derived from the manufacturer's pump curve for this application:

- the impeller diameter to meet the design point is between 10 and 10.5 inches
- the pump is about 85% efficient at the design point
- the power draw on the motor is slightly less than 30 hp

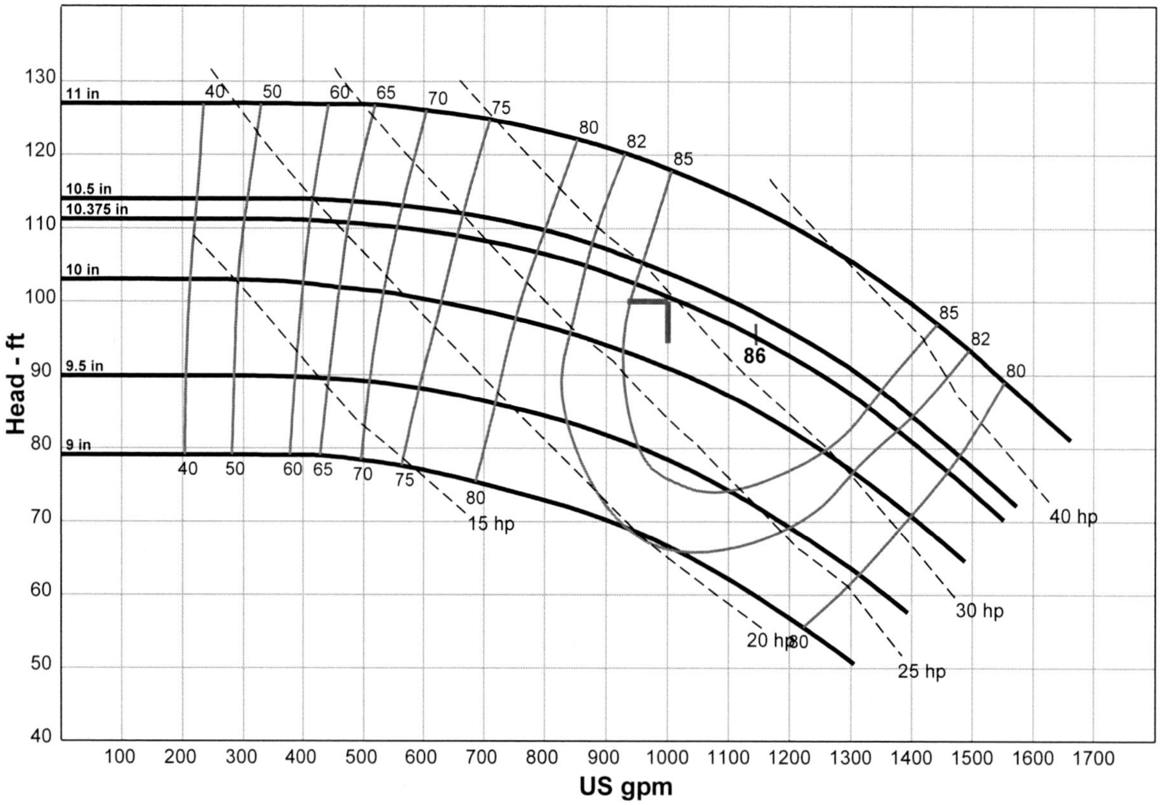

Figure 4-25. A typical manufacturer's published curve for a given pump size and speed, showing the available range of impeller diameters in an iso-efficiency format.

Manufacturers test their pumps with water at 68° F (20° C) unless a different test fluid is specified by the customer. If a fluid other than water is to be pumped and a water-based curve is provided, some information on the manufacturer's published curve must be adjusted for the fluid's density and viscosity.

Figure 4-26 is another example of a manufacturer's published curve with key landmarks highlighted. This curve shows the pump performance for only the impeller size that is installed in the pump. A separate power and NPSHr curve is graphed along with a separate scale for the pump efficiency.

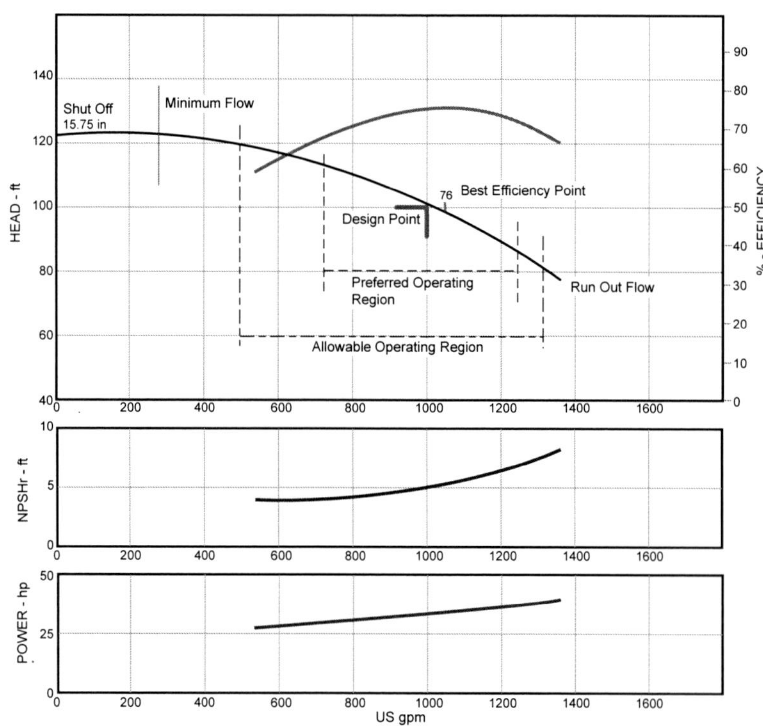

Figure 4-26. A pump curve for a single impeller with the various landmarks highlighted.

A certified pump performance curve may be called out in the customer's purchase specification to ensure that the head produced by the pump at the design flow rate is achieved by the actual pump that will be installed in the customer's piping system. The pump that will be delivered to the customer is tested by the manufacturer in accordance with the pump standard called for in the pump specification. The certified curve will only provide flow rates at or around the specified design point. Unlike the published curve, which can be applied for a typical pump type, size, and speed, the certified curve is developed for the specific pump being supplied under the purchase order.

Pump Curve Operating Data and Landmarks

The operating data and landmarks found on a typical manufacturer's published pump curve can include:

- Total Head vs. flow rate
- Pump input power
- Pump output power (must be calculated using pump curve data)
- Pump efficiency and the Best Efficiency Point
- Shut off head
- Minimum flow
- Maximum flow
- Allowable operating range
- Preferred operating range
- Net Positive Suction Head required

Total Head and Flow Rate

The total head developed by the pump is graphed over a range of flow rates. Recall that "head" is the energy content per unit weight of the liquid, measured from some reference datum plane. The unit for total head is feet of liquid being pumped. Flow rate, or capacity, is the total volumetric flow per unit time at suction conditions, assuming that there are no entrained gases.

The pump's total head curve is developed by placing the pump in a test system using water at 68° F and measuring the volumetric flow rate and suction and discharge pressures. The elevations of the pressure gages are recorded, along with the suction and discharge pipe sizes to calculate the fluid velocities. The Total Head equation, Equation 4-1, is then used to calculate the total head produced by the pump at the test flow rate. The test and calculations are repeated at various flow rates to plot the pump's total head as a function of flow rate through the pump.

Other variables that affect the pump curve are the rotational speed and diameter of the pump impeller. In order for a specific pump to meet the needs of customers over a broader range of operating conditions, the manufacturer tests the pump at various incremental nominal speeds and impeller diameters. Since the majority of pumps are run using AC motors, the manufacturer provides curves for the various synchronous motor speeds: 3600, 1800, 1200 rpm for 60 Hz power and 3000, 1500, 1000 rpm for 50 Hz power. If the pump's actual speed is not at the tested nominal speed, the pump curve should be adjusted.

In addition, the manufacturer tests the pump with various impeller diameters that can be used with the pump by trimming the impeller in increments and repeating the pump tests. The pump curves shown in Figure 4-25 graphs the pump performance curves for 9, 9.5, 10, 10.5, and 11-inch impeller trims. If the desired design point is between a published impeller diameter, the pump manufacturer should be contacted to see if the pump impeller can be trimmed to go through the desired design point. Some pumps are only available in specific impeller diameters, while other pump's impellers can be trimmed for a specific head and flow rate. If the impeller can be trimmed, the manufacturer typically interpolates between tested curves to determine the actual impeller trim needed to meet the design point.

Pump Input Power

Over the years, various terms have been used to describe the amount of power delivered to the pump from the driver: brake horse power (*bhp*), shaft horse power (*shp*), and the currently used term in the Hydraulic Institute standards: the pump input power. During the pump test, the input power of the pump is also calculated at the various flow rates so that the power curve can be included with the published pump curve. Pump input power is calculated by measuring the electrical power going into the AC motor or variable speed drive and using an equation similar to Equation 4-3 to calculate the pump input power.

$$Pump\ Input\ Power = \frac{P_{electrical} \times \eta_{motor} \times \eta_{VSD}}{0.746\ kW/hp} \qquad \text{Equation 4-3}$$

Pump Input Power = power applied to the pump shaft (hp)

$P_{\text{electrical}}$ = power added to the motor or drive (kW)

η_{motor} = nameplate efficiency of the motor (decimal)

η_{VSD} = nameplate efficiency of the variable speed drive, if installed (decimal)

Once the power curves are developed and graphed on the pump curve, the user can interpolate between the power lines to estimate the input power based on the flow rate of the pump. However, on many pump curves it can be fairly difficult to obtain a reasonably accurate value due to the scale on the power curve. Equation 4-4 can be used to obtain a more accurate value of the pump input power using the actual values of flow rate, pump total head, fluid density, and the pump efficiency at the operating point. The value 247,000 in Equation 4-4 combines all the unit conversion factors into one constant to arrive at horse power as the unit for the pump input power. "Bhp" will be used in the equations in this book.

$$bhp = \frac{Q \times H \times \rho}{247{,}000 \times \eta_P} \qquad \text{Equation 4-4}$$

bhp = brake horse power, or the power applied to the pump shaft (hp)

Q = flow rate through the pump (gpm)

H = Total Head of the pump (feet of fluid)

ρ = fluid density (lb/ft^3)

η_p = pump efficiency (decimal)

Pump Output Power

The pump output power is the amount of power added to the liquid by the impeller. It has also been called the "water horse power (*whp*)". The pump output power can be easily calculated with Equation 4-5. The constants used in the equation combine the conversion factors into one numerical value, using U.S. units. If other units are used for these variables, the numerical constants must be re-calculated.

$$whp = \frac{Q \times H \times \rho}{247{,}000} = \frac{Q \times dP_{pump}}{1715.3} = \frac{Q \times H \times SG}{3960} \qquad \text{Equation 4-5}$$

Although not specifically shown on the pump curve, the pump output power can be visualized on the pump curve by a rectangle with its corner at the operating point, as shown in Figure 4-27 with an operating point of 6,000 gpm and 250 feet TH. Note that the scale for the pump head starts at 100 feet, so the rectangle would actually extend down to zero feet.

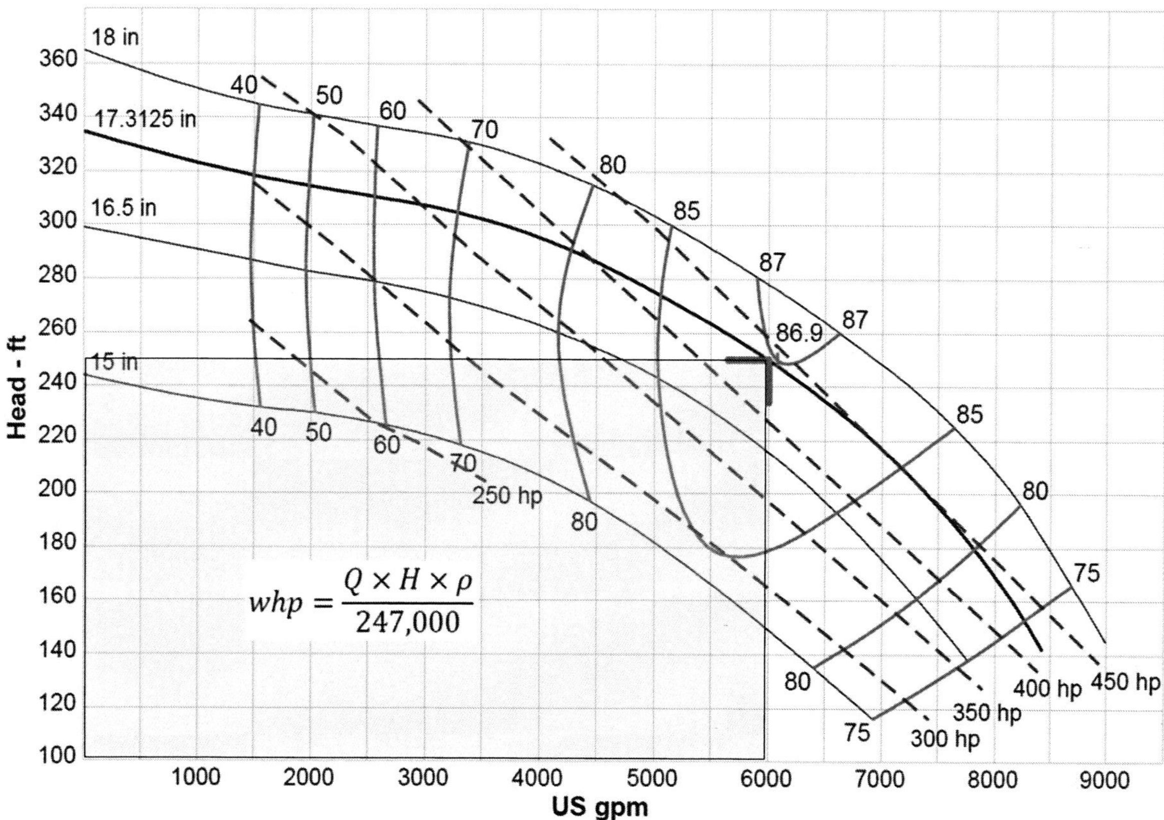

Figure 4-27. Visualizing the amount of power added to the liquid.

Example 4-1: Calculating Pump Output Power

Calculate the pump output power of the pump (whp) in Figure 4-27 using Equation 4-5. The pump has an impeller diameter of 17.3125 inches and is pumping water at 60 °F with a density (ρ) of 62.4 lb/ft^3.

$$whp = \frac{Q \times H \times \rho}{247{,}000} = \frac{(6{,}000\ gpm)(250\ ft)(62.4\frac{lb}{ft^3})}{247{,}000} = 378.9\ hp$$

Example 4-2: Calculating Pump Input Power

Calculate the pump input power (bhp) in Figure 4-27 using Equation 4-4.

$$bhp = \frac{Q \times H \times \rho}{247{,}000 \times \eta_{Pump}} = \frac{(6{,}000\ gpm)(250\ ft)(62.4\frac{lb}{ft^3})}{(247{,}000)(0.87)} = 435.6\ hp$$

Pump Efficiency and the Best Efficiency Point (BEP)

The manufacturer also calculates the pump efficiency for each operating point during the pump tests and graphs the pump's efficiency over the range of operating flow rates. Pump efficiency is the ratio of the energy added to the liquid by the pump impeller (pump output power, or whp) to the energy delivered to the pump shaft (pump input power, or bhp), expressed as a percent or in decimal form, as shown in Equation 4-6.

$$\eta_{Pump} = \frac{whp}{bhp} = \frac{QH\rho/247{,}000}{bhp} \qquad \textit{Equation 4-6}$$

The pump input power, which is the motor output power if directly coupled, is determined from the measured electrical power and motor efficiency as shown previously in Equation 4-3. The pump output power, or water horse power, is calculated from the flow rate, total head, and fluid density.

The efficiency of a pump varies considerably over the allowable range of flow rates. In looking at the pump curve in Figure 4-27, for the 17.3125 inch diameter impeller the pump efficiency ranges from 40% at the minimum flow to about 87% at the best efficiency point, and is under 75% at the end of the curve.

The Best Efficiency Point (BEP) is the highest efficiency of the pump over its range of operating flow rates. The BEP of the pump in Figure 4-27 is about 87% for the 17.3125 inch diameter impeller, and it occurs at approximately 6,000 gpm. The manufacturer designs the impeller so that at the flow rate corresponding to the BEP, the fluid enters the impeller vanes and casing diffuser area in a shock free manner. Flow through the impeller and diffuser sections is uniform and free of separation.

Even though the pump can operate through the published range of flow rates, it is always best to operate a pump close to its best efficiency point. Not only does this save energy, but it also causes less shaft deflection and less wear on the pump's bearings and seals, therefore less downtime and maintenance for the pump, as was seen with the Barringer Curve.

One additional point should be made about pump efficiency. There is no typical efficiency for all pumps. Pumps designed for smaller flow rates, higher heads, and faster rotational speeds are typically less efficient than pumps used to pass large quantities of fluid with relatively low head and slower rotational speeds.

The efficiency of a pump can also be affected by its application. For example, grinder pumps and non-clog pumps used in water collection and treatment systems are designed to pass large objects found in the fluid stream. As a result, these pumps are less efficient than a frame mounted end suction pump designed to pass a clear fluid.

When comparing pump efficiency, it is always best to compare the efficiency for similar types of pumps for given applications.

Shutoff Head

Shutoff is a condition where no liquid is flowing through the pump even though the pump is primed and running. This can be achieved if the pump discharge valve is completely closed while the pump is operating. The head produced by the pump at zero flow rate is the shutoff head of the pump. Even though it is undesireable to operate at this condition continuously, it is an important landmark used in determining the slope of the pump curve. Some pumps can be operated for a brief time at shutoff to obtain the shutoff head for troubleshooting purposes, but the pump should never be operated at shutoff without first consulting the pump supplier.

Minimum Flow

The minimum flow is the lowest flow rate at which the manufacturer recommends the pump to be continuously operated to ensure the pump does not fail. Without adequate flow through the pump, the heat added to the fluid will cause the shaft to expand and deflect, which greatly increases the stresses on the bearings and seals. The pump could also cavitate at low flows due to the heated fluid.

The minimum flow rate is typically accommodated by designing the piping system with a minimum flow recirculation line from the pump discharge back to the pump's supply tank. The recirculation line is sized to ensure at least the minimum flow is obtained if the flow to the rest of the system is completely shut off. The recirculation line may be left open during normal operations, or closed during normal operations and then opened by an operator or automatically when the minimum flow rate is reached.

Although the pump should not be allowed to operate below the manufacturer's minimum flow, certain operating conditions such as system start up or shut down may result in the pump operating below the minimum flow rate.

Small pumps may not have minimum flow limits displayed on the pump curve. Contacting the pump manufacturer is recommended prior to running a pump in an area on the pump curve with no published efficiency or NPSHr data.

Maximum Flow Rate

The end of the manufacturer's published pump curve is the maximum flow rate for the pump and is commonly referred to as the "run out" of the pump. Operating beyond this point can result in tremendous radial forces on the impeller, severe pump vibration, and excessive wear and tear on the bearings and seals. In addition, the pump is more susceptible to cavitation when operated beyond the maximum flow rate.

Allowable Operating Region

The Allowable Operating Region (AOR) is the range of flow rates recommended by the pump manufacturer in which the service life of the pump is not seriously reduced by continued operation. The manufacturer provides this AOR based on the pumped fluid being a non-viscous, non-corrosive pure fluid with no vapor, gas, suspended solids, or abrasives. Whenever a pump is operated with a fluid exhibiting any of the aforementioned conditions, the manufacturer should be contacted about the suitability of the pump for that specific application.

The AOR may be specifically marked on the manufacturer's published pump curve. If it is not specified, a reasonable AOR may be defined by the limits of the efficiency curve or the selection chart.

Preferred Operating Region

The Preferred Operating Region (POR) is a more restrictive operating region that may be defined by the pump user to minimize the amount of maintenance and downtime associated with their pumps. The POR is typically expressed as a percentage of the BEP and will vary depending on the pump type and application. The Hydraulics Institute has recommendations for the POR for different types of pumps. For example, for centrifugal pumps a POR between 70% and 120% of the BEP flow rate is reasonable. For pumps of 5 HP or less, the manufacturer may recommend a wider POR. Vertical pumps have a narrower range of preferred operation, falling between 80% and 115% of the BEP flow rate.

Net Positive Suction Head Required (NPSHr)

Another key aspect of pump performance that the manufacturer tests their pumps for is the Net Positive Suction Head required (NPSHr) as a function of the flow rate through the pump. The NPSHr test is conducted after the Total Head vs. Flow Rate curve is obtained. The procedure involves placing the pump in a test system with a supply tank in which a vacuum can be drawn with a vacuum pump. The test pump is operated at a given flow rate and the vacuum in the supply tank is increased until the pump starts to cavitate, as defined by a 3% drop in the pump's total head compared to the total head at normal conditions at that flow rate. The NPSH is then calculated and the test repeated at various flow rates to obtain a NPSHr curve.

A typical NPSHr curve can be seen in Figure 4-26. Some manufacturers have the NPSHr data displayed as iso-NPSH lines similar to the iso-power lines in Figure 4-25. A key point observation is that as the flow rate through the pump increases, the NPSHr increases as well, as can be seen in Figure 4-26. This means that the higher the flow rate through the pump, the more susceptible the pump is to cavitation.

However, the opposite is not necessarily true. Even though the NPSHr curve in Figure 4-26 shows a lower NPSHr value at a low flow rate, this does not mean that the NPSHr continues to decrease from lowest value shown on the curve. In fact, many pumps have sharply increasing NPSHr at flow rates below what is shown on the published curve. If a manufacturer does not publish data for a specific area of the pump curve, this indicates that the pump should not be operated in that region of the pump curve.

Cavitation and Net Positive Suction Head

Cavitation and Net Positive Suction Head are perhaps the least understood concepts about pump operation for those who are new to pumps. NPSH is a key concept in preventing cavitation, which is perhaps one of the most damaging aspects of improper pump operation. Cavitation and Net Positive Suction Head must be further explored to better understand its relevance to centrifugal pump operation.

Cavitation

Cavitation is the formation and subsequent collapse of vapor bubbles as a liquid's static pressure drops below, then rises above, the vapor pressure of the liquid. As shown in Figure 4-3, the pressure at the eye of the impeller is the lowest point of pressure in the pump. If the fluid pressure drops below the vapor pressure of the liquid, the liquid will change phase to a vapor and small vapor bubbles will form. As the vapor bubbles travel along the impeller vane, the pressure goes back above the vapor pressure and the bubbles collapse. If the bubbles collapse on the surface of the impeller (or farther out in the pump volute), a high-velocity jet of liquid is created and implodes on the surface, removing a small bit of material.

Figure 4-28. Severe cavitation damage to a pump impeller (courtesy of Gorman-Rupp).

Continued long-term cavitation results in eroding the impeller vanes, as can be seen in Figure 4-28. Pump head and efficiency degrades as cavitation damage affects the hydraulic performance of the impeller.

Cavitation has additional impacts on pump performance. Since vapor bubbles occupy more volume for a given mass of liquid, the volumetric flow rate through the pump is reduced. The collapsing vapor bubbles will also make noise: barely audible for slight cavitation or as loud as gravel passing through the pump for severe cavitation. The pump discharge pressure may oscillate and the pump may vibrate excessively.

Net Positive Suction Head

Exactly what is "net positive suction head"? Since "head" is the energy content of the liquid per unit weight, "suction head" is the amount of fluid energy at the pump suction. The term "net positive" refers to the amount of energy above an absolute zero energy state. So NPSH is the amount of fluid energy at the pump suction in reference to absolute zero energy.

In relation to the pump curve and pump testing, Net Positive Suction Head required (NPSHr) has already been described as the point at which the pump begins to cavitate. NPSHr is the amount of fluid energy at the pump suction when the pressure at the eye of the impeller drops below the vapor pressure and vapor bubbles begin to form. The pump is cavitating if run at NPSHr.

To prevent cavitation from occurring, the piping system on the suction side of the pump must provide the fluid with enough energy to keep the pressure at the eye from dropping below the fluid's vapor pressure. The amount of fluid energy the piping system provides to the pump suction is called the Net Positive Suction Head available (NPSHa). NPSHa is a function of the following characteristics of the piping system on the suction side of the pump:

- Elevation difference between the liquid level in the supply tank and the eye of the impeller
- Pressure on the surface of the liquid in the supply tank
- Head loss in the pump's suction pipelines
- Vapor pressure of the fluid being pumped
- Density of the fluid being pumped

Calculating NPSHa

Equation 4-7 can be used to calculate NPSHa:

$$NPSH_a = \left[\left(P_{tank} + P_{atm} - P_{vp} \right) \times \frac{144}{\rho} \right] + \left(Z_{tank} + Z_{Level} - Z_{pump} \right) - h_L \qquad \textit{Equation 4-7}$$

P_{tank} = pressure on the liquid surface of the supply tank (psig)

P_{atm} = local atmospheric pressure (psia)

P_{vp} = vapor pressure of the liquid entering the pump suction (psia)

ρ = fluid density (lb/ft^3)

Z_{tank} = elevation of the bottom of the supply tank, measure from the reference plane (ft)

Z_{Level} = liquid level measured from the bottom of the tank (ft)

Z_{pump} = elevation of the center line of the pump suction (ft)

h_L = head loss in the suction pipeline between the tank and the pump suction (ft)

If elevations, pressures, or level are measured in other units, appropriate unit conversions must be applied to Equation 4-7.

A reasonable approximation can be calculated using Equation 4-8 if a pressure gage is installed at the suction of the pump, assuming the elevation of the gage is the same as the center line of the pump.

$$NPSH_a \cong \left[\left(P_{in} + P_{atm} - P_{vp} \right) \times \frac{144}{\rho} \right] \qquad \textit{Equation 4-8}$$

P_{in} = pump inlet suction pressure (psig)

Example 4-3: Calculating NPSHa for a Pump with a Flooded Suction

Consider the system in Figure 4-29 with the eye of the pump impeller located below the liquid level in the tank. This is considerd a "flooded suction" configuration.

The system consists of a Supply Tank open to atmosphere, located at an elevation of 100 ft, with a liquid level of 5 ft. The pump is located at an elevation of 95 ft, and the suction pipeline has 1.7 ft of head loss at a flow rate of 400 gpm of 60 °F water (ρ = 62.4 lb/ft^3, P_{vp} = 0.256 psia). The local atmospheric pressure is 14.7 psia.

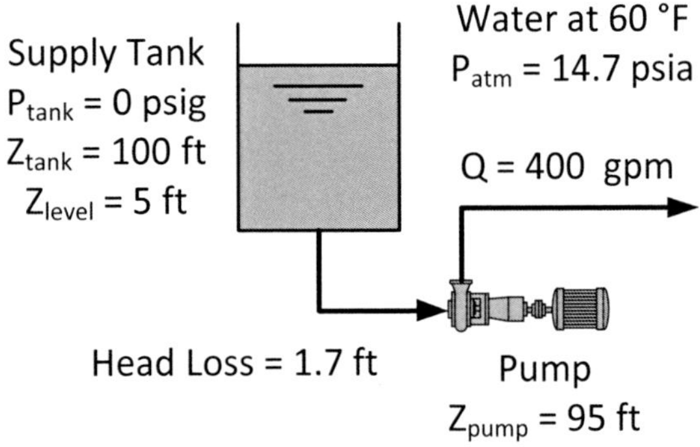

Figure 4-29. Calculating NPSHa for a pump with a flooded suction.

Using Equation 4-7, the NPSHa can be calculated as follows:

$$NPSH_a = \left[(0 + 14.7 - 0.256)\frac{lb}{in^2} \times \frac{144\,\frac{in^2}{ft^2}}{62.4\,\frac{lb}{ft^3}}\right] + (100 + 5 - 95)\,ft - 1.7\,ft = 41.6\,ft$$

Example 4-4: Calculating NPSHa for a Pump with a Suction Lift

Now consider the same system except that the Supply Tank is lowered by 15 feet so that the eye of the pump impeller is above the liquid level in the tank, as shown in Figure 4-30. This is considered a "suction lift" configuration. All other variables are the same: tank pressure and level, flow rate and head loss, fluid density and vapor pressure, and local atmospheric pressure.

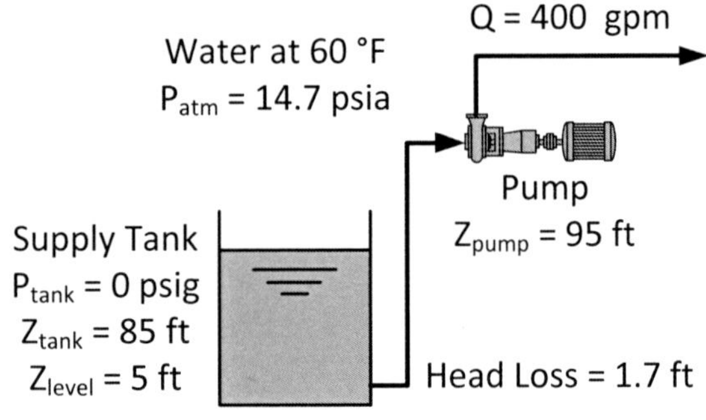

Figure 4-30. Calculating NPSHa for a pump with a suction lift.

Again using Equation 4-7, the NPSHa can be calculated as follows:

$$NPSH_a = \left[(0 + 14.7 - 0.256)\frac{lb}{in^2} \times \frac{144\,\frac{in^2}{ft^2}}{62.4\,\frac{lb}{ft^3}}\right] + (85 + 5 - 95)\,ft - 1.7\,ft = 26.6\,ft$$

Solutions for a Cavitating Pump

As can be seen with these two examples, for every one foot change in the elevation of the supply tank, there is a one foot change in NPSHa. Because the system in Figure 4-29 has more NPSHa than the one in Figure 4-30, it is less susceptible to cavitation. Understanding this example and evaluating the NPSHa equation provides some guidance for what to do for a pump that is cavitating.

Raise the Elevation of the Tank

The elevation of the bottom of the tank that supplies the pump will have a one-to-one impact on the NPSHa: for every one foot increase in the tank elevation, there is a one foot increase in NPSHa. This is more easily done during the design phase of a piping system project, when calculations for NPSHa should initially be performed. When a pump is being considered for the system, if the available NPSHa is less than the pump's NPSHr a decision can be made to select another pump or change the tank elevation. Once the system is built, it is much more costly and difficult to fix a cavitating pump by changing the tank elevation.

Lower the Elevation of the Pump

Similarly, the elevation of the pump in relation to the liquid level in the tank has a one-to-one impact on NPSHa. Again, changing the pump elevation is much easier to do when designing the system than after the system is built and operating. If necessary, the pump can be installed in a pit rather than above ground to increase the NPSHa.

Increase the Liquid Level of the Tank

A one foot increase in the liquid level of the tank gives a one foot increase in the NPSHa for the pump. During the design phase, this may require specifying a taller tank than one that was being considered. For an operating system, if it is feasible to run the system with a higher tank level without adversely affecting the process, this solution may be adequate to provide enough fluid energy to the pump suction to prevent or alleviate a cavitating pump.

Increase the Operating Pressure of the Tank

This solution is only available if the tank is specifically designed to operate at a pressure above atmospheric pressure and the increased pressure does not adversely affect the process requirements of the system. The increase in NPSHa will depend on the fluid density, but for water at 60 °F, every 1 psi increase results in 2.3 feet additional NPSHa.

Another condition that affects the NPSHa is the local atmospheric pressure. At sea level, the local atmospheric pressure is 14.7 psia, but if the pumping application is located in Denver, Colorado, at 5,200 feet above sea level, the local atmospheric pressure is 12.1 psia. The installation in Denver will have a lower NPSHa compared to an identical installation at sea level. When designing piping systems at locations with higher elevations, always factor in the lower atmospheric pressure value in the NPSHa calculation.

Reduce the Head Loss in the Suction Piping

Some applications require a strainer to be installed in the suction piping. If installed, the strainer should be cleaned on a routine basis to prevent cavitation problems.

Head loss in pipelines, valves, and fittings will be discussed in detail in the next couple of chapters, but reducing the head loss by one foot increases the NPSHa by one foot. This can be accomplished by selecting low resistance isolation valves if appropriate for the application (ball, gate, or butterfly valves instead of globe valves) and by minimizing the number of elbows and other fittings from the tank to the pump.

The suction pipeline diameter can also be increased to reduce the fluid velocity and therefore the head loss in the pipeline. As will be explained later, the head loss is a function of the fluid velocity squared, so a small reduction in fluid velocity results in a large reduction in the pipeline head loss. This is why many pumps are installed with a suction pipeline diameter that is larger than the discharge.

Reduce the Flow Rate

Reducing the flow rate has two effects on NPSHa. Recall from Figure 4-26 that the NPSHr of the pump typically increases with an increasing flow rate. Reducing the flow rate may reduce the NPSHr enough to eliminate the cavitation.

In addition, reducing the flow rate reduces the fluid velocity and therefore reduces the amount of head loss in the suction piping. Again, since head loss is a function of the fluid velocity squared, a small reduction in the flow rate will have a larger impact on the NPSHa. The combination of the reduction of NPSHr and increase in NPSHa may stop the pump from cavitating.

Reduce the Fluid Temperature (for most liquids)

If reducing the fluid temperature does not impact the process, a lower temperature will reduce the vapor pressure of the liquid. This effect will tend to increase the NPSHa according to Equation 4-7, but there is another impact that must be considered. For most fluids, reducing the fluid temperature also results in a slight increase in the pipeline head loss, the magnitude of which depends on how much the fluid's density and viscosity changes. The reduced vapor pressure and increased head loss are competing influences on NPSHa. The actual effect on NPSHa must be evaluated for the actual working fluid and the temperature change being considered.

Table 4-1 shows an analysis of three liquids that could be pumped in the flooded suction system in Example 4-3: water, ethanol, and Therminol 55 (a viscous heat transfer fluid). Each liquid is cooled from 160 °F to 60 °F and the changing fluid properties are evaluated. For water and ethanol, the change in vapor pressure is significant: water vapor pressure changes by 4.5 psi (approximately 10 feet of head) and ethanol vapor pressure changes by 10.3 psi (approximately 30 feet of head). The change in density and viscosity of water and ethanol results in only a small change in the head loss in the pipeline. The net effect is an increase in the NPSHa for water of almost 10 feet and over 29 feet increase in NPSHa for ethanol for the same 100 °F change in fluid temperature.

Table 4-1: Effect of Fluid Temperature on NPSHa PF

Fluid	Temp (°F)	Vapor Pressure (psia)	Density (lb/ft^3)	Viscosity (cP)	Head Loss in suction line (ft)	NPSHa (ft)
Water	160 °F	4.745	61.0	0.4	1.6	31.9
Water	60 °F	0.256	62.4	1.1	1.7	41.7
Ethanol	160 °F	10.92	46.3	0.5	1.6	20.1
Ethanol	60 °F	0.651	49.7	1.3	1.8	49.0
Therminol 55	160 °F	0.0009	52.3	5.6	2.1	48.4
Therminol 55	60 °F	0.00002	54.6	54.8	3.6	45.2

Now consider the impact that the same 100 °F change in temperature has on the NPSHa for a pump that's pumping Therminol 55. The vapor pressure only changes by 0.00088 psi, or about 0.002 feet of head. However, the increased viscosity causes the head loss in the suction piping to increase by 1.5 feet. Combined with the density change, the net effect on NPSHa is a decrease of over 3 feet, rather than an increase in NPSHa.

This analysis shows that the actual fluid properties and how they change must be evaluated to understand the affect that a change in temperature will have on NPSHa. The amount that the NPSHa changes will depend on the properties of the working fluid and the magnitude of the temperature change.

Install an Inducer

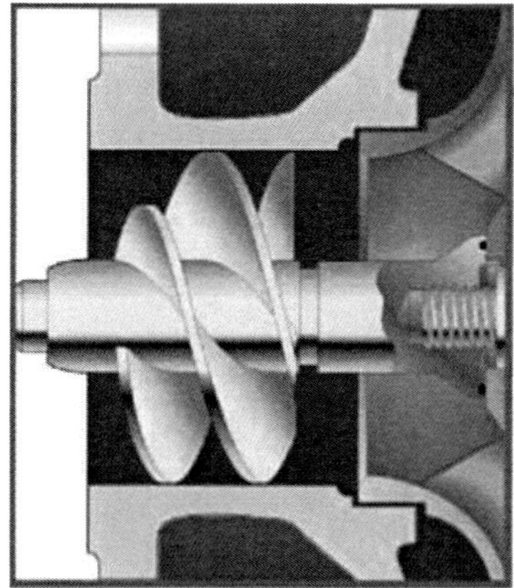

Figure 4-31. Inducer installed on centrifugal pump impeller (courtesy of Goulds Pumps).

An inducer is an axial flow impeller that is mounted to the central hub at the eye of the pump impeller. The inducer adds energy to the fluid just ahead of the main impeller, providing it with sufficient energy to prevent the static pressure at the eye from falling below the vapor pressure and therefore preventing cavitation. However, inducers are not adaptable to all impellers, so the pump manufacturer should be consulted if this option is being considered.

Select a Different Pump with Lower NPSHr

Low speed pumps typically have a lower NPSHr than higher speed pumps. If a 3600 rpm pump is experiencing cavitation, an 1800 rpm pump that meets the same flow rate and head requirements may not cavitate in the same system because its NPSHr would be lower.

In addition, similar pumps that operate at the same speed may have a different NPSHr throughout their operating ranges. This is why it's important to evaluate a piping system design for NPSHa before selecting a pump for the system. It's better to buy the right pump the first time rather than install a pump and then find out its cavitating and the only solution is to buy another pump.

Apply Protective Coating to Impeller and Casing

There have been significant technological advances in composite materials that can be used for industrial protective coatings. Cavitation resistant elastomers can dissipate the energy created by the collapse of vapor bubbles during cavitation and provide resistance to other forms of erosion and corrosion. These polymers can be applied to the pump casing and impeller to minimize the damaging effects of cavitation and eliminate the need to replace costly impellers or the entire pump.

Pump Affinity Rules

The pump curve describes how the pump will operate at the speed at which the pump is tested. If the pump is operating as designed and tested, the pump must operate at a point on its curve. The total head that the pump develops is determined by the amount of flow through the pump. Another way to look at it is that the pump delivers the amount of flow based on the hydraulic resistance of the system: how much pressure the piping system on the suction side provides to the pump inlet and how much back pressure is applied to the outlet of the pump by the piping system on the discharge side, at that flow rate.

The shape of the pump curve is a result of the various options used by pump designers to create a product that can be used for a range of expected operational requirements. There are few pump design options available to the user that will change the shape of the pump curve. To increase the utility of a pump design, the manufacturer allows the user to change the pump speed and impeller diameter. These two options allow the same pump to run under a wider range of conditions.

The pump affinity rules describe how changing the impeller diameter and speed affects the pump performance data. It is important to look at each pump curve as a series of test data points connected together to form a smooth line. When pumps are tested to develop the manufacturer's curve, distinct flow rate and head data is obtained to create a curve that describes the operation of the pump throughout its allowable operating region. Therefore, it is important to adjust the head and flow rate curve by applying the affinity rules to a series of individual points on the pump curve.

Changes in Impeller Speed

When changing a pump's rotational speed, the head, capacity, and power for a point on the pump curve vary according to the pump affinity rules, given in Equation 4-9, Equation 4-10, and Equation 4-11.

$$\frac{Q_1}{Q_2} = \left(\frac{N_1}{N_2}\right)$$

Equation 4-9

$$\frac{H_1}{H_2} = \left(\frac{N_1}{N_2}\right)^2$$

Equation 4-10

$$\frac{bhp_1}{bhp_2} = \left(\frac{N_1}{N_2}\right)^3$$

Equation 4-11

Figure 4-32 shows how a pump curve changes as the test speed drops from 2400 rpm to 1450 rpm. All points on the pump curve drop down and to the left on a second order relationship between flow rate and total head, which can be seen mathematically by substituting Equation 4-9 into Equation 4-10.

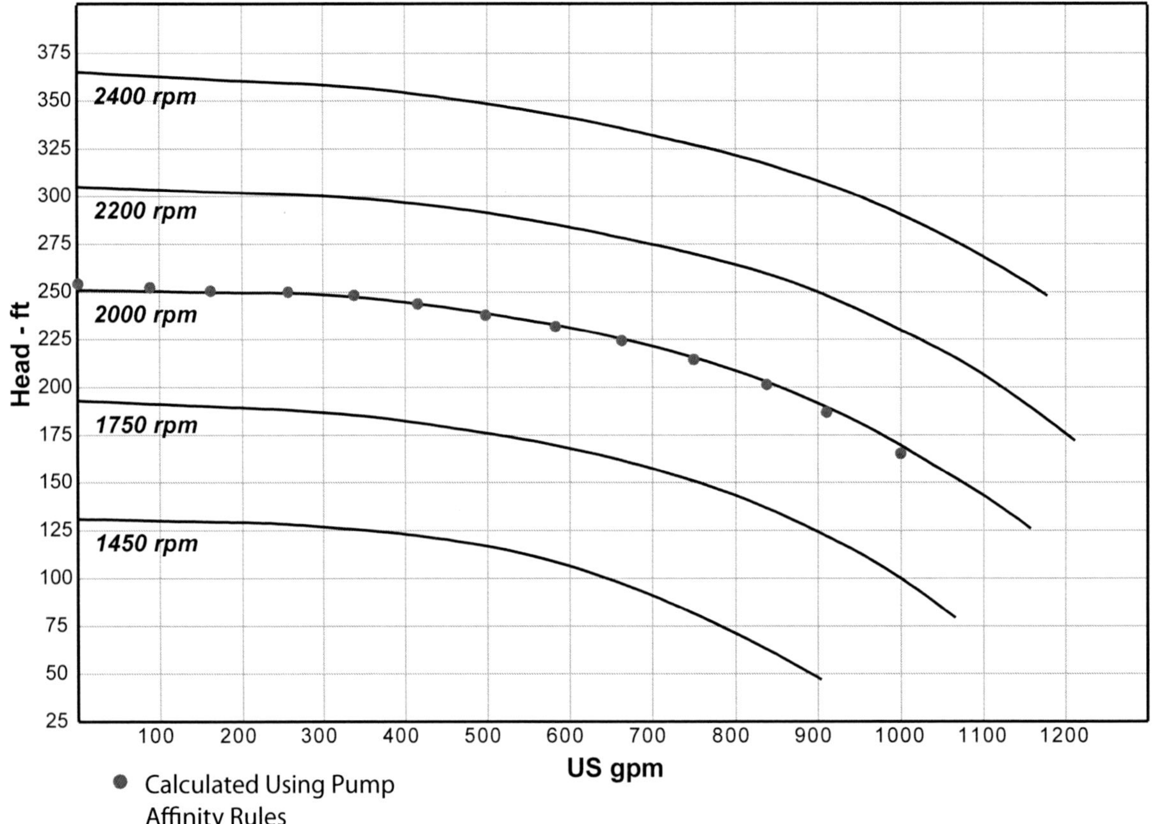

Figure 4-32. Manufacturer's pump performance curves at various speeds compared to discrete values calculated using the affinity rules from 2400 rpm to 2000 rpm.

Figure 4-32 also compares discrete values calculated using the affinity rules for a speed change from 2400 rpm to 2000 rpm. The calculated values correspond closely to the manufacturer's test, which shows that the pump affinity rules for a change in pump speed is highly accurate.

The pump affinity rules do not describe what happens to the efficiency as the pump speed changes, but once the flow rate, head, and power are calculated with the affinity rule equations, Equation 4-6 can then be used to calculate the pump efficiency at the new speed, as shown in Equation 4-12.

$$\eta_{Pump_2} = \frac{Q_2 \times H_2 \times \rho}{247{,}000 \times bhp_2} \qquad \textit{Equation 4-12}$$

The pump manufacturer should be contacted if efficiency data is needed for speeds other than the test speed of the pump. In addition, because the manufacturer tests their pump over a range of speeds, when considering changing the speed of a pump, check with the manufacturer to ensure that the pump will be operating within the allowable range of pump speeds.

The pump affinity rules do not specifically address NPSHr either, but manufacturers will use Equation 4-13 to adjust NPSHr for changes in pump speed. Others will use an exponent of 1.5 in Equation 4-13 when adjusting NPSHr.

$$\frac{NPSHr_1}{NPSHr_2} = \left(\frac{N_1}{N_2}\right)^2 \qquad \textit{Equation 4-13}$$

Misconception About the Affinity Rules

One of the main misconceptions about the use of the pump affinity rules is that they can be used to determine what speed the pump must operate to obtain a given flow rate in the system. The affinity rules describe how the pump's performance will change for a given change in speed, but the hydraulic resistance of the piping system determines how much head the pump must produce at a given flow rate.

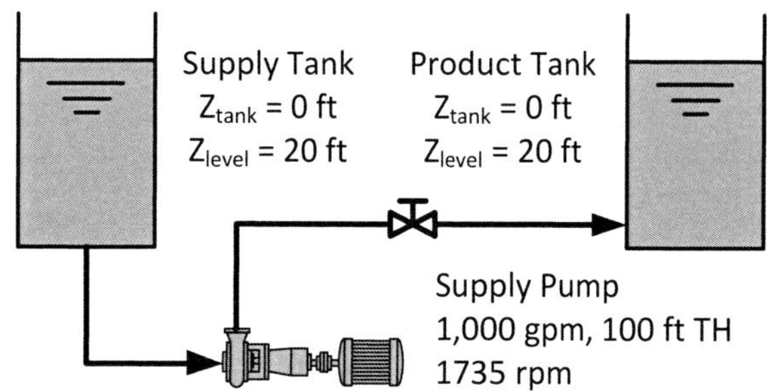

Figure 4-33. System with no static head.

To illustrate this, consider the simple piping system in Figure 4-33. The system consists of a Supply Tank, a Product Tank, a Supply Pump, and associated pipelines, valves, and fittings. The Supply Tank and Product Tank are open to atmosphere and are at the same elevations and have the same liquid levels, so there is no static head associated with these systems. The pump operates at 1735 rpm and produces 100 feet of total head to deliver 1,000 gpm from the Supply Tank to the Product Tank. All the energy the pump adds to the fluid is used to overcome the friction losses in the system, or the dynamic head.

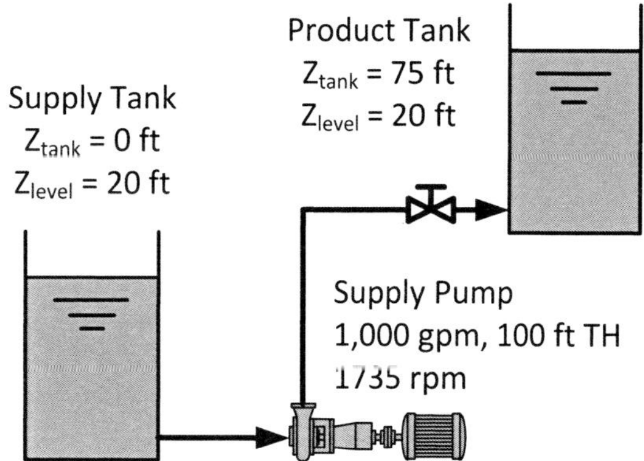

Figure 4-34. System with 75% static head and 25% dynamic head.

Now consider a similar system shown in Figure 4-34. The elevation of the Product Tank is raised to 75 feet so that the static head accounts for 75% of the total head of the pump. The pipe lengths are shortened so that the dynamic head requirements of the system account for 25% of the total head. The same pump is selected for this system so it operates at 1735 rpm to produce 100 feet of total head to deliver 1,000 gpm of liquid to the Product Tank.

A "System Resistance Curve" is a graph of the static and dynamic head of the piping system over a range of flow rates and can be used to visualize the energy requirements of the system. When plotted on the pump curve, where the system resistance curve and pump curve intersect is the operating point of the pump. The system resistance curve and use of the terms "static head" and "dynamic head" will be covered in more detail in later chapters.

The pump and system resistance curves of these two piping systems are plotted on the pump curve in Figure 4-35. The operating point of the pump is at 1,000 gpm and 100 feet of total head.

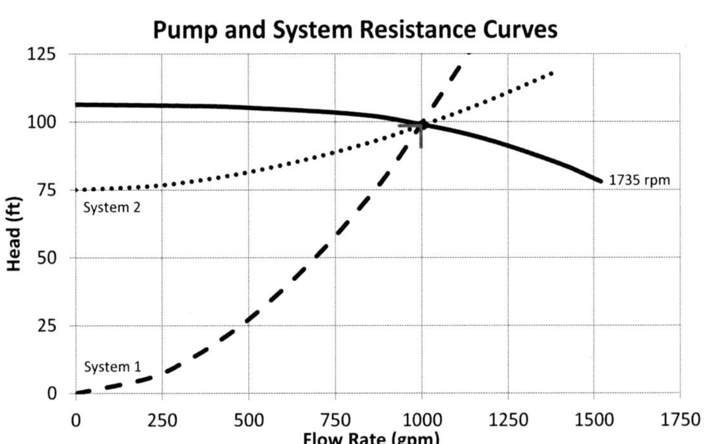

Figure 4-35. Pump and System Resistance Curves for Systems 1 and 2 operating at 1,000 gpm.

If the pump speed is controlled by a variable frequency drive, the speed of the pump can be adjusted to meet the flow rate requirements of the system. This is where the misconception about the affinity rules comes into play.

Consider a change in the flow rate to 500 gpm for both systems. If the pump affinity rule for flow rate (Equation 4-9) is applied (actually misapplied), the speed would calculate to 867.5 rpm. However, the hydraulic resistance of the piping system determines how much head the pump must produce at a given flow rate.

At 867.5 rpm, using Equation 4-10, the pump would only produce 24.6 feet of total head. Looking at Figure 4-35, System 1 requires slightly more than 25 feet of total head and System 2 requires around 80 feet of total head.

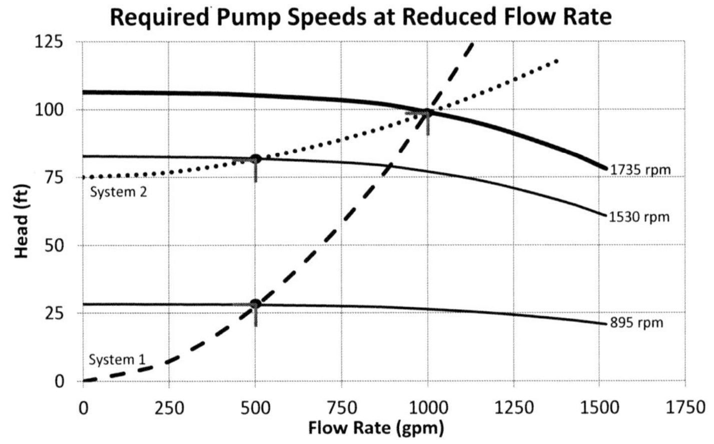

Figure 4-36. Pump and System Resistance Curves for Systems 1 and 2 operating at 500 gpm.

Figure 4-36 shows the actual pump speeds needed to meet the head requirements of the systems. The pump would have to operate at 895 rpm for System 1 to deliver 500 gpm, and the pump in System 2 would have to operate at 1530 rpm.

Calculating the pump speed needed to achieve a given flow rate is an iterative procedure which is more easily done with computer software.

Example 4-5: Applying the Pump Affinity Rules for a Known Change in Speed

Consider a pump that runs at 1780 rpm and requires 35 hp power input at 150 feet total head while delivering 500 gpm of 60 °F water. Calculate the flow rate, total head, power consumption, and efficiency if the pump speed was reduced to 1500 rpm.

Re-arranging and using Equation 4-9:

$$Q_2 = Q_1\left(\frac{N_2}{N_1}\right) = 500\left(\frac{1500}{1780}\right) = 421\ gpm$$

Re-arranging and using Equation 4-10:

$$H_2 = H_1\left(\frac{N_2}{N_1}\right)^2 = 150\left(\frac{1500}{1780}\right)^2 = 106.5\ ft$$

Re-arranging and using Equation 4-11:

$$bhp_2 = bhp_1\left(\frac{N_2}{N_1}\right)^3 = 35\left(\frac{1500}{1780}\right)^3 = 20.9\ hp$$

Using Equation 4-12:

$$\eta_{Pump_2} = \frac{Q_2 \times H_2 \times \rho}{247{,}000 \times bhp_2} = \frac{421 \times 106.5 \times 62.4}{247{,}000 \times 20.9} = 54.2\%$$

Pump Affinity Rules fo Changes in Impeller Diameter

When the impeller diameter of a pump is changed, the head, flow rate, and power for points on the pump curve varies *approximately* in accordance with similar pump affinity rules:

The affinity rules for changing the impeller diameter are not as accurate as the change in the speed of

$$\frac{Q_1}{Q_2} = \left(\frac{D_1}{D_2}\right)$$

Equation 4-14

$$\frac{H_1}{H_2} = \left(\frac{D_1}{D_2}\right)^2$$

Equation 4-15

$$\frac{bhp_1}{bhp_2} = \left(\frac{D_1}{D_2}\right)^3$$

Equation 4-16

the impeller for two reasons. When an impeller is trimmed to a new diameter, the vane angle between the outer surface of the impeller and the impeller vane changes and the width of the impeller vane becomes thicker. After trimming, the impeller is not geometrically and hydraulicaly similar to what it was before trimming. In addition, as the impeller diameter is reduced, the gap at the cutwater becomes larger, allowing more flow to recirculate around the volute instead of exiting the pump at the discharge.

These two conditions cause the pump to deliver less flow and produce less head than what is calculated by the affinity rules in Equation 4-14 and 4-15. In addition, the efficiency of the pump is reduced, resulting in a larger power requirement than what is calculated in Equation 4-16.

The pump curves in Figure 4-37 show a manufacturer's provided test curves at various impeller diameters, along with two curves that were calculated by applying the affinity rules for a change in impeller diameter from 11 inches to 10.5 inches and from 11 inches to 10 inches. These two calculated curves *over-estimate* the amount of head the pump would produce at a given flow rate, and the larger the change in the impeller diameter, the greater the over-estimation. This shows why if the affinity rules for impeller diameter are used, they should be used for small changes in impeller diameters only.

A better approach to more accurately calculate the impeller trim needed to meet a design flow rate and total head is to interpolate between curves that were developed by the manufacturer's pump tests at actual impeller diameters.

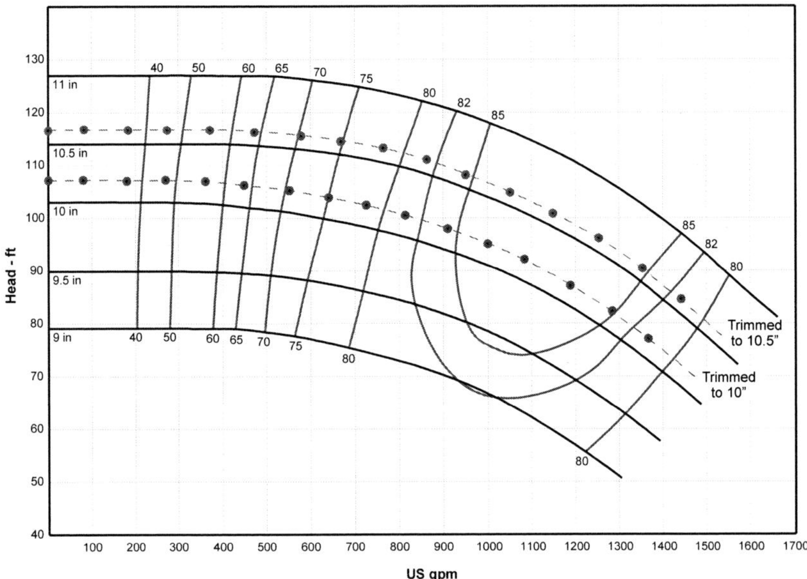

Figure 4-37. Comparing pump curves produced using affinity rules for a change in impeller diameter to actual published curves.

For example, to meet a design point of 1,000 gpm and 95 feet of total head on Figure 4-37, by interpolation between the 10 inch and 10.5 inch test curves, the impeller would have to actually be trimmed to about 10.2 inches. If the affinity rules were used, they would predict an impeller trim of 10 inches. In critical operations, this error would have resulted in over-trimming the impeller and may require the purchase of a new full-sized impeller and then trimming the impeller again in an effort to get it right the second time.

Pump and System Interaction

The interaction between the pump and the piping system was briefly touched upon in the discussion about the pump and system resistance curve and the affinity rules for changing pump speed and shown in Figures 4-35 and 4-36. The pump and system interaction will be explored in detail throughout the remaining chapters of this book. But there are two concepts that warrent further discussion in this chapter: operating pumps in parallel and in series.

Parallel Pump Operation

When two or more identical pumps are operated in parallel, the hydraulic performance of the multiple pumps can be viewed using a single pump curve that represents the addition of the individual pump curves.

Figure 4-38 shows the pump curve for a single pump, along with the curves representing the hydraulic performance of two, three, and four identical pumps operating in parallel. If the piping system on the suction side and discharge to the common header were symmetrical, the total head produced by each pump would be the same and the flow rate would be

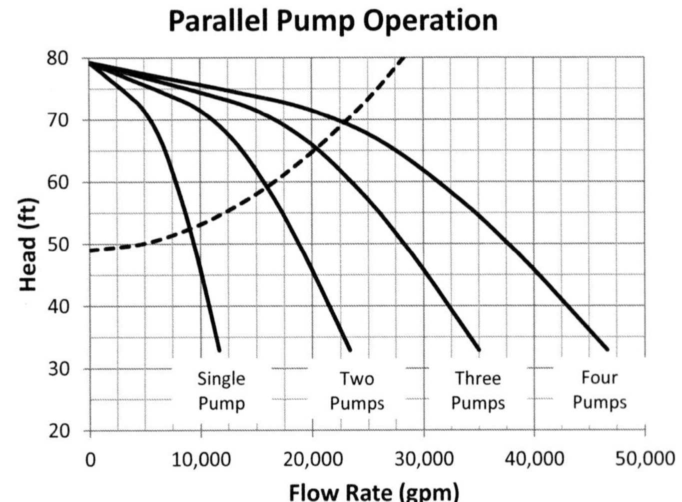

Figure 4-38. Pump curves are added "horizontally" for pumps operated in parallel.

equally divided between the number of operating pumps. To develop the combined curves, the flow rate of a single pump at a given total head is multiplied by the number of pumps that are operating in parallel. In other words, the curves are added "horizontally".

Given the system resistance curve shown in Figure 4-38, if just one pump was operating it would produce about 53 feet of total head and deliver about 9,000 gpm. If a second pump was turned on (and no other changes made to the piping system), the two pumps together would deliver 16,000 gpm at a total head of about 59 feet. This flow would be split equally between the two pumps, or 8,000 gpm through each one. Notice that the flow did not double, but increased by only 7,000 gpm. The hydraulic resistance of the piping system is determining the total head requirements of the pumps and therefore the flow rate.

If three pumps were operating, the total flow would be 20,000 gpm (an increase of 4,000 gpm) and the pumps would produce about 65 feet of total head. With four pumps on line, the pumps would produce 69 feet of head at a total flow rate of 22,500 gpm, an increase of 2,500 gpm. Notice that the amount of capacity that is added with each additional pump is getting smaller.

The key point is that the capacity of the system cannot always be increased by adding more and more pumps to the lineup. It is the hydraulic resistance of the piping system that is determining the performance of the pumps. If more capacity is needed, something will have to be done to the piping system to either lower the system resistance curve (by reducing static head) or flattening out the system resistance curve (by reducing dynamic head losses). These concepts will be discussed in more depth in later chapters.

Series Pump Operation

When two or more identical pumps are operated in series, the flow rate through each pump will be the same and the total amount of energy added to the working fluid will be the sum of the total head of each individual pump.

The hydraulic performance of the multiple pumps can be viewed using a single pump curve that represents the addition of the individual pump curves.

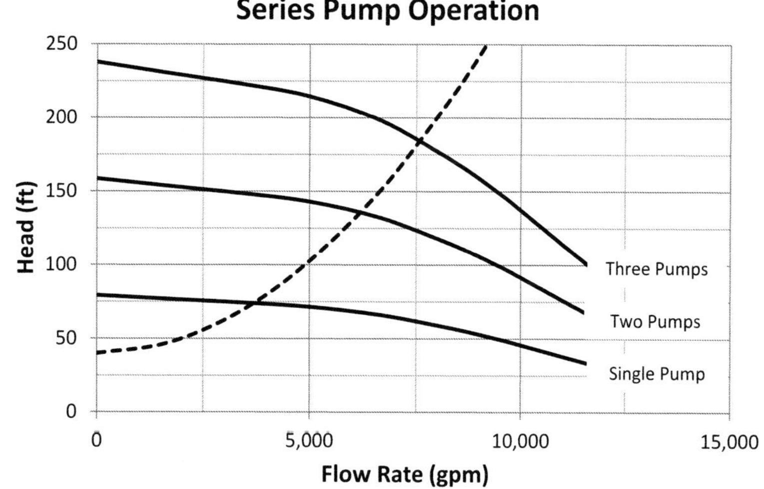

Figure 4-39. Pump curves are added "vertically" for pumps operated in series.

Figure 4-39 shows the pump curve for a single pump, two identical pumps operating in series, and three identical pumps operating in series. A system resistance curve is also shown. If all three pumps were operating, the flow rate through each pump would be about 7,500 gpm and the total amount of energy added to the fluid would be around 180 feet of head, with each pump adding 60 feet of head.

Multi-stage pumps can be thought of as several pumps operating in series but with all the impellers located in one casing. The total head of the pump is the sum of the energy that is added to the fluid by each impeller stage.

Multi-stage pumps and multiple pumps that are installed in series are used in systems that have to overcome a large pressure or elevation difference, such as boiler feedwater pumps and vertical turbine pumps used to pump water from a deep well, or overcome a large amount of friction head, such as pumps used in the petroleum industry.

One concern in series pump operation that must be considered is the pressure rating of the seals on the second and subsequent pumps in the series. The discharge pressure of one pump is applied to the suction of the next pump, so each pump must have a seal that is rated for the pressure to which it will be exposed. The pressure rating of the pump volutes must also be considered due to the increased pressure.

Dissimilar Parallel or Series Pump Operation

The previous discussion on parallel and series pump operation assumed that the multiple pumps were identical. If the pumps are not identical, their pump curves are combined in the same way, either "horizontally" for parallel pumps or "vertically" for series pumps.

However, operating dissimilar pumps in parallel has a risk of exceeding the limits of one of the pumps. Consider the two dissimilar pumps operating in parallel shown in Figure 4-40. Pump 1 has a higher shutoff head and a steeper curve than Pump 2. Their combined curves are represented by the dotted pump curve. Figure 4-40 also shows two system resistance curve: the System 1 curve represents the pumps operating at a high flow rate and the System 2 curve represents the system operating at a low flow rate.

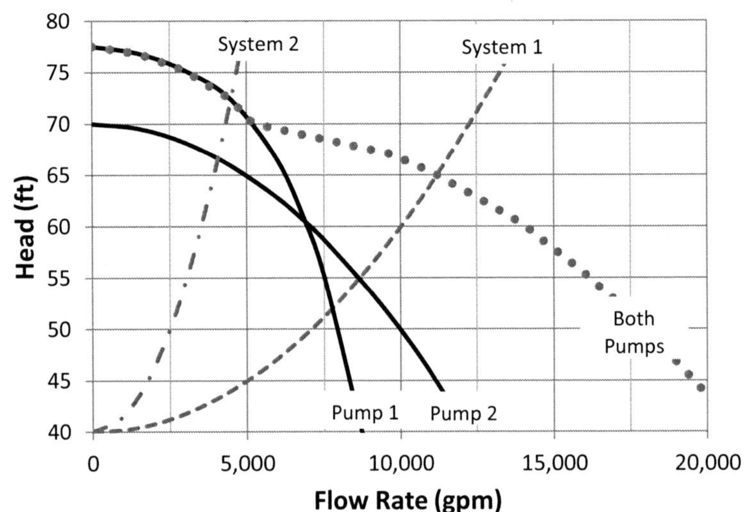

Figure 4-40. Operating dissimilar pumps in parallel.

Below about 5,000 gpm and 70 feet of head, Pump 1 produces more total head than Pump 2, so its discharge pressure will be greater than that of Pump 2. If both pumps have check valves on their discharge, which is often the case in parallel pump operation, below 5,000 gpm the higher discharge pressure on Pump 1 will keep the check valve on the discharge of Pump 2 closed. Pump 2 would be operating at shutoff head with no flow through the pump. This operating point is indicated by the intersection of the System 2 system resistance curve and the dotted combined pump curve. The smaller pump (Pump 2) can often be forced out of its allowable operating region if operated in parallel with a larger pump.

Above 5,000 gpm, Pump 2 would then produce enough total head to match that of Pump 1 and open its discharge valve. The flow rate would be divided between the two pumps based on the required total head for the piping system at the total operating flow rate. For example, if the system was operating at about 11,200 gpm, both pumps would be producing 65 feet of total head, but Pump 1 would be delivering about 6,200 gpm and Pump 2 would deliver about 5,000 gpm. This operating point is located at the intersection of the System 1 resistance curve and the dotted combined pump curve.

Effect of Fluid Properties on the Pump Curve

The pump curve is typically developed during tests using water at 60 °F at a density of 62.37 lb/ft^3. However, there are numerous applications in which pumps are used to transport fluids other than water. The pump's performance will be affected by the properties of the fluid passing through it.

Process fluids with grit or small solids can cause mechanical erosion in the pump, and special consideration should be made concerning material selection when pumping slurries. In addition, a change in fluid vapor pressure can have a detrimental effect on the NPSHa at the pump suction.

If the fluid is not water at ambient temperature, it is advisable to perform a detailed analysis of the pump system requirements and to contact the pump manufacturer to ensure the pump will operate properly and satisfy the process conditions.

Fluid Density

The amount of head developed by the pump is dependent on the velocity of the fluid at the tip of the impeller vane, which is a function of the rotational speed of the impeller and the impeller diameter. The total head developed by the pump is not affected by density of the fluid flowing through the impeller.

The pressure gain across the pump is affected by the fluid density. Equation 4-2 can be used to see that for a given amount of head produced, a liquid with a higher density than water (specific gravity greater than one) will produce a greater pressure gain across the pump and therefore a higher discharge pressure. A pump delivering a liquid with a lower density than water will have a lower discharge pressure compared to the same pump that's pumping water.

Another effect of fluid density is on the power requirements of the pump. The greater the density of the liquid, the more power required by the pump. This can be seen mathematically in the pump input power equation, Equation 4-4.

Fluid Viscosity

The viscosity of the fluid can have a significant impact on the performance of a centrifugal pump. A fluid with a higher viscosity than water will produce less head at a given flow rate, have a lower efficiency, a higher power requirement, and a higher NPSHr. Figure 4-41 shows the general trend for the head, efficiency, power, and NPSHr with increasing viscosity.

The ANSI/HI Standard 9.6.7 describes an emperical method to adjust the pump curve base on test data taken over a wide-range of high viscosity applications. The viscosity correction standard provides equations to calculate correction factors to adjust the head, efficiency, power, and NPSHr based on the fluid viscosity, pump speed, and head and flow rate at the best efficiency point on the water curve.

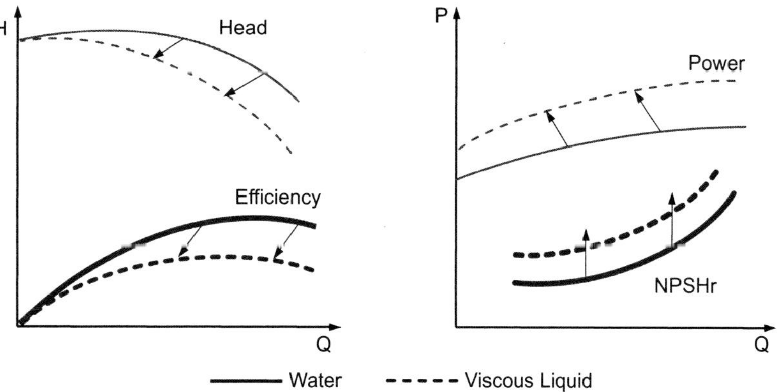

Figure 4-41. Effect of viscosity on the pump performance curve.

There are some limitations to the viscosity correction method, including:

- Viscosity between 1 centistocke (cSt) and 3,000 cSt (with increased uncertainty if applied up to 4,000 cSt)
- Flow rate at the BEP between 13 gpm and 1,800 gpm (with increased uncertainty if applied up to 10,000 gpm)
- Head per stage at the BEP between 20 feet and 430 feet
- Additional limitations based on the pump specific speed and the value of the "B" parameter calculated by the standard's methodology

Most pump selection and evaluation software will automatically perform the viscosity correction to the manufacturer's pump curves.

Pump Selection Process

Selecting the right pump for any given application can be a daunting task and one that could lead to inefficienct operation and reduced reliability if the wrong pump is installed in a piping system. The pump must be selected to meet the hydraulic requirements of the piping system. In other words, a pump must be chosen that produces the amount of total head that the system requires at the desired flow rates.

Flow Rate Requirements

One of the key pieces of information that must be known is the amount of flow rate that the pump must deliver. This includes not only the normal operating flow rate, but the maximum and minimum operating flow rates if the pump will be operating under variable conditions. The pump should be selected so that the range of operating flow rates is within a reasonable band around the BEP to minimize problems that will reduce pump reliability.

Total Head Requirements

The total amount of energy that the pump must add to the fluid includes the energy that is used to overcome the elevation and pressure differences in the system (static head) and the energy losses due to friction and changes in fluid momentum (dynamic head). The static head and dynamic head of the system must be calculated, and a reasonable design margin added, to determine the total head requirements of the pump.

The total head requirements will also be used to determine the impeller diameter of the pump. The same pump can be used for various applications by trimming the impeller diameter to meet the system total head requirements.

Uncertainties in these calculations, or an excessive design margin, may result in over-sizing the pump with adverse effects on the power consumption and efficiency of the overall system.

NPSHr and NPSHa

The NPSHa must be calculated during the design phase of the piping system before the pump is selected. Once NPSHa is calculated, the NPSHr of the pump being considered can be evaluated to determine if there will be any cavitation problems with the pump. It is a good practice to add a design margin, or NPSH margin, to ensure the pump will have sufficient NPSHa. This margin may be a percentage or an additional amount of head added to NPSHr.

Fluid / Material Compatibility

In addition to the hydraulic aspects of the pump, there are fluid / material compatibility issues that must be addressed. The material used for all components that will come into contact with the fluid must be compatible with the properties of the fluid that will be pumped. The casing, impeller, shaft, and seals must be able to withstand the corrosive and abrasive effects of the fluid.

The pump supplier must be consulted to select the right pump to meet the requirements of any given application.

Operating Pumps Properly

Once a pump is installed in a fluid piping system, it must be operated properly in order to minimize maintenance and unexpected downtime. Below are a few items one should be aware of to ensure continued trouble free operation.

Startup and Shutdown

Starting up and shutting down centrifugal pumps must be done using the manufacturer's recommendations. When starting a pump, the driver exerts a tremendous amount of energy on the rotating elements of the pump. If an electric motor is used to drive the pump, then the motor must overcome the inertia of the idle pump. This results in a brief but tremendous amount of inrush current. On some very large motors, this may limit the number of starts per hour to prevent excessive heat caused by the inrush current from damaging the motor windings. When shutting down the pump, it is important to follow any shutdown sequence that is required by the pump manufacturer or the plant operating procedures.

Minimum Flow Issues

Pumps are designed to operate for a range of flows, but for every pump, there is a minimum flow rate for continued operation specified by the manufacturer. It is important to operate all centrifugal pumps above the minimum flow rate. The minimum flow rate is provided so that the pump can be operated safely at low flow conditions during startups and shutdowns. The minimum flow does not mean the pump can be continually operated at this condition. If a pump needs to be operated at a low flow rate for any length of time, the manufacturer should be contacted to ensure the pump will not be damaged.

Many small pumps may not have a published minimum flow rate, but it is safe to assume that no pump can be run with the discharge valve shut for any length of time. For a pump with an efficiency of 40% to 80%, for every kW of power supplied to the pump by the motor, 60% to 20% of that energy is transferred to the pump by turbulence and friction. This excess energy manifests itself in the form of heat. The heat is normally removed by the fluid passing through the pump, but if the discharge valve is closed and no liquid is passing through the pump, it will overheat, which causes excessive wear.

Often, minimum flow recirculation pipelines are installed on the pump discharge prior to the discharge isolation valve. The minimum flow bypass line removes the heat and ensures that the pump minimum flow requirements are met. The minimum flow recirculation line should be directed back into the tank where the pump is drawing its suction. This will ensure the pump, operating at its minimum flow rate, will not drain the suction tank. This also allows the fluid to return to the tank, which acts like a large heat sink to dissipate the heat.

Under no circumstances should the minimum flow recirculation line be connected directly back into the pump suction pipeline. This disturbs the smooth flow of liquid into the pump suction and does not allow for the removal of excess heat from the pump.

Pump Run Out

Just as every pump has a minimum flow value, it also has a maximum flow value, oftentimes referred to as "run out." As mentioned earlier, a pump is designed for a best efficiency flow rate, and when the pump is run to the left of the BEP, the efficiency of the pump decreases. As the pump runs further to the right of the BEP, the same problems occur.

It is important to know the maximum flow allowed through each centrifugal pump and to ensure the pump is not run beyond this point. Pump run out flow may also vary with impeller diameter.

NPSH

The majority of centrifugal pumps are not designed to cavitate for extended periods. As a result, the pump must always have sufficient NPSHa for the entire range of flow rates, suction pressures, tank levels, and fluid properties it may face. The difficulties in determining whether there is adequate NPSHa for a pump comes from the fluctuation of NPSHa with varying suction conditions and the variation in a pump's NPSHr with changing flow rate.

Pump Power & Cost of Operation

In the flow path of energy from the source to the working fluid, power can be calculated at various points as given by Equation 4-4 for the pump input power (bhp) and Equation 4-5 for the pump output power (whp). Calculating the amount of electrical power needed to deliver the pump input and output power is extremely important in determining the annual operating cost of the pump, considering the fact that the lifetime operating cost is typically twenty times the cost of purchasing a pump. This cost information should be considered when comparing the advantages of a specific pump or different methods of flow control through the pump.

The annual operating cost consists of the cost of maintaining the pump and the cost of the energy needed to run the pump. The cost of maintenance can vary considerably and be very difficult to estimate, but the energy cost can be determined directly from the amount of power that is being drawn by the motor (and variable speed drive, if installed) to drive the pump to deliver the fluid at the operating flow rate and total head.

Calculating Pump Energy Cost

The cost of the energy used by the motor during a given amount of time is given by Equation 4-17:

$$Operating\ Cost = (P_{electrical})(Operating\ Hours)(\$/kWh) \qquad \textit{Equation 4-17}$$

Operating Cost = cost of energy to drive the pump (in units of currency for the utility rate)

$P_{electrical}$ = electrical power added to the motor or variable speed drive (kW)

Operating hours = number of hours of operation under consideration (hours)

$/kWh = utility rate for the plant during the hours of operation (currency/kWh)

The amount of electrical power can be calculated by re-arranging Equation 4-4 to arrive at Equation 4-18:

$$P_{electrical} = \left(\frac{Pump\ Input\ Power}{\eta_{motor}\ \eta_{VSD}}\right)\left(\frac{0.746\ kW}{hp}\right) = \left(\frac{bhp}{\eta_m\ \eta_{VSD}}\right)\left(\frac{0.746\ kW}{hp}\right) \qquad \textit{Equation 4-18}$$

Substituting the equation for *bhp* in Equation 4-4 into Equation 4-18 gives an equation for the amount of electrical power that a pump consumes at a given flow rate and total head, shown in Equation 4-19:

$$P_{electrical} = \frac{(0.746)QH\rho}{(247{,}000)\ \eta_P\ \eta_m\ \eta_{VSD}} \qquad \textit{Equation 4-19}$$

Equation 4-19 can now be substituted back into Equation 4-17 to provide an equation to calculate the cost of energy based on flow rate, total head, fluid density, and the pump, motor, and variable speed drive efficiencies, shown in Equation 4-20:

$$Operating\ Cost = \frac{(0.746)QH\rho}{(247{,}000)\ \eta_P\ \eta_m\ \eta_{VFD}}(Operating\ Hours)(\$/kWh) \qquad \textit{Equation 4-20}$$

If units other than those given are used for flow rate, head, or density, the constants in Equation 4-20 will need to be re-calculated.

Example 4-6: Calculating Electrical Power Consumption

Calculate the amount of electical power for the pump in Examples 4-1 and 4-2, given a motor efficiency of 93% (fixed speed pump with no variable speed drive installed). Using Equation 4-18:

$$P_{electrical} = \left(\frac{bhp}{\eta_m\ \eta_{VSD}}\right)\left(\frac{0.746\ kW}{hp}\right) = \left(\frac{435.6\ hp}{0.93\ \times 1.0}\right)\left(\frac{0.746\ kW}{hp}\right) = 349.4\ kW$$

Example 4-7: Calculating the Cost of Pumping Power

Calculate the cost of the power for Example 4-6 assuming the power operates for 8,000 hours with an average utility rate of \$0.08/kWh. Using Equation 4-17:

$$Operating\ Cost = (P_{electrical})(Hours)(\$/kWh) = (349.4\ kW)(8000\ hrs)(\$0.08/kWh) = \$223{,}616$$

Alternatively, using Equation 4-20:

$$OC = \frac{(0.746)(6000\ gpm)(250\ ft)(62.4\frac{lb}{ft^3})}{(247{,}000)(0.87)(0.93)(1.0)}(8000\ hrs)(\$0.08/kWh) = \$223{,}612$$

Fixed Speed Flow Control

One way to vary the flow rate of a pump operating at fixed speed is to use a control valve downstream from the pump. In a fixed speed operation, the pump curve shows that the pump produces greater head at lower flow rates. Additionally, the system has less dynamic head at the lower flow rate. As a result, additional energy must be removed from the fluid by the control valve in the form of head loss, or heat, noise, turbulence and vibration. The energy removed by the control valve is paid for in increased pump operating cost.

When calculating the operating cost for fixed speed operation, one must consider the higher head that the pump produces at lower flow rates, along with the reduced pump efficiency.

Example 4-8: Fixed Speed Pump Operating Cost

Consider a pump that operates at variable flow rates throughout the year with a pump curve, efficiency curve, power curve, and system resistance curve shown in Figure 4-42. The pump operates at 1,000 gpm, 800 gpm, 600 gpm, and 400 gpm using a control valve to regulate the flow rate. The dashed line between the pump and system curves represents the amount of head loss across the control valve at each flow rate. Notice that the head loss across the control valve increases with decreasing flow rate due to the increasing pump head and decreasing dynamic head in the system.

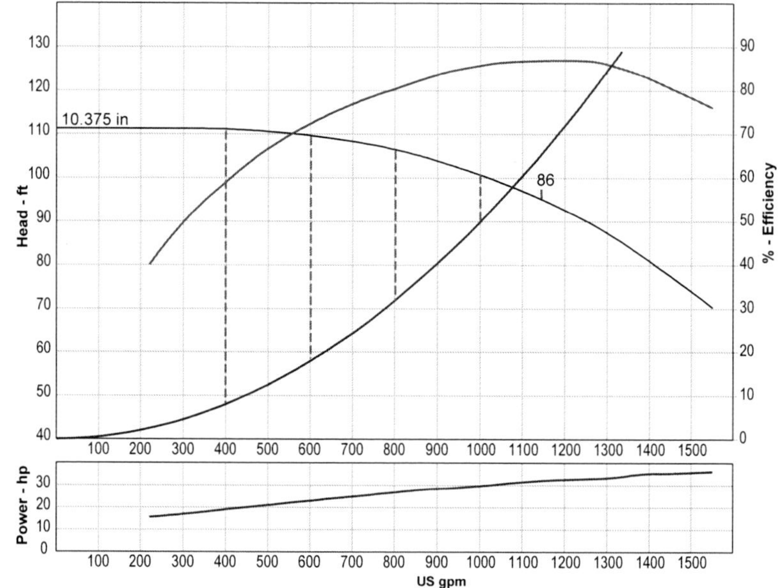

Figure 4-42. Fixed speed pump operating at various flow rates.

Assume the pump operates for 2,000 hours/year at each flow rate with a utility rate of $0.10/kWh and a motor efficiency of 93%.

Table 4-2 summarizes the various calculations presented in this chapter to arrive at an operating cost for the pump. The total operating cost for this flow profile is about $15,800.

Table 4-2. Fixed Speed Operating Costs

Q (gpm)	H (feet)	Density (lb/ft^3)	Pump Output Power (whp)	Pump Efficiency	Pump Input Power (bhp)	Motor Efficiency	Motor Input Power (hp)	Motor Input Power (kW)	Operating Time (hrs)	Power Consumed (kWh)	Utility Rate ($/kWhr)	Operating Cost
1000	100	62.4	25.3	0.85	29.7	0.93	32.0	23.8	2000	47,663	$ 0.10	$ 4,766
800	106	62.4	21.4	0.80	26.8	0.93	28.8	21.5	2000	42,944	$ 0.10	$ 4,294
600	110	62.4	16.7	0.72	23.2	0.93	24.9	18.6	2000	37,137	$ 0.10	$ 3,714
400	111	62.4	11.2	0.59	19.0	0.93	20.4	15.2	2000	30,488	$ 0.10	$ 3,049
									Total	158,232	Total	$ 15,823

Variable Speed Flow Control

When operating with a variable speed drive, the pump speed is adjusted so that the head produced by the pump equals the static head plus the dynamic head loss in the system at the desired flow rate. Variable speed drives are integrated into the process control scheme in order to continually adjust the pump speed to meet changing flow rate demands in the process. In other words, the pump curve is being continually adjusted to meet the needs of the system.

When using a variable speed drive, the pump only produces the total head needed to transport the liquid through the piping system. Since there is no excess energy to remove, the pump consumes less power and is less expensive to operate.

Example 4-9: Variable Speed Pump Operating Cost

Consider the same pump in Example 4-8 that operates at the same flow rates for the same amount of time throughout the year, except that the pump is now controlled with a variable speed drive that changes the pump speed to meet the needs of the piping system.

The pump operates at 1,000 gpm, 800 gpm, 600 gpm, and 400 gpm for 2,000 hours at each flow rate. Figure 4-43 shows the system resistance curve and the pump curve at the various speeds needed to meet the system's hydraulic resistance. Notice that the pump efficiency at each operating point is higher than those for Example 4-8.

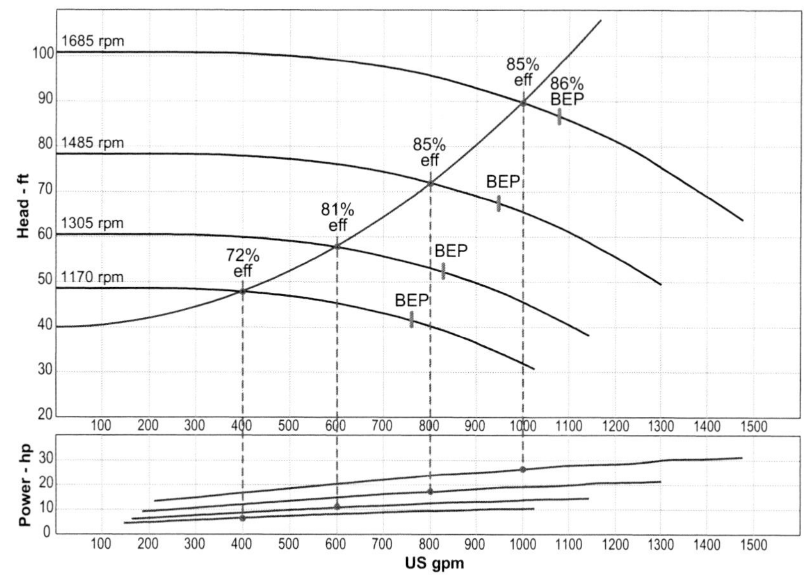

Figure 4-43. Variable speed pump operating at various flow rates.

Table 4-3 summarizes the various calculations presented in this chapter to arrive at an operating cost for the pump. The total operating cost for this flow profile is about $10,000.

Table 4-3. Variable Speed Operating Costs

Q (gpm)	H (feet)	Density (lb/ft^3)	Pump Output Power (whp)	Pump Efficiency	Pump Input Power (bhp)	Motor Efficiency	Motor Input Power (hp)	Motor Input Power (kW)	VFD Efficiency	VFD Input Power (kW)	Operating Time (hrs)	Power Consumed (kWh)	Utility Rate ($/kWhr)	Operating Cost
1000	89	62.4	22.5	0.85	26.5	0.93	28.4	21.2	0.98	21.6	2000	43,286	$ 0.10	$ 4,329
800	72	62.4	14.6	0.85	17.1	0.93	18.4	13.7	0.98	14.0	2000	28,014	$ 0.10	$ 2,801
600	58	62.4	8.8	0.81	10.9	0.93	11.7	8.7	0.98	8.9	2000	17,761	$ 0.10	$ 1,776
400	48	62.4	4.9	0.72	6.7	0.93	7.2	5.4	0.98	5.5	2000	11,024	$ 0.10	$ 1,102
											Total	100,085	Total	$ 10,008

The $5,800/year savings may justify the expenses of buying and installing a variable speed drive for this application. This type of hydraulic and economic analysis should be done when designing a new piping system or optimizing an existing one.

NOTE: The motor and drive efficiencies were held constant for the calculations in Table 4-2 and Table 4-3. In actuality, the motor and drive efficiencies will vary slightly with percent load. If known, actual performance should be used to provide more accurate results.

Chapter Five

Pipelines

Pipelines connect the components of the piping system together and transport the working fluid throughout the system. Because the components are hydraulically connected by the pipeline, it is important to understand the effect that the flow of fluid in the pipeline has on the overall performance of the total system. A good understanding of the impact of the pipeline performance will improve operational knowledge and troubleshooting skills.

Pipelines are a source of non-recoverable energy loss from the working fluid. The amount of energy loss depends not only on the physical properties of the pipeline, but also on the properties of the fluid itself.

This chapter covers the terminology associated with pipelines, how to calculate the amount of energy loss due to the fluid flow, and how the properties of the pipeline and fluid influence the amount of energy loss.

Pipe Terminology

The terms used to decribe a pipeline can often generate confusion among those who work with piping systems, especially those who are new to the field. It is important to have clear definitions for those terms and to be as concise as possible when using them to avoid misunderstandings that could lead to costly mistakes in the design, construction, operation, and maintenance of the system.

Pipe and Tubing

For the purposes of this book, a pipe is a conduit with a circular cross-section defined with two non-dimensional numbers: a Nominal Pipe Size (NPS) and a schedule (SCH). Pipe has a fixed outside diameter for a given nominal size and is described by its material of construction, the wall thickness, and its inside and outside diameters, as shown in Figure 5-1.

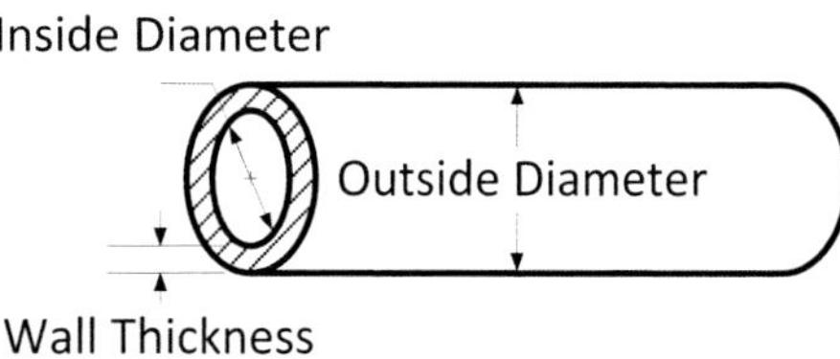

Figure 5-1. Pipe terms.

Tubing is similar to piping and from a hydraulical perspective, pipe and tube can be considered interchangeable. Pipe is generally described by its nominal pipe size and tubing is typically defined by its outside diameter (OD). For example, a 4-inch nominal pipe manufactured to the ANSI 36.10 standard has an outside diameter of 4.500 inches, whereas 4-inch nominal sanitary stainless steel tubing used in the food and pharmaceutical industries has an outside diameter of 4.000 inches.

Nominal Pipe Size (NPS)

Nominal Pipe Size is a set of standard pipe sizes used for pressure piping in North America. The nominal pipe size refers to the approximate size of the pipe expressed in inches for U.S. units and millimeters for metric units. The values of nominal pipe sizes from 1/8 to 12 inches roughly equate to the inside diameter, but for 14 inch pipelines and larger, the NPS equals the outside diameter.

In the United States, pipe sizes are documented in API 5L and ANSI/ASME B36.10M, and internationally documented in ISO 65. The European equivalent of NPS is the Diametre Nominal (DN) standard sizes. When converting nominal pipe sizes from U.S. units to metric units, the converted value is truncated. For example, a 4-inch nominal pipe diameter in U.S. units is referred to as a DN 100 nominal pipe for metric units, even though the exact conversion of four inches is 101.6 mm.

Pipe Inside Diameter (ID)

The inside diameter is the actual pipe diameter when measured at the inside surface of the pipe, as shown in Figure 5-1. The inside diameter is the most significant pipe parameter influencing the hydraulic calculations for fluid flow through a pipe. The inside diameter is equal to the outside diameter minus two times the wall thickness.

Pipe Outside Diameter (OD)

The outside diameter is the diameter when measuring from the outside surface of the pipe, as shown in Figure 5-1. For a given nominal pipe size, the outside diameter is a fixed value regardless of the schedule, or wall thickness. This makes it easier to manufacture valves and fittings to connect to the pipelines. For example, a 4-inch globe valve can mate with a 4-inch pipe, regardless of whether the pipe is schedule 40, 80, or 120.

How thick the wall must be is determined by the maximum fluid pressure the pipe must be able to withstand.

Wall Thickness and Schedule

The wall thickness describes the thickness of the pipe material. The pressure of the fluid in the pipe will determine the required thickness of the pipe wall and therefore the schedule of the pipe.

The wall thickness is characterized by the pipe schedule. Typical pipe schedules include Schedule 5, 10, 20, 30, 40, 60, 80, 100, 120, 140, and 160. The most commonly used schedules are 40, 80, and 160. Another variation on pipe schedule is the use of the suffix "S" to indicate stainless steel pipe. For example, 40S would indicate a schedule 40 stainless steel pipe.

Instead of using the Nominal Pipe Size, some specifications are based on the Iron Pipe Size (IPS) schedule, which characterized the wall thickness as Standard Wall (STD), Extra Strong (XS), and Double Extra Strong (XXS).

Pipe Standard Specifications

The majority of pipe used in piping systems is defined by a pipe standard specification. The standard specification is created by a standards organization such as ASTM International, ISO, ANSI, ASME, or DIN. These standards are developed by a committee consisting of representatives from companies that manufacturer, design, and use the products covered by the standard. The primary hydraulic information found in a pipe standard is the available pipe sizes, schedules, and the inside diameter for the pipe material.

The pipe specification for different materials defines the nominal pipe sizes and schedules used for that standard. For example, the ASTM D-1785 Standard Specification for Poly Vinyl Chloride (PVC) Plastic Pipe covers sizes up to 16-inch and schedules 40, 80, and 120.

Some pipe, such as lined pipe, is proprietary in nature. For example, the Resistoflex® division of the Crane Company manufactures a proprietary plastic lined pipe for use in chemical processing applications. This pipe material is only available from Crane Resistoflex; hence, the available sizes are determined by the manufacturer. When proprietary pipe is used, the pipe manufacturer must provide the appropriate dimensions to perform head loss and pressure drop calculations.

Absolute Roughness

Absolute roughness (ε) is the average height of the irregularities and imperfections on the pipe surface that protrude into the flow stream and is defined in units of feet, inches, or millimeters. The absolute roughness varies with the pipe material, method of construction, and corrosion and mineral build-up.

Relative Roughness

Relative roughness (R_r) is a ratio of the absolute roughness to the inside diameter of the pipe and is a dimensionless value.

Pipeline Head Loss Calculations

As discussed in Chapter 2, as fluid flows through a pipeline, friction and changes in fluid momentum cause some of the hydraulic energy to be converted into non-recoverable energy in the form of heat, noise, and vibration. This energy loss, or head loss, is no longer capable of producing work and results in a reduction of the static pressure of the fluid.

Head loss is energy that was originally added to the fluid by the pump and this head loss generated by the pipeline contributes to the total dynamic head requirements of the pump.

Calculating the amount of head loss in a pipeline for a given flow rate is important in designing the piping system, sizing and selecting a pump, understanding the operation of the system, and for troubleshooting problems in the system.

There are two widely recognized methods for calculating the head loss in a fully charged circular pipe: the Hazen-Williams method and the Darcy-Weisbach method.

The Hazen-Williams method was developed from empirical methods using 60° F water running through cast iron pipe. Over the years, a material correction factor has been applied so that this method can be used for pipe materials other than cast iron. Since it is only valid for water, the Hazen-Williams method is typically used for systems involving municipal water distribution and fire sprinkler systems.

The Darcy-Weisbach method is a much more robust method that can be used for any single phase Newtonian fluid and with any pipe material. It is valid for laminar and turbulent fluid flow and has no restrictions for incompressible liquids. If used for compressible gases and vapors, the following limitations apply:

- $(P_{inlet} - P_{outlet}) < 10\%$ of P_{inlet} : can use the fluid density at the inlet or outlet and still obtain results within reasonable accuracy
- $10\% < (P_{inlet} - P_{outlet}) < 40\%$ of P_{inlet} : use the average of the fluid density at the inlet and outlet
- $(P_{inlet} - P_{outlet}) > 40\%$ of P_{inlet} : Darcy method should not be used

The Darcy method will be used throughout this book since it can be used for a wide variety of fluids and pipe materials.

Darcy Head Loss Calculation

The Darcy equation calculates the head loss due to the friction between the flowing fluid and the pipe wall using Equation 5-1:

$$h_L = f \frac{L}{D} \frac{v^2}{2g}$$ *Equation 5-1*

where:
h_L = Head loss (feet of fluid)
f = Darcy friction factor (unitless)
L = Pipe length (feet)
D = Pipe inside diameter (feet)
v = Fluid velocity (feet/sec)
g = Gravitational constant (32.2 feet/sec^2)

Evaluating the Darcy equation provides insight on the obvious factors that influence the amount of energy that is lost as fluid flows through the pipeline, specifically the length of the pipeline, the velocity of the fluid flowing through the pipeline, and the pipe inside diameter. Evaluating the impact of just one variable at a time without considering the effect on the remaining variables:

- If the length of the pipeline is doubled, the head loss will double
- If the velocity of the fluid in the pipeline is doubled, the head loss will quadruple
- If the pipe diameter is doubled, the head loss in the pipeline will decrease by half

From every day experiences, it is intuitive to most people that there are additional factors that affect the flow of fluid in a pipe, namely the properties of the fluid and the properties of the pipeline. For example, it takes longer to pour viscous lubricating oil out of a bottle than it does to pour the same amount of water. Also, there is more flow through a new steel pipe than a highly corroded one. It is the friction factor in the Darcy equation that accounts for the fluid and pipeline properties. This friction factor is a function of both the Reynolds Number and a pipe's roughness.

Before describing how the friction factor accounts for fluid and pipe properties in the Darcy head loss calculation, an alternative form of the Darcy equation is shown in Equation 5-2. This form of the Darcy equation uses typical units for flow rate and pipe diameter encountered in most applications and assumes piping of circular cross-section.

$$h_L = 0.0311\frac{fLQ^2}{d^5}$$ *Equation 5-2*

where:
h_L = Head loss (feet of fluid)
f = Darcy friction factor (unitless)
L = Pipe length (feet)
d = Pipe inside diameter (inches)
Q = volumetric flow rate (gpm)

To derive the 0.0311 constant, substitute Equation 2-10 into Equation 5-1 and include the conversion of feet to inches.

Reynolds Number

The Reynolds number is used to account for the fluid properties in determining the Darcy friction factor. The Reynolds Number (R_e) is a dimensionless ratio that characterizes the flow regime in a pipeline and is given in Equation 5-3, with an alternative form using more common units shown in Equation 5-4.

$$R_e = \frac{Dv\rho}{\mu_e}$$

Equation 5-3

where: Re = Reynolds Number (unitless)
D = Pipe inside diameter (feet)
v = Fluid velocity (feet/sec)
ρ = Fluid weight density (lb/ft^3)
μ_e = Absolute fluid viscosity (lbm/ft•sec)

$$R_e = 50.6\frac{Q\rho}{d\mu}$$

Equation 5-4

Re = Reynolds Number (unitless)
Q = volumetric flow rate (gpm)
ρ = Fluid density (lb/ft^3)
d = Pipe inside diameter (inches)
μ = Absolute (dynamic) viscosity (cP)

To derive the 50.6 constant, substitute Equation 2-10 into Equation 5-3 and include the conversion of feet to inches and $\mu = 1488.2\ \mu_e$.

For low values of the Reynolds Numbers, the flow is considered laminar and the fluid particles flow in slipstreams with little or no lateral movement between slip streams. For high values of Reynolds Numbers, the flow is considered turbulent and the fluid particles move in the primary direction of flow, but they also move laterally between slip streams.

The difference between laminar and turbulent flow can be demonstrated by dropping colored dye into a fluid stream. If the dye makes a straight line in the flowing fluid, the flow is laminar. If the dye quickly mixes with the other fluid particles forming a cloud of dye in the flowing fluid, then the flow is considered turbulent.

It has been experimentally determined that, for Reynolds Numbers less than 2100, the flow will be laminar. For values greater than 4000, the flow will be transitional or fully turbulent. The zone between the laminar and turbulent regions (2100 to 4000) is the critical zone. In this area, the fluid can shift back and forth between laminar and turbulent flow.

Individually evaluating the factors in the Reynolds Number equation in Equation 5-4 shows that:

- Increasing the fluid flow rate in the pipe increases the Reynolds Number
- Increasing the fluid density increases the Reynolds Number
- Increasing the pipe diameter decreases the Reynolds Number
- Increasing the fluid viscosity decreases the Reynolds Number

Relative Roughness

The Relative Roughness (R_r) is used to account for the pipeline properties in determining the Darcy friction factor. Relative roughness is a dimensionless ratio of the pipe absolute roughness to the inside diameter of the pipe as shown in Equation 5-5:

$$R_r = \frac{\varepsilon}{d} \qquad \textit{Equation 5-5}$$

where: R_r = Relative Roughness (unitless)
d = pipe inside diameter (inches)
ε = absolute roughness of pipe wall irregularities (inches)

When comparing the roughness of pipe material in relation to pipe diameter, it can be seen that as the pipe diameter increases, the effect of pipe roughness decreases. For example, the relative roughness of a ¼-inch nominal pipe is larger than that of an 8-inch nominal pipe, so roughness has a larger effect on the head loss for a smaller pipe compared to a larger pipe.

Determining the Darcy Friction Factor

After calculating the Reynolds Number and the Relative Roughness, the Darcy friction factor in Equations 5-1 and 5-2 can be determined. However, the method for determining the friction factor depends on whether the flow is laminar or turbulent.

For laminar flow, ($Re < 2100$), the Darcy friction factor can be calculated using Equation 5-6 then inserted into the Darcy equation, Equation 5-1 or Equation 5-2, to determine the head loss for that pipeline.

$$f = \frac{64}{R_e} \qquad \textit{Equation 5-6}$$

The determination of the Darcy friction factor in the turbulent regime is much more difficult. In the early 20th Century, a variety of individuals performed experiments on fluid flowing through pipes and developed an equation describing the friction factor in the turbulent regime. (Any textbook on fluid dynamics can provide the details for this research.)

Colebrook, an early researcher in the study of fluid dynamics, was able to arrive at an expression describing the friction factor as shown in Equation 5-7, which is known as the Colebrook Equation. A modified form of the Colebrook Equation is shown in Equation 5-8.

$$\frac{1}{\sqrt{f}} - 2\,log\left(\frac{d}{\varepsilon}\right) = 1.14 - 2\,log\left[1 + \frac{9.28}{R_e\left(\frac{\varepsilon}{d}\right)\sqrt{f}}\right]$$ *Equation 5-7*

$$\frac{1}{\sqrt{f}} = -2\,log\left(\frac{\varepsilon}{3.7d} + \frac{2.51}{R_e\sqrt{f}}\right)$$ *Equation 5-8*

The Darcy friction factor, the relative roughness, and the Reynolds number are all included in Equations 5-7 and 5-8. However, this equation is not suitable for direct engineering calculations because the friction factor term appears on both sides of the equation and would have to be solved iteratively.

The Swamee-Jain Equation shown in Equation 5-9 is an explicit equation that is within reasonable accuracy of the implicit Colebrook Equation, and is more suitable for solving using a calculator, computer software, or a spreadsheet.

$$f = \frac{0.25}{\left[log\left(\frac{\varepsilon}{3.7d} + \frac{5.74}{R_e^{0.9}}\right)\right]^2}$$ *Equation 5-9*

L.F. Moody, in a paper entitled "Friction Factors for Pipe Flow" graphed the Colebrook friction factor equation as a function of Reynolds number and relative roughness. The Moody Diagram, shown in Figure 5-2, provides a graphical means to arrive at the Darcy friction factor. The Moody Diagram plots the friction factor on the left-hand vertical axis, the Reynolds Number on the logarithmic horizontal axis, and the Relative Roughness on the right-hand vertical axis.

There are four zones on the Moody Diagram: the laminar zone, the critical zone, the transition zone, and the zone of complete turbulence.

In the laminar zone, the friction factor is only a function of the Reynolds Number, as was shown in Equation 5- 6. On the Moody Diagram, this equation is a linear relationship with a negative slope. Determine the friction factor based on the intersection of the line in the laminar zone with the calculated Reynolds Number. For example, a Reynolds Number of 1000 (10^3) gives a friction factor of 0.064.

In the critical zone, the flow can change from laminar to turbulent then back to laminar, so the friction factor will fluctuate accordingly. This gives a much greater uncertainty for determining the amount of head loss for the pipeline, so this region should be avoided when designing and operating piping systems.

In the transition zone, the friction factor is a function of the Reynolds Number and the Relative Roughness of the pipe. For a given Relative Roughness, the friction factor decreases with increasing Reynolds Number. For a given Reynolds Number, the friction factor decreases with a decreasing Relative Roughness. To determine the friction factor in the transition zone, follow the calculated Relative Roughness line to the left and up until it intersects the calculated Reynolds Number, then read the friction factor

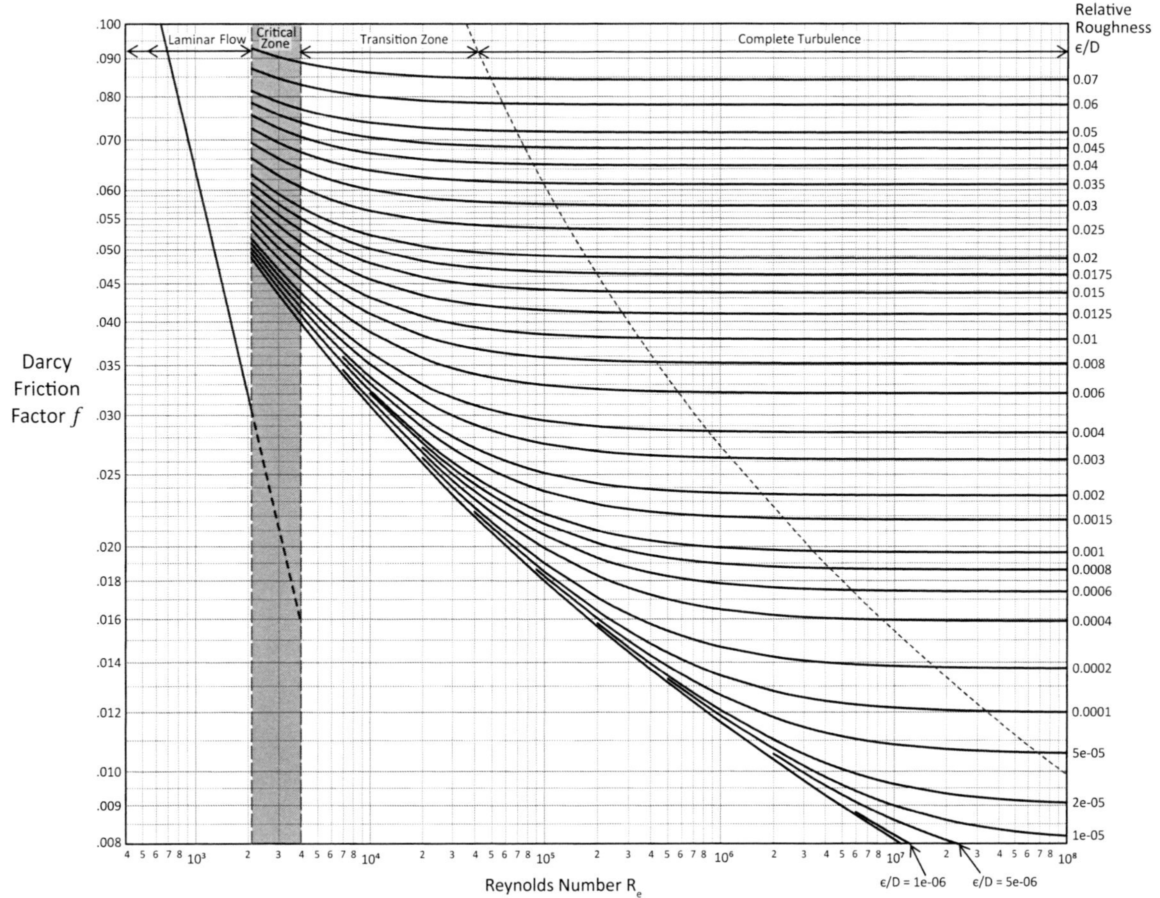

Figure 5-2. The Moody Diagram (courtesy of Crane Technical Paper No. 410).

directly off the left-hand vertical axis. For example, for a calculated Reynolds Number of 10,000 (10^4) and Relative Roughness of 0.004, the friction factor is about 0.036.

In the zone of complete turbulence, the friction factor is only a function of the Relative Roughness. For a given Relative Roughness, the friction factor is constant regardless of the Reynolds number. To determine the friction factor in the completely turbulent zone, follow the Relative Roughness line directly across to the friction factor axis. For example, for a calculated Reynolds Number of 10,000,000 (10^7) and Relative Roughness of 0.003, the friction factor is about 0.026.

Example 5-1: Calculating Head Loss and Pressure Drop for a Pipeline

Calculate the head loss in a 100 foot length of horizontal 4-inch schedule 40 clean steel pipeline with a flow of 400 gpm of 60° F water given the following fluid and pipeline properties (these can be obtained from the Crane TP-410 or other hydraulics text books):

Fluid Properties for 60° F water

- Density: $\rho = 62.4$ lb/ft^3
- Viscosity: $\mu = 1.1$ cP

Pipeline Properties for 4-inch Schedule 40

- Inside Diameter: $d = 4.026$”
- Absolulte roughness: $\varepsilon = 0.0018$”

First calculate the Reynolds Number using Equation 5-4:

$$R_e = 50.6\frac{Q\rho}{d\mu} = 50.6\frac{(400\ gpm)\left(62.4\frac{lb}{ft^3}\right)}{(4.026")(1.1\ cP)} = 2.85 \times 10^5$$

Calculate the Relative Roughness using Equation 5-5:

$$R_r = \frac{\varepsilon}{d} = \frac{0.0018"}{4.026"} = 0.000447$$

Calculate the Darcy friction factor using Equation 5-9 (or the Moody Diagram):

$$f = \frac{0.25}{\left[log\left(\frac{\varepsilon}{3.7d} + \frac{5.74}{R_e^{0.9}}\right)\right]^2} = \frac{0.25}{\left[log\left(\frac{0.0018"}{3.7(4.026")} + \frac{5.74}{(2.85 \times 10^5)^{0.9}}\right)\right]^2} = 0.01809$$

Now calculate the amount of head loss using Equation 5-2:

$$h_L = 0.0311\frac{fLQ^2}{d^5} = \frac{(0.0311)(0.01809)(100\ ft)(400\ gpm)^2}{(4.026")^5} = 8.51\ ft$$

Example 5-2: Calculating the Pressure Drop Due to Head Loss

The head loss is a loss of fluid energy that manifests itself as a decrease in the static pressure of the fluid. Equation 2-20 can be used calculate the amount of pressure drop that will be seen as a result of the head loss in the previous example:

$$dP = \frac{\rho\ h_L}{144} = \frac{(62.4\ lb/ft^3)(8.51\ ft)}{144\ in^2/ft^2} = 3.69\ psi$$

Check of Operational Understanding

Question: If there were pressure gages mounted at the inlet and outlet of this pipeline and the pressure difference was 5 psi instead of the calculated 3.69 psi, what could be the cause?

Answer: A higher pressure drop than calculated by the Darcy method would indicate partial pluggage, a rougher pipe due to corrosion, a smaller inside diameter due to sedimentation, or possibly different fluid properties than was used in the calculation. It is also possible that the pressure gages are not properly calibrated.

Example 5-3: Calculating the Fluid Velocity

Calculate the average fluid velocity for the flow rate and pipeline in Example 5-1 using Equation 2-10:

$$v = 0.4085\frac{Q}{d^2} = 0.4085\frac{400\ gpm}{(4.026")^2} = 10.08\ ft/sec$$

Pipeline Head Loss Graph

The amount of head loss generated by the flow of fluid through a pipeline can be graphed as a function of the flow rate. This graph is the basis of the system resistance curve discussed in the pump chapter. Figure 5-3 shows the head loss produced for 60 °F water for various lengths of 4-inch Schedule 40 piping over a range of flow rates.

Note that the head loss for the 100 foot length of pipe at 400 gpm is about 8.5 feet, which is what was calculated in Example 5-1.

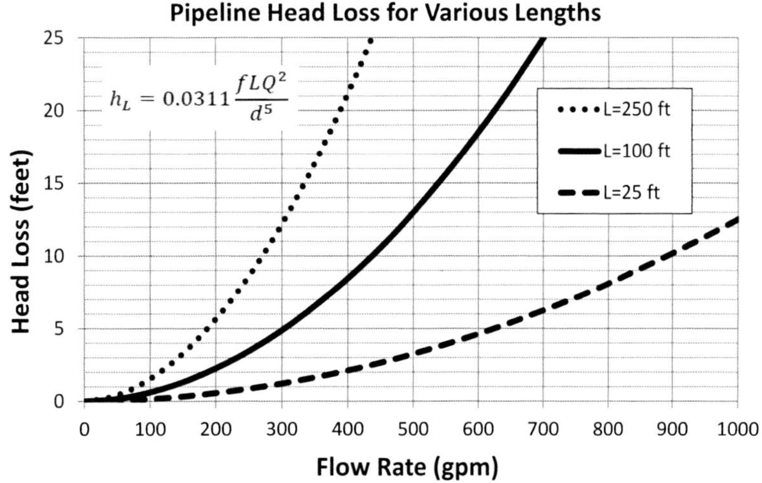

Figure 5-3. Pipeline head loss as a function of flow rate for various lengths of 4-inch Schedule 40 piping.

Figure 5-3 shows that the longer the pipeline is, the steeper the head loss curve will be. In other words, the longer pipe offers more resistance to flow than the shorter pipe.

In addition, the head loss is a second order function of the flow rate. If the flow rate is doubled, the head loss will increase by a factor of four. Although the shape of the curves in Figure 5-3 appear to be second order, as would be indicated by the head loss equation, Equation 5-2, the curves are not quite second order because the Darcy friction factor is also a function of the flow rate.

Head Loss for Series and Parallel Piping

The head loss for pipelines in series and parallel can be added in a fashion similar to how pump curves are added.

Pipelines in Series

For pipelines in series, as shown in Figure 5-4, the flow rate is the same through each segment of the pipeline. The head loss for each pipe can be calculated independently and the total head loss across all three segments is the sum of the head loss for each individual pipeline.

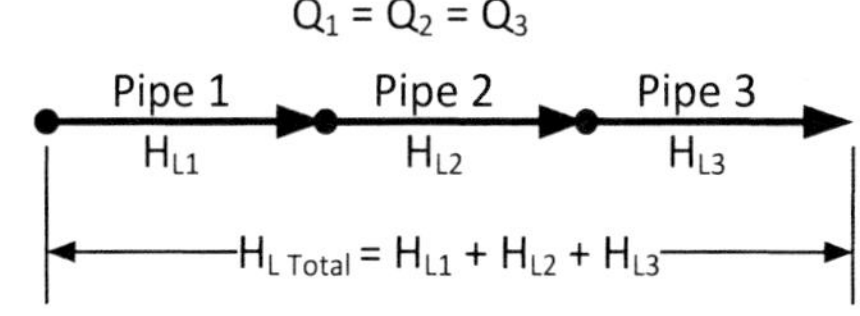

Figure 5-4. Pipelines in series.

Pipelines in Parallel

For pipelines in parallel, as shown in Figure 5-5, there is only one pressure associated with the inlet junction and one pressure for the outlet junction, so the differential pressure across Pipe 1 must equal the differential pressure across Pipe 2, which is equal to that across Pipe 3. That means that the head loss across Pipe 1 due to the flow rate Q_1 must equal the head loss of Pipe 2 caused by the flow rate Q_2, which is equal to the head loss generated by the flow rate Q_3 in Pipe 3.

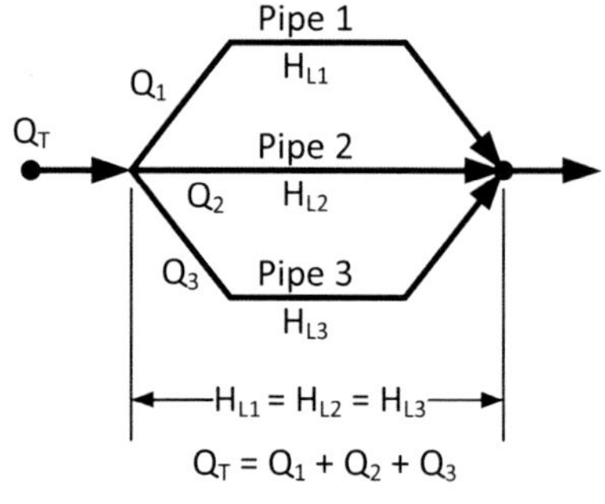

Figure 5-5. Pipelines in parallel.

The total flow rate through the common header is the sum of the flow rates through each pipeline.

Factors Affecting Pipeline Head Loss

As can be seen in Equations 5-1 through 5-5, the properties of the working fluid and the pipe properties affect the amount of head loss generated by the flow of fluid through the pipeline. Specifically, the fluid density and viscosity have a direct impact on the calculation of the Darcy friction factor, along with the flow rate, inside diameter, and the absolute roughness of the pipe wall. In addition, the pipe length, inside diameter, and the flow rate (or fluid velocity) have a direct impact on the Darcy head loss equation. These properties are shown in Figure 5-6.

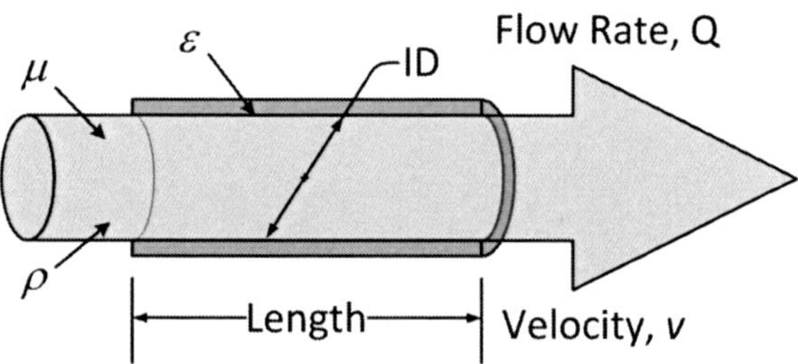

Figure 5-6. Factors affecting pipeline head loss.

It is important to understand the relative impact of these factors on the hydraulic resistance of the pipeline. Some factors are clearly seen just by evaluating the Darcy equation, as was discussed earlier. Other factors are more difficult to judge. To get a true feel for the magnitude of the impact of each factor, a quantitative analysis should be done. This analysis can be performed by comparing the amount of head loss that was calculated in Example 5-1 to the head loss calculated when various factors are changed.

Effect of Fluid Properties on Head Loss

The Darcy method used to calculate the head loss is based on two assumptions: the fluid is Newtonian and the density of the fluid remains constant as it passes through the pipeline. A Newtonian fluid is one in which the viscosity is constant regardless of the amount of shear stress. In other words, the fluid continues to flow regardless of the forces acting on it. For example, water (a Newtonian fluid) in a bottle that is turned over immediately starts flowing. However, catsup (a non-Newtonian fluid) in a bottle that is turned over does not flow until the fluid is agitated (the bottle is tapped on the side). The majority of industrial liquids and gases are Newtonian fluids.

The fluid density and viscosity are used in calculating the Reynolds Number, and the fluid temperature has a major impact on the value of both of these properties. As the temperature of a liquid increases, the density and viscosity typically decrease. The impact of these properties can be evaluated independently.

Density Impact

As the density decreases, the Reynolds Number decreases since density is in the numerator of Equation

5-4. In the laminar and transition zones, as the Reynolds Number decreases, the Darcy friction factor increases, as can be seen on the Moody diagram. Increasing the friction factor results in greater head loss as can be seen in Equation 5-2.

Viscosity Impact

As the viscosity decreases, the Reynolds Number increases since viscosity is in the denominator of Equation 5-4. In the laminar and transition zones, as the Reynolds Number increases, the Darcy friction factor decreases, as can be seen on the Moody diagram. Decreasing the friction factor results in less head loss as can be seen in Equation 5-2.

Taken separately, the impact of density and viscosity compete against each other. Since both the density and viscosity are a function of the fluid temperature in industrial fluids, both properties must be evaluated together to understand the net effect on head loss and pressure drop.

Combined Effect of Changing Density and Viscosity on Head Loss

Table 5-1 shows the combined effect of changing the fluid density and viscosity due to an increase in fluid temperature from 60 °F to 160 °F for the flow of 400 gpm of fluid through 100 feet of 4-inch Schedule 40 piping.

Table 5-1. Effect of Fluid Properties on Pipeline Head Loss

Fluid	Temp (°F)	Density (lb/ft^3)	Viscosity (cP)	Re (x10^4)	Friction Factor	Head Loss (feet) dP (psi)
Water	60	62.37	1.1	28.5	0.018	8.5 ft (3.69 psi)
Water	160	61.01	0.39	78.6	0.017	8.0 ft (3.40 psi)
40% NaOH	60	91.97	24.8	1.86	0.027	12.9 ft (8.21 psi)
40% NaOH	160	89.5	4.8	9.37	0.020	9.6 ft (5.95 psi)
Therminol 55	60	54.61	54.8	0.501	0.038	18.1 ft (6.85 psi)
Therminol 55	160	52.27	5.6	4.69	0.023	10.7 ft (3.87 psi)

For water, the 100 degree temperature change reduces the density from 62.37 lb/ft^3 to 61.01 lb/ft^3 and reduces the viscosity from 1.1 cP to 0.39 cP. Although these are competing influences, the net effect is to increase the Reynolds Number from 28.5 to 78.6 (x10^4), which reduces the friction factor from 0.018 to 0.017 and decreases the head loss from 8.5 feet to 8.0 feet. This corresponds to a reduction in the pressure drop from 3.69 psi to 3.4 psi.

For 40% NaOH, the same 100 degree change in temperature reduces the density slightly, but there is a much larger change in viscosity. The combined effect increases the Reynolds Number and reduces the friction factor, with a corresponding decrease in head loss and pressure drop.

The same effect is seen with Therminol 55, a heat transfer fluid. There is a small change in fluid density but a much larger change in viscosity. The Reynolds Number increases, the friction factor decreases, and the head loss and pressure drop decrease.

With these three fluids, the change in viscosity has a larger impact on the pipeline head loss than the change in fluid density. The magnitude of the change will depend on the fluid and the amount of temperature change. For this 100 degree temperature change, the head loss decreased by 6% for water, by 26% for NaOH, and by 41% for Therminol 55.

Whether an engineer takes a temperature change into account when calculating head loss will depend on the experience of the engineer, the amount of attention to detail that goes into the calculations, and the magnitude of the temperature change that the fluid will undergo.

The Effect of Pipe Properties on Head Loss

Pipe is available in a variety of materials, schedules, and nominal sizes. For a particular pipe, the manufacturing process and the standard to which it is made defines the pipe's physical characteristics and ultimately affects its hydraulic performance. These characteristics include the roughness of the pipe's internal surface, the schedule that defines its wall thickness, and the nominal size of the pipe.

Some design parameters have a greater effect on the hydraulics of the pipeline than others and it is important to understand the relative impact of these factors. Again, some factors are clearly seen just by evaluating the Darcy equation, but others are more difficult to judge. A quantitative analysis that uses the results of Example 5-1 will provide more insight into the magnitude of the effect of the pipe properties on the amount of head loss.

The following analyses use the flow of 400 gpm of 60° F water in a 100 foot length of pipelines with various pipe properties.

Material Roughness

The pipe material, manufacturing process, amount of corrosion, and erosive effects of fluid flow determines the pipe roughness. For example, a cast iron pipe has an extremely rough surface when compared to a steel pipe, and a PVC pipe is much smoother than the steel pipe. And a new steel pipe would have a smoother surface than an old corroded steel pipe.

The pipe roughness is used to calculate the Darcy friction factor using Equation 5-9, which directly affects the amount of head loss, as can be seen in Equations 5-1 and 5-2. Values of absolute roughness for various pipe materials can be found in a graph in Appendix A of the Crane Technical Paper 410 entitled "Relative Roughness of Pipe Materials and Friction Factors for Complete Turbulence." One important note is that the absolute roughness values in the graph are in units of feet.

Table 5-2 shows the quantitative analysis for the flow of 400 gpm of 60° F water in 100 foot lengths of 4-inch Schedule 40 pipelines made of various materials. The line for the clean commercial steel pipe shows the head loss that was calculated in Example 5-1, which is used as the reference pipeline to compare the calculated head loss for the other pipelines. Although the pipeline may not be available in a particular nominal size or schedule, this analysis assumes that it is so that comparisons can be made using the same inside diameter in Example 5-1 ($d = 4.026$").

Table 5-2 shows that PVC piping and drawn tubing is 97% smoother than clean commercial steel and this results in reducing the head loss from 8.5 feet to 6.9 feet, or a 19% reduction in the amount of head loss for the same flow rate, nominal size, and schedule.

Likewise, asphalted cast iron pipe is 167% rougher and increases the head loss by 19%. Galvanized

Table 5-2. Effect of Material Roughness on Pipeline Head Loss

Pipe Material	Absolute Roughness (inches)	% change in Absolute Roughness	Head Loss (feet)	% change in Head Loss from Clean Commercial Steel Pipe
PVC pipe & drawn tubing	0.00006	- 97%	6.9	- 19%
Clean steel	0.0018	0%	8.5	0%
Asphalted cast iron	0.0048	+ 167%	10.2	+ 19%
Galvanized iron	0.006 to 0.0072	+ 233% to + 300%	10.6 to 11.1	+ 25% to + 30%
Cast iron	0.0102	+ 467%	12.1	+ 42%
Concrete	0.012 to 0.12	+ 567% to + 6567%	12.6 to 26.9	+ 48% to + 216%

iron pipe is 233% to 300% rougher and results in a 25% to 30% increase in head loss. Cast iron has an internal surface that is 467% rougher than clean commercial steel pipe and produces 42% more head loss. Concrete can have a wide range of surface roughness depending on how it is manufactured, resulting in roughness somewhere between 567% to 6,567% greater than steel. This results in 48% to 216% more head head loss for the same flow rate, pipe size, and schedule. This analysis shows that a large change in the pipe roughness has a relatively small effect on the head loss.

Again, this analysis was done assuming each pipe in Table 5-2 had the same inside diameter of 4-inch Schedule 40 steel pipe (4.026"), although some pipe made of these materials may not be available with this exact inside diameter. For example, a 4-inch nominal size ANSI H23.1-67 Seamless Copper Tube with K thickness class has an inside diameter of 3.857 inches, but 4.026 inches was used in the calculation.

Pipe Schedule & Wall Thickness

Pipe of the same material is often provided with different wall thicknesses or schedules. This is because pipe may be subjected to a variety of temperatures and pressures, so various wall thickness options are provided to accommodate these needs. In general, pipes made of the same material with thicker pipe walls can withstand greater temperature and pressure.

The calculation of the pipe wall thickness is based on the allowable stress the pipe material can withstand. These calculations are usually performed by a piping stress group. A different group often performs the hydraulic calculations and uses the pipe wall thickness values specified by the pipe stress group.

The selected pipe material determines the available schedules or wall thickness for that material. For example, carbon steel pipe built to the ANSI B36-10 standard is available in schedules 10, 20, 30, 40, 80, 100, 120, 140, and 160. Each schedule has a different wall thickness. Since the outside diameter is the same for the same nominal size, increasing the wall thickness reduces the inside diameter.

Pipe of a particular nominal size may not be available in all pipe schedules. For example, in the ANSI B36-10 standard, 4-inch nominal pipe is only available in schedule 40, 80, 120, and 160, whereas 16-inch nominal pipe is available in all pipe schedules.

Table 5-3 compares the head loss for the flow of 400 gpm of 60° F water in 100 foot lengths of 4-inch steel pipelines made to various pipe schedules. The line for the schedule 40 steel pipe shows the head loss that was calculated in Example 5-1, which is used as the reference pipeline to compare the calculated head loss for the other pipelines.

Table 5-3. Effect of Pipe Schedule on Pipeline Head Loss

Schedule	ID (inches)	% change in ID	Head Loss (feet)	% change in Head Loss	Fluid Velocity (ft/sec)
40	4.026	0%	8.5	0%	10.08
80	3.826	- 5%	11.0	+ 30%	11.16
120	3.624	- 10%	14.5	+ 71%	12.44
160	3.438	- 15%	19.0	+ 123%	13.82

Schedule 80 pipe has a 5% smaller inside diameter than Schedule 40, but this increases the head loss from 8.5 feet to 11.0 feet, an increase of 30%. The reason the head loss increased by such a large amount can be seen by evaluating the head loss equations, Equation 5-1 and 5-2. The pipe diameter is in the denominator of the head loss equation, so a smaller diameter results in a greater value of head loss. In addition, the fluid velocity is squared in the head loss equation. The calculated values of the fluid velocity in Table 5-3 show about a 10% increase in the velocity of Schedule 80 pipe compared to Schedule 40 pipe. The squaring of the increased velocity has a large effect on the pipeline head loss.

Similarly, 4-inch Schedule 120 pipe has a 10% smaller inside diameter compared to 4-inch Schedule 40 pipe, which results in a 71% increase in the amount of head loss for the same flow rate. Schedule 160 pipe has a 15% smaller insided diameter, which increases the head loss by 123%. The change in inside pipe diameter has an extremely large effect on the head loss of the pipe.

Pipe Nominal Size

For general-purpose applications, pipe is only available in selected nominal sizes for a given material and schedule. As a result, there are a limited number of available pipe sizes to choose from when sizing a pipeline requiring specific pipe material.

Often, certain available pipe sizes are not used based on preferences or customs. For example, in many piping applications, a 5-inch nominal pipe diameter will not be selected, even though it may be available. Five-inch pipe is not a popular size in many industries for reasons that are now lost in time. Therefore, the valves and fittings for a 5-inch pipe typically cost more than similar valves and fittings for 6-inch pipe. In addition, the pipe, valves, and fittings typically have a longer delivery schedule. As a result, people often opt for the larger and less expensive 6-inch pipe. However, industries in which the weight of the pipe is a critical factor (for example, ship building) will commonly use 5-inch pipe if optimal for their application.

As was seen in the previous analysis of the effect of the pipe schedule on the head loss, the inside diameter plays a major role in the amount of head loss for a given flow rate in the pipeline. The nominal pipe size has a similar effect, as can be seen in Table 5-4 which compares the head loss generated by the flow of 400 gpm of 60° F water in 100 foot lengths of Schedule 40 steel pipelines with various nominal pipe sizes. The line for the 4-inch nominal pipe size shows the head loss that was calculated in Example

5-1, which is used as the reference pipeline to compare the calculated head loss for the other pipelines.

Table 5-4. Effect of Pipe Nominal Size on Pipeline Head Loss PF

Nominal Pipe Size	ID (inches)	% change in ID	Head Loss (feet)	% change in Head Loss	Fluid Velocity (ft/sec)
3.5	3.548	- 12%	16.2	+ 90%	12.98
4	4.026	0%	8.5	0%	10.08
5	5.047	+ 25%	2.7	- 68%	6.41
6	6.065	+ 51%	1.1	- 87%	4.44
8	7.981	+ 98%	0.3	- 97%	2.57

Table 5-4 shows that 3.5-inch pipe has a 12% smaller inside diameter compared to the 4-inch pipe, which results in increasing the head loss from 8.5 feet to 16.2 feet, a 90% increase. A 5-inch pipe is 25% larger and produces 68% less head loss than the 4-inch pipe. The 6-inch pipe has a 51% larger inside diameter and creates 87% less head loss for the same 400 gpm flow of water. The inside diameter of the 8-inch pipe is 98% larger than the 4-inch pipe and as a result, the head loss is 97% less.

Again, one of the major influences is the fluid velocity, which is squared in the head loss equation.

Pipe Sizing and Selection

One conclusion that could be drawn from the previous analyses is to select the largest, smoothest pipe that is available for all applications. However, there are many variables that go into selecting the right pipe for any given application.

One obvious variable is the cost of the pipe. Larger sized pipe typically costs more than smaller pipe, not only because there is more material, but it is also more expensive to manufacture, will require stronger pipe supports, have a larger footprint, and be more expensive to build.

Many of the factors affecting pipe selection are not based on the hydraulics of the system. Fluid and material compatibility will go into determining which pipe material is the right one for a given application. The pressure and temperature of the process fluid also affect the choice of pipe material and wall thickness, based on the allowable stress in the pipe.

Other variables may limit the available options for selecting the pipe. For example, pipes come in a wide variety of materials and schedules. The chosen material may limit the available schedules and the chosen schedule may limit the available pipe diameters.

Pipe Material Selection

The selection of the pipe material has more to do with the fluid, process needs, and cost than with the head loss. The pipe material selected must be appropriate for the fluid and process requirements. For example, steel pipe material may work well for water, but would not work as well with a highly concentrated acid because of the corrosive chemical reaction between the pipe material and fluid. A high purity stainless steel tubing material may be selected for the flow of water in a pharmaceutical process, but if the water is ultra-pure water used in the manufacturing of electronic integrated circuits, then a high purity plastic may be needed.

Many companies will have specific guidelines to help select the right piping material for the processes in their facilities. These specifications may be based on the experience of the engineers, lessons learned from previous projects, or industry standards.

Pipe Sizing

Once the options for the material of construction is determined, the available schedules and pipe sizes can be considered. A company's pipe specification may include sizing criteria to size the pipeline. Some ways to size the pipe is to specify a fluid velocity, head loss per 100 feet of pipe, or differential pressure per 100 feet of pipe.

The velocity, head loss, or dP sizing criteria may vary depending on the application and the location of the piping in the system. For example, pump suction piping is typically sized larger than the pump discharge piping to minimize the head loss in the pump suction line and increase the Net Positive Suction Head available for the pump.

Table 5-5 shows some typical values of fluid velocity for various applications.

Table 5-5. Typical Values of Fluid Velocity for Various Applications.

Application	Velocity Criteria (feet/sec)
Water (Pump Discharge)	5 to 10
Water (Pump Suction)	2.5 to 5
Steam (0-25 psig)	67 to 100
Steam (25 psig and higher)	100 to 167
Steam (Superheated)	117 to 333
Air and Gases	67 to 250

Fluid Velocity Sizing Equation

Equation 2-10 can be re-arranged and used to develop an equation to size a pipeline for a given flow rate. Equation 5-10 can be used to determine the pipe size (in inches) for a given flow rate (in gpm) and velocity criteria (in feet/sec).

$$d = \sqrt{\frac{0.4085\ Q}{v}} \qquad \textit{Equation 5-10}$$

Example 5-4: Sizing a Pipe

Determine the pipe size needed to deliver 1,000 gpm of flow with a velocity criteria of 8 feet/sec. The pipe will be Schedule 80.

Using Equation 5-10:

$$d = \sqrt{\frac{0.4085\,Q}{v}} = \sqrt{\frac{(0.4085\,)(1{,}000)}{(8)}} = 7.15\ inches$$

The inside diameter of pipe is tabulated in many hydraulics books, including the Crane Technical Paper No. 410. An 8-inch nominal pipe size in Schedule 80 has an inside diameter of 7.625 inches, whereas the 6-inch pipe has an inside diameter of 5.761 inches. The 8-inch pipe would have to be selected to keep the fluid velocity under 8 feet/sec.

Ecomonics of Selecting a Pipe Size

In addition to the hydraulic aspects of the piping system, choosing the pipe diameter for a given application is often a matter of economics. Figure 5-7 shows the generalize life cycle cost as a function of the pipe diameter.

The capital cost of the pipe increases as the pipe diameter gets larger. In addition, as the pipe size increases, the cost of the valves and fittings, the material cost, and the labor cost for fabricating and installing the pipe all increase. If a pipe size was chosen based on the capital cost alone, the smallest pipe size would be selected.

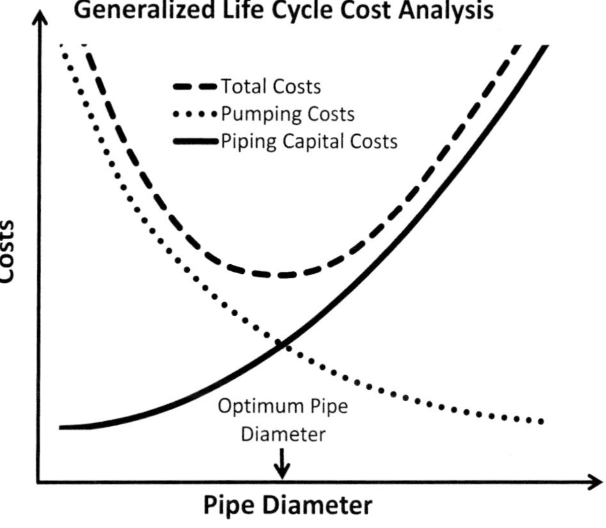

Figure 5-7. Generalized life cycle cost of selecting a pipe.

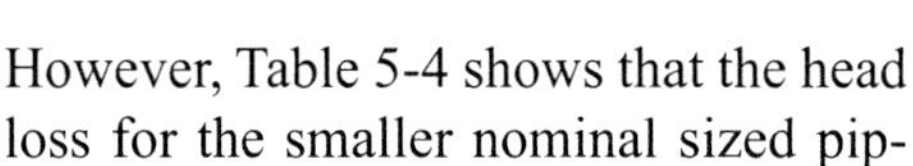

However, Table 5-4 shows that the head loss for the smaller nominal sized piping is much greater than the larger pipe. Since head loss is energy that was initially added to the fluid by the pump, the greater the amount of pipeline head loss, the more energy the pump must add to the fluid and the greater the cost of the energy consumed by the pump's driver. Therefore, the pumping costs decrease with an increasing pipe nominal size.

One final point to mention is that the operating cost must be paid during the entire life of the project, whereas the capital cost is only a onetime expenditure.

The optimum pipe diameter for a given application occurs when both the capital cost of the project and annual operating cost for the life of the plant are considered. When the cost of the pipe material and construction, along with the lifetime pumping cost for the various pipe diameters are added together, the optimum pipe diameter occurs at the lowest value in the total cost curve.

It is possible to perform a life cycle cost analysis to determine the optimum pipe diameter, but in most cases it takes more effort than most customers are interested in investing in the initial engineering. As a result, most pipe specifications include general economic considerations in the pipe sizing rules.

Another concern when determining the pipe diameter for a new pipe design is the need for additional capacity in the future. When a system is designed and built, a design flow rate is determined based on the amount of product that must be pumped. If the future demand for the product increases, the process can be changed to allow for a greater throughput. If smaller pipe diameters were initially selected to minimize the capital cost, then there is a smaller margin for an increase in capacity in the future. If the pipes were initially oversized, the system capacity can more easily be increased. When sizing individual pipelines, care must be taken to include possible future design changes to the system.

Pipe Aging

Another thing to consider when evaluating the hydraulic performance of a pipeline is the age of the pipe. Over the years, the inside of a pipe may change due to corrosion, mineral deposits, or sedimentation. Many of these problems can be corrected by using proper water chemistry or periodically cleaning the pipe.

There are no specific methods to accurately account for the effect of aged pipe on the head loss of a pipeline. For example, if a process fluid only affects the surface corrosion of the pipe, then a change in the roughness value of the pipe material can be used to accurately model aged pipe. If the process fluid deposits sediment or chemical scale on the inside of the pipe, this not only affects the pipe wall roughness, but also reduces the effective inside diameter of the pipe. Corrosion and erosion results in the removal of material from the insided surface of the pipe, causing an increase in the pipe's inside diameter.

Marine growth can also affect the head loss in a pipeline. In many parts of North America, zebra mussels have grown on the inside of cooling water piping, resulting in a blockage. The growth of these mussels within a pipeline can have a major effect on the flow rate and head loss through the pipeline.

The best way to evaluate a suspect pipeline is to either perform a head loss test on the pipeline or open a section of pipeline to evaluate its physical characteristics. For example, you would check for obstructions and changes to the roughness and inside diameter.

Calculating the Cost of Pipeline Head Loss

The amount of head loss created by the flow of fluid through the pipeline is a part of the dynamic head loss of the entire piping system. This head loss is energy that was originally added to the fluid by the pump. A portion of the energy cost for the pump driver can be allocated to the head loss dissipated as the fluid flows through the pipeline.

Equation 4-20 can be configured to calculate the cost of the energy dissipated in the form of head loss in the pipelines, as given in Equation 5-11:

$$\begin{matrix} Cost\ of \\ Head\ Loss \end{matrix} = \frac{(0.746)\ Q\ h_L\ \rho}{(247{,}000)\ \eta_P\ \eta_m\ \eta_{VFD}} (Operating\ Hours)(\$/kWh) \qquad \textit{Equation 5-11}$$

Example 5-5: Calculate the Cost of Head Loss for 4-inch Pipe

Calculate the cost of the energy dissipated as head loss in the pipeline from Example 5-1 with a flow of 400 gpm of 60 °F water in 100 feet of 4-inch schedule 40 clean steel pipe given a pump efficiency of 75%, motor efficiency of 95%, variable speed drive efficiency of 97%, for 8000 hours of operation annually with an average utility rate of \$0.08 / kWh.

Using Equation 5-11 and the 8.51 feet of head loss calculated in Example 5-1:

$$\begin{matrix} Cost\ of \\ Head\ Loss \end{matrix} = \frac{(0.746)(400\ gpm)(8.51\ ft)(62.4\ lb/ft^3)}{(247{,}000)(0.75)(0.95)(0.97)} \left(8000\ \frac{Hrs}{year}\right)(\$0.08/kWh) = \frac{\$594.07}{year}$$

Example 5-6: Calculate the Cost of Head Loss for 3.5-inch Pipeline

As a comparison, calculate the cost of the energy dissipated as head loss if the pipeline was 3.5-inch schedule 40 with the same flow rate of 400 gpm of 60 °F water and same pump efficiency, motor efficiency, variable speed drive efficiency, for the same amount of time and average utility rate.

Again using Equation 5-11, except with the head loss of 16.2 feet calculated for 3.5-inch pipe in Table 5-4.

$$\begin{matrix} Cost\ of \\ Head\ Loss \end{matrix} = \frac{(0.746)(400\ gpm)(16.2\ ft)(62.4\ lb/ft^3)}{(247{,}000)(0.75)(0.95)(0.97)} \left(8000\ \frac{Hrs}{year}\right)(\$0.08/kWh) = \frac{\$1{,}130.90}{year}$$

This half inch reduction in pipe size results in a 90% increase in the energy consumption cost for the same flow rate. These operating costs will be paid each year for the entire life cycle of the plant and should be considered when selecting a particular pipe size for a given application.

Chapter Six

Valves and Fittings

Valves and fittings are used to connect pipelines, redirect flow, diverge and converge flow, isolate equipment or parts of a system, or prevent reverse flow in a pipeline. Any valve or fitting installed in a pipeline adds additional resistance to the flow of fluid and therefore the amount of energy dissipated (head loss) and the pressure drop across the pipeline. There is a wide array of types and sizes of valves and fittings.

Many manufacturers perform bench tests on their products to characterize the hydraulic performance of the valves and fittings that they sell. For example, the Crane Valve Company performed a variety of pressure drop tests for a wide range of types and sizes of valves and fittings. The results of this study were published in the Crane Technical Paper 410: Flow of Fluids through Valves, Fittings, and Pipe. For many decades, this publication has served as a key source for engineers needing to calculate head loss for the design, operation, and troubleshooting of piping systems.

Characterizing the Hydraulic Performance of Valves and Fittings

The head loss of a valve or fitting is caused by four factors: the friction between the fluid and the internal surfaces, changes in the direction of the flow path, obstructions in the flow path, and any changes in the cross-sectional size and shape of the flow path.

Because the amount of friction is typically minor compared to the other three factors, the total resistance can be considered independent of the friction factor or Reynolds Number. The Crane Technical Paper No. 410 treats the hydraulic resistance as a constant for any given obstruction under all conditions of flow. Other studies have shown that the resistance increases at lower flow rates, so a correction factor is added based on the Reynolds Number.

Over the years, various methods have been used to characterize the hydraulic performance of valves and fittings. The most common methods are the *Equivalent Length* (*L/D*), *Flow Coefficient* (C_V), and the *Resistance Coefficient* (*K*). More complex methods are available but with marginal improvements.

Equivalent Length (*L/D*)

Valves and fittings are tested under various flow conditions to determine the equivalent length (L_{eqv} in feet) of straight horizontal pipe that will give the same pressure drop that is seen across the component. The equivalent length is typically reported as a ratio of that length of pipe to the inside diameter (*D* in feet). The amount of head loss can then be calculated for a given fluid velocity (*v* in feet/sec) with a modified form of the Darcy Equation, as shown in Equation 6-1.

$$h_L = f\frac{L_{eqv}}{D}\frac{v^2}{2g}$$ *Equation 6-1*

Flow Coefficient (C_V)

Some manufacturers may provide a flow coefficient (C_V) to characterize the hydraulic performance of their equipment. The flow coefficient is determined by measuring the amount of 60 °F water flow (*Q* in gpm) and the pressure drop across the component (P_{in} and P_{out} in psi), then using Equation 6-2. The larger the flow coefficient, the lower the resistance to flow, and therefore the higher the capacity of the component.

$$C_V = \frac{Q}{\sqrt{\dfrac{P_{in} - P_{out}}{SG}}}$$ *Equation 6-2*

Equation 6-2 is a generalized form of the the flow coefficient equation that is used by control valve manufacturers. A more detailed equation for use with control valves is published in the ISA S75.01 standard, *Flow Equations for Sizing Control Valves*. The concept of the flow coefficient was originally developed in the 1940s by Masonelian to characterize the performance of their control valves.

Other equipment can be characterized by the flow coefficient as well. For example, some heat exchangers, strainers, nozzles, and sprinkler heads use the flow coefficient to define their hydraulic performance.

Other Uses of the Flow Coefficient

The concept of the flow coefficient is a powerful tool in analyzing the performance of equipment in the piping system. It can also be used to characterize the performance of numerous fixed resistance components in a pipeline.

Example 6-1: Using of the Flow Coefficient to Represent the Performance of Fixed Resistance Components

Consider a portion of a piping system shown in Figure 6-1 with four isolation valves, two elbows, a check valve, a heat exchanger, a venturi flow meter, and various lengths of piping connecting all the components. There are pressure gages measuring the inlet and outlet pressures of the series of fixed resistance components.

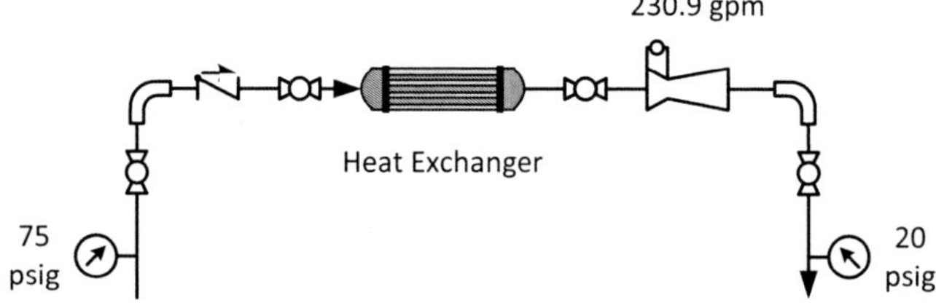

Figure 6-1. Portion of a piping system with fixed resistance components.

Given the flow rate of 230.9 gpm of water at 60 °F and the inlet and outlet pressures, an equivalent C_V can be calculated to characterize the hydraulic performance of the portion of the system between the two pressure gages, using Equation 6-2:

$$C_V = \frac{Q}{\sqrt{\frac{P_{in} - P_{out}}{SG}}} = \frac{230.9}{\sqrt{\frac{75 - 20}{1.0}}} = 31.1345$$

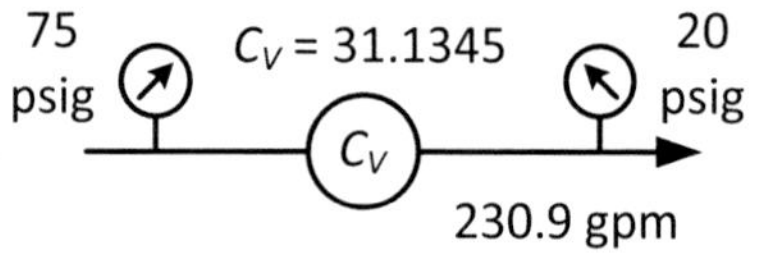

75 psig — C_V = 31.1345 — 20 psig

C_V

230.9 gpm

This equivalent C_V can be represented graphically as shown in Figure 6-2 as a C_V component in a very short length of pipe (no resistance due to the pipe since this was included in the calculation of the flow coefficient).

Figure 6-2. Graphical representation of the equivalent flow coefficient.

Now consider what happens if the pressure drop across the system is increased to 60 psid by reducing the outlet pressure to 15 psig and increasing the flow while maintaining the inlet pressure at 75 psig, as shown in Figure 6-3.

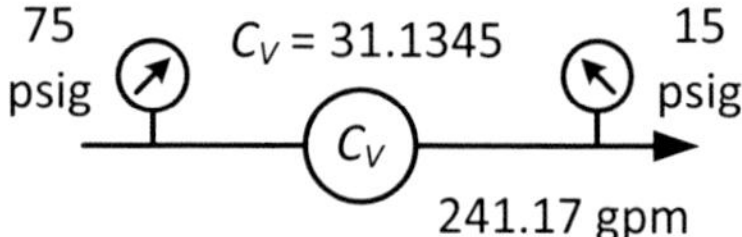

Figure 6-3. Graphical representation of the equivalent flow coefficient at increased flow and dP.

The flow rate can be calculated using the equivalent flow coefficient and the values of pressure at the inlet and outlet, and re-arranging Equation 6-2:

$$Q = C_V \sqrt{\frac{P_{in} - P_{out}}{SG}} = (31.1345)\sqrt{\frac{75 - 15}{1.0}} = 241.17\ gpm$$

This flow rate would be seen on the flow meter, as shown in Figure 6-4.

One note about using an equivalent flow coefficient to represent fixed resistance components. Because of the square root in Equation 6-2, the value of the flow coefficient is sensitive to the number of significant digits used. To increase the accuracy of calculations done with the equivalent flow coefficient, increase the number of significant digits in its numerical value.

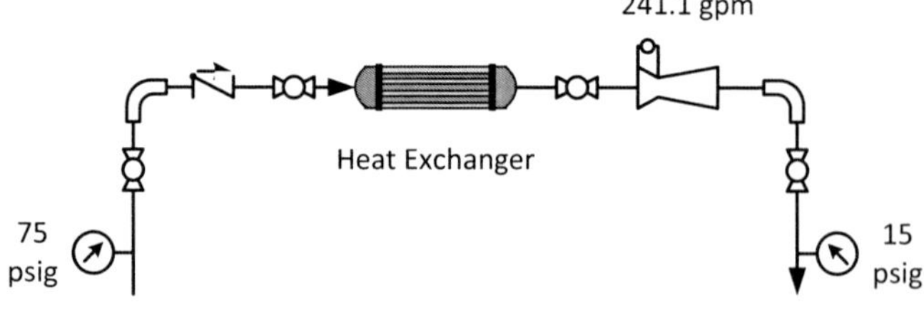

Figure 6-4. Increased pressure differential results in an increased flow rate.

Adding Flow Coefficients

The flow coefficients of components in series and parallel can be added together to obtain an equivalent flow coefficient that represents the performance of the numerous devices.

Equation 6-3 can be used to calculate the equivalent flow coefficient for *n* components in series.

$$\frac{1}{C_{v\,Total}^2} = \frac{1}{C_{v\,1}^2} + \frac{1}{C_{v\,2}^2} + \cdots \frac{1}{C_{v\,n}^2} \quad \textit{Equation 6-3}$$

Equation 6-4 can be used to calculate the equivalent flow coefficient for *n* components in parallel.

$$C_{v\,Total} = C_{v_1} + C_{v_2} + \cdots C_{v_n} \quad \textit{Equation 6-4}$$

Resistance Coefficient (*K*)

Another way to characterize the hydraulic performance of valves and fittings is with the resistance coefficient (*K*). The resistance coefficient combines the equivalent length with the completely turbulent friction factor of clean commercial steel pipe, as shown in Equation 6-5.

$$K = f_T \frac{L}{D} \quad \textit{Equation 6-5}$$

Given the value of the resistance coefficient, the amount of head loss can be calculated for a given fluid velocity using Equation 6-6.

$$h_L = K \frac{v^2}{2g} \quad \textit{Equation 6-6}$$

Using the more common units of flow rate in gallons per minute, Equation 6-7 can be used to calculate the head loss for a given resistance coefficient using the inside diameter (*d* in inches) of the connecting piping.

$$h_L = 0.00259 \frac{KQ^2}{d^4} \quad \textit{Equation 6-7}$$

The resistance coefficient is the opposite way to view hydraulic performance compared to the flow coefficient. Where the flow coefficient describes how much flow capacity the valve or fitting allows, the resistance coefficient describes how much resistance it offers to the flow. Equation 6-8 shows the mathematical relationship between the two concepts.

$$K = 891 \frac{d^4}{C_V^2} \quad \textit{Equation 6-8}$$

The Crane Technical Paper No. 410 treats the resistance coefficient as constant for all flow conditions since the flow is in the transitional or fully turbulent fluid zone in most industrial systems, but other hydraulic references apply a correction factor to increase the K value at low Reynolds Numbers.

Adding Resistance Coefficients

Just as with the flow coefficients, the resistance coefficients of components in series and parallel can be added together to obtain an equivalent value that represents the performance of the numerous devices together.

Equation 6-9 can be used to calculate and equivalent resistance coefficient for *n* components in series.

$$K_{Total} = K_1 + K_2 + K_3 + \cdots K_n \qquad \textit{Equation 6-9}$$

Equation 6-10 can be used to calculate and equivalent resistance coefficient for *n* components in parallel.

$$\frac{1}{\sqrt{K_{Total}}} = \frac{1}{\sqrt{K_1}} + \frac{1}{\sqrt{K_2}} + \frac{1}{\sqrt{K_3}} + \cdots \frac{1}{\sqrt{K_n}} \qquad \textit{Equation 6-10}$$

Determining the Turbulent Friction Factor

For calculating the resistance coefficient using Equation 6-5, the completely turbulent friction factor for clean commercial steel pipe is used as the scaling factor for the valve and fitting size.

Table 6-1 shows the completely turbulent friction factor for various sizes of valves and fittings. These values are obtained by using the Swamee-Jain equation, Equation 5-9, and taking the Reynolds Number to infinity so that it drops out of the equation. Equation 6-11 shows the resulting equation that can be used to calculate the turbulent friction factor.

$$f_T = \frac{0.25}{\left[log\left(\frac{\varepsilon}{3.7d}\right)\right]^2} \qquad \textit{Equation 6-11}$$

The turbulent friction factor is the value on the Moody diagram where the friction factor becomes constant at sufficiently high Reynolds numbers.

Notice that as the pipe size increases, the turbulent friction factor decreases. In other words, larger valves offer less resistance to flow than smaller valves.

Table 6-1: Turbulent Friction Factor for Various Valve and Fitting Sizes

Nominal Size	f_T
½″	0.026
¾″	0.024
1″	0.022
1 ¼″	0.021
1 ½″	0.020
2″	0.019
2 ½″	0.018
3″	0.017
4″	0.016
5″, 6″	0.015
8″	0.014
10-14″	0.013
16-22″	0.012
24-36″	0.011

Resistance of Valves and Fittings

Valves and fittings are selected to perform a certain function in the piping system, whether it is to isolate equipment, redirect flow, or prevent reverse flow. When installed, they add additional resistance to the flow of fluid through the pipeline. The resistance of some fittings depends on size, for others the resistance is only a function of geometry.

The following graphics and resistance values are taken from the Crane Technical Paper No. 410, with permission.

Reducers and Enlargers

Reducers (Figure 6-5) and enlargers (Figure 6-6) are used to connect pipelines of different sizes. When the fluid passes through the fitting, a change in fluid momentum occurs, resulting in an energy loss (head loss), and an associated pressure drop.

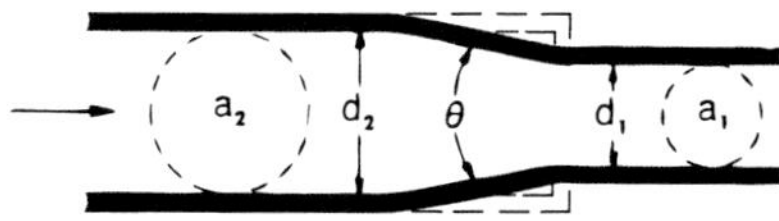

Figure 6-5. Reducer (courtesy of Crane Valve Co.)

The amount of resistance offered by the change in pipe size depends on how much the pipe diameter changes (beta ratio, β = the smaller pipe diameter divided by the larger pipe diameter), how quickly the change occurs (indicated by the angle of approach, θ, and approach length, L) and in which direction the fluid flows.

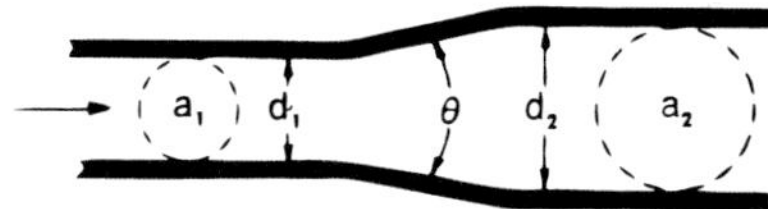

Figure 6-6. Enlarger (courtesy of Crane Valve Co.)

For a reducer or enlarger specified by dimensions d_2 x d_1 x L, the angle of approach can be calculated using trigonometry and is given by Equation 6-12.

$$\theta = 2\,tan^{-1}\left(\frac{d_2 - d_1}{2L}\right)$$ *Equation 6-12*

Equation 6-13 gives the resistance coefficient (K_2) for reducers with an angle of approach $\theta \leq 45°$, expressed in terms of the fluid velocity in the larger pipe size.

$$K_2 = \frac{0.8\left(sin\frac{\theta}{2}\right)(1-\beta^2)}{\beta^4}$$ *Equation 6-13*

Equation 6-14 gives the resistance coefficient (K_2) for enlargers with an angle of approach $\theta \leq 45°$, expressed in terms of the fluid velocity in the larger pipe size.

$$K_2 = \frac{2.6\left(sin\frac{\theta}{2}\right)(1-\beta^2)^2}{\beta^4}$$ *Equation 6-14*

Consult the Crane Technical Paper No. 410 for the appropriate equations for reducers and enlargers with the angle of approach $\theta > 45°$.

The numerator in Equations 6-13 and 6-14 expresses the resistance coefficient in terms of the fluid velocity in the smaller pipe, designated as K_1. In other words, if the head loss is calculated using Equation 6-6, the K_2 value would be used if the calculation uses the velocity in the larger pipe. The K_1 value would be used if the head loss is calculated with the velocity of the smaller pipe.

Pipe Entrances and Exits

The change in fluid momentum that occurs at a tank entrance or exit also adds resistance to flow.

The losses for the pipe entrances from a tank into the pipeline shown in Figure 6-7 vary based on the smoothness of the flow transition. A pipe projecting into a tank has the highest loss, and losses decrease if the entrance is sharp-edged and as the entrance becomes more rounded.

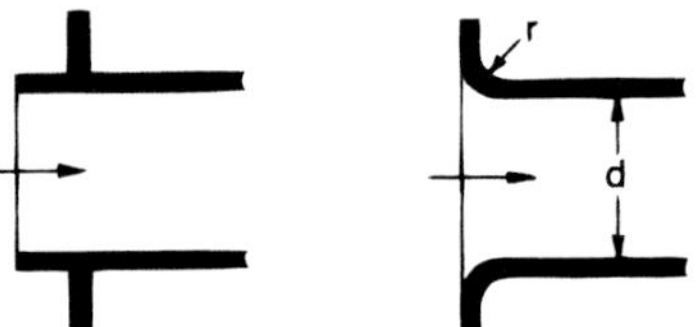

Figure 6-7. Pipe entrances: protruding (left) and bell-mouthed with rounding using r/d (right).(courtesy of Crane Valve Co.)

For the case in which the pipe protrudes into the tank, as shown in left-hand drawing in Figure 6-7, the resistance coefficient, $K = 0.78$, regardless of the pipe size.

For pipe entrances that are bell-mouthed, as shown in the right-hand drawing of Figure 6-7, Table 6-2 shows the resistance coefficient as a function of the r/d value. For sharp-edge pipe entrances, the r/d value is zero and the resistance coefficient, $K = 0.5$, regardless of the pipe size.

For all fluid exits from a pipeline into the tank, as shown in Figure 6-8, the resistance coefficient, $K = 1.0$ for all designs because this takes into account the fact that the fluid will slow down from the velocity it has in the pipeline to zero feet/sec in the tank.

Table 6-2: Sharp-edged and Bell-mouthed Pipe Entrance Resistance Coefficients

r/d	K
0.00*	0.5
0.02	0.28
0.04	0.24
0.06	0.15
0.10	0.09
0.15 and up	0.04

*sharp-edged entrance

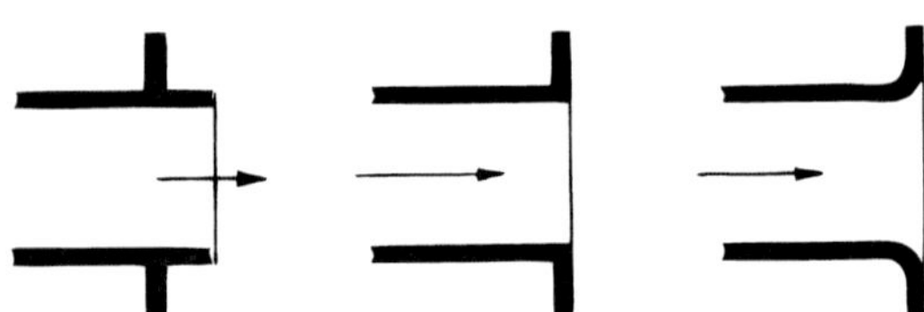

Figure 6-8. K = 1.0 for all pipe exits into a tank: protruding (left), sharp edged (center), and bell-mouthed (right). (courtesy of Crane Valve Co.)

Elbows and Bends

The losses for elbows and bends are caused by a change of fluid momentum when the fluid changes direction as it flows through the bend. The larger the change in direction (i.e. the larger the angle), the greater the change in fluid momentum, the greater the resistance offered by the elbow, and therefore the greater the head loss. The resistance due to the distance traveled through the elbow is also included in the head loss.

Standard Elbows

For the standard elbows shown in Figure 6-9, the resistance coefficient depends on the angle and the pipe size of the elbow.

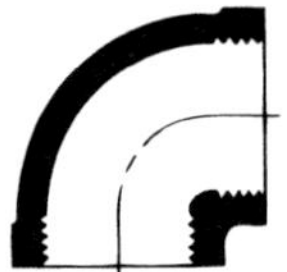

Figure 6-9. Standard threaded elbows: 90° (left), 45° (right). (courtesy of Crane Valve Co.)

For 90° standard elbows, the resistance coefficient is calculated using Equation 6-15. The constant in Equation 6-15 is the *L/D* value. The turbulent friction factor (f_T) is determined by the elbow size using Table 6-1.

$$K = 30\ f_T \qquad \textit{Equation 6-15}$$

For 45° standard elbows, the resistance coefficient is calculated using Equation 6-16. Notice that the *L/D* value is smaller than for the 90° elbow, which means that for the same size, the 45° elbow has less resistance to flow and less head loss than the 90° elbow because there is a smaller change in fluid momentum.

$$K = 16\ f_T \qquad \textit{Equation 6-16}$$

90° Pipe Bends and Flanged or Butt-Welded 90° Elbows

For 90° pipe bends that are flanged or butt-welded, as shown in Figure 6-10, the resistance coefficient depends not only on the pipe size, but also on the r/d of the bend. Table 6-3 shows the equations to calculate the resistance coefficient based on the r/d value. Notice that the *L/D* value initially decreases with increasing r/d for r/d < 3 as the change is more gradual, but then increases with increasing r/d above 4. This occurs because the length of pipe required to make a 90° turn increases with higher r/d, which adds more resistance to the flow.

Figure 6-10. Flanged or butt-welded 90° elbow (courtesy of Crane Valve Co.)

Table 6-3: Resistance Coefficients for Flanged or Butt-welded 90° Elbows as a Function of r/d

r/d	K	r/d	K
1	20 f_T	8	24 f_T
1.5	14 f_T	10	30 f_T
2	12 f_T	12	34 f_T
3	12 f_T	14	38 f_T
4	14 f_T	16	42 f_T
6	17 f_T	20	50 f_T

Close Pattern Return Bends

For the 180° close pattern return bend shown in Figure 6-11, the resistance coefficient is dependent on the pipe size and can be calculated with Equation 6-17.

$$K = 50\ f_T \qquad \textit{Equation 6-17}$$

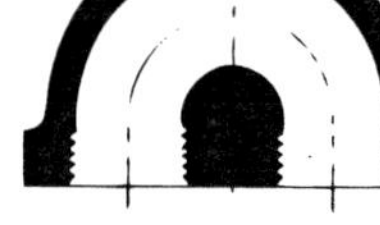

Figure 6-11. Close pattern return bend (courtesy of Crane Valve Co.)

Mitre Bends

The resistance coefficient of a mitre bend shown in Figure 6-12 depends on the mitre angle and the pipe size. Table 6-4 shows the equations to calculate the resistance coefficient of the bend as a function of the mitre angle. Notice that the greater the mitre angle, the larger the *L/D* value.

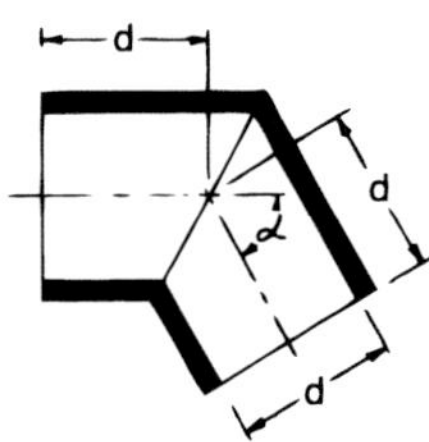

Figure 6-12. Mitre bend (courtesy of Crane Valve Co.)

Table 6-4: Resistance Coefficients for Mitre Bends as a Function of Angle

α	K
0°	$2\,f_T$
15°	$4\,f_T$
30°	$8\,f_T$
45°	$15\,f_T$
60°	$25\,f_T$
75°	$40\,f_T$
90°	$60\,f_T$

Isolation Valves

Isolation valves are used to start and stop flow and to isolate a component or part of the piping system. There are a variety of types of isolation valves to choose from and the amount of resistance they offer when in the fully open position varies with their design.

The resistance increases when there are restrictions in the cross sectional area through the valve, the valve disk remains in the flow stream, or there are changes in direction of flow within the valve.

Ball Valves

A ball valve consists of a spherical ball with a hole drilled through it to allow passage of the fluid. A ball valve is a quarter turn rotary valve that goes from fully open to fully closed with a quarter turn of the handle. The advantage of a ball valve is that it offers the lowest resistance to flow of any standard valve design when fully open.

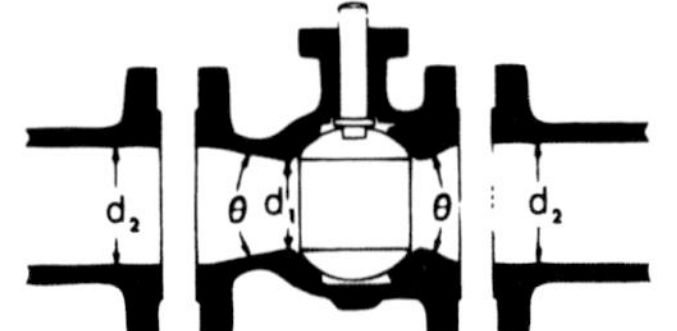

Figure 6-13. Reduced ported ball valve (courtesy of Crane Valve Co.)

The valve shown in Figure 6-13 is a reduced ported ball valve, also known as a venturi ball valve, in which the diameter of the port is smaller than the diameter of the connecting piping ($\beta < 1.0$). A full ported ball valve is one in which the port diameter is equal to the connecting pipe diameter.

The resistance coefficient for a fully open full port ball valve is a function of the valve size and can be calculated with Equation 6-18. The Crane Technical Paper No. 410 should be consulted for calculating the resistance coefficient for reduced ported ball valves.

$$K = 3\,f_T \qquad \text{Equation 6-18}$$

Ball valves are used for on/off isolation valves and can be used for moderate throttling, but do not have the best throttling characteristics. They can be used in applications with non-abrasive liquids or gases, slurries, and chemicals in piping systems that are pressurized or under a vacuum.

Gate Valves

A gate valve is a linear motion valve that has a flat disk that is inserted and withdrawn from the valve seat perpendicular to the direction of the flow. When the valve is open, the valve disk is fully removed from the flow stream through the valve. A gate valve can also be full ported or reduced ported, as shown in Figure 6-14

Gate valves also have a very low resistance to flow because the disc is completely removed from the flow stream when the valve is fully open. The resistance coefficient for full ported gate valves can be calculated with Equation 6-19. The Crane Technical Paper No. 410 should be consulted for calculating the resistance coefficient for reduced ported gate valves.

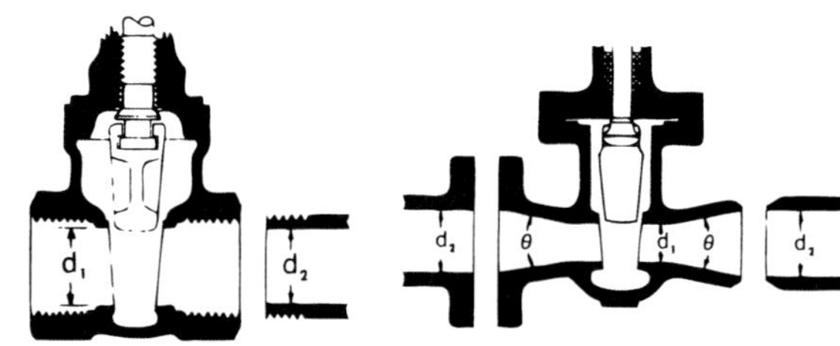

Figure 6-14. Full port and reduced ported gate valves (courtesy of Crane Valve Co.)

$$K = 8\,f_T \qquad \text{Equation 6-19}$$

Gate valves are primarily used for on/off isolation valves because they have extremely poor throttling characteristics. They are used in liquid and gas applications, for powders, or with slurries that have entrained solids. They can be used in pressurized systems or systems under vacuum.

Gate valves are difficult to open when there is a high differential pressure across the valve. Large gate valves typically have a bypass valve installed for system startup to equalize the pressure across the valve prior to opening. Equalizing the differential pressure by "cracking open" the gate valve could lead to excessive erosion of the seat and disc, especially in high temperature and pressure steam applications.

In addition, the disc guide is susceptible to plugging and fouling in applications with fluids that have particulates.

Plug Valves

Plug valves are also a quarter turn rotary valve in which the plug rotates 90° from fully closed to fully open. There is a passage through the valve plug allowing fluid to flow, and can be a straight through design or a 3-way design, as shown in Figure 6-15. Plug valves can also be full ported or reduced ported.

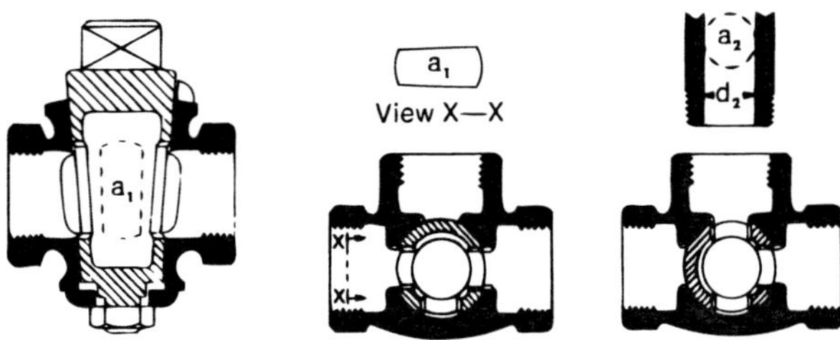

Figure 6-15. Straigh through plug valve (left), 3-way plug valve positioned for straight through flow (center), and positioned for 90° flow (right). (courtesy of Crane Valve Co.)

The large opening through the plug yields a low resistance to flow. The resistance coefficient for the straight through design in which the flow area of the plug equal to the pipeline flow area ($\beta = 1.0$) is given by Equation 6-20.

$$K = 18\,f_T \qquad \text{Equation 6-20}$$

For the 3-way plug valve with straight through flow, shown in the center drawing of Figure 6-15, the resistance coefficient is calculated using Equation 6-21. For the case in which the flow takes a 90° turn through the 3-way plug valve, the resistance coefficient is calculated using Equation 6-22.

$$K = 30\,f_T \qquad \text{Equation 6-21}$$

$$K = 90\,f_T \qquad \text{Equation 6-22}$$

The Crane Technical Paper No. 410 should be consulted for calculating the resistance coefficient for reduced ported plug valves.

Plug valves can be used as on/off isolation valves and can also be used in moderate throttling applications. Multi-port plug valves are used for diverting applications.

Plug valves are typically used in systems under vacuum and at low pressures and temperatures, although some designs allow for high pressures and temperatures. They can also be used in non-abrasive liquids or gases, or with slurries and chemicals.

Butterfly Valves

Butterfly valves are rotary valves with a waffle shaped valve disc that closes and opens. The centerline of the shaft of the centric butterfly valve shown on the left is located at the centerline of disc, which is the same as the centerline of the pipeline, as shown in Figure 6-16.

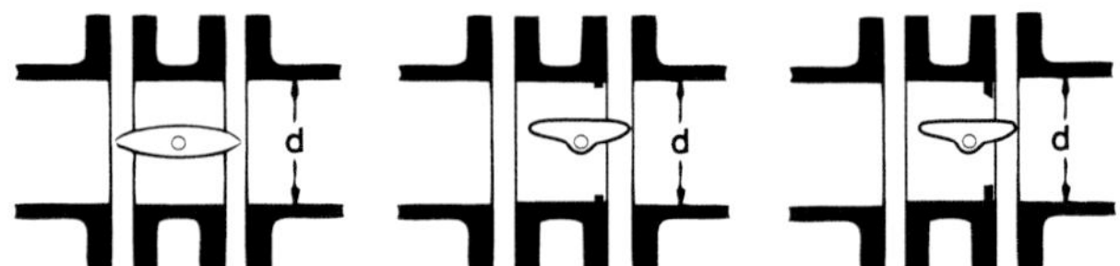

Figure 6-16. Various butterfly valve designs: centric (left), double offset (center), and tripple offset (right). (courtesy of Crane Valve Co.)

With double offset butterfly valves (center image of Figure 6-16), the disc and seat are offset from the shaft centerline, and the shaft itself is offset from the centerline of the pipeline. The triple offset design (image on the right of Figure 6-16) also incorporates an offset between the valve seat and the disc sealing surface to minimize rubbing during opening and closing and to improve the sealing integrity over the life of the valve.

Because the rotating disc of the butterfly valve is always in the flow path, it offers a greater resistance to flow and a larger pressure drop compared to ball and gate valves. The resistance coefficient depends not only on the valve design, but also on the valve size. The equations to calculate the resistance coefficients for fully open butterfly valves are shown in Table 6-5. Notice that for a given valve design, the resistance coefficient decreases with increasing size, not only due to the decreasing turbulent friction factor, but also due to the valve size iteslf. This is because the valve disc has a lesser influence on the overall resistance in an increasingly larger flow passage.

Table 6-5: Resistance Coefficients for Butterfly Valves as a Function of Valve Size and Design

Size Range	Centric	Double Offset	Triple Offset
2" – 8"	45 f_T	74 f_T	218 f_T
10" – 14"	35 f_T	52 f_T	96 f_T
16" – 24"	25 f_T	43 f_T	55 f_T

Butterfly valves are used for on/off isolation valves and in throttling applications when the differential pressure across the valve is relatively small since they are susceptible to cavitation at high differential pressures. They are used for both liquids and gases, as well as for powders and slurries. They can be used in fluids under vacuum or in pressurized systems. Other advantages of butterfly valves include their low cost and small installation width in the pipeline.

Globe and Angle Valves

A globe valve is a linear motion valve in which the fluid flowing through the valve body takes a more tortuous path through the valve, depending on the valve design. In addition, the valve disc remains in the flow path even when the valve is fully open. These two factors cause the globe valve to have a higher resistance to flow.

In the standard straight through design shown in Figure 6-17, the flow actually makes roughly two 90° changes of direction in quick succession. The resistance coefficient for full ported globe valves can be calculated using Equation 6-23.

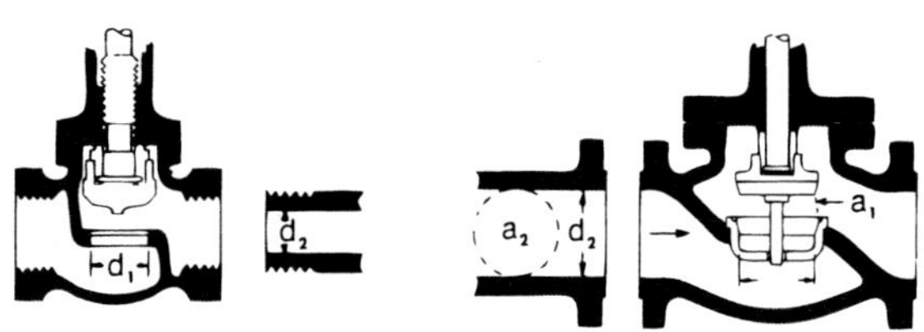

Figure 6-17. Standard straight through globe valves (courtesy of Crane Valve Co.).

$$K = 340\ f_T \qquad \textit{Equation 6-23}$$

Another type of globe valve is the Y-pattern angled globe valve shown in Figure 6-18. The flow essentially makes two 45° changes in fluid direction, so its resistance coefficient would be less than the design shown in Figure 6-17. The resistance coefficient for a full ported Y-pattern angled globe valve is given by Equation 6-24.

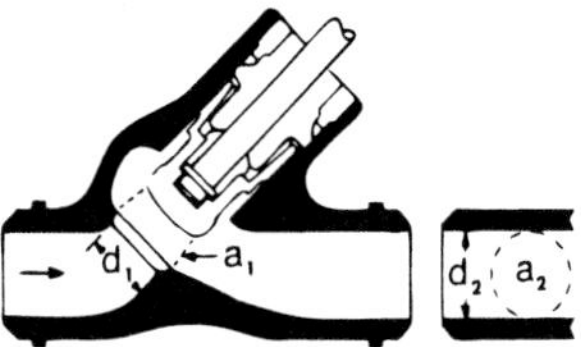

Figure 6-18. 45° Y-pattern angled globe valve (courtesy of Crane Valve Co.).

$$K = 55\ f_T \qquad \textit{Equation 6-24}$$

If a globe valve needs to be installed at the connection between a vertical pipeline and a horizontal pipeline, a 90° angled globe valve such as the ones shown in Figure 6-19 may be used. The flow makes a single 90° change in direction as it flows through the angled globe valve. If the valve plug of the angled globe valve remains in the flow stream as shown on the left, its resistance coefficient can be calculated using Equation 6-25.

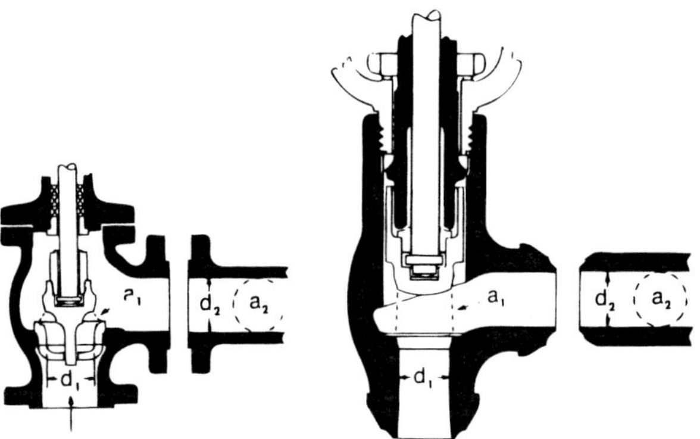

Figure 6-19. 90° angled globe valves. (courtesy of Crane Valve Co.)

$$K = 150\ f_T \qquad \textit{Equation 6-25}$$

The valve plug of the angled globe valve on the right in Figure 6-19 is almost fully removed from the flow stream, so it will offer less resistance to flow, as can be seen in the *L/D* value used for calculating its resistance coefficient in Equation 6-26.

$$K = 55\ f_T \qquad \textit{Equation 6-26}$$

The above equations for calculating the resistance coefficient for globe valves assumes fully open full port valves. The Crane Technical Paper No. 410 should be consulted for calculating the resistance coefficient for reduced ported globe valves.

Globe valves are good choices for on/off isolation valves and for throttling the flow rate through the valve. They can be used in non-abrasive liquids and gases at a wide range of temperature and pressure or under vacuum. They are not as susceptible to cavitation at high differential pressures as butterfly valves.

Diaphragm and Pinch Valves

Diaphragm and pinch valves are very similar in design and operation. Both contain a flexible diaphragm that deforms to change the shape of the flow path and restrict the fluid flow as the valve is closed. Figure 6-20 shows two types of diaphragm valves. The weir type (left) contains a solid weir at the bottom that reduces the amount of travel required by the flexible diaphragm. It's fully open resistance coefficient can be calculated with Equation 6-27.

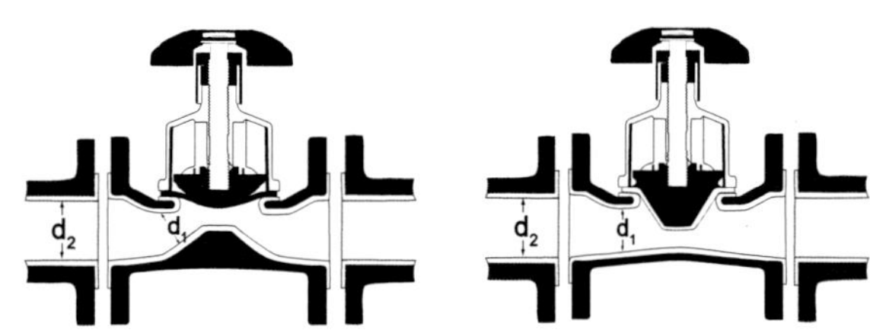

Figure 6-20. Weir type (left) and straight through (right) diaphragm valves (courtesy of Crane Valve Co.).

$$K = 149\ f_T \qquad \textit{Equation 6-27}$$

The straight through diaphragm valve has a more flexible membrane that allows the diaphragm to stretch farther, allowing a larger flow area when fully open. The resistance coefficient for a fully open straight through diaphragm valve is calculated with Equation 6-28.

$$K = 39\ f_T \qquad \textit{Equation 6-28}$$

Pinch valves are similar in that they contain a flexible tube through which the fluid flows. An external bar or pnuematic or hydraulic pressure compresses the tube to pinch off the fluid flow. The valve manufacturer should be consulted to obtain the resistance coefficient for the pinch valves they produce.

Diaphragm and pinch valves are excellent choices to use with fluids with particulates, slurries, or chemicals. Pinch valves are not good choices for systems under vacuum or at high pressures or with a high differential pressure across the valve. Both types are typically used in low pressure applications, but diaphragm valves can be used at higher pressures than pinch valves.

Diaphragm and pinch valves are good isolation valves and can be used for throttling in the last 50% of their stroke, but throttling close to the closed seat should be avoided because of high velocity erosion of the rubber sealing surfaces.

Check Valves

Check valves prevent the reversal of flow in a pipeline which could result in damage to equipment. When fully open, the check valve still offers resistance to flow depending on the type and design. The check valve resistance tends to be greater if the disc remains within the flow stream or if there are multiple changes of direction within the check valve.

When selecting a check valve it is important to ensure there is sufficient flow through the check valve to fully open the disc.

Swing Check Valves

A swing check valve consists of a hinged disc that allows flow in one direction, as shown in Figure 6-21. The hinged disc is opened by the fluid passing through the valve and is pushed out of the main flow passage by the moving liquid.

The resistance coefficient for a swing check valve depends on the design. For the swing check valve in which the disc seats at an angle, as shown in the left hand drawing of Figure 6-21, the fluid makes two 45° changes in direction, and its resistance coefficient is calculated by Equation 6-29.

$$K = 100\, f_T \qquad \text{Equation 6-29}$$

Figure 6-21. Various designs of swing check valves: disc seats at an angle (left) or vertically (right). (courtesy of Crane Valve Co.)

The resistance coefficient for the swing check valve in which the disc seats vertically, as shown in the right hand drawing of Figure 6-21, is calculated by Equation 6-30. Since the fluid essentially passes straight through the valve, its resistance coefficient would be smaller, as indicated by the smaller *L/D* value.

$$K = 50\, f_T \qquad \text{Equation 6-30}$$

Tilting Disc Check Valves

The tilting disc check valve shown in Figure 6-22 is typically the least expensive design and consists of a hinged disc that remains tilted at an angle as the fluid flows through the valve. The resistance to flow is increased because the disc remains in the flow passage. The resistance coefficient for a tilting disc check valve is a function of the angle at which the disc sits when fully open, as well as the check valve size, as shown in the equations for the resistance coefficients in Table 6-6.

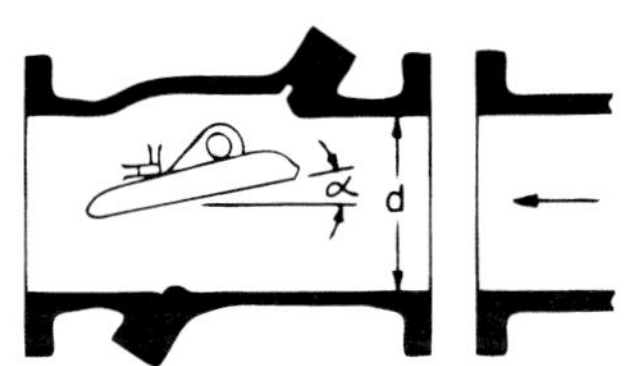

Figure 6-22. Tilting disc check valves. (courtesy of Crane Valve Co.)

Table 6-6: Resistance Coefficients for Tilting Disc Check Valves as a Function of Valve Size and Disc Angle

Size Range	$\alpha = 5°$	$\alpha = 15°$
2" – 8"	$40\, f_T$	$120\, f_T$
10" – 14"	$30\, f_T$	$90\, f_T$
16" – 48"	$20\, f_T$	$60\, f_T$

Lift Check Valves

With lift check valves, shown in Figure 6-23, the force of the fluid flowing through the valve causes the disc to open and the disc "floats" on the fluid as it passes through the valve.

As in every valve or fitting, the greater the change in direction of the flow, the greater the head loss. The lift check valve on the left in Figure 6-23 is similiar to a globe valve in that there is essentially two 90° changes in fluid direction. Its resistance coefficient is calculated using Equation 6-31 for a full ported valve.

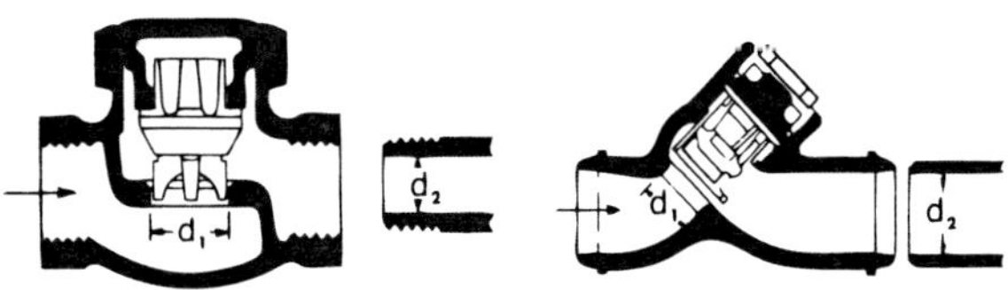

Figure 6-23. Lift check valves: globe type (left) and Y-pattern (right). (courtesy of Crane Valve Co.)

$$K = 600\, f_T \qquad \text{Equation 6-31}$$

Fluid flowing through the Y-pattern lift check valve shown on the right in Figure 6-23 makes two 45° changes in direction. Its resistance coefficient is less than the globe type lift check valve as seen with the smaller *L/D* value used to calculated the resistance coefficient for a full port valve in Equation 6-32.

$$K = 55\ f_T \qquad \textit{Equation 6-32}$$

The Crane Technical Paper No. 410 should be consulted for calculating the resistance coefficient for reduced ported lift check valves.

Foot Check Valves

Foot check valves are typically installed in the suction line of a pump to prevent it from losing its prime when the pump is turned off and the fluid flows back into the supply tank.

The poppet disc type of foot check valve shown in Figure 6-24 has a higher resistance coefficient because the disc remains in the flow stream and is an obstruction to the flow compared to the hinged disc type in which the disc is partially moved out of the flow stream. This can be seen with the higher *L/D* value for calculating the resistance coefficient for the poppet disc foot check valve in Equation 6-33.

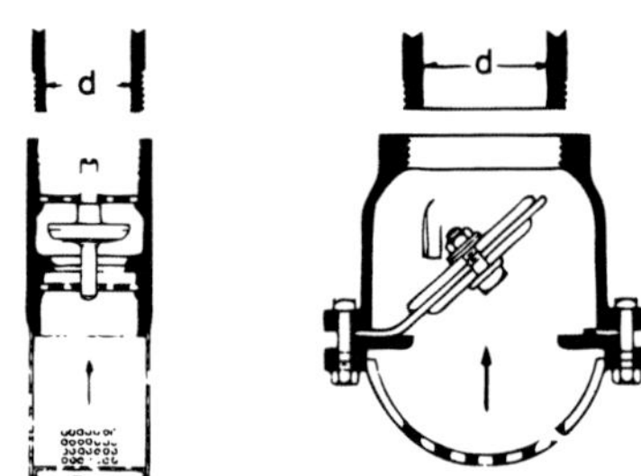

Figure 6-24. Foot check valves: poppet disc type (left) and hinged disc type (right). (courtesy of Crane Valve Co.)

$$K = 420\ f_T \qquad \textit{Equation 6-33}$$

The resistance coefficient for the hinged disc foot check valve is given in Equation 6-34.

$$K = 75\ f_T \qquad \textit{Equation 6-34}$$

Stop Check Valves

A stop check valve fulfills two functions in a single valve in that it is an isolation valve and a check valve combined in one valve body. When fully open, the disc can drop to the closed position automatically in the event of a flow reversal, or it can be manually closed by a valve actuator.

Stop check valves can have either a globe type body or a Y-pattern, as shown in Figures 6-25, and they can be either full ported or reduced ported valves. The design of the valve will have a big impact on the resistance coefficient of the valve.

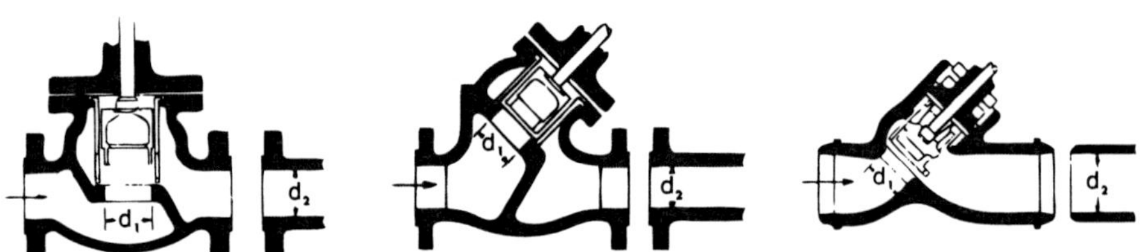

Figure 6-25. Stop check valves: globe type (left), Y-pattern with cage guide (center), and Y-pattern with disc fully removed from the flow path (right). (courtesy of Crane Valve Co.)

Equation 6-35 is used to calculate the resistance coefficient for the globe type stop check valve shown on the left in Figure 6-25.

$$K = 400\ f_T \quad \text{Equation 6-35}$$

Equation 6-36 is used to calculate the resistance coefficient for the Y-pattern stop check valve with a cage guide shown in the center in Figure 6-25.

$$K = 300\ f_T \quad \text{Equation 6-36}$$

Equation 6-37 is used to calculate the resistance coefficient for the Y-pattern stop check valve in which the disc is fully removed from the flow path shown on the right in Figure 6-25.

$$K = 55\ f_T \quad \text{Equation 6-37}$$

Stop check valves can also be mounted at the corner intersection of a vertical and horizontal pipe and have an angled body design as shown in Figure 6-26.

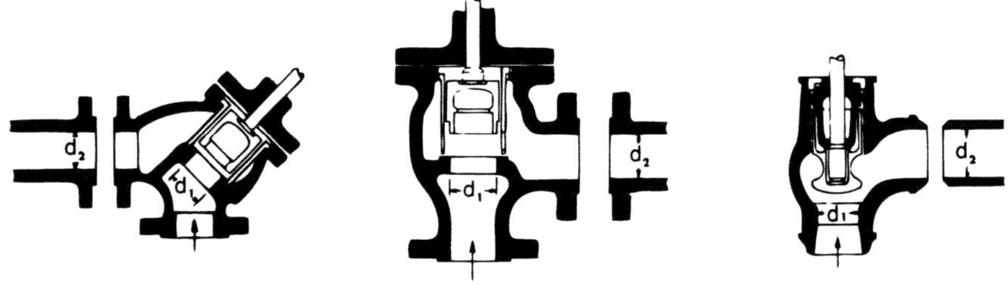

Figure 6-26. Angled body stop check valves: cage guided with actuator mounted at 45° (left), cage guided with actuator mounted at 90° (center), and angled with disc fully removed from the flow path (right). (courtesy of Crane Valve Co.)

Equation 6-38 is used to calculate the resistance coefficient for the cage guided angled stop check valve with the actuator mounted at 45° as shown on the left in Figure 6-26.

$$K = 350\ f_T \quad \text{Equation 6-38}$$

Equation 6-39 is used to calculate the resistance coefficient for the cage guided angled stop check valve with the actuator mounted at 90° as shown in the center in Figure 6-26.

$$K = 200\ f_T \quad \text{Equation 6-39}$$

Equation 6-40 is used to calculate the resistance coefficient for the angled stop check valve with the actuator mounted at 90° and the disc fully removed from the flow path as shown on the right in Figure 6-26.

$$K = 55\ f_T \quad \text{Equation 6-40}$$

Notice that for all the cases for calculating the resistance coefficient, the more tortuous the flow path is through the valve, the more resistance it offers to the fluid and the higher the *L/D* value.

As before, the equations for stop check valves presented above are for full ported valves. The Crane Technical Paper No. 410 should be consulted for calculating the resistance coefficient for reduced ported stop check valves.

Example 6-2: Calculating the Hydraulic Performance of Valves and Fittings PF ⓢ

To demonstrate how to use these concepts and equations, calculate the resistance coefficient, head loss, associated pressure drop, and equivalent flow coefficient of a standard full port 4-inch globe valve that is fully open with a 400 gpm flow of water at 60°F, as shown in Figure 6-27. The inside diameter of the attached 4-inch nominal pipe is 4.026". The density of the water is 62.4 lb/ft³.

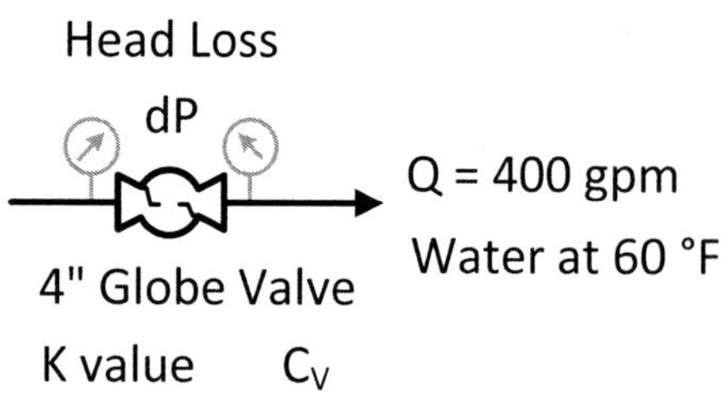

Head Loss
dP
Q = 400 gpm
Water at 60 °F
4" Globe Valve
K value C_V

Figure 6-27. 4-inch globe valve with 400 gpm of water flow.

Resistance Coefficient

The resistance coefficient is calculated with the proper form of Equation 6-5 for a globe valve. The *L/D* value is 340 as shown in Equation 6-23. The turbulent friction factor (f_T) is determined using Table 6-1 for a 4-inch valve size.

$$K = f_T \frac{L}{D} = 340 f_T = (340)(0.016) = 5.44$$

Head Loss

The head loss can be calculated with Equation 6-7 since the flow rate (in gpm) and the inside pipe diameter (in inches) are known:

$$h_L = 0.00259 \frac{KQ^2}{d^4} = \frac{(0.00259)(5.44)(400\ gpm)^2}{(4.026")^4} = 8.58\ ft$$

Pressure Drop

The pressure drop associated with the head loss across the valve can be calculated using Equation 2-20.

$$dP = \frac{\rho h_L}{144} = \frac{(62.4\ lb/ft^3)(8.58\ ft)}{144\ in^2/ft^2} = 3.72\ psi$$

Equivalent Flow Coefficient, C_V

The equivalent flow coefficient can be calculated using the flow rate and pressure drop with Equation 6-2, or with the relationship between the resistance coefficient and flow coefficient by re-arranging Equation 6-8.

$$C_V = \frac{Q}{\sqrt{dP/SG}} = \frac{400\ gpm}{\sqrt{3.72\ psid/1.0}} = 207.39$$

$$C_V = \sqrt{891 \frac{d^4}{K}} = \sqrt{891 \frac{(4.026")^4}{5.44}} = 207.44$$

As mentioned before, the accuracy of the calculation of the flow coefficient is sensitive to the number of significant digits used for the variables because of the square root function.

Example 6-3: Comparing the Hydraulic Performance of Valves and Fittings

Table 6-7 shows the comparison between the *L/D* value, resistance coefficient, flow coefficient, head loss, and pressure drop across various types of 4-inch valves with 400 gpm of 60 °F water flow. Notice that the *L/D* value and resistance coefficient increase linearly with each other, whereas the flow coefficient decreases exponentially with an increasing resistance coefficient. The greater the resistance coefficient, the greater the amount of head loss and associated pressure drop.

Table 6-7: Comparing the Hydraulic Characterization and Performance of Various Types of Valves

Valve Type	L/D	K	C_V	Head Loss (feet)	Pressure Drop (psi)
Ball	3	0.05	2208	0.08	0.03
Gate	8	0.13	1352	0.20	0.09
Plug	18	0.29	902	0.45	0.20
Butterfly	45	0.72	570	1.14	0.49
Globe	340	5.44	207	8.58	3.72

Valve and Fitting Head Loss Graph

The amount of head loss created by the flow of fluid through a valve or fitting can be graphed as a function of the flow rate, as shown in Figure 6-28. The graph is a second order curve as indicated by the head loss equation, Equation 6-7. The steepness of the curve depends on the resistance coefficient of the valve or fitting.

As with the pipeline head loss graph, the graph of the valve and fitting head loss is a basis for the system resistance curve that was discussed in Chapter 4 on centrifugal pumps.

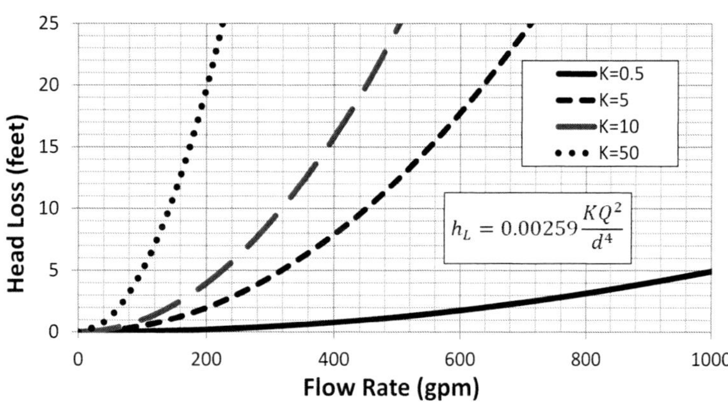

Figure 6-28. Graph of valve and fitting head loss as a function of flow rate and increasing resistance coefficient.

Cost of Head Loss Across Valves and Fittings

The head loss across a valve or fitting is dissipated energy that was initially added to the fluid by the pump. A portion of the operating cost of the energy added by the pump can be allocated to the head loss across each valve and fitting in the system using Equation 6-41.

$$Cost\ of\ Head\ Loss = \frac{(0.746)\ Q\ h_L\ \rho}{(247{,}000)\ \eta_P\ \eta_m\ \eta_{VFD}} \begin{pmatrix} Operating \\ Hours \end{pmatrix} (\$/kWh) \qquad \textit{Equation 6-41}$$

Comparing the Operating Cost of Valves and Fittings

Table 6-8 puts into perspective the cost of the energy being dissipated as head loss across various valves and fittings. This table shows the amount of head loss and the associated energy cost for a 4" fitting with 400 gpm of 60 °F water flow with a pump efficiency of 70%, motor efficiency of 90%, and a utility rate of $0.10 / kWh, operating for 1,000 hours, using Equations 6-7 and 6-41.

The head loss across a long radius elbow is 0.35 feet at an energy cost of $4.23, compared to 0.50 feet of head loss at a cost of $6.04 for a short radius elbow.

For entrances, the head loss of a rounded entrance costs $0.75, a sharp edged entrance costs $9.43, and an inward projecting entrance costs $14.72.

The head loss across a ball valve costs $0.91, $2.41 for a gate valve, $5.43 for a plug valve, $13.58 for a butterfly valve, and $102.63 for a globe valve.

Table 6-8: Comparing the Operating Cost of Various Types of Valves and Fittings

Valve Type	*Head Loss (feet) of a 4-inch Fitting With 400 gpm*	*Cost ($) per 1,000 hours of Operation*
Elbow LR	0.35	$4.23
Elbow SR	0.50	$6.04
Entrance (rounded)	0.06	$0.75
Entrance (sharp edged)	0.79	$9.43
Entrance (protruding)	1.23	$14.72
Ball	0.08	$0.91
Gate	0.20	$2.41
Plug	0.45	$5.43
Butterfly	1.14	$13.58
Globe	8.58	$102.63

This is not an argument to replace all short radius elbows in an existing piping system with long radius elbows, or all globe valves with ball valves. Operating cost isn't always the deciding factor when designing a system and selecting valves and fittings. A particular valve or fitting is selected for a specific function in a system and that function has to be accomplished in order for the system to work as intended. However, if there are multiple valve types that are suitable for a particular application, the operating cost should be considered in the selection.

These operating costs, and potential energy savings, will be paid for the entire life of the system.

Graphing the Energy Costs of Valves and Fittings

Another way to view the operating costs of valve and fitting head loss is using a graph of energy cost versus flow rate, as shown in Figure 6-29. This curve is based on a 4-inch valve with 60 °F water flow with a pump efficiency of 70%, motor efficiency of 90%, and a utility rate of $0.10 / kWh, operating for 1,000 hours.

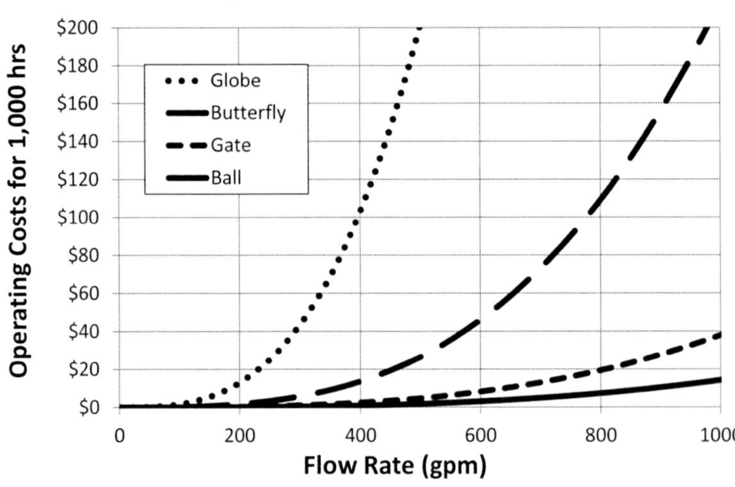

Figure 6-29. Graph of the energy cost of the head loss for various valves as a function of flow rate.

For a given flow rate, the operating costs vary dramatically with the valve type. In addition, the operating cost for a particular valve increases by the second order of the flow rate. This last observation emphasizes the need to select low resistance valves and fittings wherever possible for a particular application.

Selecting Valves & Fittings for a Given Application

Valves and fittings are required to redirect and isolate the flow in a piping system. There are many things to consider when choosing a valve or fitting for a given application. The selection of a valve type has an effect on the amount of head loss across the valve for a given flow rate, but the head loss should not be the sole consideration for the valve selected.

When selecting a valve type for an application in a piping system, the service requirements must be considered, including the valve's sealing capability under various pressures, the number of times a valve is opened and closed, how much time it takes to close the valve, hand-wheel torque, and the consequences of valve stem leakage, among other considerations.

The costs of the valve or fitting are often a primary concern. These costs include not only the life time energy cost, but the initial capital cost and anticipated maintenance cost as well.

Valves and fittings come in a wide array of types and sizes and are produced by many manufacturers around the world. The *L/D* values and the equations for resistance coefficients presented in this chapter are based on the pressure drop tests performed by the Crane Valve Company. When selecting and purchasing a particular valve or fitting, the manufacturer should be consulted to determine if they have equivalent lengths, resistance coefficients, or flow coefficients for their products. In the absence of specific data, the resistance coefficients presented in this chapter may be used, or approximations may be made based on good engineering principles and experience.

Chapter Seven

Control Valves

Control valves play a crucial role in the total piping system. Isolation valves and control valves share many physical characteristics, but where an isolation valve's primary purpose is to allow flow when fully open or to stop flow when fully closed, the control valve operates between the extremes to regulate the flow rate, pressure, temperature, tank level, chemical composition, or some other system process variable.

Role of the Control Valve

A piping system exists to transport mass and energy in order to perform work or make a product, and the working fluid may undergo many processes that change its physical, thermal, or chemical properties. Various instruments are used to measure processes occuring in the piping system, processes that are subject to disturbances that cause the property of the fluid to deviate from a desired value. Control loops are installed to automatically respond to these disturbances and a control valve is a common device used to maintain the measured property in a steady state condition.

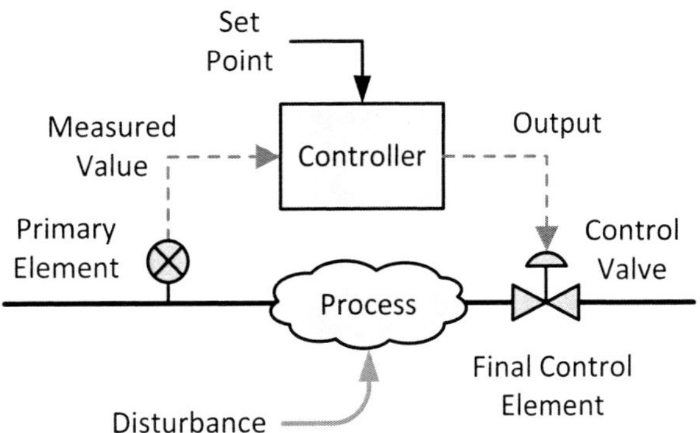

Figure 7-1. Block diagram of a typical process control loop.

Figure 7-1 shows the key elements of a typical process control loop, including the primary element (or sensor), the controller, and the final control element. These elements will be explained in detail in Chapter 8: Process Measurements and Controls, and the actual processes that occur in the piping system will be covered in Chapter 9: Processes and Process Equipment.

The control valve plays a major role as the final control element of the process control loop. In a piping system, a control valve will be called upon to regulate the flow rate, upstream or downstream pressure, fluid temperature or pH, tank level, chemical reaction rate, or some other important process parameter.

How a Control Valve Works

The control valve is designed to change the shape and size of the flow passage within the valve, thereby adjusting its hydraulic resistance and the amount of energy dissipated across the valve. This energy, or head loss, is dissipated in the form of heat, noise, and vibration in the valve.

A control valve's variable resistance is accomplished by inserting an adjustable obstruction in the flow path within the valve. This obstruction can be a moveable plug such as in a globe valve, a fluted disc in butterfly valve, or a vee-notched ball in a ball valve, just to name a few.

To better understand how a control valve dissipates hydraulic energy to control a process occuring in a piping system, consider the generalized energy grade profile, the hydraulic grade profile (pressure profile), and velocity profile shown in Figure 7-2 as the fluid travels through a control valve with an inlet and outlet reducer attached. (Note: The valve shown is a single seated globe valve, but the same principles apply to all types of control valves.)

The energy grade profile shows the total hydraulic energy in the fluid and consists of the velocity head, pressure head, and elevation head as described by the Bernoulli equation. Any reduction in the energy grade line indicates energy loss due to friction and changes in fluid momentum and is energy dissipated as head loss in the form of heat, noise and vibration.

Chapter 2 mentioned that hydraulic grade represents static head, which is the sum of the elevation and pressure head of the fluid. Since the elevation is not changing from the inlet to the outlet, the hydraulic grade line in Figure 7-2 represents just the pressure head component, or the fluid's static pressure.

The velocity profile represents the dynamic head component of the fluid's total energy. The sum of the static head (hydraulic grade) and dynamic head (velocity) is the total energy of the fluid.

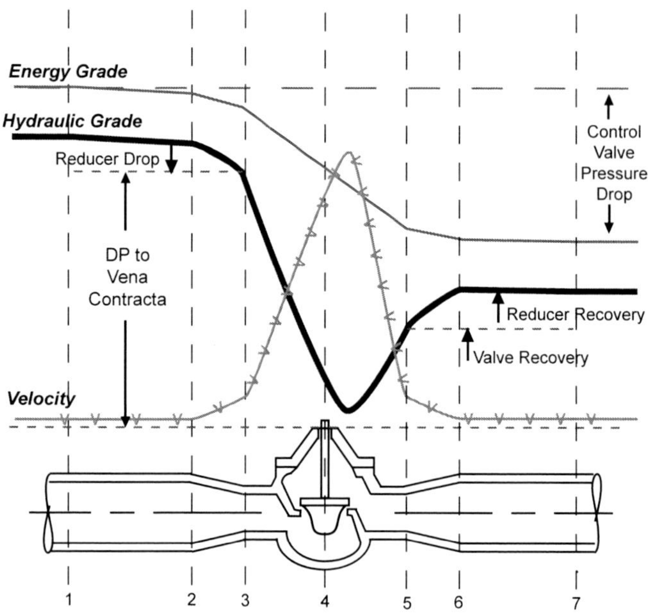

Figure 7-2. Total energy grade, hydraulic grade (pressure), and velocity profiles through a control valve.

In Figure 7-2, Position 1 represents a point in the inlet pipe upstream from the valve assembly. Pipeline head loss from Position 1 to the inlet of the reducer at Position 2 results in a small drop in the total energy grade line. Since the velocity is constant in the inlet pipeline, this energy loss results in an equivalent drop in the hydraulic grade line, which is seen as a pressure drop in the fluid. The energy grade line and hydraulic grade lines are parallel.

As the fluid enters the inlet reducer of the control valve at Position 2, the flow area decreases, resulting in an increase in the fluid velocity according to the Bernoulli Theorem. This increased fluid velocity results in a momentum change and head loss across the reducer, which is seen as a decrease in the energy grade and hydraulic grade lines from Position 2 to Position 3.

As the fluid flows past the inlet at Position 3 it quickly changes direction by 90° to flow up through the valve seat and past the plug at Position 4, resulting in momentum change, head loss, and a reduction in the fluid's total energy. In addition to the change in direction, there is often a reduction of the cross-sectional flow area between the valve inlet and the flow passage through the valve seat, resulting in a large increase in the fluid velocity, additional change in fluid momentum, additional head loss, and associated drop in pressure and total energy. For the globe valve shown in Figure 7-2, the flow path is actually a donut-shaped annulus between the seat and plug. The point of highest velocity and lowest pressure occurs at the vena contracta, which is slightly downstream of the narrowest point in the flow path.

Between Position 4 and 5, there is another 90° change of direction as the fluid moves through the valve seat to the valve outlet. The change of direction results in a momentum change and head loss. In addition, the fluid velocity decreases from the vena contracta to the valve outlet and this momentum change results in head loss. However, the decreased fluid velocity results in an increase in the static pressure of the fluid according to the Bernoulli Theorem, so there is an overall pressure recovery from the vena contracta to the valve outlet, even though there is a continuous drop in the total energy of the fluid.

As the fluid flows past the valve outlet at Position 5 and through the reducer to Position 6, there is an increase in the flow path's cross-sectional area, which decreases the velocity and increases the fluid static pressure. This pressure recovery across the reducer is the conversion of the velocity head to pressure head in accordance with the Bernoulli Theorem. However, this change in velocity is also a change in the momentum of the fluid, resulting in additional head loss and an associated drop in total fluid energy grade line across the outlet reducer.

From Position 6 at the discharge of the outlet reducer to a point farther downstream represented by Position 7, the pipeline head loss results in a constant decrease in the fluid's total energy and static pressure.

The position of the valve plug in relation to the seat will determine the size of the flow passage and the amount of resistance the valve offers to the fluid flow, and therefore the amount of head loss across the control valve. Consider the change to the energy profiles for a control valve that is farther open, as shown in Figure 7-3.

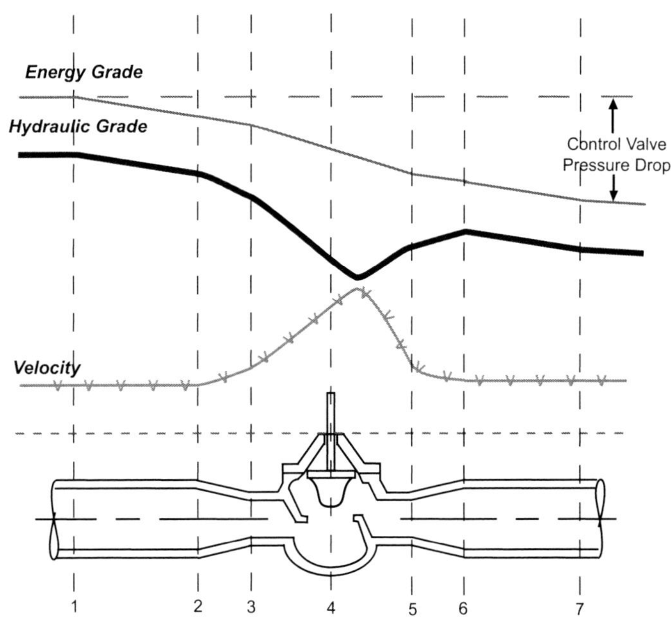

Figure 7-3. Total energy grade, hydraulic grade (pressure), and velocity profiles through a control valve that is farther open.

Because there is more distance between the seat and plug, there is a larger flow path and less resistance to flow through the valve and a higher flow rate through the piping and control valve (assuming the same inlet pressure at Position 1 as in Figure 7-2). The fluid velocity at Position 1 will be higher than in Figure 7-2 due to the higher flow rate. The hydraulic grade and energy grade lines for the pipelines will have a steeper slope due to the greater amount of head loss in the pipeline from Position 1 to Position 2 and from Position 6 to Position 7.

In additon, because the flow path is larger in the valve, the velocity at the vena contracta does not increase as high as it did in the previous example, so there is less momentum change and therefore less head loss across the valve. This results in a smaller drop in the hydraulic grade line from Position 2 to just past Position 4, and a smaller pressure recovery from Position 4 to Position 5.

The net effect of a wider open control valve is a higher flow rate through the valve, less head loss (energy dissipated) across the valve, and a smaller pressure drop from the inlet to the outlet of the valve.

Major Parts of a Control Valve

The major parts of a control valve can be seen in Figure 7-4 which shows an air operated sliding stem globe valve. The two main components are the valve body assembly and the valve actuator.

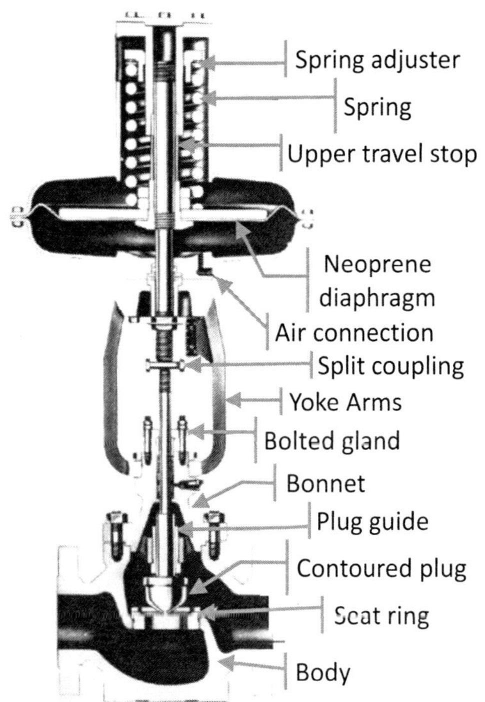

Figure 7-4. Cross-sectional drawing showing major parts of a control valve (courtesy of Fisher Controls International, LLC).

Valve Body Assembly

The valve body assembly consists of the valve body

and the valve bonnet, both of which form the fluid pressure boundary. The valve trim components are contained within the body assembly.

Valve Body

The valve body contains the inlet and outlet connections to the piping system and its shape forms the internal fluid flow passage. The body also contains supports for the valve seat and provides room for the valve closure members (plug or disc).

Valve Bonnet

The bonnet is bolted on top of the valve body and contains the packing box, stem seal, and a means to attach the valve actuator. The bonnet also provides support for the plug guide.

The valve gland consists of packing that is inserted into the packing box between the bonnet and the stem. The packing is held into place by a bolted gland.

Valve Trim

The valve trim consists of the components that are in contact with the process fluid flowing through the valve and include the valve seat, the plug or disc, plug guide, and valve stem. The valve seat is typically screwed into position in the valve body, allowing the seat to be replaced when necessary. In addition, the valve seat and plug can be replaced as a set and come in reduced sizes, allowing for a wider range of performance for the same valve body.

For cage guided valves, as shown in Figure 7-5, the cage is also a part of the valve trim and can be designed to give the valve various hydraulic characteristics.

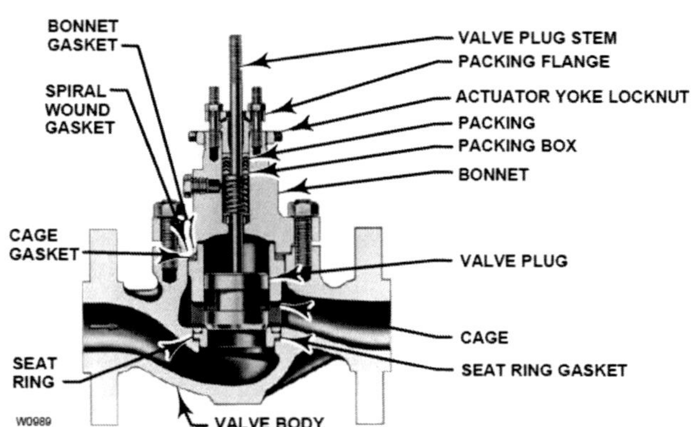

Figure 7-5. Cage guided globe valve (courtesy of Emerson Process Management).

Valve Actuator Assembly

The most common actuator installed on a control valve is a pnuematic actuator as shown in Figures 7-4 and 7-6. The actuator can also be an electric motor or solonoid, or use a hydraulic piston to move the valve stem.

The pneumatic actuator consists of a diaphragm motor, a spring chamber, an actuator stem, and yoke arms to connect the actuator to the valve bonnet. The actuator may also have a positioner installed to control the position of the valve stem.

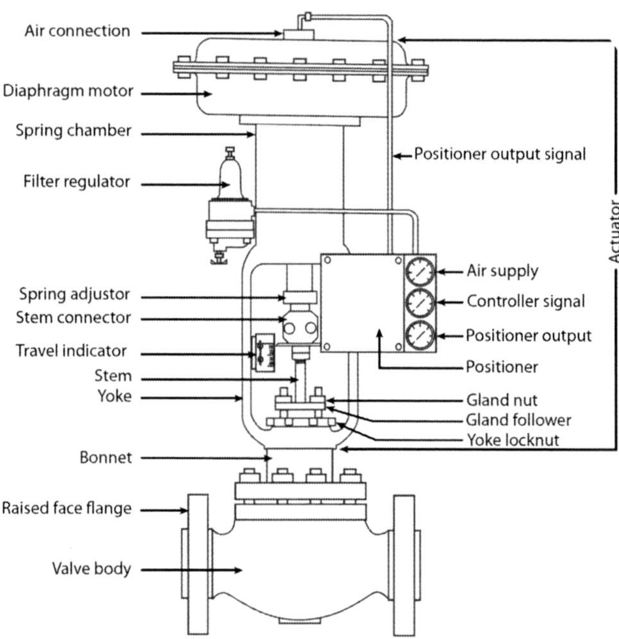

Figure 7-6. External components of a linear control valve (courtesy Fisher Controls International LLC).

Figure 7-7. Pneumatically operated automatic control valve with digital positioner (courtesy of Emerson Process Management).

Diaphragm Motor

The diaphragm motor contains a neoprene diaphragm that separates the spring chamber from a chamber that is pressurized by an external supply of instrument air. Air pressure can either act to open the valve (Figure 7-4) or close the valve (Figure 7-6).

Spring Chamber

The spring chamber contains a spring, a spring adjuster, and an upper travel stop. The spring chamber can be mounted at the top of the actuator as shown in Figure 7-4, or below the diaphragm as shown in Figure 7-6. The force exerted by the spring is in the opposite direction of the force exerted by the air pressure on the diagphragm.

Actuator Stem

The net force exerted by the air pressure and spring is tranmitted by the actuator stem to the valve stem to position the plug within the valve body. In steady state conditions, the two forces are equalized and valve plug is held in a fixed position. If the control valve position needs to be adjusted by the loop controller, the air pressure will be increased or decreased to create an unbalanced force between the air pressure and spring force, causing the valve to either open farther or close slightly until the process reaches steady state at the desired value.

The actuator stem may also contain a position indicator that can be compared to a scale mounted on the yoke arm to give a visual indication of the approximate valve position, as can be seen in Figure 7-6.

Positioner

The control valve may also have a positioner installed on the valve actuator that has a magnetic or mechanical linkage to the shaft to measure the actual position of the valve travel. The positioner is a position controller that receives its set point from the loop controller, compares it to the measured valve position, and adjusts the air pressure to the actuator to adjust the valve to the desired position.

The positioner can be pneumatic, electro-pneumatic, or a digital positioner (intelligent or smart position), as shown in Figure 7-7. Positioners will be covered in more detail in Chapter 8: Process Measurement and Controls.

Classifying Control Valves

There are numerous ways to classify control valves with the various attributes that can be used to describe them. They can be classified according to how the valve disc or plug is caused to move, how the valve performs hydraulically, by its body style, or by the ASME or ANSI ratings.

Classifying Control Valves Based on Valve Actuation

Control valves fall into three generaly types according to how the force is applied to the valve stem and disc to cause them to move and change the shape and size of the flow path. Actuated valves use an external source of power to apply the force, self-contained regulators use the energy of the working fluid, and manually-adjusted valves use the force applied by a human "actuator" to move the valve stem and plug.

Actuated Control Valves

Figure 7-7 shows a typical actuated control valve that uses air as the external source of energy to adjust the position of the valve stem and plug. The valve actuator can be pneumatically powered, use an electric solonoid or motor, or use a hydraulic cylinder to move the valve stem.

It is important to remember that an actuated control valve is part of an external control loop, consisting of a sensor and a transmitter. Because of the variety of supporting equipment required for the control loop, using a control valve to maintain a process variable is expensive. However when the process variable must be maintained within a tight range, using an external control loop and properly sized control valve is necessary because of the degree of control they provide.

The actuated control valve will be the main focus of the majority of this chapter.

Self-contained Regulators

A self-contained regulator, such as the pressure regulator shown in Figure 7-8, is a control valve in which the process fluid provides the energy required to adjust the valve stem and plug. The set screw at the top adjusts the force exerted by the main spring on the diaphragm element. The downstream fluid pressure is applied to the underside of the diaphragm via a pitot tube. A spring below the valve plug provides a counter force that adds to the force of the fluid pressure and balances the force of the main spring to maintain the position of the valve plug.

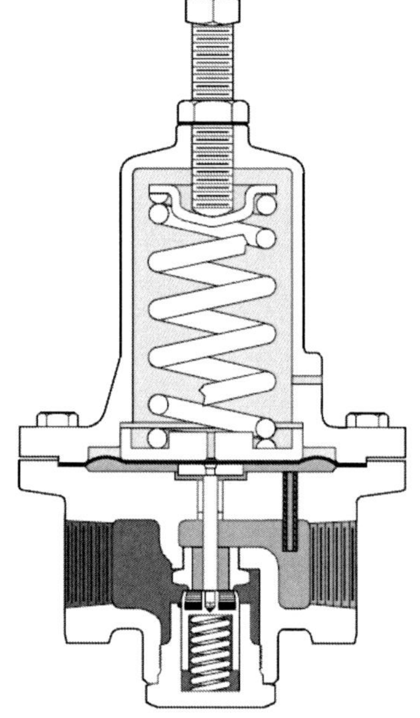

Figure 7-8. Self-contained pressure regulator (courtesy of Emerson Process Management).

As the downstream fluid pressure drops due to an increase in flow demand to downstream users, the main spring pushes the diaphragm and valve plug down to further open the valve, allowing more of the higher pressure upstream fluid to flow through the valve, thus maintaining the downstream pressure at a constant value.

Advantages of self-contained regulators include cost, excellent frequency response, good rangeability, space savings, limited valve leakage, and not requiring electricity or air to operate.

The disadvantages of self-contained regulators are a fixed proportional band, no reset action, limited size, and pressure rating, along with a limited choice of material and end connections.

Manually Operated Throttle Valves

In many applications, the cost of an automatic control valve or a regulator is not justified for the process. In these cases, a manually operated valve is often used to allow an operator to adjust the position of the valve based on a process variable that the operator observes.

For example, if a desired level is required for a tank with a site glass installed, the operator can adjust the flow rate of the liquid entering the tank based on the actual tank level and the desired tank level. For these manually operated valves, the operator acts as the transmitter, controller, and valve actuator.

Manually operated throttle valves are often used in systems where the process variables do not significantly change. The tolerances and speed of a manual control are limited. As a result, manually operated throttle valves are used on steady-state processes that do not require a tight range of control.

Any isolation valve that is used by an operator to manually adjust the flow rate, pressure, tank level, temperature, or any other process variable can be considered a control valve.

Classifying Control Valves Based on Characteristic Trim

The design of the valve trim affects the hydraulic performance of the valve, called the characteristic trim. Different types of valves will have a specific characteristic trim, but there are some design changes the manufacturer can make to obtain specific characteristics for some valve types.

Inherent Characteristic Curves

The manufacturer tests their control valves in a test system with 60 °F water to determine the *inherent characteristic* of the valve, or the characteristic with a constant differential pressure across the valve. This is done by measuring the flow rate through the valve with a 1 psi pressure drop from the valve inlet to the valve outlet and calculating the valve's flow coefficient (C_V). The test is repeated at various valve positions to obtain a profile of the hydraulic performance of the valve defined by its flow coefficient as a function of the valve position, or the inherent characteristic curve.

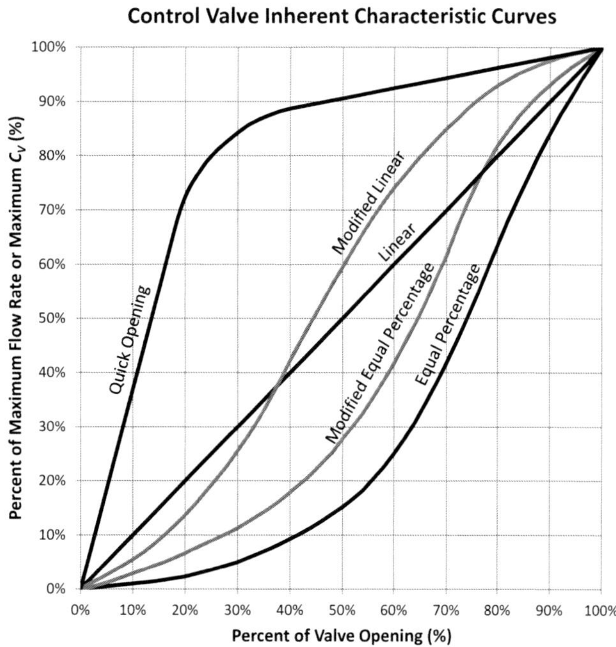

Figure 7-9. Control valve flow characteristic curves.

The most common characteristic curves are the quick opening, linear, and equal percentage curves shown in Figure 7-9. Trim can be installed to produce a modified linear and modified equal percentage curve as well.

Installed Characteristic Curves

When the control valve is installed in a piping system with a centrifugal pump, the differential pressure across the control valve will not be held constant as it is in the initial testing of the valve. Due to the shape of the pump curve, the *installed characteristic curve* will shift because the inlet pressure of the control valve changes with the flow rate. How the curve shift can be seen in Figure 7-10.

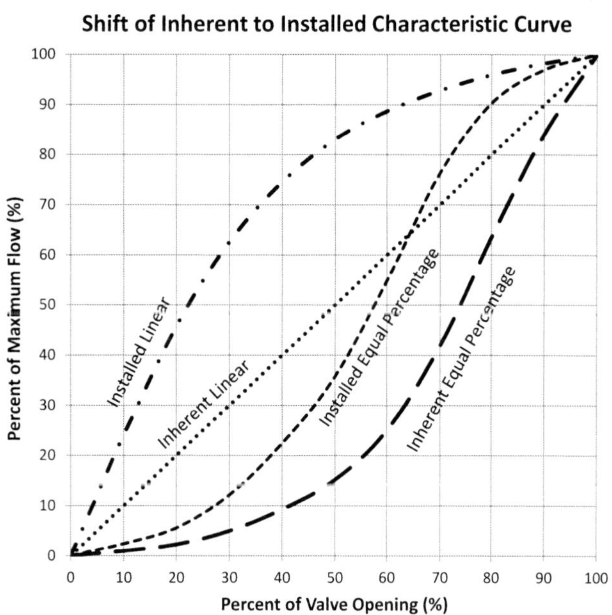

Figure 7-10. Shift of the inherent characteristic curve when installed in a piping system with a pump.

Quick Opening Characteristic

Quick opening valves are used in applications when a large change in the flow rate is needed for very little valve travel, such as on-off valves, pressure relief valves, or safety valves.

Linear Characteristic

Linear valves are used when the pressure at the valve inlet is expected to remain fairly constant, such as with level control and some flow control applications.

Equal Percentage Characteristic

Equal percentage valves are ones in which the flow coefficient changes by an equal percentage for a given change in valve position. This is the most common type of characteristic used in flow, pressure, and temperature control applications due to how inherent characteristic curve shifts when installed in a piping system.

Trim Designs to Obtain Various Characteristics

The geometry of the internal trim will determine how the control valve performs over its range of travel. For the globe valve shown in Figure 7-4, the shape of the contoured plug will determine the valve's inherent characteristics, as shown in Figure 7-11. A relatively flat plug will produces a quick opening characteristic, a parabolic shaped plug gives a linear characteristic, and a linear shaped plug produces an equal percentage characteristic.

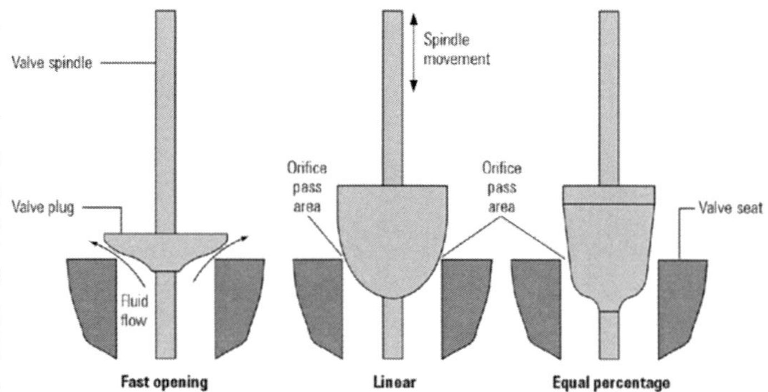

Figure 7-11. Contour of the plug determines the inherent flow characteristic of the control valve (courtesy of Spirax Sarco).

For the cage guided globe valve shown in Figure 7-5, the shape of the flow windows determines the flow characteristic of the valve. Figure 7-12 shows the various shapes that produce a quick opening, linear, and equal percentage characteristic.

Figure 7-12. Shape of the flow window determines the inherent flow characteristic of the control valve (courtesy of Emerson Process Management).

For ball valves, the ball can be contoured with a V-notch or designed with various shapes of the flow passage to obtain different flow characteristics. Similarly, for butterfly valves, the disc can be designed to provide the desired flow characteristic.

Classifying Control Valves Based on Valve Body Style

Control valves can also be classified according the style of the valve body. In general, valve body styles fall into two categories based on the motion used to change the shape of the flow path: linear motion and rotary motion.

In a linear motion control valve, the flow rate is controlled by the linear motion of the plug attached to a valve stem. The plug is moved closer to or farther away from the valve seat, resulting in a change of the flow path area through the seat. When the valve plug is moved closer to the seat, the flow area decreases and the velocity of the fluid flowing past the valve seat increases. This increase in velocity causes greater turbulence in the valve, resulting in more energy dissipated across the valve (head loss) and a larger pressure drop. Linear motion control valves include single and dual ported globe valves, cage trim globe valves, diaphragm valves, and pinch valves.

In a rotary motion control valve, the flow rate is controlled by turning the control element (ball, disc, or plug) in the flow stream. When the valve is fully open, the controlling element presents the smallest resistance to flow. As the controlling element is rotated, the cross-sectional area of the flow passage decreases. Rotary valves have a larger flow capacity and some are less expensive than linear motion control valves. In addition, since there are fewer obstructions in the flow path, the rotary valve design works well with slurries, paper stock, and solids in suspension. Rotary valves are more susceptible to flashing and cavitation in high-pressure drop applications due to their high-pressure recovery. Under these conditions, the fluid velocity through the valve can cause noise and excess wear. Rotary motion control valves include butterfly valves, ball valves, and rotating plug valves.

Single Port Globe Valves

Globe valve bodies tend to have a compact spherical shape. Figure 7-13 shows a typical single ported globe valve. The valve consists of a valve body, bonnet, stem, and plug. As previously mentioned, the seat can be removed for repair. In addition, a reduced ported plug can be inserted into the valve in order to change its control characteristics.

As the fluid flows through the valve, the turbulence between the valve seat and plug can cause lateral forces on the plug, resulting in a bend of the stem, as well as vibration. A guide is used in the bonnet in order to steady the plug under varying flow rates and minimize its lateral movement.

Finally, there is considerable unbalanced force on the plug because of the difference in area between the bottom and top of the plug caused by the differential pressure across the valve. This exerts additional force upon the valve stem and may require a thicker stem and a larger actuator.

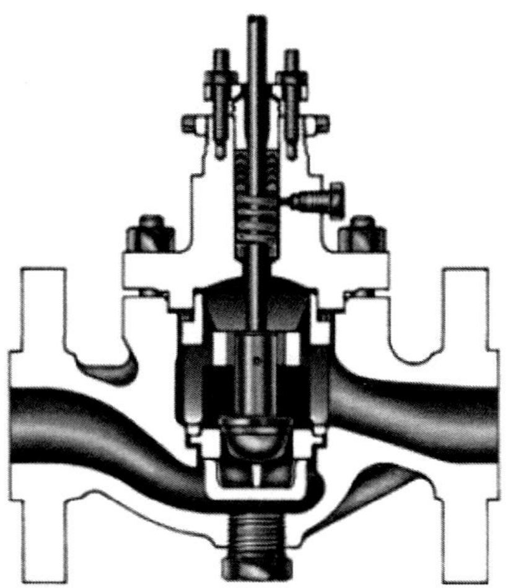

Figure 7-13. Single port globe valve (courtesy of Fisher Controls International, LLC).

Single ported globe valves are also manufactured in a 90° angle and inline style. The 90° angle valve is useful when the pipeline with the control valve needs to make a change of direction, eliminating the need for an additional elbow. The inline valve pattern has the valve stem, plug, and seat on an oblique angle, minimizing the number of directional changes of the fluid.

Dual Port Globe Valves

Figure 7-14 shows a cross section of a dual port globe valve with two seats and a plug that has two seating areas. The flow enters the valve through the inlet port, diverges through each of the valve seats, travels around the plug, and then converges before leaving the valve.

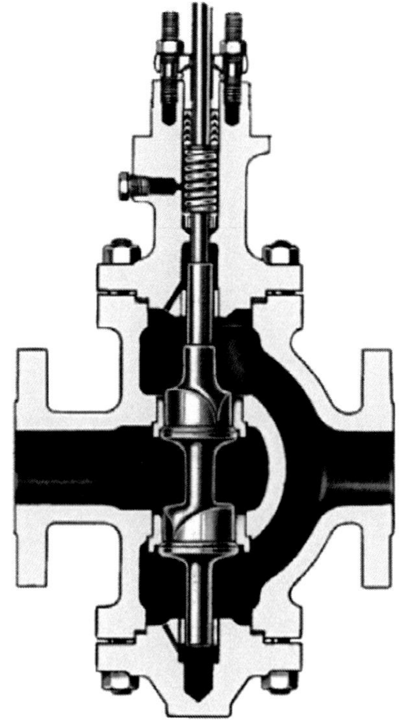

Figure 7-14. Dual port globe valve (courtesy of Fisher Controls International, LLC).

The advantage of the dual port valve is its ability to balance the hydrostatic and hydrodynamic forces. The pressure differential acts both upward and downward upon the upper and lower plug areas, canceling out the hydrostatic and hydrodynamic forces upon the plug. The only unbalanced force on the dual ported plug is that caused by the difference in area of the valve stem passing through the valve gland to the atmosphere. Any difference in pressure must be overcome by the valve actuator. Since this unbalanced force is smaller on the dual port valve than the single port valve, the actuator can be smaller.

Cage-Trim Globe Valves

The cage trim design eliminates many of the problems associated with the single port and dual port globe valves. Cage trim valves have the following advantages over single and dual port valves:

- Greater capacity for a given body size
- Less prone to vibration from the fluid passing through the valve
- Reduced susceptibility to cavitation and the damage caused by cavitation
- Less noise
- Greater serviceability

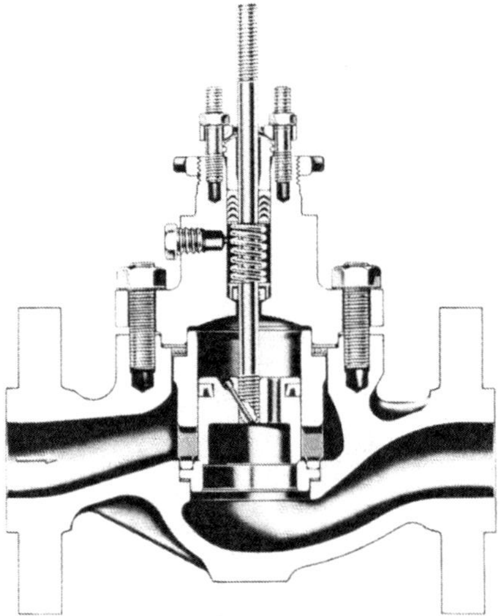

Figure 7-15. Cage trim globe valve (courtesy of Fisher Controls International, LLC).

As shown in Figure 7-15, the plug is guided in the cage as it opens and closes. This increases the lateral stability and reducing vibrations in the valve. By drilling balancing holes in the plug, the process pressure acts equally upon both sides of the plug, thus minimizing problems with unbalanced pressures.

As was seen in Figure 7-12, the shape of the ports in the cage can be varied to provide the desired characteristic trim. In addition, special cages are designed to reduce noise or cavitation in the valve. Also, the manufacturer can change the number and size of the holes in the cage to change the capacity of the valve without having to change out the valve body.

Multi Port Globe Valve

Multi port globe valves, such as the one shown in Figure 7-16, allow diverting or mixing of fluids. These valves always have two seats. The plug can be a double-ended single plug or two separate plugs. The valve body has three ports. For diverting applications, one port serves as the inlet and the other two as the outlets. These valves are often used in HVAC chilled water applications. When the multi port valve is used for mixing two fluids, two of the ports serve as inlets, and the mixture exits the remaining port.

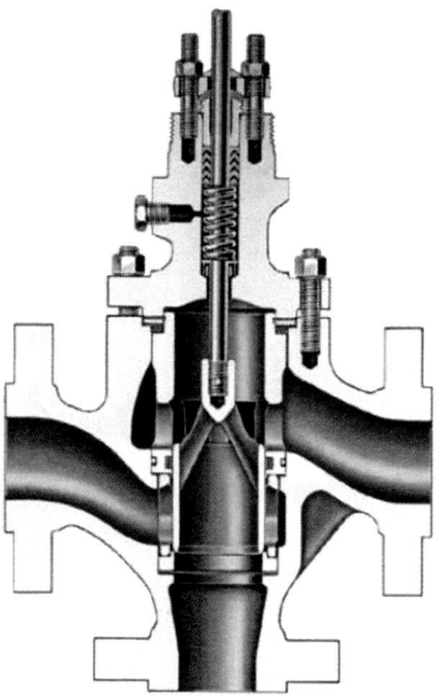

Figure 7-16. Multi-port globe valve (courtesy of Fisher Controls International, LLC).

Pinch Valves

The pinch valve shown in Figure 7-17 consists of a valve body that holds a flexible sleeve, which is the only component exposed to the process fluid. The valve operates when the sleeve is compressed, reducing the cross-sectional area of the sleeve. Compression of the sleeve can occur by a mechanical bar that pinches the flexible sleeve and restricts the flow, or by an external pressure source around the sleeve that compresses the sleeve and reduces the flow area to throttle the flow.

Diaphragm Valves

Diaphragm valves can be a straight through design such as the one shown in Figure 7-18, or have a weir built into the body of the valve. A flexible diaphragm is the closing member that deforms as the actuator is closed to change the shape and size of the flow passage and vary the amount of energy dissipated across the valve and throttle the flow rate. Diaphragm valves can operate at positive pressure or under high vacuum. The flexible diaphragm provides a tight seal at shutoff, even for liquids with solid particles.

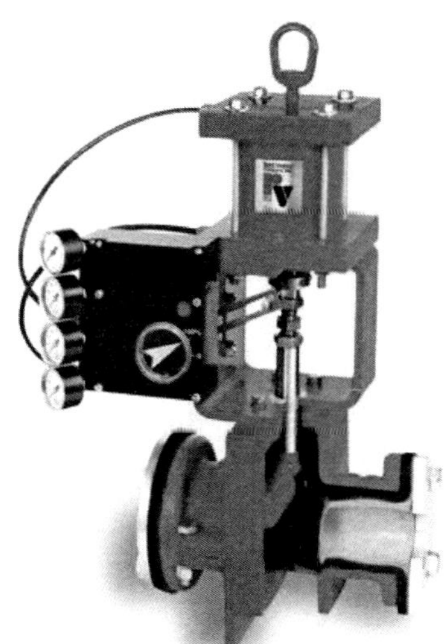

Figure 7-17. A typical pinch valve, (courtesy of the Red Valve Company).

Figure 7-18. A manually operated diaphragm valve, (courtesy of Crane Saunders).

Ball Valves

Ball valves are rotary valves consisting of a spherical closing member with a flow passage, as shown in Figure 7-19. In addition to the V-notch segmented ball shown in Figure 7-19, the rotating member can be a full ball, a characterized V-notch, or a V-notch ball with an attenuator for cavitation and noise reduction, as shown in Figure 7-20.

Figure 7-19. Segmented V-notch ball valve (courtesy of Emerson Process Management).

Ball valves are used to control flow, pressure in gas distribution systems, and pressure reduction in gas storage systems.

Ball valves are designed as full port and reduced port valves. The full port ball valves are primarily used in oil and gas distribution systems to allow a cleaning "pig" to be sent through the pipeline and pass through fully open ball valves without requiring the valve to be disassembled. One disadvantage of the full port ball valve is its poor flow control characteristics.

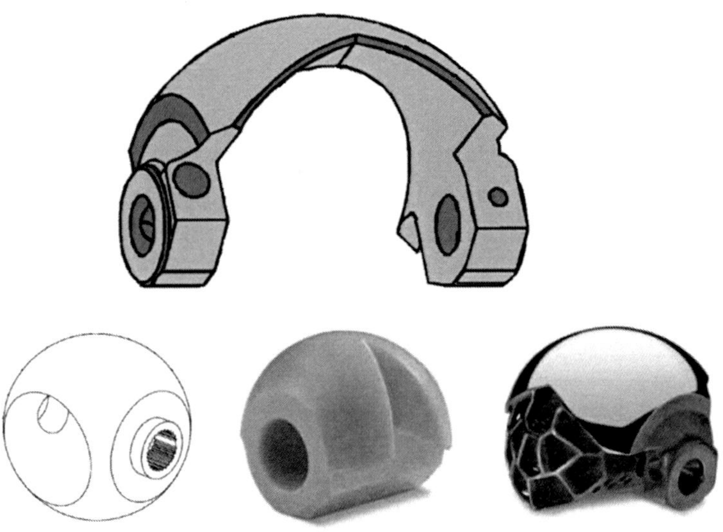

Figure 7-20. Segmented V-notch ball (top), full port ball (bottom left), characterized V-notch (bottom center), and V-notch with cavitation and noise attenuator (bottom right) (courtesy of Emerson Process Management).

The flow control characteristics of ball valves can be greatly improved by characterizing the rotating ball by designing them with a V-notch. The V-notch gives the ball valve an equal percentage inherent flow characteristic.

In addition, the V-notch prevents clogging of partially open ball valves in applications with particulates in the liquid. The V-notch design makes the valve suitable for paper stock, fibrous materials, and slurries.

V-notch ball valves have a high capacity and rangeability. They have a very tight shutoff and can operate in high temperature applications. They can be used for the control of gas, steam, clean or dirty liquids, and abrasive chemicals.

For applications which result in high noise levels through the ball valve, or if there is cavitation occuring in the ball valve, the ball can be designed with a cavitation and noise attenuator as shown in Figure 7-20.

Butterfly Valves

Butterfly valves consist of a thin wafer or contoured disc that rotates 90 degrees from the closed position to the fully open position, as shown in Figure 7-21. They are suitable for gas and liquid applications for a wide range of temperatures and pressures, and work well as both control and isolation valves.

Figure 7-21. Fisher® Control-Disk butterfly valve (courtesy of Emerson Process Management).

There are a variety of disc designs that can be used for the butterfly valve. The conventional butterfly valve has a disc with geometric symmetry, as shown on the left in Figure 7-22. The disadvantage of this type of disc is the high torque that is produced on the shaft due to the flow of the fluid over the disc from about 60 to 90 degrees of valve travel. This torque can be reduced by changing the shape of the disc, such as with the fish tail design shown in the center drawing of Figure 7-22.

Figure 7-22. Butterfly valve disc designs: conventional (left), fish tail (center), and contoured (right) (courtesy of Emerson Process Management).

High performance butterfly valves have eccentric contoured discs (shown on the right in Figure 7-22) to produce an equal percentage inherent flow characteristic. These can incorporate a single, double, or triple offset with the valve body, shown in Figure 7-23. A single offset means that the centerline of the shaft is offset from the plane of the sealing surface of the disc. This allows the disc to rotate away from the seal on the body in the initial 10 degrees of rotation, with no contact in the remainder of the rotation.

A double offset incorporates an offset between the centerline of the valve shaft with the centerline of the flow passage, or disc face. This allows the disc to pull away from the seal in the valve body at initial opening, minimizing the torque required to adjust the position of the disc.

The triple offset design has a third offset between the centerline of the shaft and the cut angle of the leading edge of the sealing surface of the disc. This ensures that the disc contacts the body seal only at the final shutoff position.

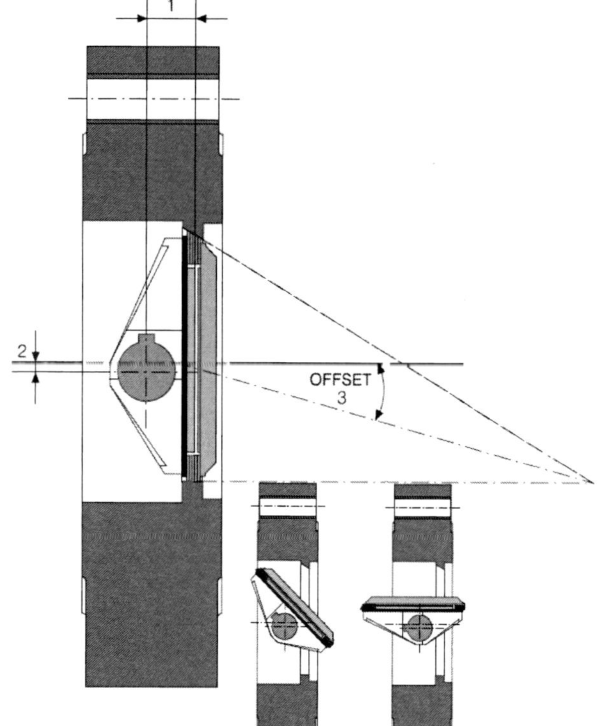

Figure 7-23. Triple offset of butterfly valve disc (courtesy of Flowseal, a Crane Co.).

Plug Valves

Plug valves are also rotary motion valves that are ideally suited for erosive fluid applications. The closing member can be a tapered or cylindrical plug with a rectangular flow passage through it, or it can be an eccentric segmented plug as shown in Figure 7-24. The plug can also incorporate various V-notch features to characterize the hydraulic performance of the valve.

Table 7-1 summarizes the features and differences between the types of control valve styles.

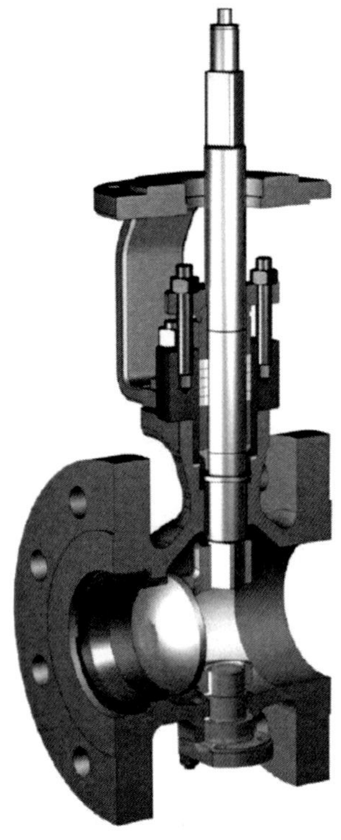

Figure 7-24. Eccentric rotating plug valve (courtesy of Flowserve).

Table 7-1: Capabilities and Features of Various Types of Control Valves (courtesy of European Valves)

	Linear motion	**Rotary Ball Valve**	**Rotary Butterfly Valve**
Size			
Nominal Size Range	¼ - 60"	½" – 48"	2" – 140"
C_V for a 4" valve	240	530	490
Maximum C_V for type	60,000	14,000	400,000
Pressure Rating			
ANSI	6,600 psi	600 psi	2,500 psi
API	20,000 psi		
Max differential pressure			
	10,000 psi	1,500 psi	2,000 psi
Operating temperature			
Maximum °F	100 to 1,500	175 to 800	300 to 1,500
Minimum (normal trim) °F	60 to -100	-20 to -115	20 to -110
End connections			
Screwed	√		
Compression fittings	√		
Flanged	√	√	√
Proprietary clamped fittings	√		
Socket weld	√		√
Butt weld	√	√	√
Wafer	√	√	√
Lug		√	√
Valve characteristics			
Equal Percentage	√	√	√
Linear	√		
Quick opening	√		√
Rangeability			
Maximum / minimum flow	50:1 to 200:1	150:1 to 300:1	100:1
Action on control failure			
Fail open	√	√	√
Fail closed	√	√	√
As-is	√	√	√
Installation options			
Space required	large	smaller	smallest
Trim servicing	in place	removal	removal
Actuator mounting	fixed	variable	variable
Operating conditions			
Corrosive	√	√	√
Abrasive	limited	X	X
Flashing	√	√	√
Cavitating	√	X	X
Hazardous emissions	bellows seal	double packing	double packing
Pulp	X	√	√
Sanitary	√	X	√

Classifying Control Valves Based on Pressure and Temperature Rating

Control valves are also classified according to the pressure and temperature of the working fluid that the valve can handle without affecting the integrity of the valve. The higher the temperature and pressure of the working fluid, the greater the wall thickness, depending on the material of construction. The valve manufacturer can increase the wall thickness of the valve or choose a different material. When the wall thickness is increased, the internal passages of the control valve may decrease which reduces the flow coefficient for a given valve size.

The American Society of Mechanical Engineers has established valve class ratings based on the allowable fluid pressure at the working temperature, as shown in Figure 7-25.

The valve class number increases with higher allowable operating pressures. Class 900, 1500, and 2500 valves are generally referred to as high pressure valves.

Also note in Figure 7-25, as the fluid temperature increases, the allowable operating pressure decreases, especially above about 750 °F. This is because the metal valve bodies become more pliable at higher temperatures, making them more susceptible to failure at higher pressures.

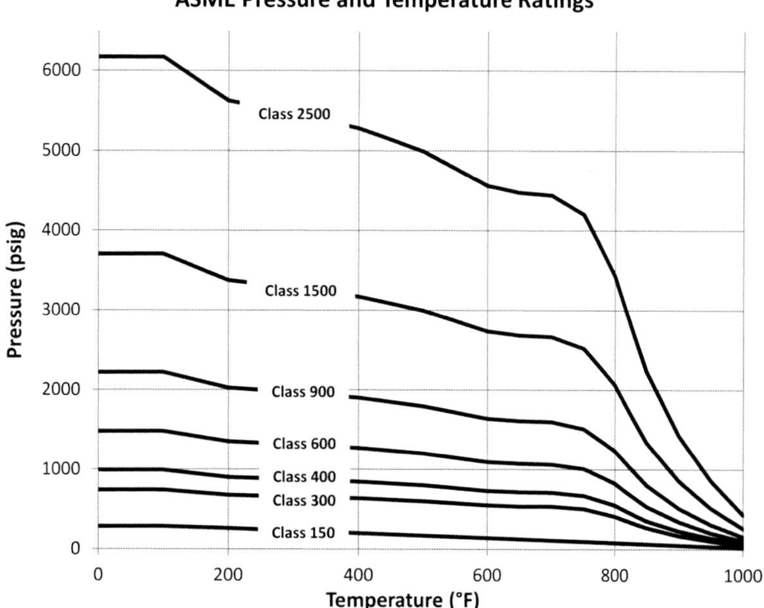

Figure 7-25. Generalized graph of the allowable pressure and temperature based on ASME valve classification.

Classifying Control Valves Based on Leak Tightness at Shutoff

Control valves can also be classified according to the amount of allowable leakage at shutoff. Many factors affect the valve's leak tighness, including whether the valve is single or double seated, how the valve plug is guided, the seating surface material, how much force the actuator can produce, the pressure differential across the closed valve, and the working fluid composition and temperature.

The ANSI valve classifications shown in Table 7-2 defines the valve class based on the tested shutoff leak rate of the valve as specified in the ANSI/FCI 70-2 standard. In addition to the maximum allowable leak rate, the standard defines the test procedure, the test fluid, and the test pressure required to meet the valve classifications.

Table 7-2: ANSI Valve Classifications Based on Leak Rate at Shutoff

Valve Class	Allowable Leak Rate (Percent of Rated Capacity)
Class I	x
Class II	0.5%
Class III	0.1%
Class IV	0.01%
Class V	0.0005 mL / minute per inch port diameter per psid
Class VI	Bubbles/min or mL/min based on valve size

Class I valves are referred to as "dust tight", but there is no actual bench test that needs to be done for these valves.

Class II, III, and IV valves are similar in type and design but have progressively lower allowable leak rates at shutoff. They are typically balanced single port or double ported valves with a metal-to-metal contact between the seat and plug.

Class V valves are tested at higher test pressures and have an extremely low allowable leak rate based on the port diameter and test pressure drop.

Class VI valves are soft seated valves where the seat and/or disc is made of a resilient material like teflon or coated with a resilient material like Stellite, a cobalt-chromium alloy designed for wear resistance. The allowable leak rate for Class VI valves is extemely low and based on the valve size.

Class IV and Class VI valves are the most commonly used control valves.

Considerations for Sizing and Selecting Control Valves

A control valve must meet the requirements of the control loop and the piping system. The design conditions are the primary sizing criteria used to select a control valve and are typically the most demanding conditions the valve will be expected to handle. The design conditions used to size the control valve represent a worst-case operating scenario.

Although sized for specific design conditions, a control valve will typically not operate continually at those conditions. For example, when a system is started, the process fluid temperature and pressure may be considerably different from the design conditions. These conditions result in changes to the density, viscosity, and vapor pressure of the fluid compared to initial design conditions. The set point may also vary greatly during startup conditions. Minimum and maximum flow conditions, as well as extended operation at conditions other than the design conditions, must be taken into account when selecting a control valve.

There are many things to consider when sizing and selecting a particular control valve for a given application, including:

- Valve size
- Flow characteristics
- Controllability
- Rangeability
- Reliability
- Fluid / material compatability
- Pressure and temperature rating
- Leak tightness

Control Valve Sizing

The valve must be properly sized to ensure it has the capacity to pass the desired flow rate. An iterative method for sizing control valves is outlined in the Instrumentation, System, and Automation Society (ISA) standard ANSI/ISA-75.01.01 *Flow Equations for Sizing Control Valves*. The standard presents the necessary information and equations needed to calculate the required flow coefficient (C_V) to size a control valve for both liquid and gas applications, in both U.S. and metric units. It also allows for adjustment of the flow coefficient for laminar flow, and for valve installations in which another valve or fitting is installed within two pipe diameters upstream of the valve inlet or six pipe diameters downstream of the valve outlet.

Sizing for Incompressible Fluid Flow

For incompressible fluid flow, Equation 7-1 is used to calculate the required flow coefficient of the control valve.

$$C_V = \frac{Q}{N_1 F_P \sqrt{\frac{P_1 - P_2}{S}}}$$ *Equation 7-1*

C_V = nominal flow coefficient

Q = volumetric flow rate

N_1 = numerical constant based on units used for flow rate and pressure

F_P = piping geometry factor

P_1 = absolute pressure measured at the valve inlet

P_2 = absolute pressure measured at the valve outlet

S = specific gravity of the fluid

The value of $N_1 = 1.0$ if units of gpm are used for flow rate and psi are used for pressure. If units other than gpm and psi are used, the standard should be consulted.

The piping geometry factor (F_P) accounts for fittings attached within two pipe diameters of the valve inlet or six pipe diameters of the outlet. The piping geometry factor is the ratio of the flow coefficient with the fittings attached, to the flow coefficient of the valve installed in a straight pipe of the same diameter, and is calculated using Equation 7-2.

$$F_P = \frac{1}{\sqrt{1 + \frac{\Sigma K}{N_2}\left(\frac{C_V}{d^2}\right)^2}}$$ *Equation 7-2*

F_P = piping geometry factor

ΣK = sum of the resistance coefficients for all attached valves and fittings

C_V = valve flow coefficient

N_2 = numerical constant based on units used for nominal valve size

d = nominal valve size

Sizing a control valve is an iterative procedure. The flow coefficient is first calculated assuming no fittings attached to the valve(the piping geometry factor $F_P = 1.0$). Control valve manufacturer data can be checked to find a valve with a fully open C_V greater than the calculated C_V. If a smaller control valve than the pipe size can be selected (for economic reasons as well as others), then reducers will need to be installed at the valve inlet and outlet.

The piping geometry factor will then need to be calculated using Equation 7-2, and the flow coefficient re-calculated using the piping geometry factor. As long as the second calculation of the flow coefficient is within the range of the selected valve, the valve will have sufficient capacity to meet the needs of the application.

If the valve is expected to be used under laminar flow conditions, an additional correction factor called the Reynolds number factor will need to be determined using the standard.

The possibility of choking and cavitation will need to be determined for the control valve being considered. This will be discussed in more detail later in this chapter.

Sizing for Compressible Fluid Flow

The sizing equations for applications involving compressible gas flow are similar to the equations for incompressible flow, with the exception that the compressible nature of the fluid is taken into account with an expansion factor, *Y*. Equation 7-3 is used to calculate the flow coefficient for a control valve in a compressible application.

$$C_V = \frac{w}{N_6 F_P Y \sqrt{x P_1 \rho}} \qquad \textit{Equation 7-3}$$

w = mass flow rate

N_6 = numerical constant based on units used for mass flow rate, pressure, and density

F_P = piping geometry factor

Y = fluid expansion factor

x = ratio of the pressure drop across the valve to the absolute inlet pressure ($\Delta P/P_1$)

P_1 = absolute pressure measured at the valve inlet

ρ = density of the fluid at the inlet pressure and temperature

The expansion factor, *Y*, is calculated using Equation 7-4.

$$Y = 1 - \frac{x}{3 F_k x_T} \qquad \textit{Equation 7-4}$$

Y = expansion factor

x = ratio of the pressure drop across the valve to the absolute inlet pressure ($\Delta P/P_1$)

F_K = specific heat ratio factor (= k /1.4, where k = specific heat ratio of the fluid)

x_T = rated pressure drop ratio factor, obtain by manufacturer testing in accordance with ANSI/ISA-75.02

Flow Characteristics

The selected control valve needs to have the right flow characteristics to ensure adequate response over the range of operating flow rates. All components of a control loop have inherent characteristics that define the relationship between the inlet and outlet of each component. The process itself (level, temperature, flow, or pressure control for example) will have inherent characteristics. A key to selecting a good valve for a given process is to choose one with the right inherent characteristics to make the entire loop and process as close to linear as possible over the range of control for the valve.

Controllability

Controllability involves the static aspects of the control valve such as the size and type, the flow characteristics, and the flow direction. It also involves dynamic aspects that determine how the valve responds to step changes in the control signal in response to disturbances in the process. These dynamic aspects include backlash and stiction that result in a dead band between when the control signal changes to when the valve plug or disc starts to move. Backlash is the loss of movement of the closure member in response to a change in control signal due to looseness in the mechanical linkages from the actuator to the valve plug or disc. Stiction is a result of the packing friction that prevents movement of the stem until enough force is applied by the actuator to overcome the friction.

Rangeability

The rangeability of the valve is the range of flow rates that the valve is expected to control from the minimum to the maximum flow rate. A control valve is typically sized to meet the maximum flow requirements but may be expected to operate over a wide range of conditions.

Reliability

Reliability is also a key performance indicator for a control valve. Cavitation, critical damage, noise, high pressure drop, and high outlet velocity are the most common reliability challenges a control valve has to deal with to minimize maintenance on the valve.

Cavitation and Choking

A control valve with incompressible fluid flow is susceptible to cavitation just like a centrifugal pump. Cavitation occurs when the localized static pressure within the control valve drops below the fluid's vapor pressure, causing some of the liquid to flash to a vapor state. When the fluid reaches a region of higher pressure above the vapor pressure, the vapor bubbles collapse, potentially causing severe erosion and damage to the valve trim. Cavitation also results in increased noise levels and vibration of the attached piping and supports.

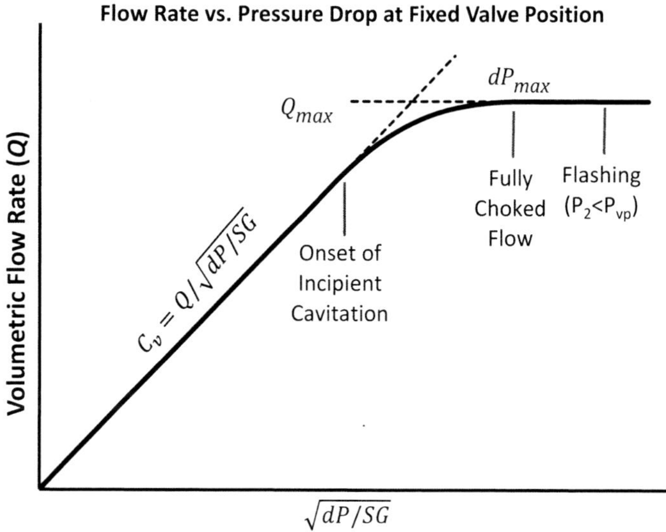

Figure 7-26. Flow vs. pressure drop at a fixed valve position showing the onset of cavitation to fully choked flow.

In addition, since the vapor bubbles occupy more volume than the same mass of liquid, the flow rate through the valve begins to become restricted and the flow rate deviates from that predicted by the flow coefficient equation. This can be seen graphically on Figure 7-26, which shows the relationship between the volumetric flow rate and the square root of the pressure drop for a valve at a fixed position. In the region where there is a linear relationship between the flow rate and the square root of the pressure drop, the fluid remains incompressible all the way through the valve. The slope of this line is the value of the flow coefficient.

As the differential pressure across the valve is increased (by lowering the downstream pressure, for example) the flow rate through the valve increases and the pressure at the vena contracta drops. At the point where the pressure reaches the vapor pressure, the onset of incipient cavitation occurs and the flow is becoming choked. As the downstream pressure continues to be lowered, a greater region around the vena contracta is filled with vapor bubbles, causing a further deviation from the linear C_V relationship. At the point where the entire region of the vena contracta has vapor flowing through it, the flow is fully choked, and no further drop in downstream pressure will result in an increase in the flow rate through the valve.

When the valve is experiencing cavitation, the vapor bubbles collapse within the valve body. If the pressure is not returned above the vapor pressure at the outlet of the valve, a condition of flashing is said to occur.

For compressible fluid applications, choked flow occurs when the fluid velocity at the vena contracta approaches the speed of sound of the compressible gas.

When selecting a control valve for a given application, it is important to check if cavitation or choking will occur throughout the range of operation of the valve. For incompressible flow, choking can be determined if the expected flow rate is above the maximum flow rate shown in Figure 7-26, or if the pressure drop across the valve is greater than the maximum pressure drop corresponding to the maximum flow rate.

Equation 7-5 can be used to calculate the maximum flow rate and Equation 7-6 can be used to calculate the maximum pressure drop for a valve without attached fittings.

$$Q_{max} = N_1 F_L C_V \sqrt{\frac{P_1 - F_F P_{vp}}{S}}$$ *Equation 7-5*

$$\Delta P_{max} = F_L^2 (P_1 - F_F P_{vp})$$ *Equation 7-6*

Q_{max} = volumetric flow rate
N_1 = numerical constant based on units used for flow rate and pressure
F_L = liquid pressure recovery factor
C_V = flow coefficient at a given valve position
P_1 = absolute pressure measured at the valve inlet
F_F = liquid critical pressure ratio factor
P_{vp} = fluid's vapor pressure
S = fluid's specific gravity

The liquid pressure recovery factor (F_L) is a function of the valve type, size, and valve position, and is determined by the valve manufacturer by testing and should be provided in the manufacturer's valve data table. For globe valves, typical values of F_L range from about 0.82 to 0.95, for ball valves from 0.55 to 0.75, and from 0.50 to 0.70 for butterfly valves.

The liquid critical pressure ratio factor (F_F) is a function of the fluid's vapor pressure and critical pressure and can be calculated using Equation 7-7.

$$F_F = 0.96 - 0.28 \sqrt{\frac{P_{vp}}{P_c}}$$ *Equation 7-7*

F_F = liquid critical pressure ratio factor
P_{vp} = fluid's vapor pressure
P_c = fluid's critical pressure

For compressible gas flow, choked flow occurs when the velocity at the vena contracta approaches the speed of sound. This occurs when $x = F_k X_T$ and therefore Y approaches 2/3 (refer to Equation 7-4).

For applications where cavitation is occuring in a control valve, or is predicted to occur, special anti-cavitation trim is available for most types of control valves. Anti-cavitation trim causes the total pressure drop across the valve to occur in stages rather than all at once, allowing some pressure recovery to occur between the stages so that the localized static pressure doesn't fall below the fluid's vapor pressure.

Fluid / Material Compatibility

The process fluid and the material of construction for the control valve must be compatible to ensure the internal trim is not adversely affected by severe duty conditions. The valve internals can be stellated to handle wear, erosion, corrosion and high temperature process conditions. Stellite alloy is a cobalt-chromium alloy designed for wear resistance.

Pressure and Temperature

When selecting a control valve, the maximum pressure and temperature must be known in order to choose the correct ASME rating for the valve.

Leak Tightness

The allowable leakage at shutoff is also a consideration for selecting a control valve. The ANSI valve classifications may influence the decision on which valve is appropriate for a given application.

Cost of Head Loss Across a Control Valve

The pressure drop across a control valve is hydraulic energy that is dissipated across the valve as head loss in the form of heat, noise, and vibration. This energy was originally added to the fluid at the pump and a portion of the operating cost of the energy can be allocated to the control valve using Equation 7-8.

$$\begin{matrix} Cost\ of\ Control \\ Valve\ Head\ Loss \end{matrix} = \frac{(0.746)\ Q\ h_L\ \rho}{(247{,}000)\ \eta_P\ \eta_m\ \eta_{VFD}} \begin{pmatrix} Operating \\ Hours \end{pmatrix} (\$/kWh) \qquad \text{Equation 7-8}$$

Examples Using the Control Valve Equations

In addition to using the control valve equations to size and select a control valve for a particular application, they can also be used to determine various operating parameters if enough information is known about the valve.

Example 7-1: Sizing a Control Valve for a Given Flow Rate and Pressure Drop

For the piping system shown in Figure 7-27, water is heated to 160 °F and pumped from the Supply Tank to the Product Tank. The flow control valve (FCV-271) must allow a maximum flow rate of 950 gpm with an inlet pressure of 75 psig and an outlet pressure of 65 psig. Fluid density at 160 °F is 61.0 lb/ft^3. Select the appropriate valve size from the manufacturer's list of equal percentage globe valves shown in Table 7-3. Assume N_I= 1.0, and F_P= 1.0.

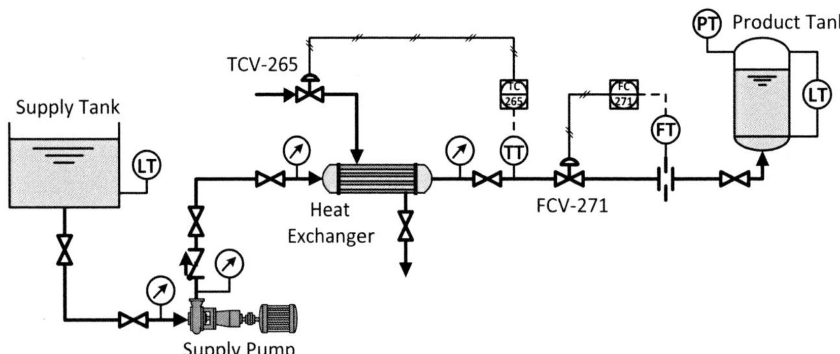

Table 7-3: Valve Sizes

Valve Size	Fully Open C_V
4"	224
6"	394
8"	818

Figure 7-27. Typical piping system with a flow control valve.

Determine Specific Gravity

$$SG = \frac{\rho_{water\ at\ 160\ °F}}{\rho_{water\ at\ 60\ °F}} = \frac{61.0\ lb/ft^3}{62.4\ lb/ft^3} = 0.978$$

Calculate the Valve's Required Flow Coefficient

$$C_V = \frac{Q}{N_1 F_P \sqrt{\frac{P_1 - P_2}{S}}} = \frac{950}{(1.0)(1.0)\sqrt{\frac{75-65}{0.978}}} = 297.1$$

From Table 7-3, a 4-inch valve would be too small, but the 6-inch and 8-inch valves have a flow coefficient greater than what is required. From an economic perspective, there is no reason to buy an 8-inch valve when a 6-inch valve would satisfy the application; also, an 8-inch valve cannot be installed in a 6-inch pipeline. The 6-inch control valve should be selected. No adjustment to the flow coefficient would be needed for piping geometry (F_P= 1.0).

Example 7-2: Calculating Pressure Drop and Head Loss

The flow control valve (FCV-271) is 65% open with a measured flow rate of 700 gpm. It is a 6-inch globe valve installed in a 6-inch pipeline with no fittings attached. A portion of its C_V profile is given in Table 7-4.

Calculate the pressure drop and associated head loss dissipated across the control valve.

Table 7-4: Control Valve Data

Position	C_V
50%	65
60%	106
70%	178
80%	270

Determine the Valve's Flow Coefficient at 65% Open

The flow coefficient at 65% open can be estimated using the values at the 60% and 70% open positions, or can be determined by linear interpolation between those values.

$$C_{V_{act}} = C_{V_1} + \frac{(Position_{act} - Position_1)}{(Position_2 - Position_1)}\left(C_{V_2} - C_{V_1}\right) = 106 + \frac{(65-60)}{(70-60)}(178-106) = 142$$

Calculate the Pressure Drop

The differential pressure across the control valve can be calculated by re-arranging Equation 7-1 and solving for the pressure drop (P_1 - P_2):

$$dP = P_1 - P_2 = \frac{Q^2\ SG}{(C_V N_1 F_P)^2} = \frac{(700)^2\ (0.978)}{(142 \times 1 \times 1)^2} = 23.8\ psi$$

Convert Pressure Drop to Head Loss

Since the pressure drop across the valve represents hydraulic energy that is dissipated across the valve, Equation 2-19 can be used:

$$h_L = \frac{144\ dP}{\rho} = \frac{144\ (23.8)}{61.0} = 56.2\ ft$$

Example 7-3: Calculating the Cost of Control Valve Head Loss

For the control valve in Example 7-2, calculate the cost of the head loss across the control valve using 8,000 hours of operation, a utility rate of \$0.10/kWh, a fixed speed pump efficiency of 70%, and motor efficiency of 95%.

$$\begin{matrix} Cost\ of\ Control \\ Valve\ Head\ Loss \end{matrix} = \frac{(0.746)\ (700)(56.2)\ (61.0)}{(247{,}000)(0.70)\ (0.95)\ (1.0)}(8{,}000\ )(\$0.10/kWh) = \$8{,}719$$

Example 7-4: Determine the Flow Rate Through a Control Valve

The flow rate through a control valve can be determined if the valve's flow coefficient and the inlet and outlet pressures of the valve are known. The flow coefficient can be determined by the valve position and the manufacturer's valve data table. The valve's inlet and outlet pressures may be measured directly with pressure gages or can be estimated using nearby pressure gages.

Determine the flow rate through FCV-271 in Figure 7-27 with the valve at 80% open and a measured inlet pressure of 80 psig and an outlet pressure of 67 psig.

From Table 7-4, at 80% open the $C_V = 270$. Re-arranging Equation 7-1 and solving for flow rate:

$$Q = C_V N_1 F_P \sqrt{\frac{P_1 - P_2}{S}} = (270)(1.0)(1.0)\sqrt{\frac{80 - 67}{0.978}} = 984.4\ gpm$$

Chapter Eight

Process Measurement and Controls

Piping systems exist to transport raw materials in order to do work or make a product. These raw materials undergo processes that change their physical, thermal, or chemical properties. Many of these processes are hazardous in nature and involve elevated energy states. In addition, disturbances may occur that affect the stability of the processes.

To ensure the safety and reliability of the operators and the facility, piping system processes must be measured and controlled. In addition, the quality of the product being produced often depends on the variability of process parameters around a desired set point.

It is critical to measure and control key system parameters in most industrial and commercial processes, whether it is tank level or pressure, fluid temperature, system flow rate, or some analytical parameter such as fluid pH, conductivity, or consistency. This chapter focuses on the instruments used to measure these key parameters, the control methods that can be implemented, and the various components that make up a process control loop.

Architecture of Process Measurement and Control

Perhaps more than any other aspect of fluid piping systems, the equipment used to measure and control processes in a facility has undergone the greatest advancements over the past several decades. Pneumatic controls have evolved to dedicated electrical wiring to digital networking. Wireless technology is becoming more accepted in industrial applications as well.

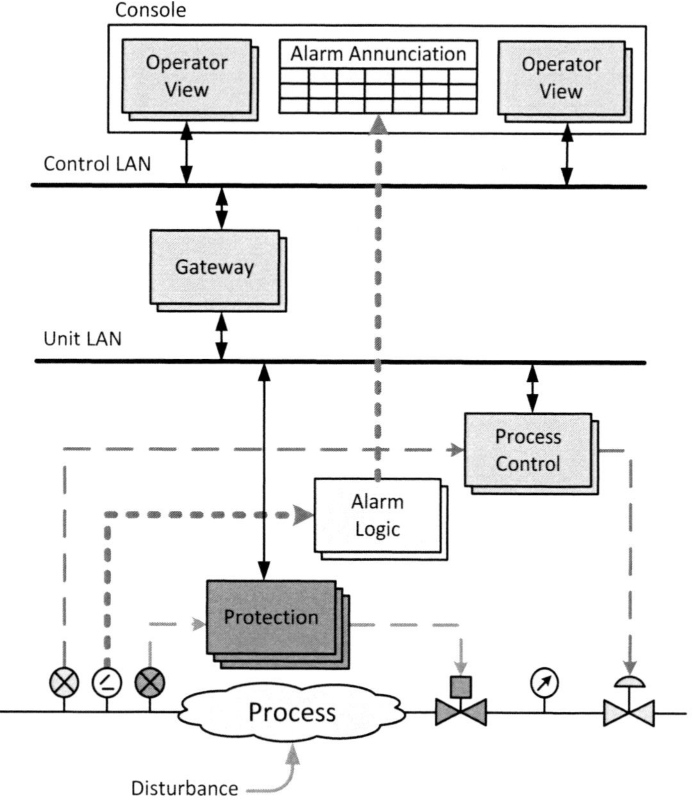

Figure 8-1. Modern architecture of Process Measurement and Controls for the petrochemical industry.

Functionalities

Depending on the industry, the overall architecture of process measurement and control at a facility can take a variety of configurations and have various levels. Figure 8-1 shows a block diagram of a typical modern architecture for the petrochemical industry and includes four key functionalities to regulate processes.

- local indication functionality
- process control functionality
- alarm functionality
- protective functionality

Other industries may implement some or all of these functionalities in their architecture depending on the nature of the processes in the industry. Some industries may require strict adherence to a very structured architecture, especially industries involving hazardous processes. Other industries may be upgrading from older technology, and some may not require dedicated functionality in their architecture.

Two key aspects of the architecture in the petrochemical industry are ***redundancy*** and the ***separation*** of the control, alarm and protective functionality. These features ensure that all functions are not impacted by the failure of any individual device. For example, if there is a failure in the basic process control loop, the alarm and protective features would still be functional.

Local Indication

Local indication functionality involves the use of gages mounted directly on the pipeline, tank, or at the inlet or outlet of individual pieces of equipment. Local gages are used to provide the operator with process measurements at the equipment or close to the final control element.

Fluid pressure may be measured locally using a bourdon tube pressure gage shown in Figure 8-2 or a diaphragm pressure gage shown in Figure 8-3.

Figure 8-2. Bourdon tube pressure gage (courtesy of Wika).

Figure 8-3. Diaphragm pressure gage (courtesy of Wika).

Fluid temperature may be measured using a glass thermometer (Figure 8-4), a bimetallic strip thermometer (Figure 8-5), or a gas-filled thermometer (Figure 8-6).

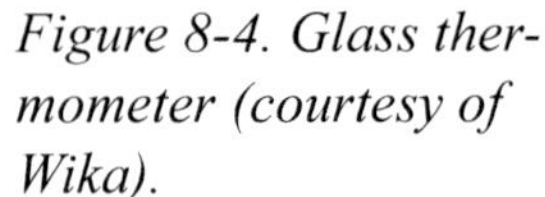

Figure 8-4. Glass thermometer (courtesy of Wika).

Figure 8-5. Bimetallic thermometer (courtesy of Wika).

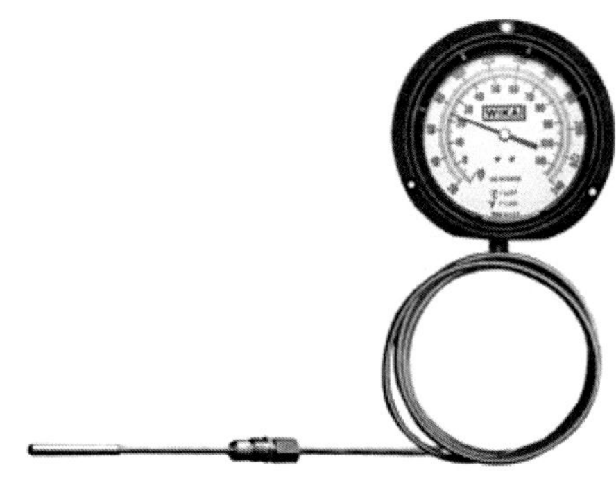

Figure 8-6. Gas-filled thermometer (courtesy of Wika).

Tank level may be measured locally using a site glass, as shown in Figure 8-7, and flow rate may be measured locally using a tapered variable area flow gage as shown in Figure 8-8.

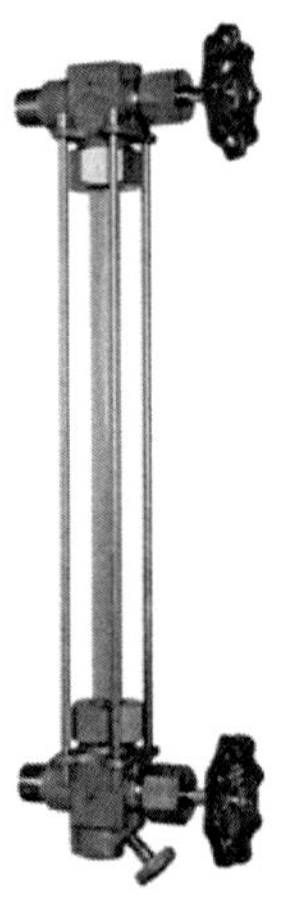

Figure 8-7. Tank site glass (courtesy of Johnernst.com).

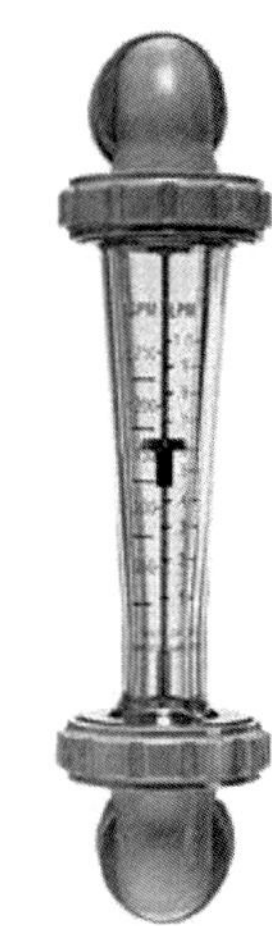

Figure 8-8. Tapered variable area flow gage (courtesy of Cole-Parmer).

Process Control

The process control functionality consists of a dedicated process sensor (or primary element), a loop controller, and a final control element (shown as the control valve in Figure 8-1).

In modern industrial controls, the loop controller is configured in a process control microprocessor, called a Distributed Control System (DCS) or a Programmable Logic Controller (PLC), that can contain a large number of configurable controllers. Since the failure of this process control microprocessor will impact a large number of loops, it is redundant as shown by a double box in Figure 8-1.

The process control loop will be examined in detail later in this chapter.

Alarms

Alarms are used to warn the operator of an abnormal operating condition. The set point of the alarm should be established to allow the operator enough time to take action before any automatic protective action is initiated.

Alarm functionality for critical alarms may use a dedicated sensor, redundant microprocessors for alarms, and an alarm annunciator or alarm panel located near the operator console. Alarm annunciators may provide a visual and audible alarm, such as the one shown in Figure 8-9, or may include event recording functionality such as the one in Figure 8-10.

Figure 8-9. Industrial alarm annunciator (courtesy of RTK Instruments).

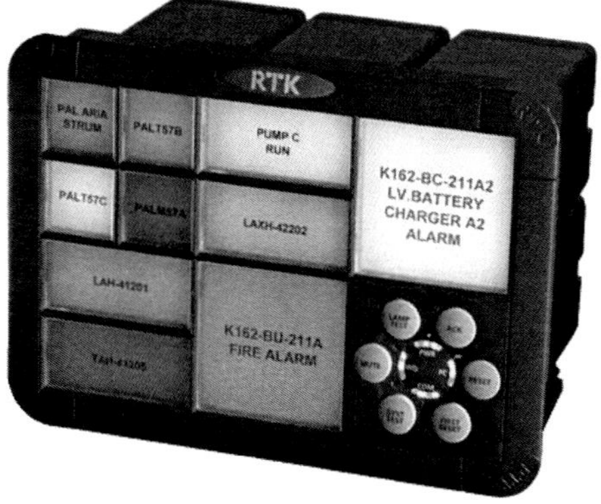

Figure 8-10. Alarm annunciator and event recorder (courtesy of RTK Instruments).

Alarms may also be activated on the operators DCS console using an audible and/or visual indication to alert the operator of an abnormal operating condition.

Protection

Protection functionality involves automatically initiating protective action to protect workers and equipment in the event that a process goes out of control and is beyond the point of intervention on the part of the operator. For example, automatic shutdown action may be initiated on low tank level, high machine rpm or vibration, or high fluid temperature.

Protective devices in the overall architecture include a dedicated sensor, microprocessors for protection logic, and a dedicated on/off block valve. The protection microprocessors are triple redundant to ensure that a large number of critical safety functions remain functional in the unlikely event of the simultaneous failure of two microprocessors.

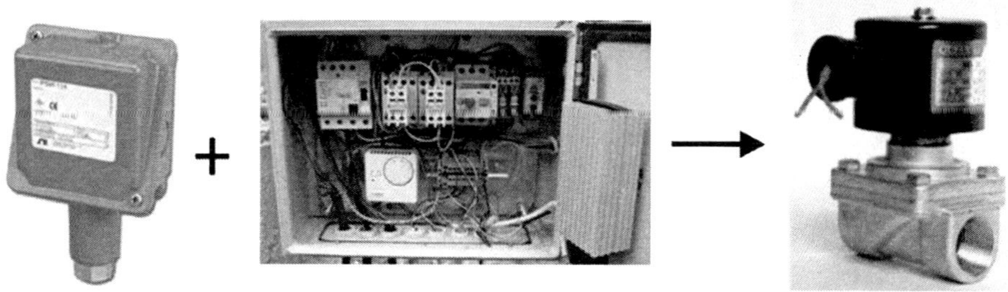

Figure 8-11. Traditional devices used for protective functionality: a pressure switch (left), relays (center), and a solonoid operated block valve (right).

The traditional method for protective functionality used switches and relays to activate an automatic block valve, as shown in Figure 8-11. These switches are considered "blind" devices in that they have an on/off state based on the calibration of the switch, so they are susceptible to human error in calibration. Relays are also susceptible to mechanical or electrical failure and environmental conditions.

Newer technology uses dedicated transmitters and logic configured in Programmable Logic Controllers (PLCs) to activate the block valve, as shown in Figure 8-12.

Figure 8-12. Protective functionality using dedicated transmitters (left) and Programmable Logic Controllers (center) to activate the solonoid operated block valve (right).

Networks

Depending on the size of the facility and the number of discrete departments within the facility, process measurement and controls may be networked together to ensure information and commands are passed between individual devices in the architecture.

Unit LANs

As shown in Figure 8-1, the process control and the protection logic microprocessors are connected via redundant Unit Local Area Networks (or Unit LANs). A Unit LAN may be dedicated to all the measurements and controls in an individual department, or unit, within the facility. For example, in a pulp and paper mill, one Unit LAN may be dedicated to the digester department, one to the bleach plant, one to the paper machine, and one to the power and recovery department.

Control LANs

The Unit LANs are connected over a redundant gateway to the Control LAN. This Control LAN communicates to a large number of devices on different Unit LANs. The Control LAN passes information and commands between the operator consoles and the process control and protection microprocessors.

Operator Consoles

The control operator works from redundant consoles that allow the operator to change control loop set points, put controllers in manual, and to remotely change the control valve position.

The operator consoles may be equipped with graphical displays that represent the piping system or process that the operator controls, as shown in Figure 8-13. The consoles may also have audible and visual alarms.

Figure 8-13. Typical operator DCS display.

Process Control

Process control functionality involves measuring a property of a process and implementing an automatic control scheme to adjust a device called the Final Control Element, to maintain the property at a desired set point when a disturbance affects the process. The process can be any one of many that will be discussed in Chapter 9, but a process can change a property of the piping system: tank level, fluid flow, pipeline pressure, fluid temperature, or some other parameter. The disturbance can be from a change in environmental conditions, an operator action, or a mechanical or hydraulic disturbance from another interconnected piping system.

In a steady state condition, there is no change over time in any of the properties of the system. The levels, pressures, flow rates, fluid temperatures, controller outputs, and even the disturbance itself, are all constant.

A block diagram of a typical process control loop is shown in Figure 8-14. The main components of a typical process control loop include:

- Primary Element
- Transmitter
- Loop Controller
- Transducer
- Final Control Element

Additional components may be included in the control loop depending on the application and the other components in the loop. For example, if a control valve is used as the final control element, a positioner may be installed as an optional component, and its performance included in understanding the operation of the entire loop.

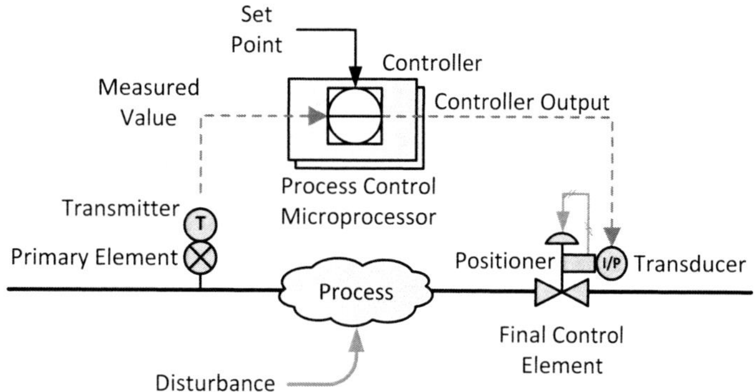

Figure 8-14. Components of the process control functionality: primary element, transmitter, controller, transducer, and final control element.

The process itself and the disturbances that affect the process must be understood as well.

Primary Elements & Transmitters

The primary element is the instrument that measures a property of the process, such as the fluid flow rate, pressure, temperature, tank level, or some other property.

Once the fluid property is measured, it has to be transmitted to the controller to provide information about the process. This is done using a transmitter that may have to convert the measurement signal into another signal form that is transmitted to the loop controller. The signal may also be sent to an alarm annunciator or to the protection loop.

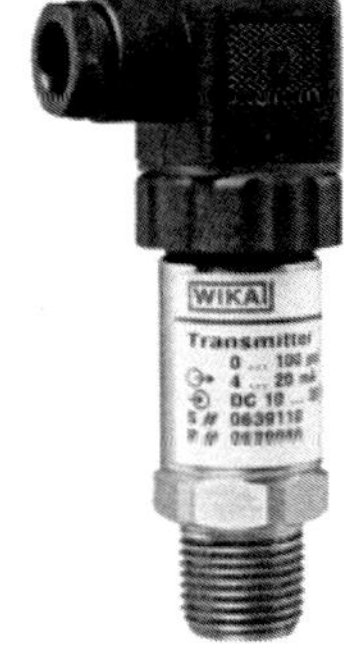

Figure 8-15. Primary element and transmitter combined into one component for measuring and transmitting fluid pressure (courtesy of Wika).

The signal may be an electrical signal, such as a 4 – 20 mA DC current, which is the defacto standard established by the ISA SP 50 standard. It can also be an electrical voltage signal, such as a 0 – 5 volt signal or 0 – 10 volt signal, or a millivolt signal. The form of the signal that is used may be specified for a particular piece of equipment or by a particular supplier (for example, the Foxboro Spec 200 infrastructure used a 0 – 10 volt signal).

The sensor and transmitter are sometimes combined into a single device, such as with the pressure transmitter shown in Figure 8-15. For other instruments, the transmitter is a dedicated device that can be easily replaced or interchanged with other brands of transmitters.

Some of the most common primary elements are used to measure flow, pressure, level, and temperature. The primary element may also be used for analytical measurement such as pH, conductivity, oxygen, or some other fluid property. Entire analyzer systems, such as gas chromatographs may be used to measure properties of the working fluid in a process. Other measurements made with primary elements include devices that measure rotational speed, equipment vibration, and the weight of an object.

Flow Rate Measurement

Flow meters come in two categories: differential pressure and linear meters.

Differential pressure meters use the Bernoulli principle that when fluid flows through a restriction, velocity increases and static pressure decreases, resulting in a differential pressure across the meter. An obstruction in the flow path is used to create the difference in pressure. The differential pressure is proportional to the flow rate squared and requires the square root of the output to be taken in order to calculate the flow rate.

Examples of differential pressure meters include orifices, flow nozzles, venturi tubes, pitot tubes, and annubars.

Linear meters have an operating principle that yields a direct linear output, or through electronics, the output is linearized to volumetric or mass flow units. Turbine meters, vortex meters, magnetic flow meters, ultrasonic flow meters, and coriolis flow meters are all linear meters.

Most flow meters, with the exception of the coriolis flow meter, provide an indication of the volumetric flow rate of the fluid flowing through the meter. The coriolis flow meter measures the mass flow rate. To obtain the mass flow rate with a meter that outputs the volumetric flow rate, the output must be density compensated, typically by measuring the fluid pressure and temperature to calculate a density compensation factor.

Orifice Plate

The concentric orifice shown in Figure 8-16 is the most commonly used differential pressure flow meter. It can be used for clean liquids, gases, and low velocity vapors, such as steam. The orifice is a flat plate with a round hole bored into it, with the centerline of the hole aligned with the centerline of the pipe. The hole can be tapered with the sharper edge located on the upstream side.

Figure 8-16. Standard orifice plate (courtesy of Rosemount).

A tab is provided on the orifice to assist in positioning the orifice between the flanges. The meter identification and diameter of the primary element is often stamped on the tab to help determine whether the proper primary element is installed.

Due to the wide application of orifice meters in a variety of industries, standards have been developed to provide installation and construction guidelines, along with methods to estimate the overall accuracy of the meter. The standards also provide formulas used to size the primary element in order to achieve a given flow rate for a specified differential pressure.

In North America, the two primary standards are the American Society of Mechanical Engineers (ASME-MFC-3M) and the American Petroleum Institute 2530. The standards also provide formulas to help calculate the size of the primary element while still achieving an accuracy of ±0.8 to ±0.5 percent, without the need to calibrate the meter.

The two most critical elements in working with orifice flow meters are the location of the pressure taps and the diameter of the primary element. The pressure taps are located upstream and downstream from the primary element. The location of the pressure taps is critical for arriving at an accurate value for the flow rate.

Pressure taps locations are standardized at defined distances on the inlet and outlet of the orifice meter, as shown in Figure 8-17. The taps measure the differential pressure created by the flow of fluid through the orifice plate. There are 3 typical arrangements for the pressure taps:

- Flange taps located 1 inch from the face of the orifice plate
- Corner taps flush with the walls of the orifice plate
- 1D - ½D taps measure the pressure 1 pipe diameter upstream and ½ pipe diameter downstream of the orifice, close to the vena contracta where the differential pressure is maximum

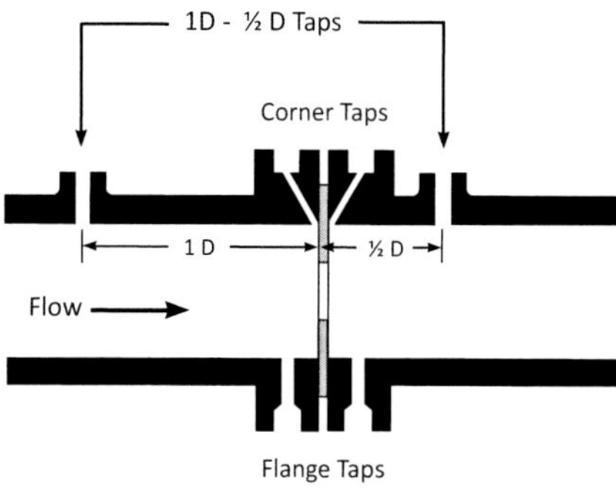

1D - ½ D Taps
Corner Taps
1 D
½ D
Flow
Flange Taps

Figure 8-17. Orifice plate tap arrangements.

Conditioning orifice plates with multiple bored holes, as shown in Figure 8-18, allows for installation in shorter runs of straight pipe.

Orifice plates can also be configured with an eccentric orifice that offsets the centerline of the orifice with the centerline of the pipe. These would be used for fluids that have entrained gases or solid particulates in the flow stream. The location of the hole in the primary element of these types of orifices prevents the buildup of entrained gases or particles from the upstream side of the meter. The size of the hole in the primary element of eccentric and segmented orifices is not covered in the concentric orifice standard. As a result, these meters must be calibrated to provide an accurate indication of flow rate.

Figure 8-18. Conditioning orifice plate (courtesy of Rosemount).

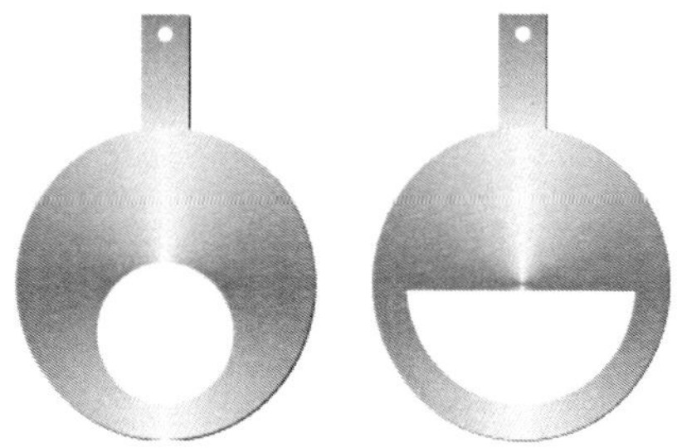

Figure 8-19. Eccentric orifice plate (left) and segmented orifice plate (right) (courtesy of Bibb Control Systems).

When calculating the size of the flow meter, it is important to use the correct formula for the pressure tap arrangements being used.

The primary disadvantage of the concentric orifice is its rather large differential pressure drop when compared to other types of flow meters, resulting in higher lifetime energy consumption and cost.

Venturi

The obstruction in a venturi flow meter is created by the converging inlet, a straight section called the throat, and a diverging outlet, as shown in Figure 8-20. This creates the restriction that causes the fluid velocity to increase and static pressure to decrease, developing a differential pressure from the venturi inlet to the throat. The gradual changes in diameter through the venturi minimize the total losses across the meter. In addition, the design allows for the passing of entrained gases and solids without clogging the metering element.

Venturis are typically used in processes with large flow rates where a low permanent pressure drop across the meter is desirable. Examples are large diameter piping in water and waste water applications.

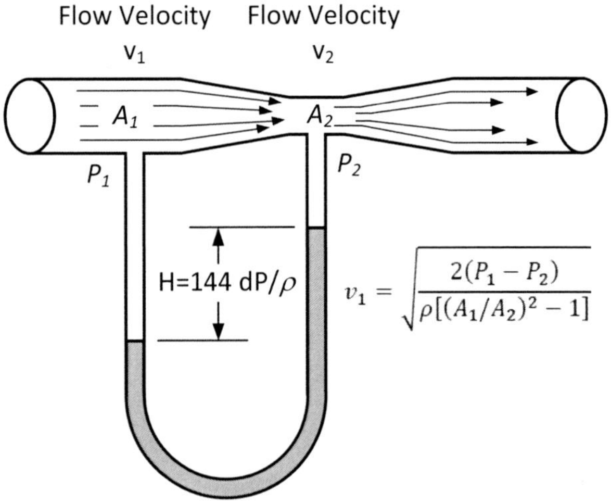

Flow Velocity V_1 Flow Velocity V_2

A_1 A_2 P_1 P_2

H=144 dP/ρ

$$v_1 = \sqrt{\frac{2(P_1 - P_2)}{\rho[(A_1/A_2)^2 - 1]}}$$

Figure 8-20. Venturi flow meter.

The venturi results in a smaller permanent pressure loss across the flow meter than an orifice plate. The sizing, design, and installation of venturi meters are also covered in the ASME-MFC-3M standard.

Flow Nozzles

A flow nozzle flow meter, shown in Figure 8-21, has a nozzle with a smaller inside diameter installed in the pipeline to create an obstruction that changes the fluid's flow path. As fluid flows through the nozzle, the fluid velocity increases due to the smaller inside diameter, and the static pressure drops due to the Bernoulli principle, resulting in a differential pressure across the nozzle.

Flow nozzles come in many designs and are typically more expensive to manufacture than the orifice plate, but are more accurate and have a smaller permanent pressure drop for a given beta ratio. In addition, flow nozzles allow almost twice the capacity as an orifice plate for the same pressure drop.

The accuracy of the flow nozzle is better sustained compared to an orifice since there are no sharp edges or protrusions that wear over time.

Figure 8-21. Flow nozzle flow meter (courtesy of Delta-T Company).

Pitot Tubes

A pitot tube, shown in Figure 8-22, measures the total pressure and static pressure of the fluid, and the difference is the dynamic pressure due to the fluid flow, which can be related to the fluid velocity and therefore the flow rate. The dynamic pressure is determined by measuring the difference between the total and static pressure using a pressure transducer.

Equation 2-13 can be re-arranged to solve for the fluid velocity, which can then be used to calculate the volumetric flow rate of the fluid.

$$v = \sqrt{\frac{2(P_{Total} - P_{statc}) \times 144\, g}{\rho}}$$

Figure 8-22. Pitot tube measures the total and static pressures.

Annubar

An annubar, shown in Figure 8-23, is an averaging pitot tube that measures the fluid's total and static pressures over a larger cross-sectional area of the pipeline. A built-in thermowell behind the total pressure chamber allows the fluid temperature to be measured and used to density compensate the volumetric flow rate to obtain the mass flow rate of the fluid.

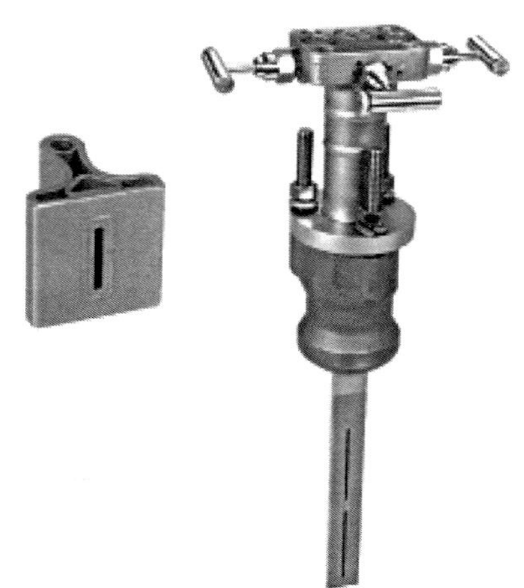

Figure 8-23. Annubar measures the total and static pressures over a larger cross-section of the pipeline (courtesy of Rosemount).

The annubar can provide a reading not only for mass and volumetric flow rates, but for totalized flow, energy flow, fluid temperature, and static pressure.

Annubars can be used in liquids, saturated or superheated steam, or with gases and vapors.

Annubars have a much lower permanent pressure drop for a given flow rate compared to orifice plates, and they have a greater range of accurate measurement.

Turbine Flowmeter

The turbine flow meter is a linear meter that contains a vaned rotor located in the flow stream. As the fluid flows past the turbine vanes, hydraulic forces cause the rotor to spin. The rotor's rotational speed is detected by an external magnet or some other sensor. The speed of rotation varies linearly with the fluid velocity.

Figure 8-24. Turbine flow meter (courtesy of Bopp & Reuther).

Turbine meters are susceptible to shifts in calibration with blade wear and bearing friction, and for liquids containing entrained air. They also have a higher permanent pressure drop due to head loss across the meter.

Turbine meters can be used for measuring the flow rate of clean liquids or gases.

Vortex Flowmeter

A vortex flow meter, shown in Figure 8-25, contains a specially designed bar inserted into the flow stream that causes the fluid to split and flow around the bar. As the fluid sheds off the bar, alternating vortexes are created. An ultrasonic signal is used to count the number of vortexes that are shed off the bar per unit time, which is linearly proportional to the fluid velocity.

Vortex meters can contain an installed temperature sensor to density compensate volumetric flow rate calculation to obtain a reading of the mass flow rate through the flow meter.

Vortex meters can be used for liquids or gases.

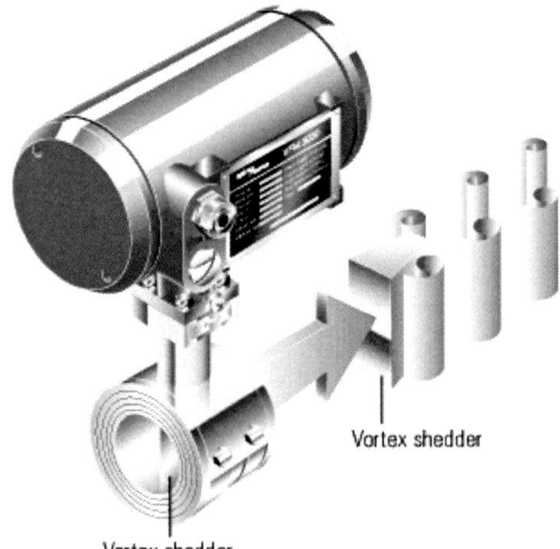

Figure 8-25. Vortex flow meter (courtesy of Spirax-Sarco).

Magnetic Flowmeter (Magmeter)

A magnetic flow meter, shown in Figure 8-26, consists of an electromagnetic coil that generates a magnetic field through the fluid flow path. Fluid flows through the magnetic field and generates a voltage which is measured by electrodes in the meter. The voltage is linearly proportional to the average fluid velocity, and the volumetric flow rate can be determined from the average fluid velocity.

There is essentially no head loss associated with a magmeter since the primary element is out of the flow stream and the flow path through the meter is essentially a straight open pipe.

The liquid must have a magnetic conductivity (>5 – 20 microsiemens/cm) in order to generate a high enough voltage to be measureable. It is ideal for applications including water (except for ultrapure water), slurries, chemicals, pharmaceuticals, foodstuffs, etc.

The accuracy of a magnetic flow meter is ±0.5 to ±1 percent, depending on application.

Figure 8-26. Magnetic flow meter (courtesy of Rosemount).

Ultrasonic Flowmeter

Ultrasonic flow meters are also linear flow meters and operate on two different principles of ultrasonic energy, the amount of time it takes for sound to travel through a fluid (time of flight), and the amount of shift in the frequency of the sound as it travels through the fluid (doppler).

Both the time of flight ultrasonic meters and the doppler ultrasonic meters use high frequency sound waves to determine the average fluid velocity across the pipeline.

The time of flight ultrasonic meter, shown in Figure 8-27, consists of two transducers that alternately transmit and receive a burst of sound energy, first in the direction of the fluid flow and then a burst of sound energy against the direction of the flow. Sound travels faster in the direction of fluid flow than against the flow, so a difference in the times of flight will occur and the fluid velocity is linearly proportional to this difference.

Time of flight meters are used in clean liquid applications where the ultrasonic sound waves will not be affected by particles within the fluid. The accuracy of a time of flight ultrasonic flow meter ranges from ±1 to ±4 percent.

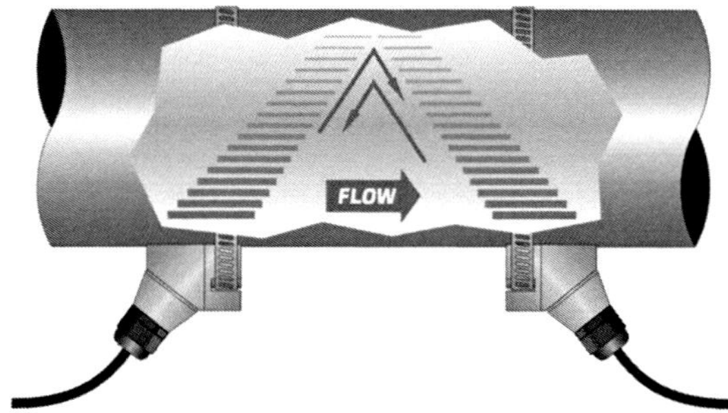

Figure 8-27. Time of flight ultrasonic flow meter (courtesy of Dynasonics).

A doppler type ultrasonic flow meter uses the fact that the frequency of a sound wave shifts as the sound bounces off a moving object. The faster the object is moving, the greater the shift in the sound frequency.

The ultrasonic flow meter in Figure 8-28 uses a shift in the frequency of the transmitted sound wave to measure the fluid velocity. Small particles in the fluid stream deflect the sound wave and shift the frequency. The difference between the transmitted frequency and the returned frequency can be used to calculate the fluid velocity.

The doppler type ultrasonic flow meter works best when the liquid has small particles or impurities within the fluid. The accuracy of a doppler type ultrasonic flow meter ranges from ±1 to ±4 percent.

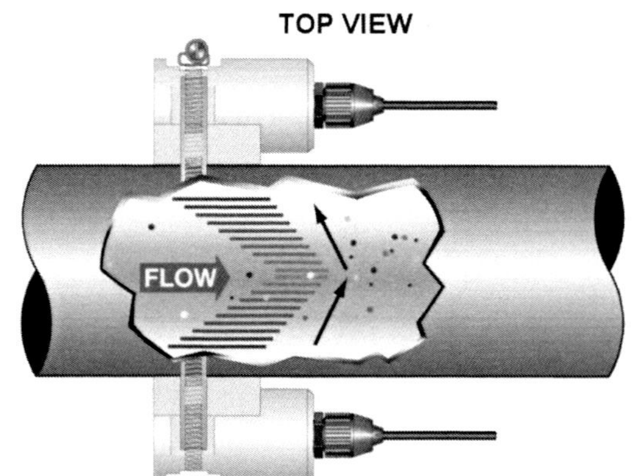

Figure 8-28. Doppler type ultrasonic flow meter (courtesy of Dynasonics).

Ultrasonic flow meters also have no head loss associated with them since the sensors are located outside the flow stream. There are also insertion ultrasonic flow meters that are mounted inside the pipeline but have a minimum amount of head loss and permanent pressure drop.

Coriolis Flowmeter

Coriolis flow meters are highly accurate flow meters that measure not only fluid velocity and volumetric flow rate, they can also measure the density and mass flow rate of the fluid as well.

The coriolis meter shown in Figure 8-29 consists of two parallel curved tubes in which the flow is split. A drive coil causes the tubes to vibrate in parallel when there is no flow through the tubes. Coriolis forces are created as the fluid flows through the curved tubes. These forces cause the tubes to twist as they vibrate.

Pickoff coils on the inlet and outlet of the flow tubes generate electrical sine waves that are out of phase due to the twisting of the tubes. The amount of phase shift between the inlet and outlet pickoff coils is proportional to the mass flow rate through the flow meter.

The coriolis flow meter is very accurate for flow rate (+/- 0.05%) and for density (+/- 0.0002 g/cc).

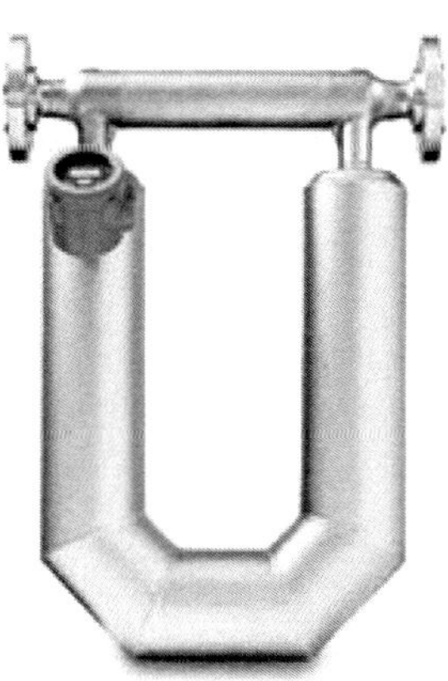

Figure 8-29. Coriolis flow meter (courtesy of Emerson Process Management).

Considerations for Selecting a Flow Meter

There are many things to consider when selecting a flow meter for any given application. The price and complexity of the meter are important. The more complex the operating principle, generally the more expensive the meter, so differential pressure meters are generally less expensive and less complex than linear meters. In addition, more complex meters are more susceptible to human error when calibrating and troubleshooting the meter.

In general, the more moving parts in the meter, the more maintenance the meter will require. For example, turbine meters have moving parts so the accuracy can drift over time. They are also very sensitive to dirt and particles in the stream.

The accuracy, turndown, and rangeability are important considerations as well. Turndown and rangeability are terms that are sometimes used interchangeably, and generally refer to the ratio of the maximum flow rate to the minimum flow rate in which the accuracy of the flow meter is within an acceptable range. For example, to measure the flow rate from a maximum of 100 gpm to a minimum of 10 gpm, the turndown or rangeability is 10 to 1.

The rangeability of differential pressure meters is more limiting than for linear meters because the pressure drop is proportional to flow rate squared. The rangeability for differential pressure meters is typically about 3:1, with a maximum up to 4:1. Linear meters can achieve a higher rangeability, typically 50:1 or as high as 80:1.

Selecting a flow meter also involves determining whether to measure the volumetric or mass flow rate of the fluid. With the exception of the corioilis and annubar flow meters, all other technologies measure volumetric flow rate. Density correction is necessary to obtain mass flow, which is often required because most often products are sold by the mass, by pounds or by molecules.

Pressure and Differential Pressure Measurement

Fluid pressure at a given point in the piping system may need to be measured and used as an input for process control. The pressure may be controlled by regulating the position of a control valve or the speed of a centrifugal pump.

Fluid pressure is measured with a pressure transmitter that can report the pressure as a gage pressure, absolute pressure, or a vacuum. A differential pressure transmitter measures the pressure at two points in a piping system and measures the difference in pressure between them.

A typical pressure transmitter (Figure 8-30) contains two modules, one for the sensor and one for the electronics. The sensor module contains a flexible isolating diaphragm to which the fluid pressure is applied. The deflection of the isolating diaphragm transmits the pressure through a silicone or inert fill fluid to a polysilicon sensing diaphragm, which then deflects to create a strain on a resistor in a Wheatstone bridge circuit. The strain changes the electrical resistance, which is converted to a digital signal. Some pressure transmitter designs use the change in electrical capacitance to relate to the change in fluid pressure.

Figure 8-30. Pressure transmitter (courtesy of Rosemount).

The electronics module of the pressure transmitter takes the digital signal from the sensor and adds correction coefficients, then linearizes the signal and converts it into an electrical DC current or voltage, then transmits it to the controller. The transmitted signal is typically a 4-20 mA electrical signal, but can also be 0 – 5 volt or 0 – 10 volt signal as well.

Differential pressure transmitters, like the one shown in Figure 8-31, use two sensing lines to measure the difference in pressure between two taps and are commonly used for flow rate and pressurized tank level measurements. Differential pressure transmitters are similar in operation to the pressure transmitter.

Figure 8-31. Differential pressure transmitter with a manifold for isolation and vent / drain valves (courtesy of Rosemount).

Liquid Level Measurement

As was mentioned in Chapter 3 on tanks and vessels, there are countless ways to measure the liquid level in a tank, and that number increases with the development of new technologies.

Direct level measurement involves a measurement of the actual liquid level from the bottom of the tank, such as with a notched dip stick, a site glass, or a float gage. Indirect level measurement involves determining the liquid level based on some property of the fluid or a property of the vapor in the space above the liquid level.

Pressure and Differential Pressure Level Measurement

A common indirect level measurement for an open tank uses a pressure transmitter as shown in Figure 8-32. For closed pressurized tanks or vessels under vacuum, a differential pressure transmitter as shown in Figures 8-33 is used. Both of these methods use the fluid density to adjust the pressure reading to units of feet of fluid, or liquid level.

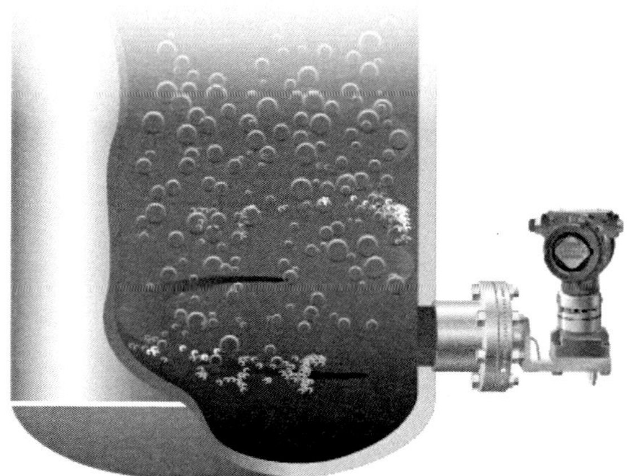

Figure 8-32. Measuring tank level with a pressure transmitter (courtesy of Rosemount).

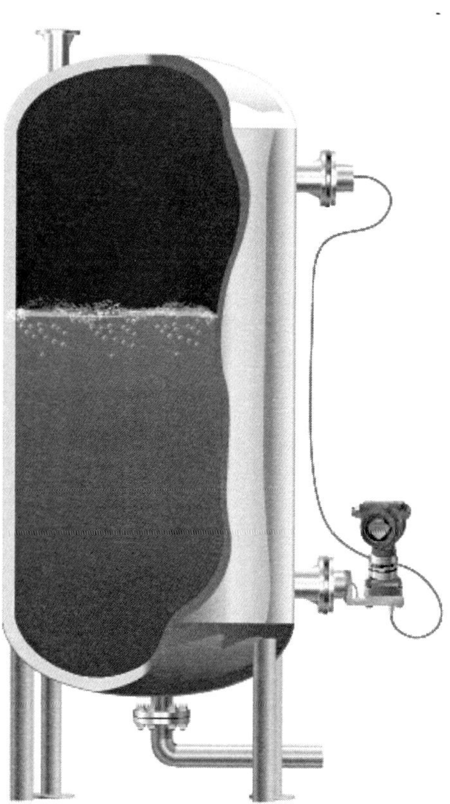

Figure 8-33. Measuring pressurized tank level with a differential pressure transmitter (courtesy of Rosemount).

Microwave Radar Level Measurement

Microwave radar is another technology that can be used to measure level of a liquid or solid in a tank. It is suitable for a wide range of temperature and pressures applications, and is unaffected by fluid properties such as density, viscosity, or the presence of dust.

A guided wave radar instrument, shown in Figure 8-34, uses microwave pulses that are sent down a probe into the liquid in the tank. Some of the signal is reflected back, and the time difference from transmitting to receiving the signal is measured and the level is derived. Guided wave radar can also be used to determine the interface level between two separate liquids in the tank.

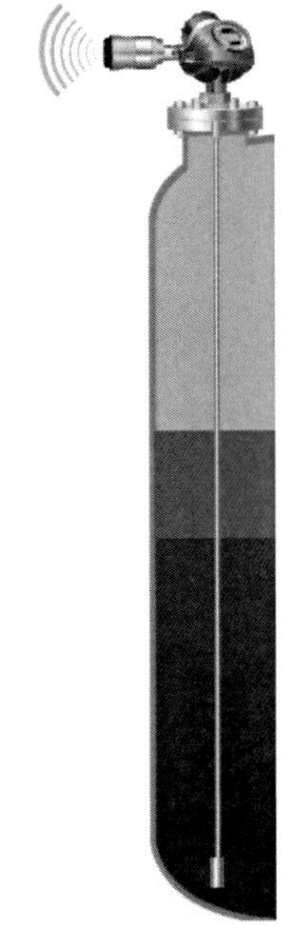

Figure 8-34. Guided wave radar (courtesy of Rosemount).

Figure 8-35. Non contacting radar (courtesy of Rosemount).

Non-contacting radar, shown in Figure 8-35, sends a microwave signal into the tank, which is reflected back from the liquid surface. The time difference or the frequency difference is used to determine the level.

Ultrasonic Level Measurement

The liquid level can also be determined by the use of ultrasonic technology. An ultrasonic level transmitter, shown in Figure 8-36, sends an ultrasonic pulse into the tank, and the time required for the pulse to bounce off the liquid surface is measured and converted into a liquid level.

The ultrasonic level measurement can be used with open tanks and reservoirs, sumps, rivers, and open channel flow.

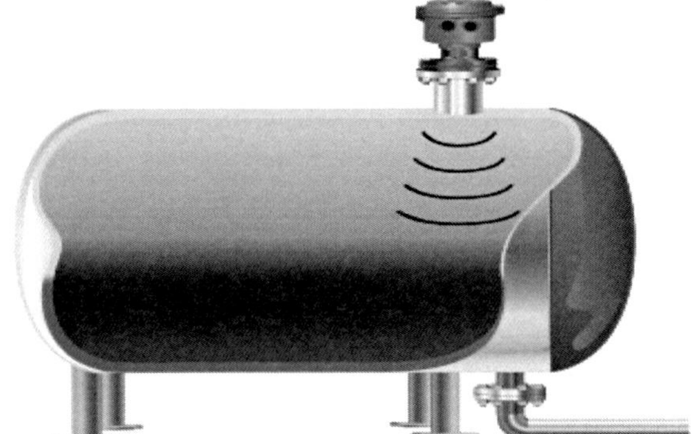

Figure 8-36. Ultrasonic level transmitter (courtesy of Rosemount).

Capacitance Level Measurement

The electrical capacitance between the two electrodes can be used to determine the liquid level in the tank. Capacitance is a measure of a material's ability to store electrical energy. The material between the two electrodes is called the dielectric and its capacitance is defined by the dielectric constant.

The capacitance level instrument, shown in Figure 8-37, can use the tank wall as one of the electrodes, called the reference electrode, and a second measurement electrode that is inserted into the tank and is submerged in the tank contents. Some installations cannot use the tank wall as the reference electrode and require two electrodes on the level instrument.

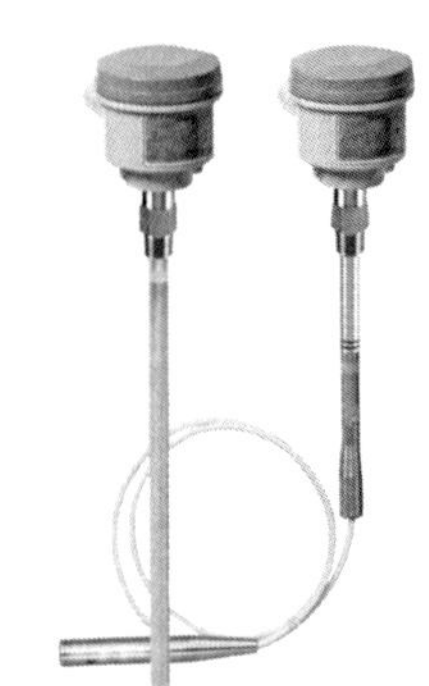

Figure 8-37. Capacitance level transmitter (courtesy of Siemens).

The contents of the tank, as well as the insulating material on the measurement electrode, make up the dielectric. The capacitance between the tank wall (or separate reference electrode) and the measurement electrode changes as the level in the tank changes the dielectric constant between the electrodes.

Capacitance level transmitters can be used in a wide variety of applications involving liquids and solids. The measurement is unaffected by gas vapors, dust, condensation, or deposits of material on the electrodes.

Gravimetric Level Measurement

Gravimetric level measurement uses load cells to measure the weight of the tank and the tank's contents. The difference between the weight of the empty tank compared to the tank at a given liquid level can be used to determine the level in the tank. The load cells are completely separated from the process fluid.

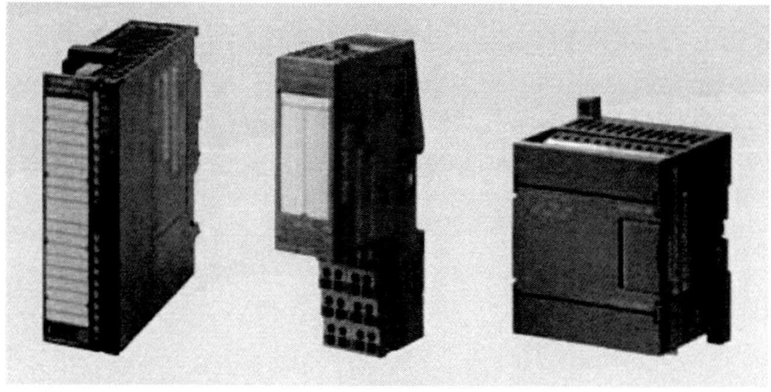

Figure 8-38. Gravimetric level measurement (courtesy of Siemens).

Laser Level Measurement

The primary element to measure the level in a tank can use laser technology to determine the level. A laser level transmitter, such as the one shown in Figure 8-39, transmits an invisible infrared light into the tank. The time it takes for the light to travel from the transmitter to the surface and back is divided by two and multiplied by the speed of light.

Figure 8-39. Laser level measurement (courtesy of K-Tek).

Nuclear Source Level Measurement

A nuclear level transmitter consists of a shielded radioisotope source attached to one side of the tank and a detector mounted on the opposite side of the tank, as shown in Figure 8-40. Gamma rays emitted from the source travel through the tank wall, the material in the tank, the opposite tank wall, and to the detector. The amount of radiation that reaches the detector will depend on the level in the tank.

Because the source and detector are located on the outside of the tank, the measurement is not affected by high process temperatures or pressures, corrosive or viscous fluids, abrasive material, or agitation.

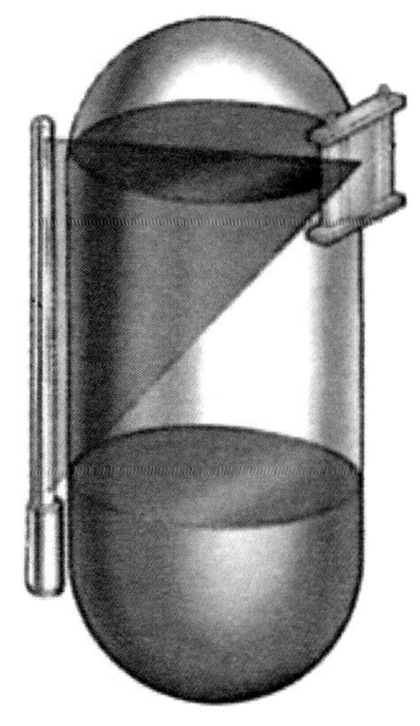

Figure 8-40. Nuclear source level measurement (courtesy of Berthold Technologies).

Temperature Measurement

The temperature of a fluid can be measured using the electrical properties of metals that vary linearly with temperature. There are two major types of temperature sensors based on what electrical property is used to convert the measured fluid temperature into an electrical signal for calibrating the temperature scale. The resistance of some metals vary linearly with the temperature of the metal over a certain range.

Temperature sensors that use this property are called Resistance Temperature Detectors (RTDs).

Another electrical property that can be used for measuring temperature is the linear relationship between the amount of voltage generated when two dissimilar metals are joined and the temperature of the junction of those metals. These temperature sensors are called Thermocouples (TC).

*Resistance Temperature Detectors (*RTDs)

Resistance Temperature Detectors (RTDs) use the fact that the electrical resistance of certain metals vary linearly with the temperature of the metal. This allows the use of a small filament made of this metal to be included as one of the resistance legs of a Wheatstone bridge circuit, where the varying RTD resistance can then be converted into an electrical current that is linearly proportional to the temperature of the measuring resistor.

The two most common metals used for the measuring resistor of the RTD are platinum (Pt) and nickel (Ni). The temperature range for a platinum RTD is -328 to +1,562 °F. Nickel RTDs can operate at temperatures from -76 to 302 °F.

The RTD shown in Figure 8-41 consists of a measuring element made of a platinum or nickel resistor that is embedded in ceramic or glass. This ceramic or glass rod is encased in a measuring insert that is spring mounted to the connection head. The measuring insert is further protected by placing it into a protective tube, or thermowell, that is mounted on the pipe or tank wall.

The thermowell can be screwed in, welded, or flanged, as shown in Figure 8-42, depending on the application.

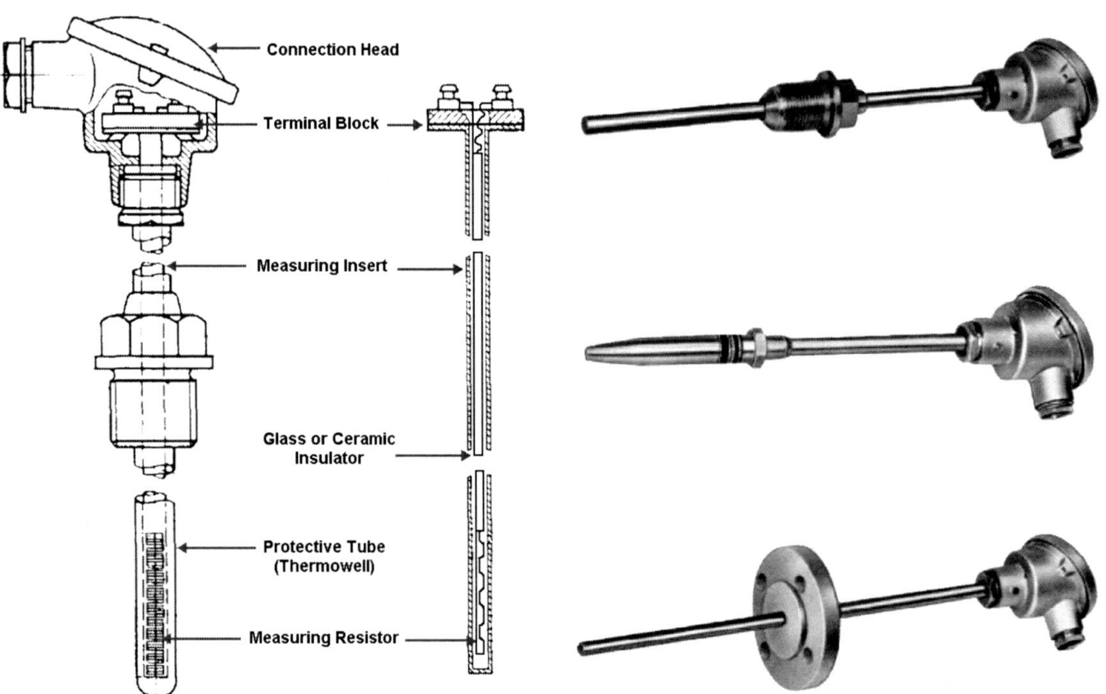

Figure 8-41. Components of a Resistance Temperature Detector (courtesy of Siemens).

Figure 8-42. Resistance Temperature Detectors (RTDs). Screw in (top), welded (middle), and flanged (bottom) (courtesy of Siemens).

Thermocouples

Thermocouples consist of a sensor element formed by the junction of two conductors made of dissimilar metals or metal alloys that are soldered or welded together at one end. The conductors are separated and insulated from each other along the length of the measuring insert by ceramic or glass insulating beads. The thermocouple is protected with a metal tube.

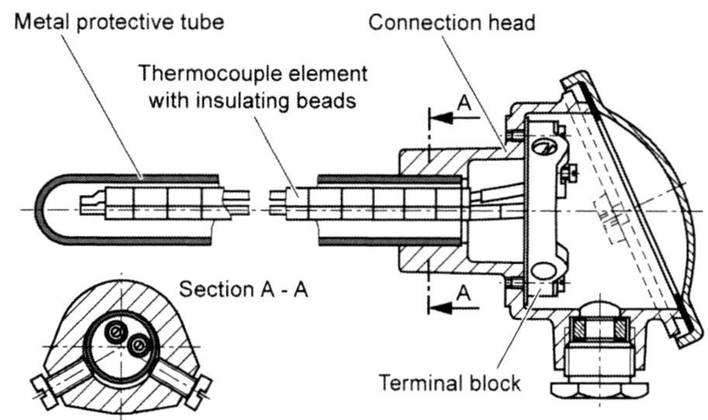

Figure 8-43. Components of a Thermocouple (courtesy of Siemens).

Thermocouples operate on the fact that when two dissimilar metals are joined together, they produce a low level voltage that is proportional to the temperature difference between the junction and the free ends. The magnitude of this voltage depends on the magnitude of the temperature difference and the materials used for the two conductors. The free end must be connected to a reference (cold) junction at a constant known temperature.

The material used for the conductors of the thermocouple depends on the range of temperatures to be measured and the application, as shown in Table 8-1.

Table 8-1: Thermocouple types, temperature range, material of construction, and application notes.

Thermocouple Type	Temperature Range	Material	Notes
Type B	32 to 3,308 °F	Pt30Rh – Pt6Rh (Platinum 30% Rodium – Platinum 6% Rhodium)	High temperature measurements up to 3,200 °F
Type C *	32 to 4,172 °F	W5Re - W26Re Tungsten 5% Rhenium – Tungsten 26% Rhenium	Vacuum furnaces, do not use in presence of oxygen above 500°F
Type D *	32 to 4,172 °F	W3Re – W25Re Tungsten 3% Rhenium – Tungsten 25% Rhenium	Very high temperature use
Type E	-328 to +1,832 °F	NiCr – CuNi (Chromel – Constantan)	Low temperature use (cryogenic), non-magnetic
Type G *	32 – 4,200 °F	W – W26Re Tungsten – Tungsten 26% Rhenium	Very high temperature use
Type J	-346 to +2,192 °F	Fe – CuNi (Iron – Constantan)	Older equipment
Type K	-382 to +2,498 °F	NiCr – Ni (Chromel – Alumel)	General purpose, low cost, most commonly used
Type L *	-328 to +1,652 °F	Fe - CuNi	Obsolete
Type M *	-58 – 2,570 °F	Ni – Ni18Mo	
Type N	-328 to +2,372 °F	NiCrSi – NiSi (Nicrosil – Nisil)	High temperature measurements without the cost of platinum
Type P *	32 – 2,550 °F	Platinel II – Platinel II	Stable but expensive substitute for Type K & N
Type R	-58 to +3,200 °F	Pt13Rh – Pt (Platinum 13 % Rhodium - Platinum)	High cost, high temperatures up to 2,900°F
Type S	-58 to +3,200 °F	Pt10Rh – Pt (Platinum 10% Rhodium - Platinum)	High cost, high temperatures up to 2,900°F
Type T	-328 to +752 °F	Cu - CuNi	Low and cryogenic temperatures
Type U *	-328 to +1112 °F	Cu - CuNi	Obsolete

* Not recognized by ANSI

Al = Aluminum, Cr = Chromium, Cu = Copper, Mg = Magnesium, Mo = Molybdenum, Ni = Nickel, Pt = Platinum, Re = Rhenium, Rh = Rhodium, Si = Silicon, W = Tungsten

Thermowells

Thermowells are tube fittings used to protect the thermocouple or RTD temperature measuring element from the environmental conditions posed by the working fluid. The thermowell, shown in Figure 8-44, is a hollow straight or tapered tube, made of a material compatible with the working fluid, and can be stellited, PTFE lined, or coated with a protective cladding like teflon or tantaline.

The material used for the thermowell must be able to withstand the temperature, pressure, and chemical properties of the working fluid. Common thermowell material include 304 and 316 stainless steel, monel, inconel, hasteloy, ceramic, nickel, tantelum, and wrought iron, depending on the application.

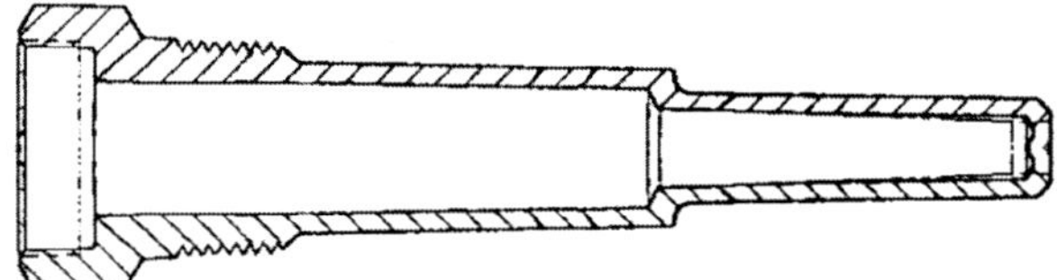

Figure 8-44. Screw in type thermowell.

The thermowell is inserted into the fluid and mounted to the pipe or tank wall by welding, a flanged connection, or by screwing in. It becomes a pressure boundary for the working fluid.

It is important that the thermocouple or RTD make contact with the bottom of the thermowell so that the fluid temperature is being measured more directly and not the air gap in the thermowell.

Analytical Measurement

A process may have other instrumentation to measure various properties of the fluid in the process, depending on the application. These analytical measurements can also be used in a process control loop as the primary element.

Dedicated analyzers are used to measure common analytical properties such as pH, conductivity, and density. Other properties such as the turbidity, color, or opacity of the fluid may also be measured and controlled. Properties of gases such as percent oxygen, ppm carbon monoxide, or ppm sulfur dioxide may also be measured and controlled. Many of these dedicated analyzers use a 4-20 mA signal to transmit the measured value to the controller.

Gas chromatograph analyzers are complex devices that may use sample conditioning to prepare the gas sample for analysis. These may be small in size or large enough to require analyzer shelters, often using datalinks and protocols to pass data from the analyzer to the distributed control system (DCS).

Speed and Vibration Measurements

Speed and vibration sensors play a very important role in the control and protection of rotating machinery, particularly large turbines and compressors. A speed and vibration system consists of speed sensors connected to the machine shaft and vibration sensors mounted on the bearing housing. These sensors send signals to a control and protection microprocessor, which often communicates to the distributed control system.

An independent over-speed protection device may also be provided with dedicated speed probes connected to the machine shaft that transmit their measurements directly to a protection microprocessor. The protection microprocessor, often triple modular redundant, contains the routine to start up and protect the rotating machine.

Final Control Elements

The final control element is the device that is adjusted to maintain the measured value in the process at the desired value. Control valves, dampers, and variable speed drives are typical final control elements used in a process control loop.

Control valves

As discussed in Chapter 7, control valves have an inherent characteristic curve that depends on the flow coefficient profile over the range of valve travel, with typical characteristics being equal percentage, linear, or a modified curve. The inherent characteristic is determined by the type of valve and the shape and design of the seat and plug in the valve.

All components of a control loop have inherent characteristics, which define the relationship between the inlet and outlet of each component. The process itself also has an inherent characteristic. A key to selecting a good valve for a given process is to choose one with the right inherent characteristics to make the entire loop and process as close to linear as possible over the range of control for the valve.

The majority of control valves have an equal percentage characteristic because they are installed in a piping system with a pump or compressor with a decreasing pressure gain with an increasing flow rate. The equal percentage characteristic of the control valve makes the complete loop and process relationship (the installed characteristic) nearly linear, which makes process control the most effective.

Positioners

A control valve positioner is a valve stem position controller that measures the position of the valve stem using a mechanical linkage or magnetic coupling.

The positioner receives a signal from the loop controller in the form of a pneumatic or electrical signal, which is the set point for the positioner. The positioner then adjusts the air pressure to the valve actuator to move the valve to the desired position determined by the loop controller.

Pneumatic positioners, shown on the left in Figure 8-45, use air pressure as the input from the loop controller and as the output to the valve actuator.

Figure 8-45. Pneumatic positioner (left) and electropneumatic positioner (right) (courtesy of Emerson Process Management).

Electro-pneumatic positioners, shown on the right of Figure 8-45, receive a 4 – 20 mA signal from the loop controller and have an installed current to pneumatic (I/P) transducer to convert the current signal to an air signal to adjust the air pressure to the valve actuator.

Intelligent or smart positioners, shown in Figure 8-46, are microprocessor based devices that receive the 4 – 20 mA signal from the loop controller and use electronics to adjust the air pressure to the actuator. Smart positioners can incorporate many features including automatic commissioning, manual valve position control at the positioner, self-diagnostic tools, and valve diagnostic communication back to the distributed control system.

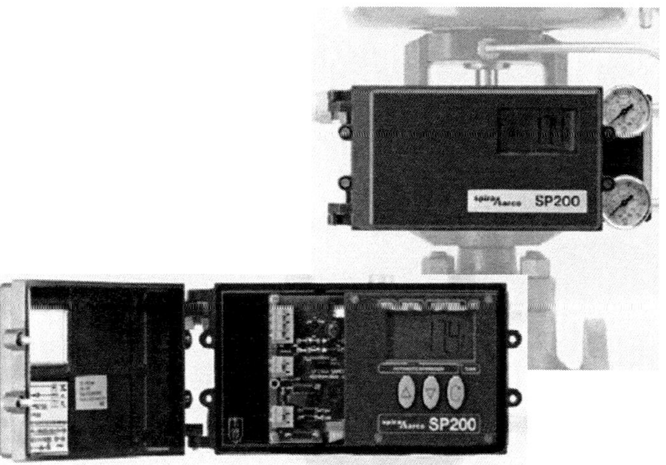

Figure 8-46. Intelligent (smart) positioner (courtesy of Spirax Sarco).

Transducers (I/P)

Transducers are devices that convert a signal from one form of energy to another and are used when components in a control loop use different forms of energy for a control signal. For example, a current to pneumatic transducer (I/P) converts a 4 – 20 mA signal to a 3 – 15 psig pneumatic air signal. The I/P is essentially a pressure regulator that maintains a linear relationship between the current and pnuematic signals.

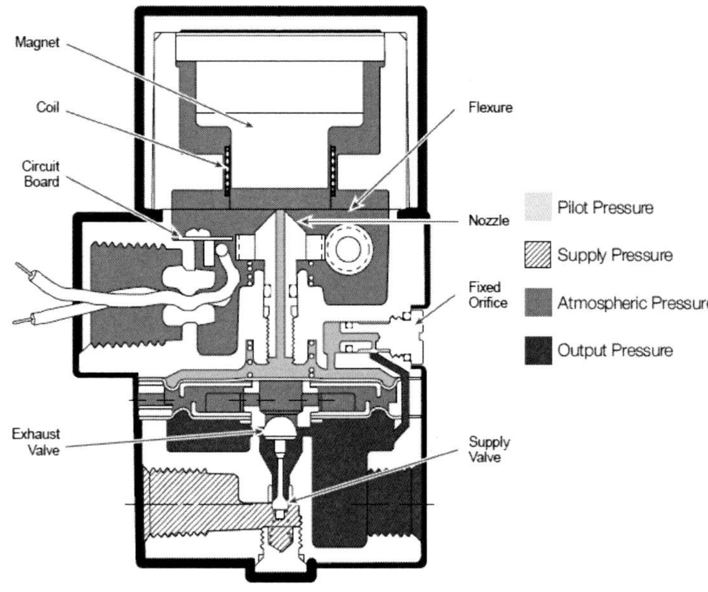

Figure 8-47. Current to pneumatic transducer (courtesy of Control Air Inc.).

The cutaway drawing in Figure 8-47 shows the main components of an I/P. An electrical coil is suspended in a magnetic field by a flexure. The amount of current flowing through the coil generates axial movement of the coil and flexure, which holds the position of the flexure in relation to the nozzle. The distance between the flexure and nozzle adjusts the back pressure, or pilot pressure, to adjust the position of the supply and exhaust valve and regulate the output pressure.

Controllers

The controller is the component in the control loop that responds to a disturbance in the process by comparing the measured value from the primary element to an operator entered set point. The controller then calculates and sends a control output to the final control element to adjust its position, if required, to maintain the measured value at set point.

Figure 8-48. Pneumatic controller (courtesy of Foxboro).

Controllers have changed in size and complexity as technology has improved over time. Pneumatic controllers (Figure 8-48) use air signals for the inputs and outputs to the controller. Electronic controllers such as Programmable Logic Controllers (PLCs) (see Figure 8-12) and Single Loop Controllers (SLCs) (Figure 8-49) use electrical signals for inputs and outputs. Distributed Control Systems (DCS) are computer-based algorithms programmed to perform the functions of the controller. The algorithms are standardized and configurable to allow the use of various control schemes.

Controllers can be configured as open loop or closed loop controllers. Open loop controllers have no feedback of the measured process variable back to the controller. Closed loop controllers use negative feedback of the process variable back to the controller.

Figure 8-49. Single loop electronic controller (courtesy of Foxboro).

Controller Algorithm

There is a basic mathematical relationship that determines how a typical controller responds to an error between the measured value and the set point, as shown in the block diagram in Figure 8-50.

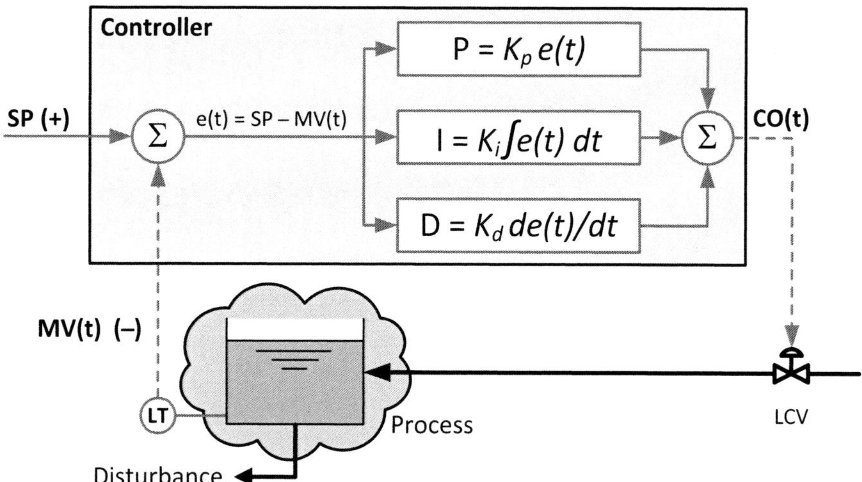

Figure 8-50. Block diagram of the Proportional - Integral - Derivative controller.

Equation 8-1 is the generalized mathematical relationship for a Proportional - Integral - Derivative (PID) controller. Many controllers respond to some, or all, of these mathematical relationships, or can be configured to use just the actions needed for a particular application.

$$CO(t) = CO_0 + K_p e(t) + K_i \int e(t)\,dt + K_d \frac{d}{dt} e(t) \qquad \textit{Equation 8-1}$$

The first thing the controller does is compare the measured value at a given time (MV(t)) to its set point (SP) to determine the magnitude of the error between the two at that point in time (e(t)). The accumulation of error over time (the integral of the error) and/or the rate of change of the error (the derivative of the error) may also be included in the controller response.

The magnitude, integral, and derivative of the error are all multiplied by proportional, integral, and derivative constants respectively and added together to produce a controller output (CO) that adjusts the final control element to maintain the measured value at set point.

Controller Actions

Controller action refers to the proportional, integral, and derivative response of a controller to an error between the measured value and set point.

Proportional action is analogous to *how much* the measured value is off of the set point. Integral action is analogous to *how long* the measure value has been off of the setpoint, and derivative action is analogous to *how fast* the measured value is going away from or toward the set point.

Controllers can be configured with proportional action only, but this will result in a permanent deviation from the set point, called an offset, after the controller has responded to a disturbance and steady state conditions are achieved. They can also be configured with proportional and integral action (PI), proportional and derivative action (PD), or proportional, integral, and derivative action (PID), depending on the application.

Proportional action only is used when a small offset from the set point has no impact on the process.

PI control is used when no offset can be tolerated, where noise (temporary error readings that do not reflect the true process variable condition) may be present, and where excessive dead time (time after a disturbance before control action takes place) is not a problem.

PID control is used in processes when no offset can be tolerated, no noise is present, and when dead time is an issue. Any time derivative action is used, the controller may be susceptible to rapid changes in the output due to spikes in the measured value or if the controller is not tuned properly.

In general, flow, level, and pressure controllers are typically configured for proportional only or proportional - integral action. Analytical controllers, such as pH or conductivity controllers, are typically proportional or proportional - integral action, but rarely include derivative action. Temperature controllers are good applications for using derivative action in addition to proportional or proportional - integral action.

Controller Tuning

Controllers must be tuned to obtain the proper response to a disturbance and quickly bring the measured value back to set point with a minimal amount of overshoot, undershoot, or oscillations. Tuning a control loop requires an understanding of the dynamic behavior of the loop components as well as the process dynamics.

Tuning determines the proportional, integral, and derivative constants of the P-I-D equation in order to minimize the variation between the set point and measured value. There are various methods used to determine the tuning constants.

The Trial and Error method consists of inputting the tuning constants, introducing an error (typically by changing the set point), then watching the response. If the response is not desirable, the constants are adjusted and the process repeated until the response is acceptable.

The Process Reaction Curve method consists of making a step change in the set point and plotting the response of the measured value until it reaches the new set point. Values are taken from the curve and the tuning constants calculated for the controller.

The Ziegler-Nichols and Cohen-Coon methods are the most common methods but are more complex. They involve making a step change in the set point while in automatic mode of the controller, and placing the controller in manual and making a step change in the controller output. The response is measured and the

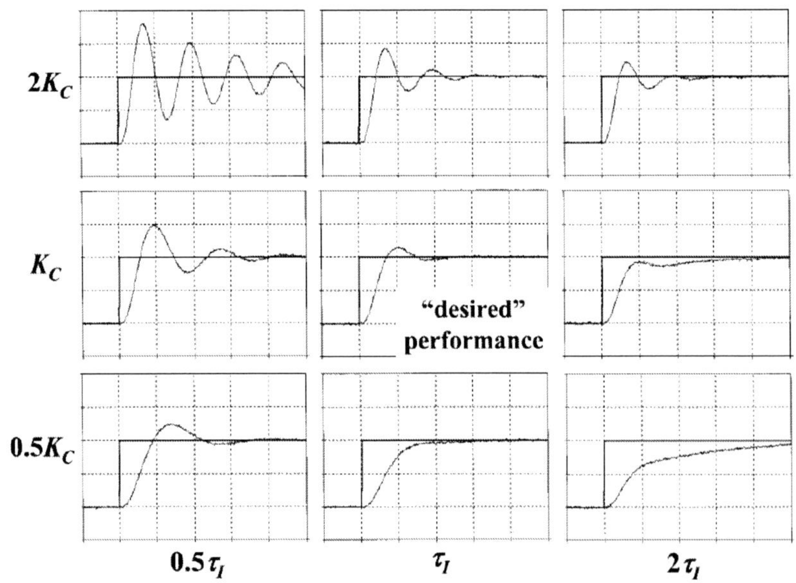

Figure 8-51. P-I controller tuning map (courtesy of Control Station, Inc).

tuning constants calculated based on the response.

The P-I controller tuning map shown in Figure 8-51 shows various responses that can be obtained with different values for the proportional and integral tuning constants. The desired performance of the graph in the center of the P-I tuning map shows the response with just the right amount of proportional action (K_C) and integral action (τ_I). With an increase in the set point, the measured value should quickly start responding and have a small overshoot of the new set point, an even smaller undershoot, and then a quick return to the new set point.

The response shown on the upper left graph in Figure 8-51 results from having double the correct amount of proportional action ($2\ K_C$) and only half the correct amount of integral action ($0.5\ \tau_I$). These incorrect tuning constants result in numerous oscillations of the measured value with a gradual converging to the set point.

If the proportional constant is too low ($0.5\ K_C$) and the integral constant is too high ($2\ \tau_I$), the response shown on the graph in the lower right hand corner of Figure 8-51 would result. This sluggish performance causes the measured value to slowly respond and gradually drift up to the new set point.

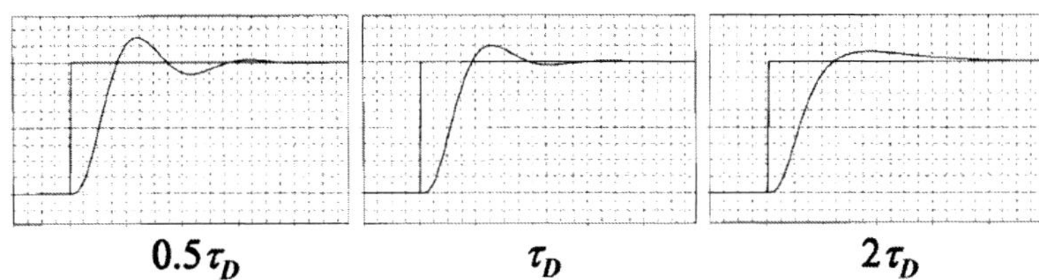

Figure 8-52. P-I-D controller tuning map (courtesy of Control Station, Inc.).

Figure 8-52 shows the PID tuning maps with derivative action added to the controller output. The center graph is the ideal response with just the right amount of derivative action added (τ_D): a rapid increase in the measured value, a little over-shoot of the set point followed by a smaller under-shoot, then a rapid return to the set point. Too little derivative action ($0.5\ \tau_D$) results in oscillations with larger over-shoots and under-shoots and a gradual converging to the set point, as shown on the left-hand graph of Figure 8-52. Too much derivative action ($2\ \tau_D$) results in a long time to reach set point, followed by a small overshoot and a gradual return to set point, as shown on the right-hand graph of Figure 8-52.

Tuning a controller can be a complex iterative process that should be performed by properly trained personnel. Many modern distributed control systems incorporate an automatic loop tuner feature that continuously monitors the loop controller performance and makes adjustments to the P-I-D tuning constants. These automatic tuners are becoming more robust and reliable.

Control Methods

Various control methods can be implemented to obtain a desired response from a controller to maintain the measured value at the set point. Which control method is implemented depends on the application, the acceptable level of variability, and the cost of implementing the control method.

The most common control methods include:

- On / off control
- Manual control (open loop)
- Automatic control (feedback)
- Feed forward control
- Cascade control
- Split range control
- Ratio control

On / Off Control

On / off control is a method in which a process measurement triggers a control action at an upper and lower control limit to either fully open or close the final control element, or turn it on or off. This method does not maintain a single set point, but instead lets the measured value oscillate between the control limits, as shown in Figure 8-53. In order to reduce the variability of the measured value, the range of the control limits must be narrowed, resulting in a more frequent cycling of the control element (pump, valve).

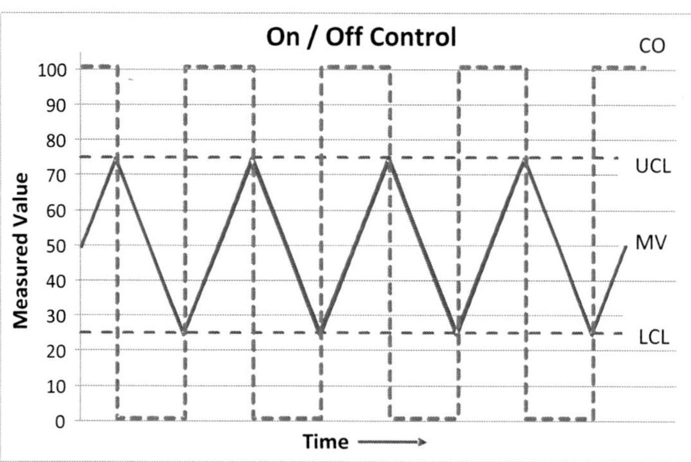

Figure 8-53. On / Off control method.

Applications where on / off control may be implemented include day tank level control, room temperature control, or air receiver pressure control.

Manual Control (Open Loop)

Manual control is a very simple, low cost control method in which an operator adjusts the final control element based on observing the system parameter and determining if the value is above or below the desired value.

For example, the tank level control method shown in Figure 8-54 shows an operator manually adjusting the position of a tank fill valve based on the level observed in the site glass.

Figure 8-54. Manual control method in which an operator adjusts the position of a tank fill valve.

An automatic controller can also be placed into the manual control mode in which the operator sets the controller output to place the final control element at the desired position.

Because there is no automatic adjustment to compensate for a disturbance in the process, the variability of the system parameter will be much higher.

Another disadvantage is that manual control requires constant operator attention to the process. Considering the large number of process controls the operator of a modern industrial plant is required to monitor, manual control is impractical except for a few steady state processes.

Automatic Control (Feed Back)

Automatic control uses feedback from a measured variable in a process to calculate the deviation from the desired set point, then determine the controller output to adjust the final control element to eliminate the error. Automatic control implements the P-I-D controller action to automatically respond to a disturbance that affects the process.

The automatic tank level control method shown in Figure 8-55 is an example where a process parameter (the tank level) is measured and transmitted to the controller. The controller compares the actual level to the set point and calculates a controller output that is transmitter via the I/P to adjust the final control element (the level control valve) to maintain the level at set point.

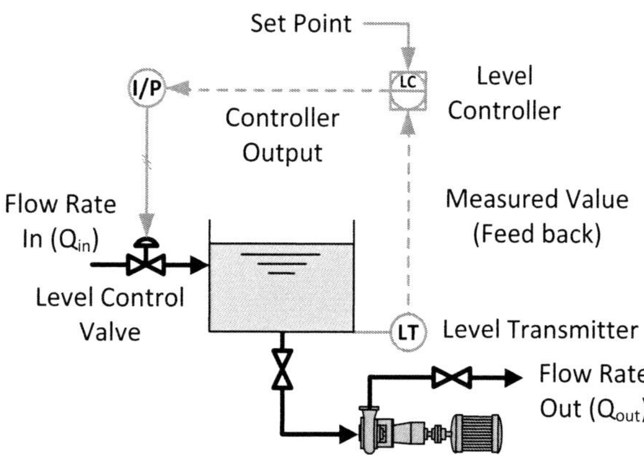

Figure 8-55. Automatic control method in which feed back from the process is used to automatically adjusts the position of a tank fill valve.

Automatic control reduces the variability in the measured value compared to the manual control method, but there is additional cost for the instrumentation to implement automatic control. In addition, it will require tuning to ensure the proper controller response to a disturbance to the process (a change in the flow rate out of the tank, for example).

Feed Forward Control

Feed forward control uses the measurement of a system parameter that is known to impact the measured process variable to cause the controller to adjust its output before an actual change in the measured value is detected. Feed forward attempts to prevent an error between the measured value and the set point, rather than just correct the error after it happens, resulting in a much more stable control of the process.

In the level control scheme shown in Figure 8-56, the flow rate out of the tank will have a direct impact on the tank level. If the flow rate is measured and transmitted to the level controller, this would be a "feed forward" signal to the controller.

When a change in flow rate from the pump is detected, the feed forward signal causes the controller output to start adjusting before the change in level is actually measured.

Because of the additional instrumentation required, there is increased complexity and expense with feed forward control.

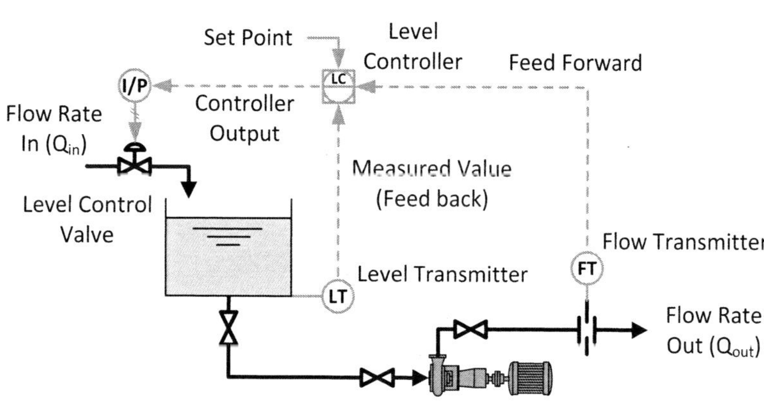

Figure 8-56. Feed forward control method uses the measurement of a different parameter (flow rate) that is known to affect the measured process variable (tank level).

Cascade Control

Cascade control is a complex control method in which the controller output of one controller become the set point of a second controller. The 2 - element steam drum level control method shown in Figure 8-57 is an example of a cascade control method.

The steam drum level is measured and tranmitted as feed back to the level controller, which calculates its controller output based on the deviation of the measured level from the set point. The level controller output is calibrated in units for the feed water flow, and transmitted to the flow controller as its set point.

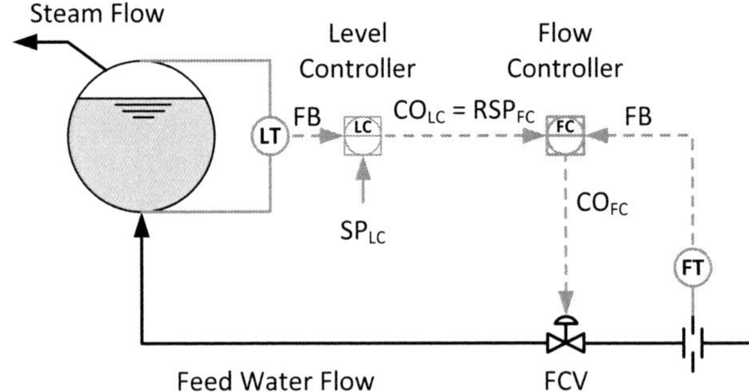

Figure 8-57. Cascade control method in which the output from one controller (level controller) becomes the set point for a second controller (flow controller).

The feed water flow is also measured and transmitted to the flow controller, where it is compared to the set point established by the level controller. The output of the feed water flow controller adjusts the position of the feed water flow control valve.

Cascade control responds more quickly to disturbances, resulting in reduced process variability. Because of the quick response, cascade control is particularly useful for systems with a lot of dead time. However, cascade control requires additional instrumentation, and because of the complexity, the tuning of the individual controllers is more difficult.

If the steam flow from the drum is measured and sent to the level controller, this would be a feed forward input into the cascade control scheme. That is known as a 3-element steam drum level control method.

Split Range Control

A split range control method uses one controller to adjust the position of two or more final control elements.

For example, if there were two sources of water to a tank, as shown in Figure 8-58, one level controller can be used to adjust the position of both level control valves.

Split range control can be achieved by scaling a portion of the output of the controller to the full stroke of one valve, and the remaining portion of the output to the full range of the second valve.

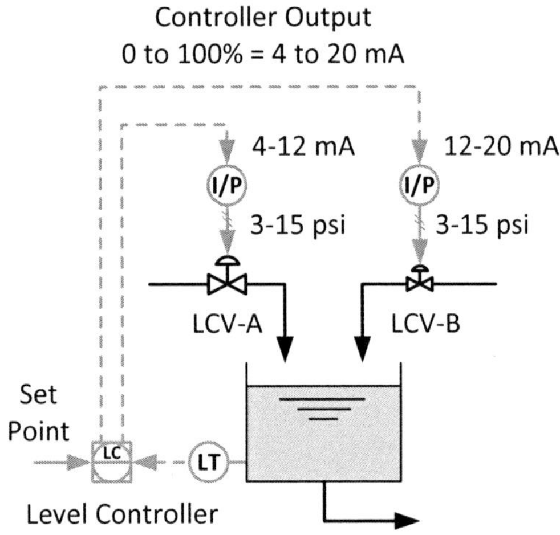

Figure 8-58. Split range control method in which the output from one controller adjusts the position of two control valves.

This scaling can occur in the calibration of the transducers (I/Ps) such that a controller output of 4-12 mA results in the full range of air pressure from 3 to 15 psi for the I/P that regulates the travel of Valve A from 0 to 100% open. The I/P for Valve B can be calibrated such that a controller output of 12-20 mA results in changing the pneumatic pressure from 3 to 15 psi to control the position of Valve B from 0 to 100% open. This is shown graphically in Figure 8-59.

This split range control method causes Valve A to open first while Valve B remains closed. When Valve A is 100% open (at 50% controller output, or at 12 mA), Valve B will then start to open to control the tank level.

The range of scaling for the controller output can be user defined. For example, Valve A can be programmed for a controller output from 0 to 75%, and Valve B be opened from a controller output of 75 to 100%.

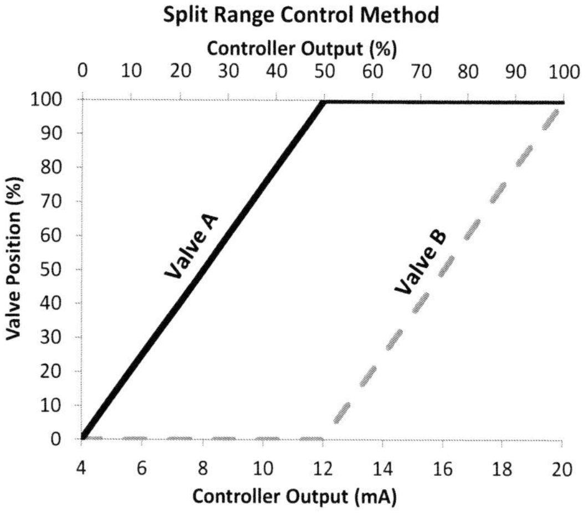

Figure 8-59. Graph of the controller output vs. the valve positions for a split range control of two control valves.

Ratio Control

Ratio control is used to automatically adjust one flow rate based on the value of another flow rate and the desired ratio between the two.

Figure 8-60 shows the flow of two fluids into a mixer. The primary flow from Source A is measured and may or may not be controlled. If it is uncontrolled, it is sometimes referred to as a "wild flow".

If the primary flow is controlled, the measured flow rate is transmitted to the primary flow controller which controls FCV - A. In addition, the measured flow rate is transmitted to the ratio controller, which has the desired ratio as the set point. The ratio controller output is then the remote set point (RSP) for the secondary flow controller that adjusts FCV-B.

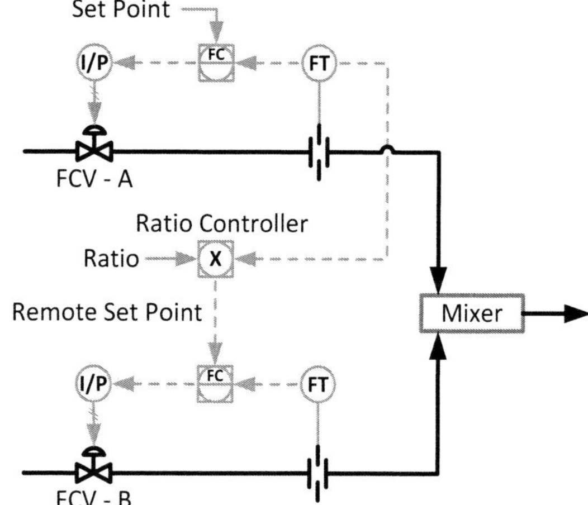

Figure 8-60. Ratio control method.

The ratio controller function may be combined with the secondary flow controller, with a fixed or a user-entered ratio programmed into the controller.

Applications for a ratio controller include the control of various chemical flow rates, mixing of several ingredients, and air / fuel flow control for boiler combustion control.

Chapter Nine

Processes and Process Equipment

Piping systems exist to transport mass and energy to do work, transfer energy, or make a product. In order to do this, piping systems connect together a variety of processes in different combinations to achieve specific functions in turning incoming raw materials into intermediate or finished products.

The mathematics describing some processes may be easily understood and will be presented in this chapter, but the mathematics behind other processes may have many variables which require complex solutions.

It's important to understand the key concepts about a process and the unique equipment designed to carry out the process in order to understand the overall hydraulic performance of the equipment in the piping system.

Processes fall into 3 broad categories: momentum transfer processes which include fluid flow, sedimentation, and mixing; heat transfer processes such as heating, cooling, drying, evaporation, and distillation; and mass transfer processes like distillation, absorption, extraction, separation, and leaching.

Momentum Transfer

As discussed in Chapter 2, momentum is a property a fluid has due to its mass and velocity, and has both a magnitude and direction. Momentum transfer involves not only the transport of a fluid (mass) from one location to another, but also a change in the direction of flow of the fluid.

The conservation of momentum applies to the flow of fluid in a pipe line. When the momentum changes, a force is exerted on the internal surface of the pipe or component wall or on a wetted part within the component.

Types of Momentum Transfer Processes

Momemtum transfer processes occur in moving fluids and includes processes such as fluid flow, sedimentation, and mixing. Many of the concepts discussed in the previous chapters of this book involve momentum transfer, including:

- Measuring a fluid's pressure as a function of depth
- Head loss
- Pump head
- Measuring fluid pressure and flow rate

Momentum Transfer Equipment

The typical open piping system shown in Figure 9-1 contains many of the the equipment involved in momentum transfer, including the pipe lines, valves, fittings, pumps, and tank & vessels.

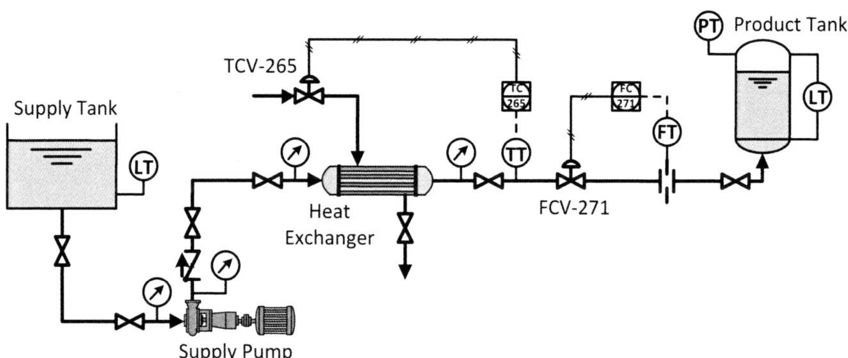

Figure 9-1. Piping system components involved in mass transfer processes.

Heat Transfer

Heat transfer is another key process that occurs in piping systems. Heat is a measure of the amount of thermal energy in a substance based on its temperature and to some degree on its pressure. Heat is designated with the letter Q in the context of heat transfer and is in units of British Thermal Unit (BTU).

Heat transfer is the transit of thermal energy from a point of higher temperature to a point of lower temperature. Heat transfer is measured in units of British Thermal Unit per hour (BTU/hr).

Types of Heat Transfer Mechanisms

Heat can be transferred by one of three mechanisms: conduction, convection, or radiation.

Conduction

In conduction, heat is transferred through a solid, liquid, or gas by the collision of molecules at a high energy state and adjacent molecules at a lower energy state, due to a temperature difference. An example of conduction heat transfer is the transfer of heat through the walls of a heat exchanger tube.

Convection

Convection is the transfer of energy by the flow of a liquid or gas resulting in the mixing of warmer portions with cooler portions of the fluid. It can also occur as the result of a liquid or gas flowing past a solid surface at a different temperature than the fluid.

Forced convection occurs when hydraulic energy must be added to cause the fluid to flow over the solid surface, such as with a pump or fan causing the flow of fluid through a heat exchanger.

Natural convection occurs as a result of a difference in fluid densities caused by a difference in fluid temperatures. Natural convection occurs in an industrial boiler and causes the feedwater to flow from the steam drum to the mud drum then back up to the steam drum as it is heated and changes phase from a liquid to a steam vapor.

Radiation

Radiation is the transfer of energy through a gas or space by electromagnetic waves due just to the temperature of a surface. Radiation occurs in the transfer of heat from the sun to the earth.

Types of Heat Transfer Processes

The mechanisms for heat transfer (conduction, convection, and radiation) can be applied to several types of heat transfer processes depending on the application and the intended result on the fluids in the system.

Heating and Cooling

Heating and cooling is the addition or removal of heat to raise or lower a fluid's temperature without creating a phase change. The fluids may be liquids such as lube oil and water in a lube oil cooler application, or they may be gases such as steam being heated in a boiler superheater or cooling air in an air handling unit.

Drying

Drying occurs when heat is added to remove the liquid from a solid material. An air dryer used to reduce the percent moisture in the production of paper in the pulp and paper industry is a good example .

Evaporation

Evaporation is the addition of heat to a liquid to change phase to a vapor to reduce the amount of liquid content and increase the percent solids of the solution. Multiple Effect Evaporators (MEEs), for example, are used in the production of sugar, in water desalination, and in the chemical recovery plant of a paper mill.

Boiling

Boiling adds heat to a liquid in order to cause a phase change to a vapor. Industrial steam boilers heat water to make steam to efficiently transfer energy to various users throughout a plant.

Condensation

Condensation is the cooling of a vapor to cause a phase change to liquid. Condensers are used to condense steam turbine generator exhaust in electrical power generation applications, for example.

Heat Transfer Equations

Consider the heat exchanger shown in Figure 9-2 that is used to cool hot oil using a supply of cold water. The rate of the water flow ($Q_{Water\ Out}$) through the heat exchanger is controlled by the oil outlet temperature ($T_{Oil\ Out}$). The rate of heat transfer out of the oil equals the rate of heat transfer into the water (neglecting heat losses from the heat exhanger to the surrounding environment).

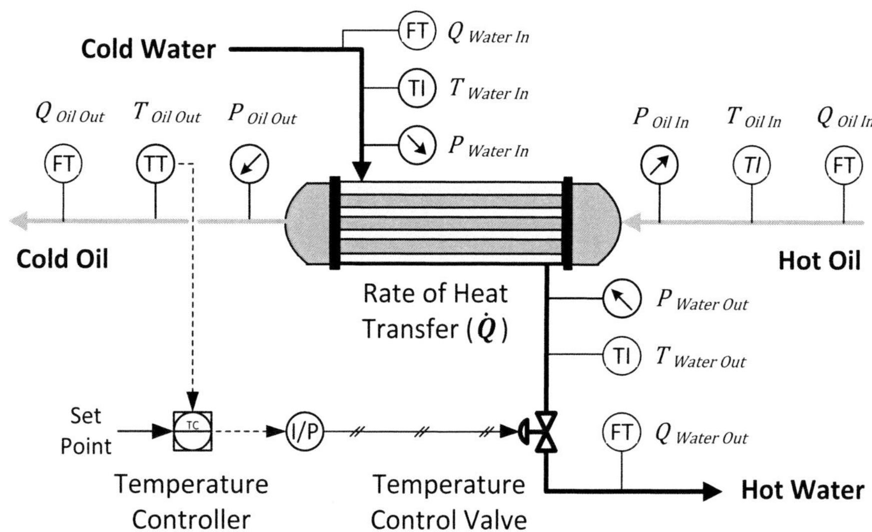

Figure 9-2. Flow diagram of a hot oil cooler.

There are several equations that can be used to quantify the amount of heat transferred from the oil to the water. Equation 9-1 applies for liquids in which no phase change occurs, and can be applied to the oil flow and the water flow.

$$\dot{Q} = w\ c_p(T_{hot} - T_{cold}) \qquad \textit{Equation 9-1}$$

$\dot{Q}$ = rate of heat transfer (BTU/hr)

w = mass flow rate of the fluid (lbm/hr)

c_p = specific heat capacity of the fluid (BTU/lbm · °F)

T_{hot} = temperature of the hot fluid (°F)

T_{cold} = temperature of the cold fluid (°F)

The specific heat capacity is the amount of heat per unit mass needed to raise the temperature of a substance by 1°F, and has units of BTU/lbm · °F.

Because the rate of heat transfer out of the oil equals the rate of heat transfer into the water, Equation 9-2 applies:

$$\dot{Q} = w_{Water}\, c_{p\,Water}(T_{Water\,Out} - T_{Water\,In}) = w_{Oil}\, c_{p\,Oil}(T_{Oil\,In} - T_{Oil\,Out})$$

Equation 9-2

The rate of heat transfer can also be calculated using properties of the heat exchanger with Equation 9-3.

$$\dot{Q} = UA(LMTD)$$

Equation 9-3

U = overall heat transfer coefficient (BTU/hr · ft² · °F)

A = heat transfer area (ft²)

$LMTD$ = Log Mean Temperature Difference (°F)

For fluids that undergo a phase change, Equation 9-4 can be used to calculate the amount of heat transfer based on the mass flow rate and the change in fluid enthalpy that occurs.

$$\dot{Q} = w\,(h_{hot} - h_{cold})$$

Equation 9-4

w = mass flow rate of the fluid (lbm/hr)

h_{hot} = enthalpy of the hot fluid (BTU/lbm)

h_{cold} = enthalpy of the cold fluid (BTU/lbm)

These are simplified forms of heat transfer equations to show the factors affecting heat transfer. More detailed equations found in thermodynamic textbooks should be used depending on the application.

Heat Transfer Equipment

Heat transfer equipment is designed to bring two fluids of different temperatures into close proximity to allow heat transfer to occur. In a typical heat exchanger, the hot fluid transfers its thermal energy by convection to the surface of the pipe wall, then by conduction through the pipe wall, and finally transferred by convection to the colder fluid.

The two fluids in a heat exchanger can flow in opposite directions of each other, called counter-flow heat exchangers. Heat exchangers can also have concurrent flow in which both fluids flow in the same direction, or cross-flow in which the fluids flow perpendicularly to each other.

Types of Heat Exchangers

There are many types of heat exchangers with various designs depending on the application. The most common types of heat exchangers include:

- Tube-in-tube
- Shell and tube
- Fin and tube
- Plate heat exchanger

Tube-in-Tube Heat Exchangers

The tube-in-tube heat exchanger shown in Figure 9-3 is typically a counter flow heat exchanger in which the fluid inside the inner pipe flows in one direction and the fluid between the inner and outer pipes flows in the opposite direction.

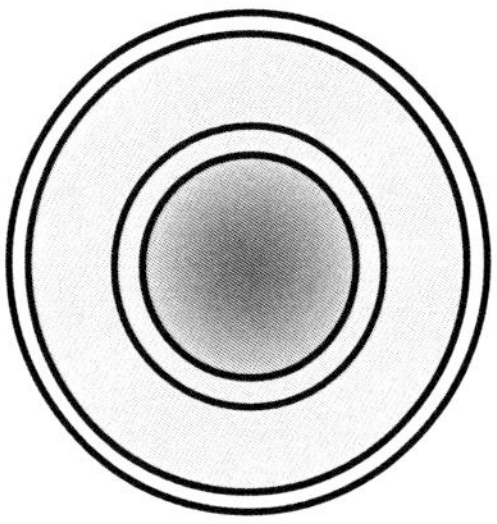

Figure 9-3. Tube-in-tube heat exchanger.

Shell and Tube Heat Exchangers

The shell and tube type heat exchanger shown in Figure 9-4 is perhaps the most common type of heat exchanger. They are versatile and used in many applications in a large number of industries.

The shell and tube heat exchanger consists of a bundle of tubes mounted in a shell, with one process fluid flowing through the tubes and the other fluid flowing around the outside of the tubes on the shell-side.

The major components on the tube-side include the heads, the tube sheet, and the tube bundle. The heads contains the inlet and outlet piping connections. The tube sheet separates the head from the shell side and consists of perforations for the fluid to enter the tubes. The tube bundle design can be a single straight through pass or a multi-pass design with 2, 4, 6, 8, or even 10 passes, based on the location and orientation of divider plates on either end of the heat exchanger.

Figure 9-4. Shell and tube heat exchanger (courtesy of ITT).

The shell contains the inlet and outlet piping connections and several baffle plates. The baffle plates provide structural support for the tubes and create an obstruction for the shell-side fluid to flow around, thereby creating a tortuous flow path to enhance heat exchanger performance and mixing.

Fin and Tube Heat Exchangers

Fin and tube heat exchangers are typically used for heat transfer between a hot fluid and cold air. The hot fluid (typically steam or hot condensate) flows inside the tubes, which are usually made of copper, aluminum, or stainless steel. The colder air flows around the outside of the tubes, which have fins in contact with the tubes to increase the heat transfer area. The fins are typically made of aluminum, but can also be made of copper.

Figure 9-5 shows a typical fin and tube heat exchanger used in the pulp and paper industry, but other applications include the HVAC industry and radiators used in automobiles.

Figure 9-5. Fin and tube heat exchanger (courtesy of Daken).

Plate Heat Exchangers

A plate heat exchanger consists of contoured metal plates placed back to back with the number and the size of the plates customizable to suit the heat transfer requirements of the application. The plates often have a chevron pattern with alternating orientations to create flow passages between the plates, as shown in Figure 9-6. Gaskets seal one plate from the next and direct the fluid into the inlet or outlet of the heat exchanger on both the hot and cold side.

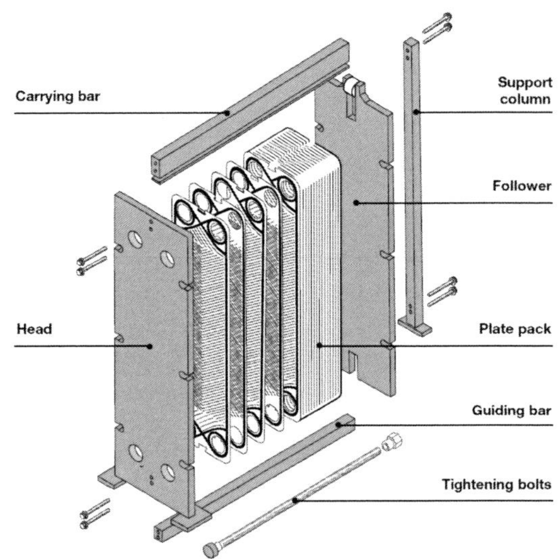

Figure 9-6. Plate heat exchanger (courtesy of Polaris Plate Heat Exchangers).

Hydraulic Performance of Heat Exchangers

In addition to its thermal performance, a heat exchanger has a hydraulic performance that defines the pressure drop across it as a function of the flow rate through each side. The pressure drop is due to head loss created by changes in the fluid velocity and direction (momentum changes), changes to the size and shape of the flow path, and friction between the fluid and the surface of the flow path.

The hydraulic performance of a heat exchanger depends on the design and application. For liquid to liquid heat transfer with no phase change, both the primary and secondary sides display a nearly-second order relationship between the flow rate and differential pressure.

For heat transfer that results in a phase change, the head loss calculation for two phase flow and the expansion or contraction of the fluid as it changes phase complicates the calculation for pressure drop across the heat exchanger.

The hydraulic performance of the heat exchanger may be provided by the manufacturer in the form of a complete head loss or pressure drop curve over a range of flow rates. However, if the manufacturer doesn't provide a curve, a single data point of pressure drop at a known flow rate can be used to create a second order curve to estimate the performance of the heat exchanger if no phase change occurs.

The second order curve can be generated by calculating the heat exchanger's equivalent flow coefficient (C_V) with Equation 9-5 using the flow and pressure drop at one test point, then re-arranging the equation to solve for pressure drop, as shown in Equation 9-6. The pressure drops over a range of flow rates can then be calculated and graphed.

$$C_V = \frac{Q}{\sqrt{dP/SG}} \qquad \text{Equation 9-5}$$

$$dP = \frac{Q^2 \times SG}{(C_V)^2} \qquad \text{Equation 9-6}$$

Because the fluid temperature (and therefore fluid density) is changing as the fluid flows through the heat exchanger, the volumetric flow rate (Q) and specific gravity (SG) will change as well. Using the average temperature, density (SG) and volumetric flow rate will result in reasonably accurate results.

Example 9-1: Generating a Second Order Curve for Heat Exchanger Performance

The heat exchanger in Figure 9-1 has a 15 psid pressure drop across it with 1,000 gpm of water flow at an average temperature of 60 °F. Determine the heat exchanger's equivalent flow coefficient and develop a second order curve to represent it's hydraulic performance.

Using Equation 9-5 to calculate the heat exchanger's equivalent flow coefficient:

$$C_V = \frac{Q}{\sqrt{dP/SG}} = \frac{1000\ gpm}{\sqrt{15\ psi/1.0}} = 258.2$$

Using Equation 9-6 to determine the pressure drop at 500 gpm and 1,500 gpm:

$$dP = \frac{Q^2 \times SG}{(C_V)^2} = \frac{500^2 \times 1.0}{(258.2)^2} = 3.75\ psid$$

$$dP = \frac{Q^2 \times SG}{(C_V)^2} = \frac{1{,}500^2 \times 1.0}{(258.2)^2} = 33.75\ psid$$

The second order curve for the heat exchanger can now be drawn:

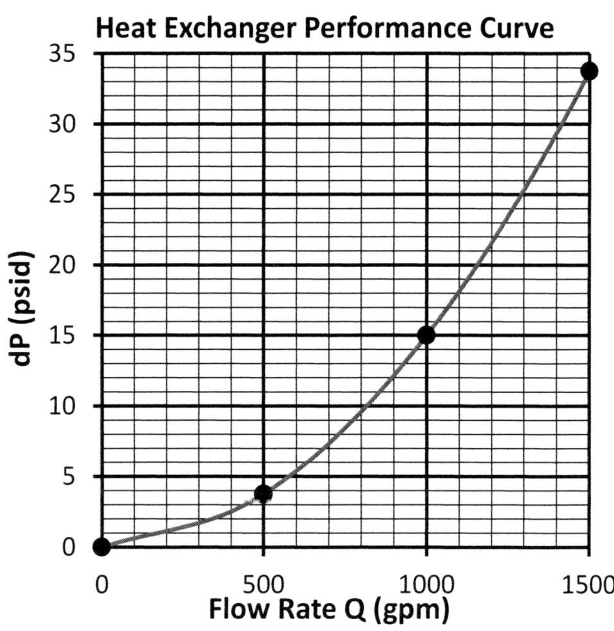

Using the performance curve, the flow rate at any pressure drop can be estimated. For example, if the pressure drop is 25 psid, the flow rate is about 1,300 gpm.

Changes to Hydraulic Performance of Heat Exchangers

Since the purpose of the heat exchanger is to change the temperature of the fluid, the fluid viscosity and density will change from the inlet to the outlet, so an average temperature can be used to determine the average fluid properties. Changes to the average fluid temperature will occur as process conditions change.

How much impact the viscosity and density change has on the hydraulic performance will depend on the magnitude of the temperature change. For small temperature changes around the normal operating temperature, the variation in the viscosity may be insignificant and have little impact on the head loss across the heat exchanger.

Larger temperature changes may be experienced during start up and shut down and may result in a significant change in viscosity and density that needs to be taken into account in the selection and sizing of the equipment in the system. For example, cold oil is more viscous than hot oil, so a pump that is selected based on head loss and pressure drop calcuations at the normal operating temperature may not produce enough head at cold start up conditions to obtain the desired flow rate. This may require heaters to be installed in the oil reservoir to heat the oil to the normal operation temperature before the system can be operated.

Heat exchangers may also experience fouling during normal operations, resulting in reduced thermal performance that will require a higher flow rate to maintain the same amount of heat transfer. The higher flow rate will result in more head loss and a larger pressure drop across the heat exchanger. Fouling also results in a reduction in the size of the flow passage through the heat exchanger, causing even more head loss and pressure drop.

Obstructions in the heat exchanger will also increase the head loss and pressure drop at a given flow rate. For example, leaking tubes are typically repaired by plugging both ends of the leaking tube. Zebra mussels or other biological growth can obstruct the flow paths in the heat exchanger. Additionally, blockage due to poor house keeping will increase its resistance to fluid flow. As a heat exchanger becomes fouled or if it has some other form of obstruction, the rest of the piping system will be affected.

Example 9-2: System Changes Due to a Plugged Heat Exchanger

The system shown in Figure 9-7 shows the values of pressures, flow, and valve position for the normal operation of the system with a clean heat exchanger. The pump produces 121 feet of Total Head at 400 gpm resulting in a discharge pressure of 53.9 psig based on an inlet pressure of 1.4 psig. At 400 gpm the heat exchanger has a pressure drop of 13.8 psid with an inlet pressure of 52.1 psig and an outlet pressure of 38.3 psig. The control valve is 75% open with an inlet pressure of 36.5 psig.

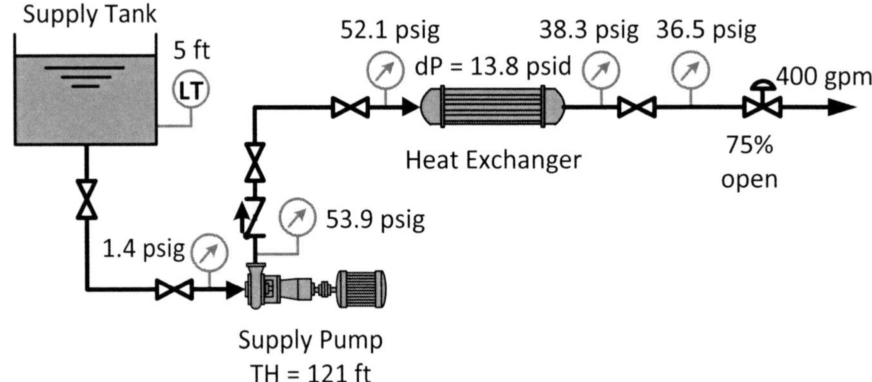

Figure 9-7. Operating conditions with a clean heat exchanger.

Now consider the system response if the heat exchanger has an obstruction and the flow is maintained at 400 gpm with an automatic control valve, shown in Figure 9-8. Because of the obstruction, the pressure drop across the heat exchanger increases, in this example to 17.9 psid. Since the flow through the pump is the same, the pump's Total Head remains constant at 121 feet and therefore the pump discharge pressure remains the same at 53.9 psig.

The heat exchanger inlet pressure stays the same at 52.1 psig because the flow rate is maintained at 400 gpm so the amount of head loss, and therefore pressure drop, across the pipelines, valves and fittings remain constant. With the higher pressure drop across the heat exchanger, the heat exchanger outlet pressure decreases to 34.2 psig, which reduces the inlet pressure at the valve to 34.2 psig. The reduced inlet pressure at the control valve requires the valve to open up to maintain a constant flow rate, in this case to 80% open.

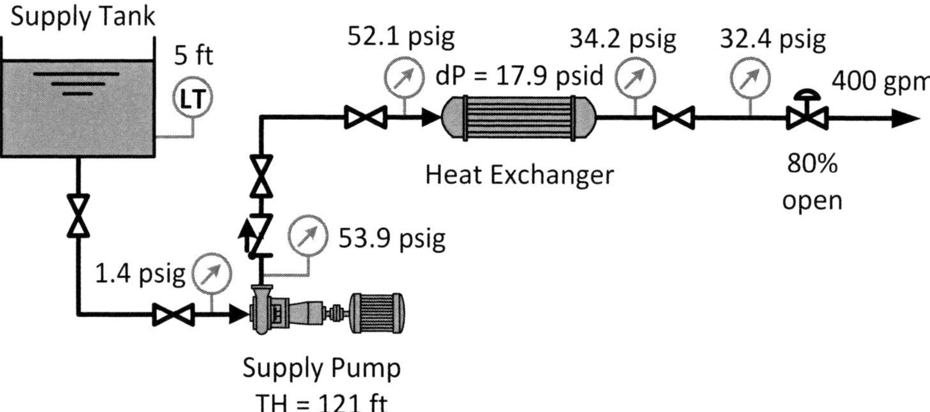

Figure 9-8. Operating conditions with a partially plugged heat exchanger and flow remained constant.

The system response will be different if the valve is not an automatic valve but is instead manually controlled, as shown in Figure 9-9. If the flow goes to a constant pressure user and the heat exchanger is plugged the same amount, the increased pressure drop across the heat exchanger causes the flow rate to decrease, in this case to 373 gpm.

The lower flow rate causes the pump to run farther back on the pump curve so the Total Head increases, in this case from 121 feet to 124 feet. The increased Total Head causes the pump discharge pressure to increase to 55.3 psig. The increased discharge pressure combined with the higher head loss and pressure drop across the heat exchanger causes the heat exchanger inlet pressure increases to 53.7 psig. Also, the lower flow rate in the suction piping causes the pump suction pressure to increase slightly due to less head loss.

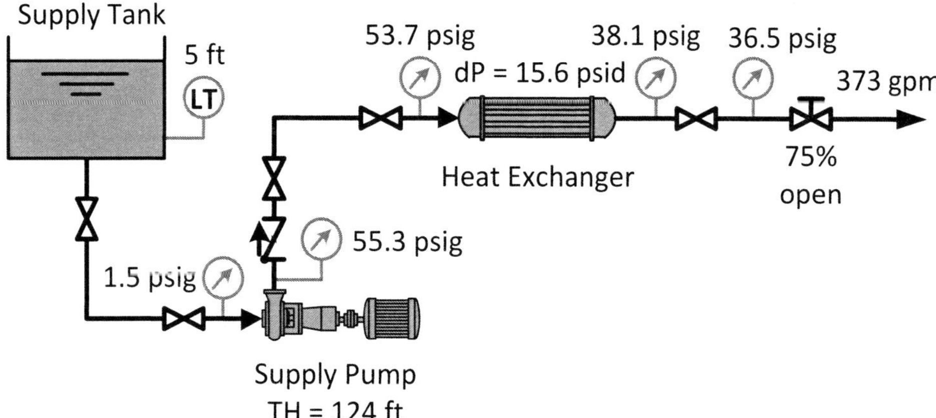

Figure 9-9. Operating conditions with a partially plugged heat exchanger with manually controlled flow and constant control valve inlet pressure.

Mass Transfer

Mass transfer is the third main category of processes that can occur in a piping system. Mass transfer occurs as a result of a difference in the concentration of various substances in a fluid. Molecules will migrate from a point of higher concentration to lower concentration. There may or may not be a change in phase from a liquid to a gas or a gas to a liquid. Mass transfer is often used in conjunction with momentum or heat transfer processes to change the physical or chemical properties of the working fluid.

Types of Mass Transfer Processes

There are various forms of mass transfer that can occur in a piping system, each with a specific mechanism that changes the physical properties of the working fluid. The mathematics that describe mass transfer mechanisms are often complex and difficult to solve and are beyond the scope of this book

Absorption

Absorption occurs when vapor molecules in a gas stream are removed by a liquid. This typically occurs in an absorption or cooling tower. For example, sulfur dioxide (SO_2) is removed from a coal fired boiler flue gas stream as it is absorbed in a wet flue gas desulfurization (FGD) system into a magnesium hydroxide solution or calcium carbonate solution.

Adsorption

Adsorption is the binding of molecules in a gas or liquid stream to a solid material. A good example of adsorption is the use of desiccant air dryers in compressed air systems to remove water from air. Common adsorbents include activated carbon, silica gels, activated alumina, and aluminosilicates.

Distillation

Distillation is a mass transfer process in which the components of a liquid mixture are separated by boiling due to different vapor pressures for the individual liquids that make up the mixture. A distillation column at a refinery is used to separate crude oil into various streams of distillates that are then processed to make gasoline, kerosene, diesel oil, fuel oil, lubricating oil, and asphalt.

Extraction

Extraction is the separation of different liquid compounds in a solution. Liquid-liquid extraction removes components dissolved in a liquid by contact with a second liquid, typically by using a solvent. Applications of liquid-liquid extraction include the production of perfumes, vegetable oils, and biodiesel fuels.

Ion exchange is also an extraction mechanism in which an ion in a liquid is transferred to a resin, and a different ion with the same charge is tranferred from the resin into the liquid. Nuclear power plant ion exhangers, demineraliziers, and water polishing systems are used to remove impurities for chemisty and radioactivity control.

Drying

Drying is not only a heat transfer process, but it is also a mass transfer process in which a liquid is removed from a solid material.

Membrane Separation

Membrane separation is the removal of a substance in a fluid by diffusion through a semi-permeable membrane. Reverse osmosis water treatment is a good example of membrane separation.

Mechanical - Physical Separation

Mechanical - physical separation involves separating solids, liquids, or gases by filtration, settling, centrifugal forces or size reduction. Settling tanks used in a water treatment plant and centrifugal cleaners in a paper mill are good examples of mechanical - physical separation.

Hydraulic Performance of Mass Transfer Equipment

There are unique equipment and devices designed and constructed to support various mass transfer mechanisms in different industries based on the application and desired outcome of the process. For example, absorption and cooling towers are tanks with a known hydraulic performance, but there are typically spray nozzles installed to support the mass transfer processes that occur in the towers.

Distillation columns, centrifuges, centrifugal cleaners, screens, filters, strainers, demineralizers, ion exchangers, reverse osmosis filters, and settling tanks are also unique devices installed to facilitate mass transfer processes.

The mathematics describing the hydraulic performance of some mass transfer equipment may be complex with many variables. However, the hydraulic performance of some equipment follow a second order (or nearly second order) relationship between flow rate and head loss (pressure drop) across the equipment.

Equipment manufacturers may provide a complete flow rate vs. pressure drop (or head loss) graph, or they may determine the equipment's equivalent flow coefficient (C_V). The equipment manufacturer should always be consulted to determine the expected hydraulic performance of their equipment.

Hydraulic Performance of Strainers and Filters

An example of a mass transfer device that follows a second order relationship between flow and pressure drop is the strainer or filter shown in Figure 9-10. Strainers and filters remove dirt and debris from the fluid to protect sensitive downstream components. The strainer or filter element presents an obstruction in the flow path, so there will be head loss and pressure drop associated with it.

Figure 9-10. Duplex strainer (courtesy of Eaton).

The differential pressure across the strainer not only increases with increased flow rate, but also as the strainer removes particulates and begins to partially plug. The strainer needs to be cleaned or replaced when the pressure drop increases to a value specified by the manufacturer (typically 5 to 20 psid).

Figure 9-11 shows a log-log graph of the hydraulic performance of the Eaton duplex strainer based on the size of the strainer. The hydraulic performance for a particular strainer size is also defined with a flow coefficient, as shown in Table 9-1.

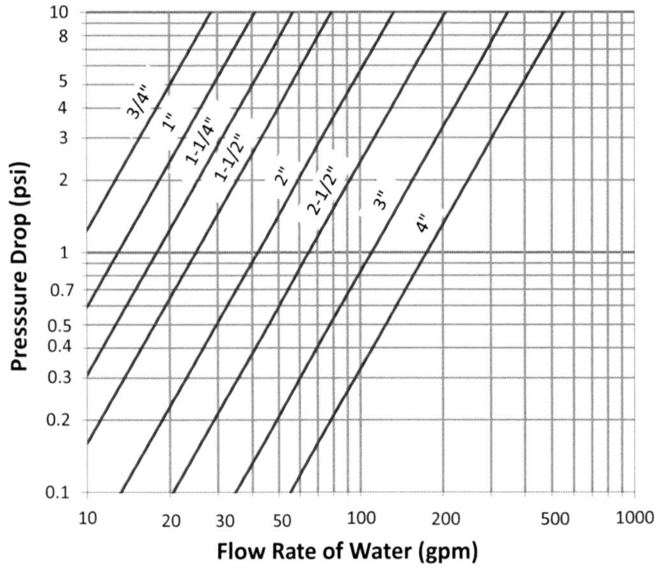

Figure 9-11. Duplex strainer hydraulic performance graphs (courtesy of Eaton).

Table 9-1: Duplex Strainer Flow Coefficients (courtesy of Eaton).

Strainer C_V Factors			
Size	Value	Size	Value
3/4"	9	2"	42
1"	13	2-1/2"	65
1-1/4"	18	3"	110
1-1/2"	25	4"	175

Hydraulic Performance of Nozzles and Sprinklers

Another device that is installed to facilitate a mass transfer process is a spray nozzle used in absorption towers, similar to the one shown in Figure 9-12.

Figure 9-12. Distribojet spray nozzle (courtesy of Spraying Systems Co.).

Nozzle and sprinkler manufacturers characterize the hydraulic performance of their equipment using a nozzle discharge coefficient (K) with Equation 9-7:

$$Q = K\sqrt{P} \qquad \textit{Equation 9-7}$$

The pressure (*P*) in the square root function of Equation 9-7 is the nozzle inlet pressure, which is the same as the differential pressure across the nozzle since it is tested while discharging into atmospheric conditions.

The nozzle discharge coefficient (*K*) in Equation 9-7 should not be confused with the resistance coefficient that is used to characterize the hydraulic performance of valves and fittings. The nozzle discharge coefficient is actually equivalent to the flow coefficient (C_V) because the test fluid is typically water close to 60 °F with a specific gravity equal to one.

In addition to providing a nozzle discharge coefficient, the manufacturer may provide a graph that represents the hydraulic performance of the nozzles. Figure 9-13 shows a graph for various nozzle sizes for a given design.

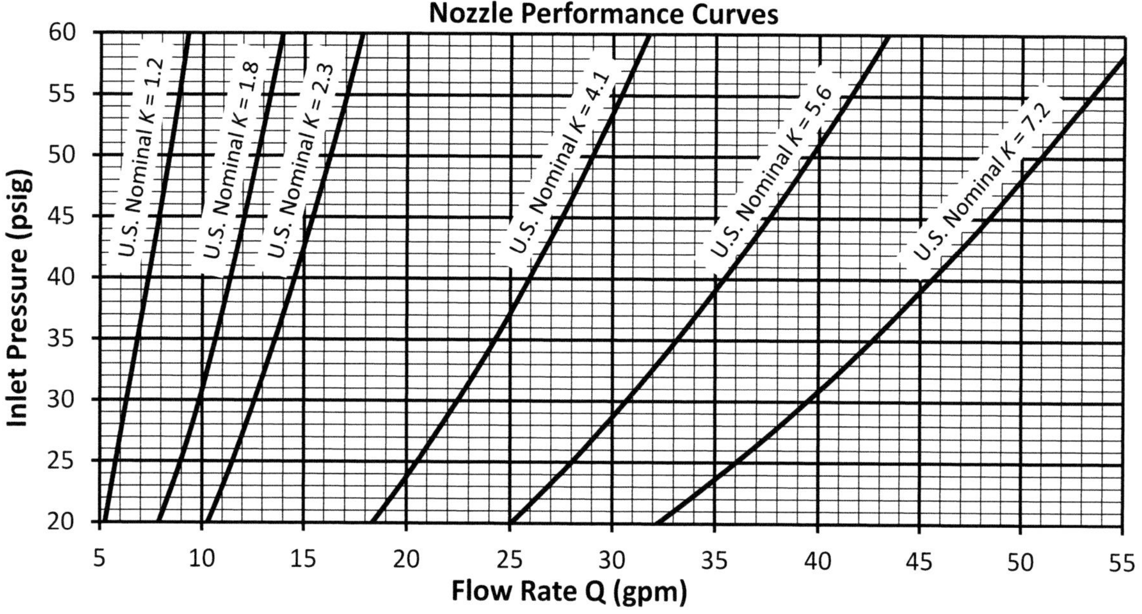

Figure 9-13. Spray nozzle hydraulic performance graph for various sizes of a given nozzle design (courtesy of Viking Group Inc.).

Unique nozzle designs may have a hydraulic performance that is not quite a second order relationship, in which case the manufacturer may provide an equation similar to Equation 9-8 to describe the performance of their nozzles.

$$Q = K \times P^n \qquad \textit{Equation 9-8}$$

In addition to providing the nozzle discharge coefficient (K), the manufacturer will provide the pressure exponent (n) in Equation 9-8. Table 9-2 provides typical pressure exponents for full cone nozzles and wide angle full cone nozzles, as well as sprinklers, swirl, and spiral nozzle designs.

Table 9-2: Spray Nozzle Pressure Exponents (courtesy of Spraying Systems Co.).

Spray Nozzle Type	Pressure Exponent (n)
Sprinklers, swirl, spiral nozzles	0.5
Full cone nozzles	0.47
Wide angle full cone	0.44

Chapter Ten

The Total System

A better understanding of how the entire system works together can be obtained with a solid foundation of how each piece of equipment operates, what processes are occuring in the system and the unique equipment installed to support those processes, and how the processes are measured and controlled. Knowing how the system operates and the expected normal operating conditions given the configuration and performance of the equipment, it will be much easier to identify abnormal operating conditions and get to the root cause of issues that may be causing production, quality, or environmental problems.

Understanding the Total Piping System

A piping system is a collection of pipelines, valves, fittings, instrumentation, and other devices used to transport mass and energy to perform work or make a product using a fluid, which can be either a gas or liquid. The system boundaries must be defined so that all flows of mass and energy into and out of the system can be measured and quantified. In addition, the processes occurring in the system must be understood, as well as the hydraulic performance of individual devices designed to facilitate those processes.

The various pieces of equipment installed in the system either add or remove energy from the working fluid. Pumps add hydraulic energy in the form of pressure head (and sometimes velocity head), whereas pipelines, valves, fittings, and other components remove energy in the form of head loss.

Types of Piping Systems

There are essentially two general types of piping systems: open and closed loop systems.

Open systems are ones in which the fluid is pumped from a source to an end user or to multiple end users. These can be single path open systems or multiple path branching systems. Applications for open systems include many process, chemical injection, transfer & distribution systems.

Closed loop systems are ones in which the working fluid circulates around a loop with no mass transfer across system boundaries. There may be a small amount of leakage through pump and valve packing or through leaking flanges, cracks at welds, or in various pieces of equipment. However, a make-up flow may maintain a constant total mass. Closed systems can be single loop or multi-loop closed systems, and are typically used for component cooling, process heating, HVAC, and hydronic applications.

The working fluid, installed components, configuration, size, and footprint will depend on the application and what the systems are required to do, but the fundamental concepts discussed in previous chapters apply to the operation of the systems. Each system has unique operating characteristics that need to be understood in order to get a clear picture of the entire piping system.

Single Path Open Systems

Figure 10-1 shows a typical single path open system. This system may be used to heat water, to cool lubricating oil, or perform some other process on the working fluid.

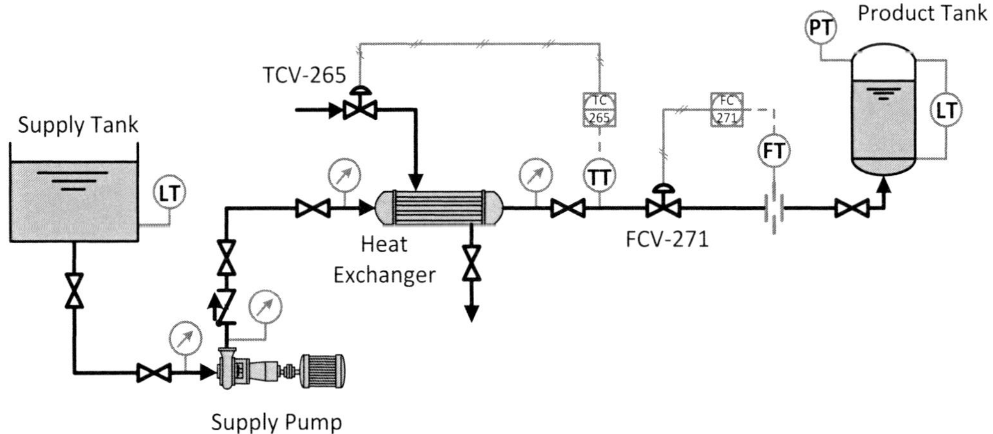

Figure 10-1. Typical single path open system used in numerous applications throughout various industries.

Branching Systems

Branching systems are a type of open system with more than one end user. Figure 10-2 shows a typical branching system that may be found in many applications throughout various industries.

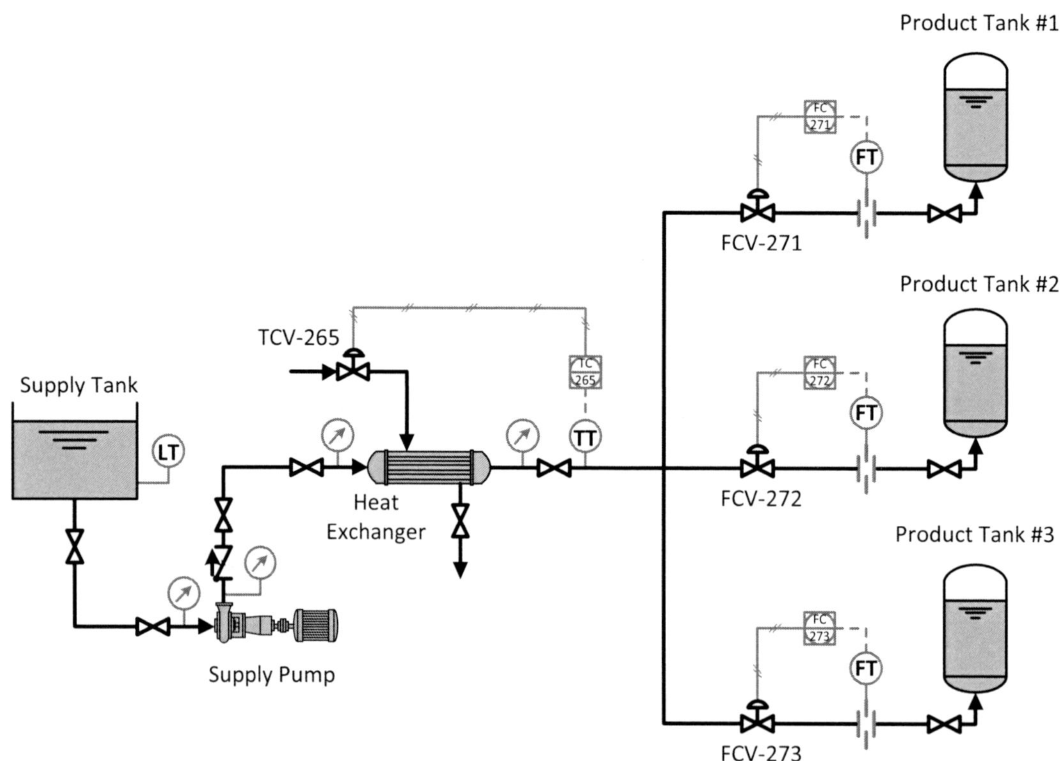

Figure 10-2. Typical branching system used to supply a fluid to multiple end users.

Single Path Closed Loop System

Figure 10-3 shows a typical single path closed loop system that circulates fluid around a loop to a dedicated user.

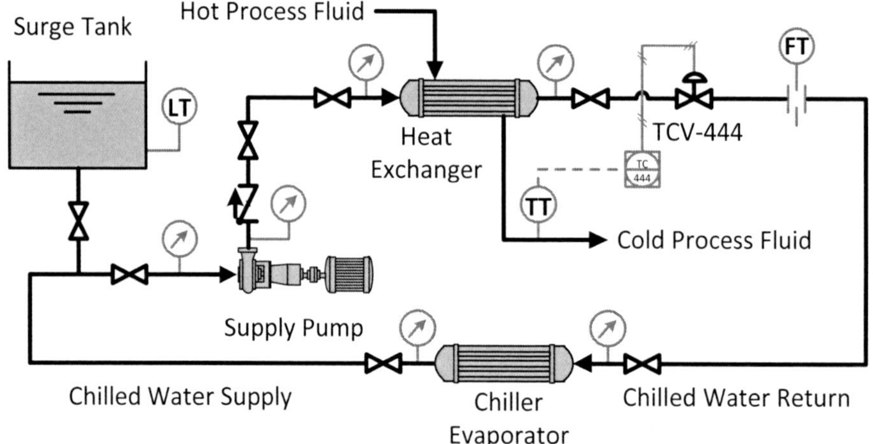

Figure 10-3. Typical single path closed loop system used to provide chilled water to cool a hot process fluid.

Multi-Loop Closed System

Multi-loop closed systems are a more common application of closed systems. Figure 10-4 shows a cooling water system in which chilled water is pumped to various heat exchangers to cool other process fluids.

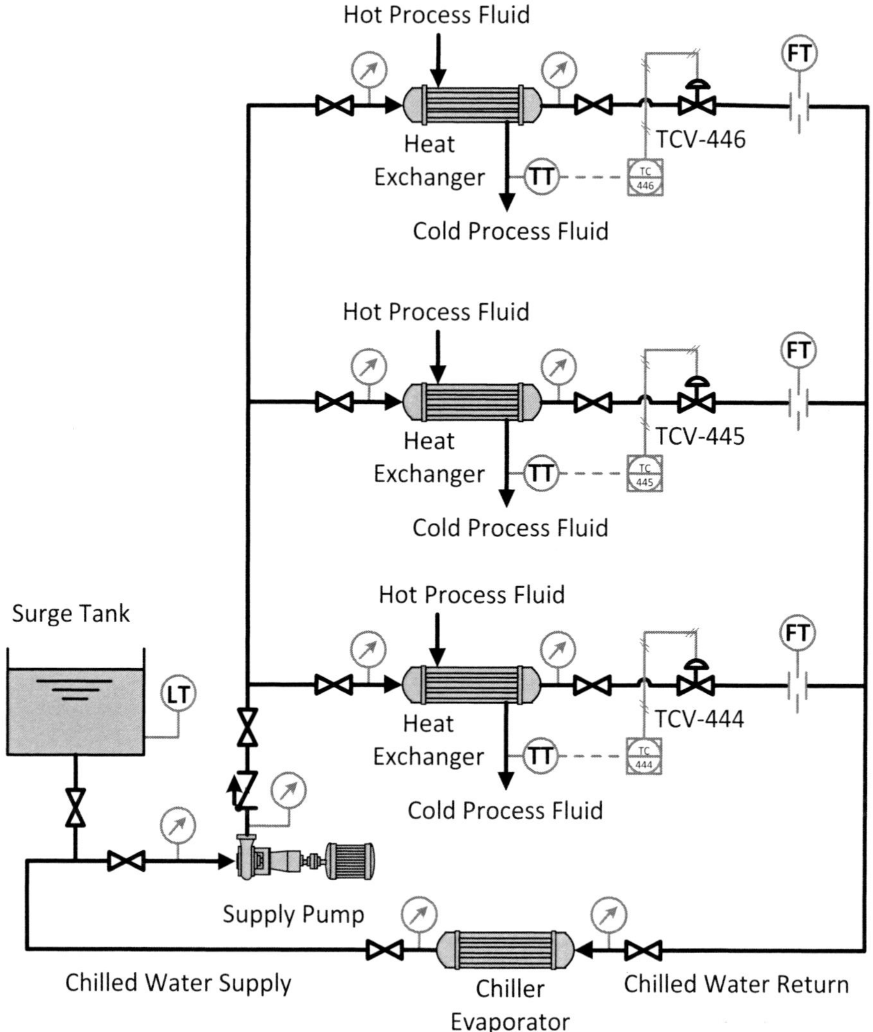

Figure 10-4. Typical multi-loop closed loop system used to provide chilled water to cool numerous hot process fluids.

Key Concepts to Understand the Performance of Piping Systems

There are several concepts that need to be understood about the piping system as a whole in order to gain a clear picture of its operation. Among these are how head loss is calculated for pipelines in series and parallel piping systems, how to determine pressures in a system with known flow rates, how to determine flow rates in a system with known boundary conditions, the siphon effect, and the concept of static and dynamic head in a system.

Head Loss for Pipelines and Components in Series

Chapter 5 briefly touched on how head loss is added together for multiple pipelines in series. The total head loss of the pipelines in series is the sum of the individual head losses for each pipeline. The same concept applies if pipelines are in series with valves, fittings, and other components in the system.

For example, Figure 10-5 shows a portion of a system consisting of a component with an inlet pipeline (Pipe 1) and outlet pipeline (Pipe 2). The total head loss for the series is equal to the sum of the head loss for Pipe 1, the component, and Pipe 2.

In addition, if the elevations and pipe sizes are the same, the total pressure drop is the sum of the individual pressure drops across each device.

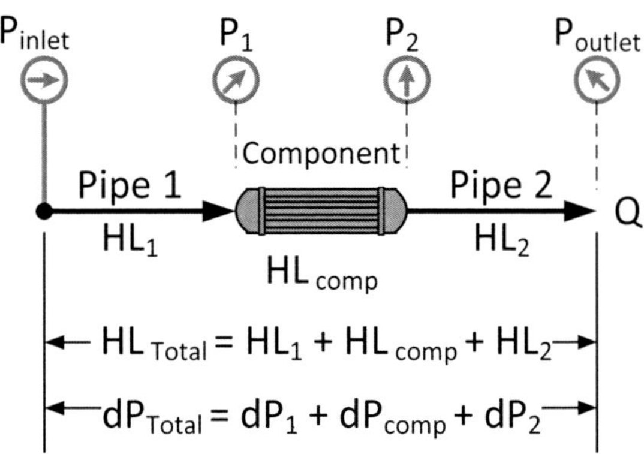

Figure 10-5. Head loss and pressure drop for pipelines and components in series.

Figure 10-6 displays the head loss curves for the individual pipelines and the component and shows how the curves are added "vertically" to obtain a System Resistance Curve (*SRC*) that represents the equivalent hydraulic performance of the series. The right hand vertical axis shows the equivalent pressure drop for the head loss based on water at 60 °F.

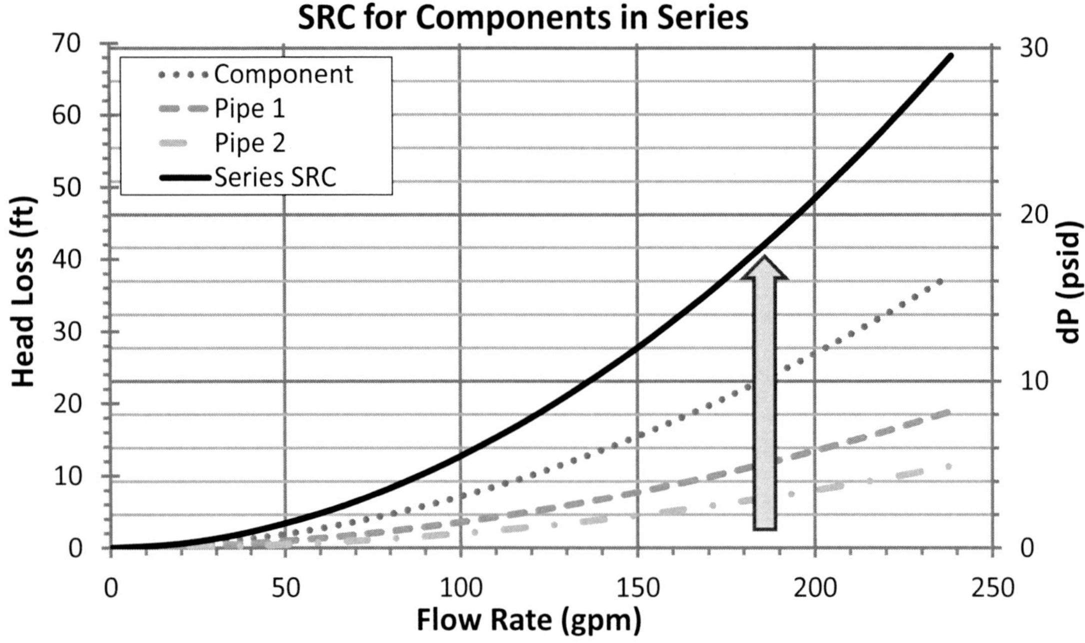

Figure 10-6. Development of the System Resistance Curve (SRC) for pipelines and components connected in series.

If the flow rate and inlet pressure of the system in Figure 10-5 are known, the head loss can be calculated using the Darcy Equation or the performance curves. The pressure drop across each device can be determined and the pressures at the component inlet (P_1), the component outlet (P_2), and the outlet pressure (P_{outlet}) can then be calculated. These can also be determined graphically using Figure 10-6.

If the elevations or pipe sizes are not the same, the Bernoulli Equation would also need to be applied to determine the pressures at the various locations.

Example 10-1: Series Head Loss and Pressure Drop

Graphically determine P_1, P_2, and P_{outlet} for the system in series shown in Figure 10-7 with a known inlet pressure of 75 psig and a flow rate of 200 gpm of water at 60 °F. There is no elevation or pipe size changes.

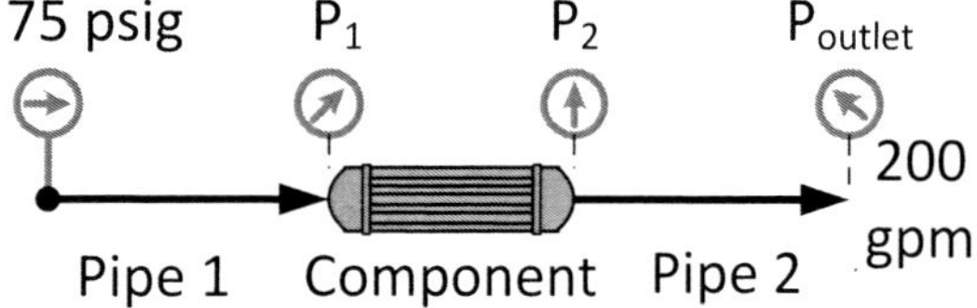

Figure 10-7. Determining pressures in a series system with known flow rates.

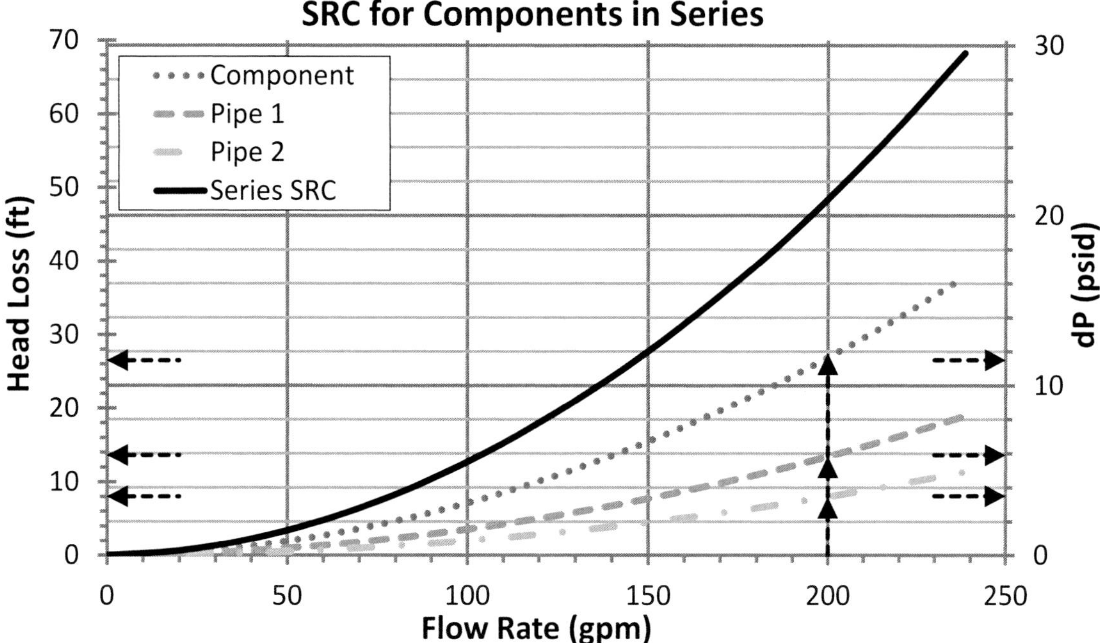

Figure 10-8. Graphically solving for head loss and pressure drop for a series system with a known flow rate.

Using the graph in Figure 10-8, the head loss and pressure drops for the individual pipelines and the component can be determined.

At 200 gpm:

- Pipe 1 has a head loss of about 13.6 feet which corresponds to about 5.9 psid. P_1 is therefore about 69.1 psig (75 - 5.9 psi).
- The component has a head loss of about 26.5 feet and a pressure drop of 11.5 psid, so P_2 is about 57.6 psig (69.1 - 11.5 psi).
- Pipe 2 has a head loss of about 8 feet and a pressure drop of 3.5 psid, making P_{outlet} about 54.1 psig (57.6 - 3.5 psi).

To get more accurate results, the Darcy Equation can be used to calculate the actual head loss and pressure drop for the pipelines, and the component flow coefficient can be used to obtain the pressure drop and head loss at 200 gpm.

> **Check of Operational Understanding**
>
> *Question*: What happens to the head losses, pressure drops, and pressures at the various locations if the flow is reduced to 150 gpm and the inlet pressure is held constant with a pressure regulator?
>
> *Answer*: The lower flow rate reduces the amount of head loss and decreases the pressure drops, so P_1, P_2, and P_{outlet} all increase.

Steady State Flow Between Two Pressure Boundaries

An unknown steady state flow rate between two pressure boundaries can be determined if enough information is known about the system. Consider the system shown in Figure 10-9 consisting of a Supply Tank with a constant level of 30 feet and an Outlet Tank with a constant level of 15 feet. The two tanks are connected by a series of three 4-inch pipelines: Pipe 1 is 100 feet in length, Pipe 2 is 50 feet, and Pipe 3 is 200 feet in length, all located at zero foot elevation.

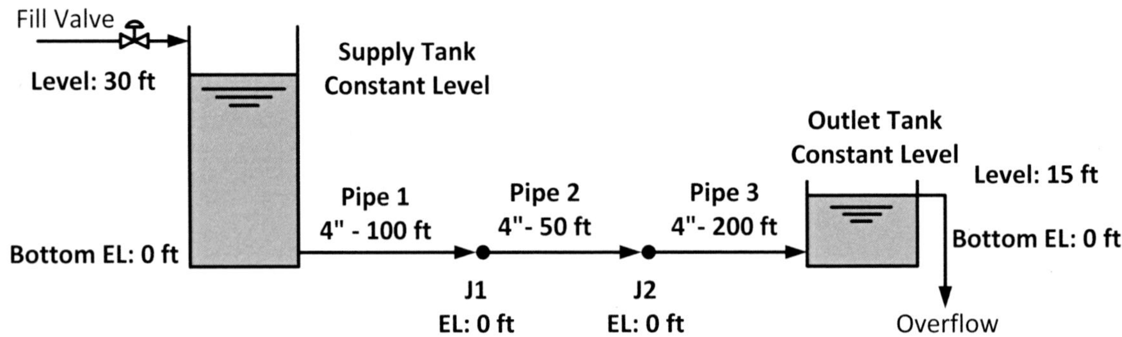

Figure 10-9. Determining the flow rate in a system with known pressure boundaries.

If the system is initially isolated and then flow is allowed to occur (for example by opening an imaginary "no resistance" valve at Junction J2 between Pipe 2 and 3), the flow will go from zero and increase to some steady state value. Under what condition does the flow stop increasing and come to steady state?

For this system, the steady state flow will be achieved when the head loss in the series of pipelines equals the difference in the "driving head" or the hydraulic grade between the two tanks. In other words, steady state flow occurs when the head loss equals 15 feet of head.

The flow rate can be solved mathematically, graphically, or by using a computer program.

Mathematical Solution

Equation 10-1 uses the Darcy Equation to obtain a mathematical solution:

$$H_{inlet} - H_{outlet} = 0.0311\left[f_1\frac{L_1}{d_1^5}Q^2 + f_2\frac{L_2}{d_2^5}Q^2 + f_3\frac{L_3}{d_3^5}Q^2\right] \qquad \textit{Equation 10-1}$$

Since the flow rate through each pipeline is the same, it looks like Equation 10-1 can easily be solved for the flow rate, *Q*. However, because the flow rate is used to calculate the Reynolds Number which is used to determine the friction factor, the solution to Equation 10-1 is not as easy as it appears.

One way to mathematically solve this problem is to take an iterative approach. The iterative method requires a guess for the flow rate, calculating the Reynolds Number and relative roughness, determining the friction factor, then solving the right hand side of Equation 10-1. If it doesn't equal 15 feet, then the flow rate is adjusted and the calculations performed again.

Table 10-1 summarizes an interative solution in which an initial guess for the flow rate of 200 gpm results in a total head loss of 7.96 feet. Since this is 7.04 feet less than the desired 15 feet, an additional 50 gpm is added for the next iteration. The second iteration using 250 gpm results in 12.14 feet of head loss, so 50 gpm is added for the third iteration, which results in 17.18 feet of head loss. Since this is greater than the 15 feet required, 20 gpm is taken off for the fourth iteration, resulting in 15.1 feet of head losss. This process can be continued depending on the accuracy required for the answer.

Table 10-1: Iterative Solution for a System with Known Pressure Boundaries

Assumed Flow Rate (gpm)	Calculated Head Loss (feet)	Difference in Head Loss (feet)	Correction (gpm)
200	7.96	15 – 7.96 = 7.04	+50
250	12.14	15 – 12.14 = 2.86	+50
300	17.18	15 – 17.18 = - 2.18	-20
280	15.1	15 – 15.1 = - 0.1	Solution

Graphical Solution

Another way to solve for the flow rate in a system with known pressure boundaries is to use the pipeline head loss graphs and the system resistance curve. Figure 10-10 shows the head loss and system resis-

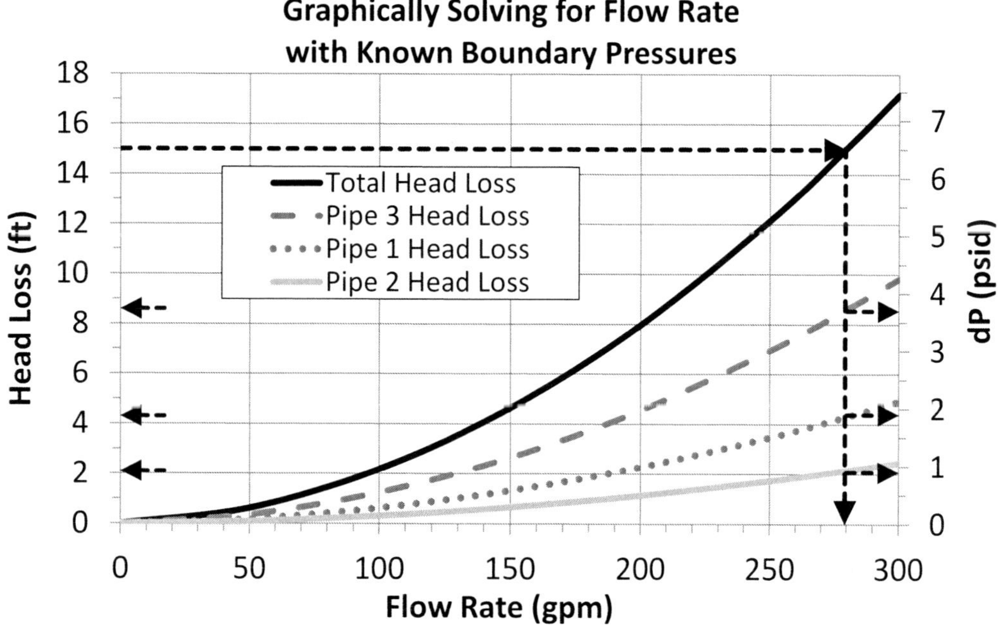

Figure 10-10. Graphical solution for flow rate in a system with known pressure boundaries.

tance curves for the pipelines in Figure 10-9. Because the head loss in the total system must equal the driving head, or 15 feet, the corresponding flow rate on the system resistance curve can be estimated at about 280 gpm.

The head loss in each individual pipeline can also be estimated using the graph. At 280 gpm, the head loss in Pipeline 1 is almost 4.5 feet, which correspond to almost 2 psid (based on water at 60 °F). Pipeline 2 has about 2 feet of head loss which is just under 1 psid, and Pipeline 3 has about 8.5 feet of head loss and 3.75 psi of pressure drop.

Computer Solution

A way to arrive at an accurate solution more quickly and solve for the flow rate in a system with known boundary pressures is to model the system in a commercially available software program such as Engineered Software's PIPE-FLO Professional® in which the user draws the system, enters the pipe and fluid data, and defines the boundary conditions. The program then uses the laws of conservation of mass and energy to solve for the flow rate, as shown in Figure 10-11.

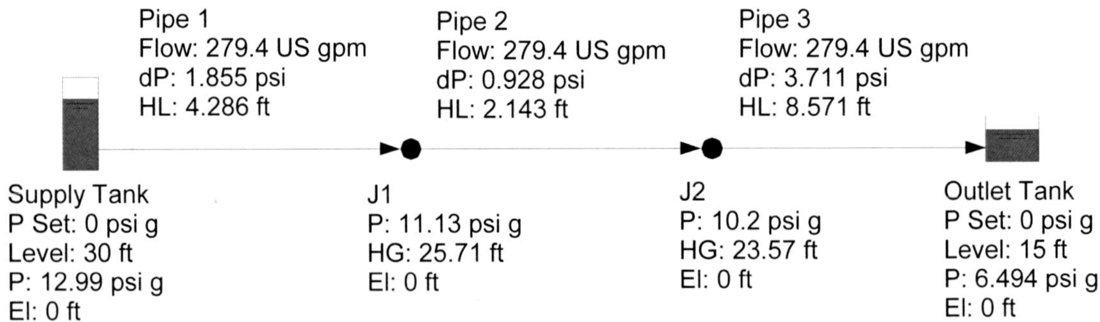

Figure 10-11. Software solution for flow rate in a system with known pressure boundaries.

The software calculates a flow rate of 279.4 gpm through the pipelines. In addition, the program more accurately calculates the head losses, pressure drops, hydraulic grade, and pressures at each junction in the system.

In evaluating the results, the pressure at the bottom of the Supply Tank is due to the density of the fluid and the level in the tank. The fluid pressure at the tank outlet is 12.99 psig. The hydraulic grade at that point is equal to the liquid level in the tank, or 30 feet.

The pressures at the pipe junctions are also calculated: 11.13 psig at J1 and 10.2 psig at J2. The pressure at the bottom of the Outlet Tank is due to the level in the tank and the fluid density, which gives 6.494 psig, which can also be calculated starting from the pressure at the bottom of the Supply tank and subtracting the pressure drops due to the head losses in all three pipelines.

Also, the hydraulic grades at J1 is the total energy at the bottom of the Supply Tank (30 feet) minus the head loss in Pipe 1 (4.286 feet), resulting in 25.71 feet of fluid energy at J1. Similarly, the hydraulic grade at J2 is the hydraulic grade at J1 minus the head loss in Pipe 2, or 23.57 feet. Subtracting the head loss in Pipe 3 from the hydraulic grade at J2 gives 15 feet, which is the total energy at the bottom of the Outlet Tank due to its liquid level of 15 feet.

The Siphon Effect

To understand the siphon effect, consider the system in Figure 10-9, except that the pipelines are flexible and junction J2 can be raised to higher elevations without changing the pipe lengths after steady state flow is established. What would happen to the flow rate, the pressure, and the hydraulic grade at J2 as the junction is raised to 23.6 feet, 30 feet, and 57 feet as shown in Figure 10-12?

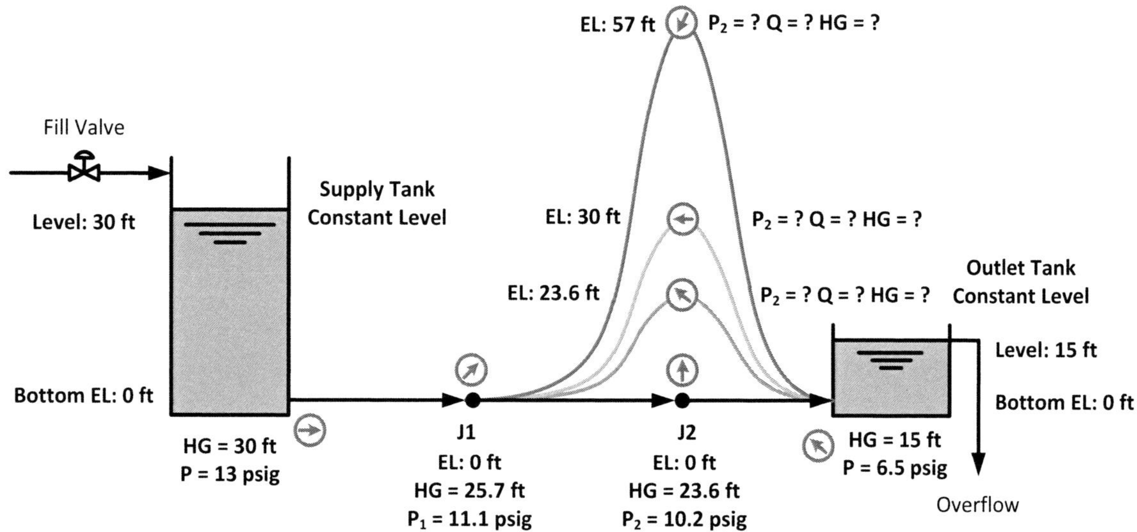

Figure 10-12. Evaluating the siphon effect as pipeline elevation is increased.

The Siphon Effect at 23.6 Feet

Even with junction J2 at 23.6 feet, the driving force is still the same, which is the elevation difference between the levels in the Supply Tank and the Outlet Tank, so the flow rate remains the same at 279.4 gpm. The hydraulic grade at J2 stays the same but now all of the hydraulic energy is in the form of elevation head, so the pressure at J2 drops to 0 psig, as shown in Figure 10-13. The energy needed to raise the fluid to the higher level is recovered as the fluid drops to the lower level.

This is essentially another application of the Bernoulli Principle in which pressure head is converted to elevation head simply by a change in the elevation of the pipeline.

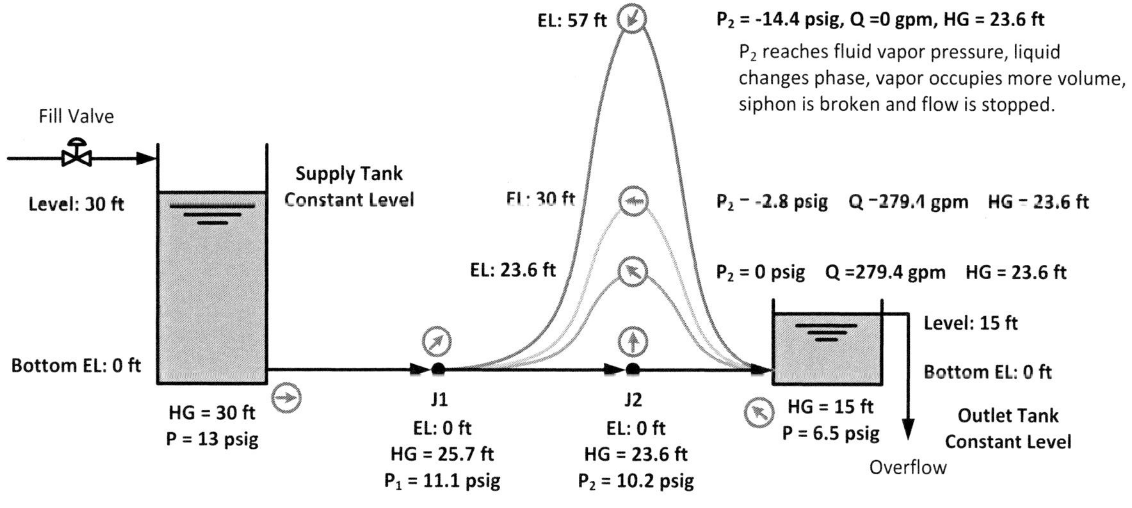

Figure 10-13. The siphon effect causes flow to remain constant until the fluid pressure drops below the vapor pressure. PF ⑤

The Siphon Effect at 30 Feet

With junction J2 at 30 foot elevation the driving force is still 15 feet, so the flow rate remains the same at 279.4 gpm. The fluid's hydraulic grade at J2 remains the same at 23.6 feet, so the pressure head must go to negative 6.4 feet, which corresponds to negative 2.8 psig. This just means that the fluid in the pipeline is below atmospheric pressure, or at a vacuum.

The Siphon Effect at 57 Feet

At 57 feet, the pressure at junction J2 drops to the fluid's vapor pressure, in this case about 0.3 psia for water at 60 °F (or -14.4 psig). At this point, the liquid changes phase to a vapor. Since vapor occupies more volume than the same mass of liquid, the volume expansion breaks the siphon and flow is stopped.

Advantages of the Siphon Effect

There are applications in which the siphon effect is utilized to facilitate a process. The rotary drum washer shown in Figure 10-14 is used in various applications in the pulp and paper industry to clean brown pulp stock or remove chemicals from bleached pulp stock.

Dirty stock is pumped into the vat of the washer where it is pulled onto a mesh wire by the vacuum created by the siphon effect as the filtrate falls into the filtrate tank.

Fresh water applied to the sheet by a shower bar filters through the pulp to remove chemicals and impurities. The clean stock leaves the washer wire for further processing.

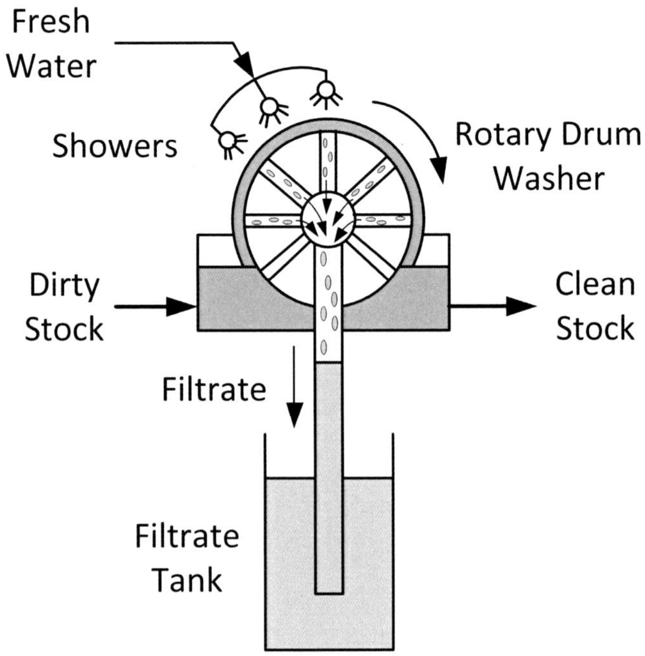

Figure 10-14. The siphon effect used to create a vacuum in a rotary drum washer.

Other applications for a siphon inculde uses in agricultural irrigation systems and steam drum rotary or stationary siphon systems.

Disadvantages of the Siphon Effect

There are piping system configurations in which the siphon effect can have unintented consequences so it's important to understand where a siphon can be formed in a piping system to avoid creating a vacuum or undesired continuous flow. Systems in which a fluid is pumped from a low elevation to a higher elevation and then back to a lower elevation are particularly susceptible to the siphon effect. Both open and closed loop systems can form siphons.

The system shown in Figure 10-15 pumps 750 gpm of water at 60 °F from a Supply Tank located at zero foot elevation to a heat exchanger and flow control valve located at 75 foot elevation. The fluid then drops down to a Product Tank located at 30 feet.

Both tanks are open to atmosphere and have a liquid level of 10 feet, so the pressure at the bottom of each tank is about 4.3 psig based on the density of water at 60 °F (neglecting the temperature change that occurs in the heat exchanger).

The total head and differential pressure at the Supply Pump are shown in parentheses indicating that 179.6 feet of hydraulic energy is added to the fluid at the pump and there is a pressure gain (or a negative pressure drop) of 77.7 psi across the pump.

The differential pressure across the pump's discharge pipe up to the inlet of the heat exchanger includes not only the pressure drop due to the head loss of 7.4 feet, but also the pressure decrease due to the elevation change of 75 feet.

The heat exchanger has a 20 psi drop across it and 46.2 feet of head loss based on its hydraulic performance.

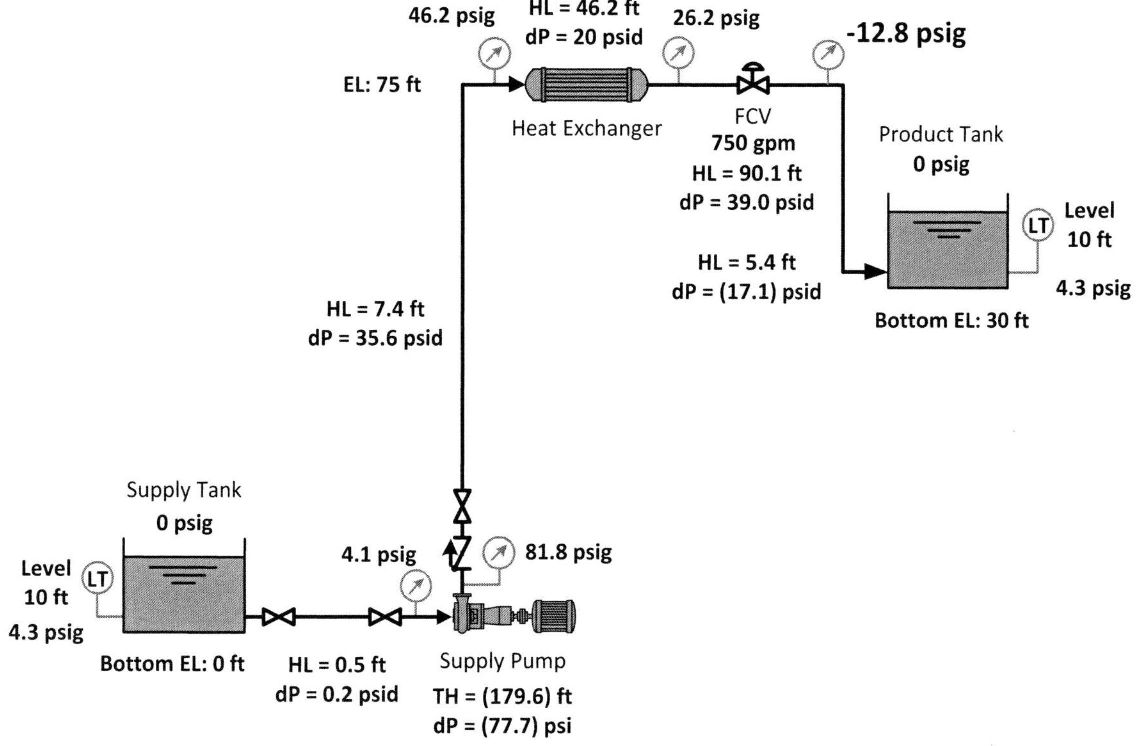

Figure 10-15. The siphon effect on an open system.

The flow control valve must dissipate 90.1 feet of head loss with a 39 psi pressure drop. This is based on the amount of fluid energy at its inlet, the final fluid energy state in the Product Tank, and the head loss in the pipeline from the control valve to the Product Tank. Even though there is 5.4 feet of head loss in this pipeline that results in a pressure drop, because the pipeline goes from 75 feet to 30 feet, there is a net pressure gain of 17.1 psi from the control valve outlet to the bottom of the Product Tank.

Because of the siphon effect on the line from the control valve to the Product Tank, the outlet pressure of the control valve is reduced to negative 12.8 psig, which is a very high vacuum. Depending on the schedule and strength of the pipeline, this may cause the pipeline to collapse or cause severe flow oscillations and water hammer.

The conserservation of energy can be evaluated for this system by starting at the Supply Tank which has a 10 foot liquid level, adding in the total head of the pump (179.6 feet), and subtracting out the head loss in the pipelines, components, and control valves (0.5 + 7.4 + 46.2 + 90.1 + 5.4 = 149.6). The final energy state of the fluid in the Product Tank is 40 feet (10 + 179.6 - 149.6 = 40), which is the 30 foot elevation of the Product Tank plus a 10 foot liquid level. This evaluation can also be done using the fluid's total pressure from the Supply Tank to the Product Tank.

There are several things that can be done to this system to prevent the adverse effect of the siphon and maintain a positive pressure at the higher elevation. One solution is to install a back pressure valve (BPV) in the pipeline close to the 30 foot elevation of the Product Tank as shown in Figure 10-16.

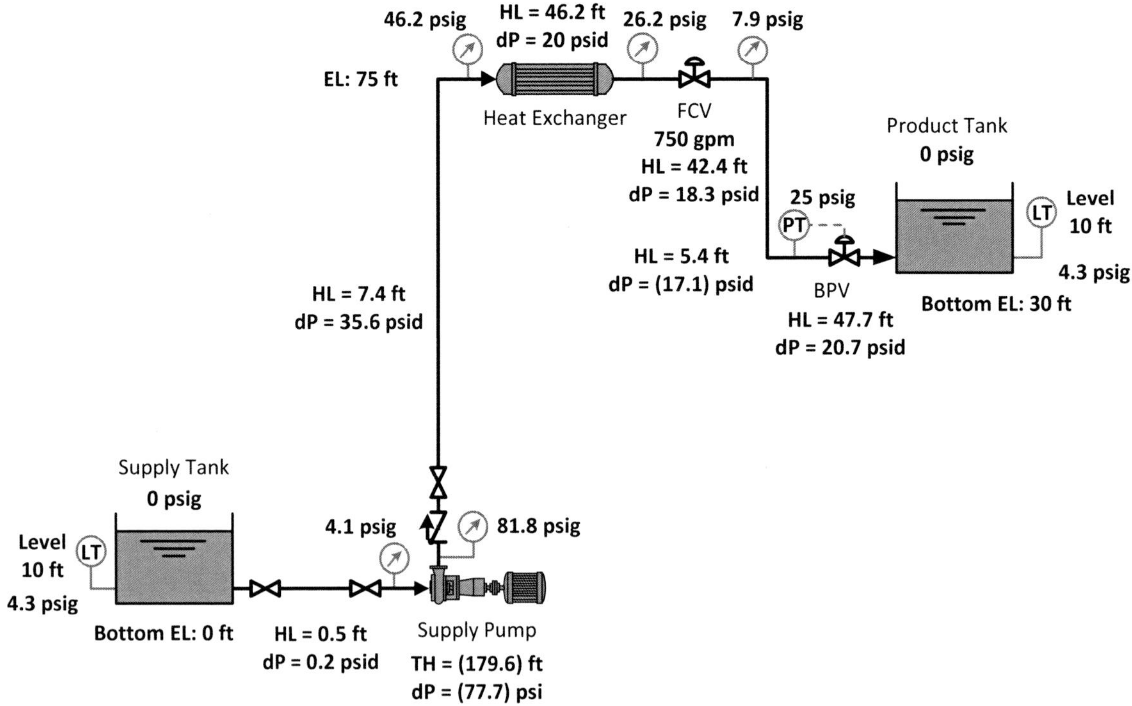

Figure 10-16. Adverse effect of the siphon resolved using a back pressure valve (BPV).

The set point for the back pressure valve will depend on the desired pressure at the high point in the system as well as the range of operation of the flow control valve. With a 25 psig set point on the back pressure valve, the pressure at the outlet of the flow control valve is 7.9 psig. This occurs because the head loss across the back pressure valve reduces the head loss across the flow control valve, which now has to be farther open, which results in a greater pressure at its outlet.

Installing a restricting orifice at the same location to dissipate some of the head loss, as shown in Figure 10-17, would have the same effect as the back pressure valve. The size of the restriction would determine the amount of head loss across the orifice and therefore how high of a back pressure it would create at the outlet of the flow control valve.

A third solution is to install the heat exchanger flow control valve at the lower elevation close to the Product Tank, as shown in Figure 10-18. The same amount of head loss and pressure drop occurs across the flow control valve, but because the valve is located at the lower elevation the pressure at the higher elevation is greater, thereby preventing a vacuum from forming at the high point.

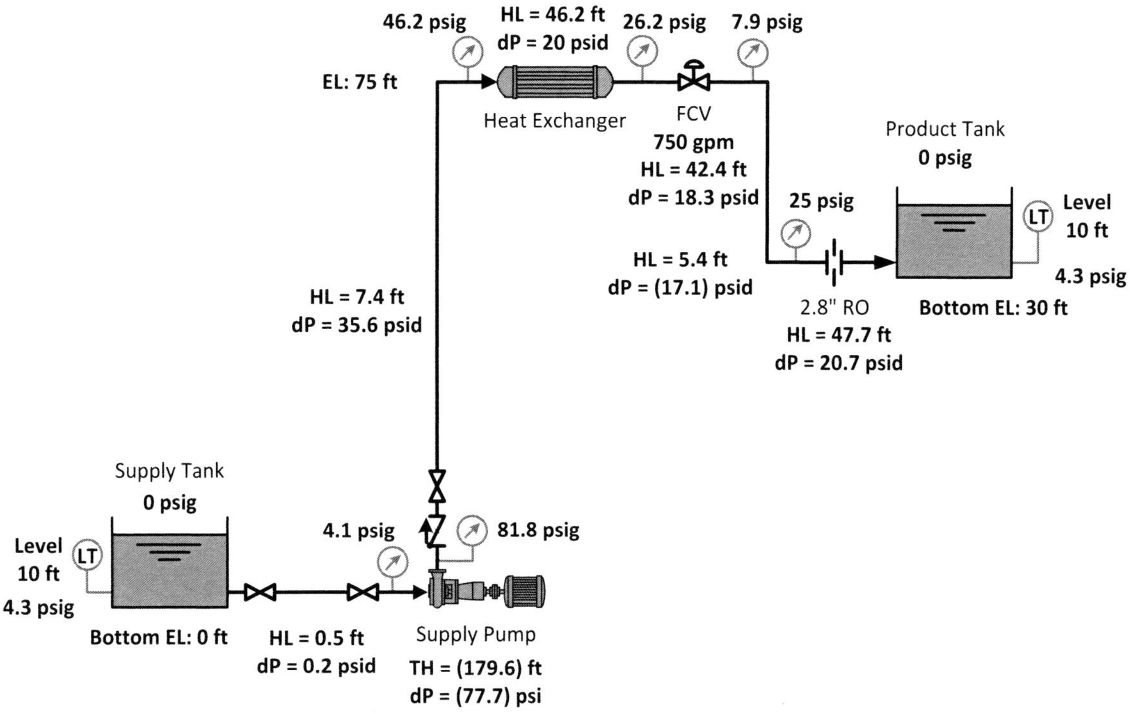

Figure 10-17. Adverse effect of the siphon resolved using a restricting orifice (RO).

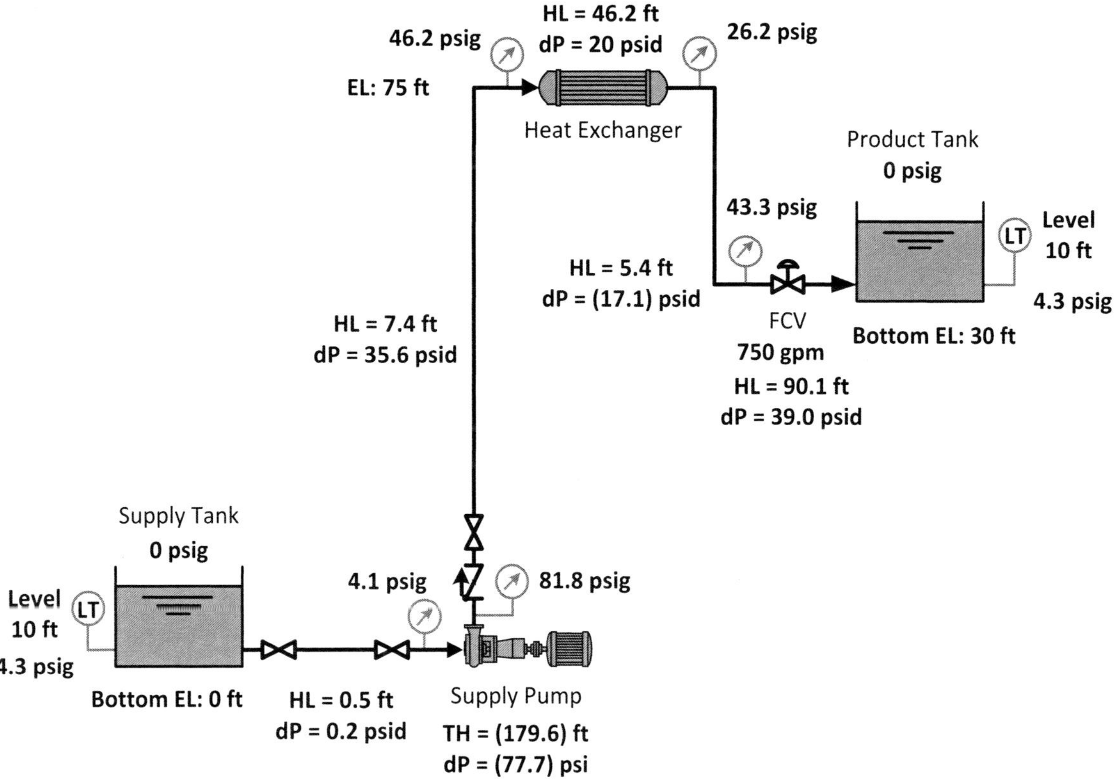

Figure 10-18. Adverse effect of the siphon resolved by installing the flow control valve at a lower elevation.

Head Loss for Pipelines and Components in Parallel

Head loss and pressure drop for pipelines configured in parallel was also briefly discussed in Chapter 5. Figure 10-19 shows a portion of a piping system in which flow from a common header is divided into three pipelines in parallel, then converges into a common return header.

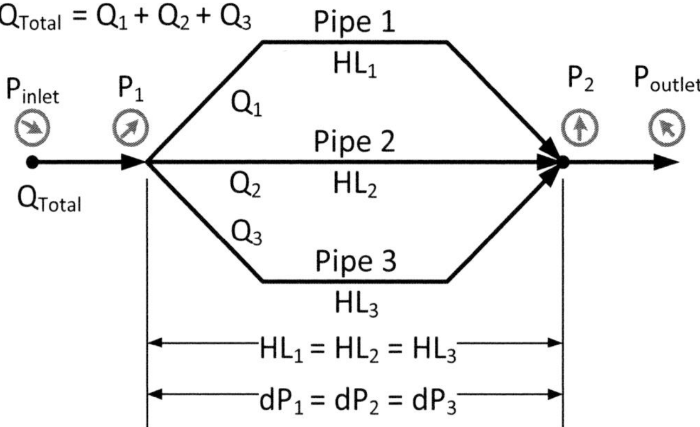

Figure 10-19. Pipelines configured in parallel.

Intuitively, the conservation of mass states that the total flow rate in the header is equal to the sum of the flow rates in the individual pipelines.

In addition, since there can only be one pressure at P_1 and one pressure at P_2, then the pressure drop across Pipe 1 has to equal the pressure drop across Pipe 2, which has to equal the pressure drop across Pipe 3. That also means that head loss across Pipe 1 equals the head loss across Pipe 2 which equals the head loss across Pipe 3. This would be the case even if there were elevation changes in the system.

Graphically, to obtain an equivalent total head loss curve, the individual pipeline head loss graphs would be added together "horizontally" as shown in Figure 10-20.

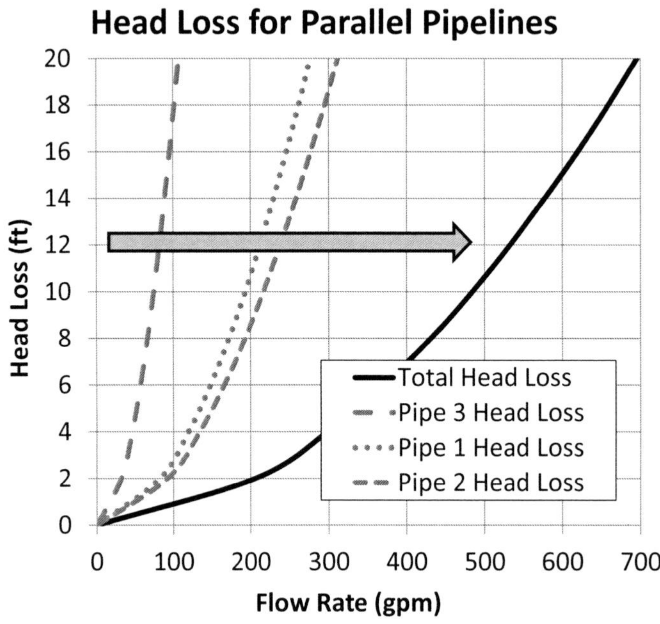

Figure 10-20. Developing a system resistance curve for pipelines configured in parallel.

If the total flow rate is known, the graph can be used to determine the head loss across the pipelines and also the individual flow rates. This is done by entering the horizontal axis at the known total flow rate, moving up to the equivalent total head loss curve, then moving to the left to the individual pipeline graphs. Dropping down to the flow rate axis will give the flow rate in each individual pipeline.

Example 10-2: Graphically Determining Parallel Pipeline Flow Rates, Head Loss, and Pressure Drop

If the graphs in Figure 10-20 represent the hydraulic performance of the system in Figure 10-21, graphically determine flow rates Q_1, Q_2, Q_3, P_{inlet}, P_1, and P_2, if the total flow rate is 600 gpm of 60 °F water and the outlet pressure is 20 psig. The inlet and outlet pipelines are 6" – 150 ft long and have a head loss of 3.5 feet at 600 gpm, which is equivalent to 1.5 psid for water.

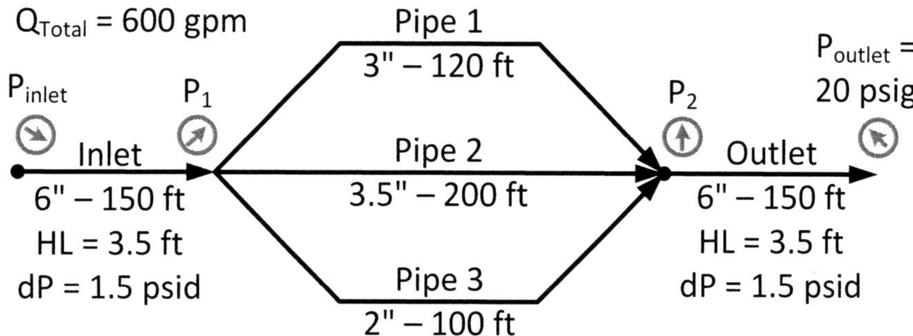

Figure 10-21. Parallel piping system in which flow rates are unknown.

Figure 10-22 shows how to graphically determine the unknown variables in the parallel pipeline system. The differential pressure scale is based on water at 60 °F.

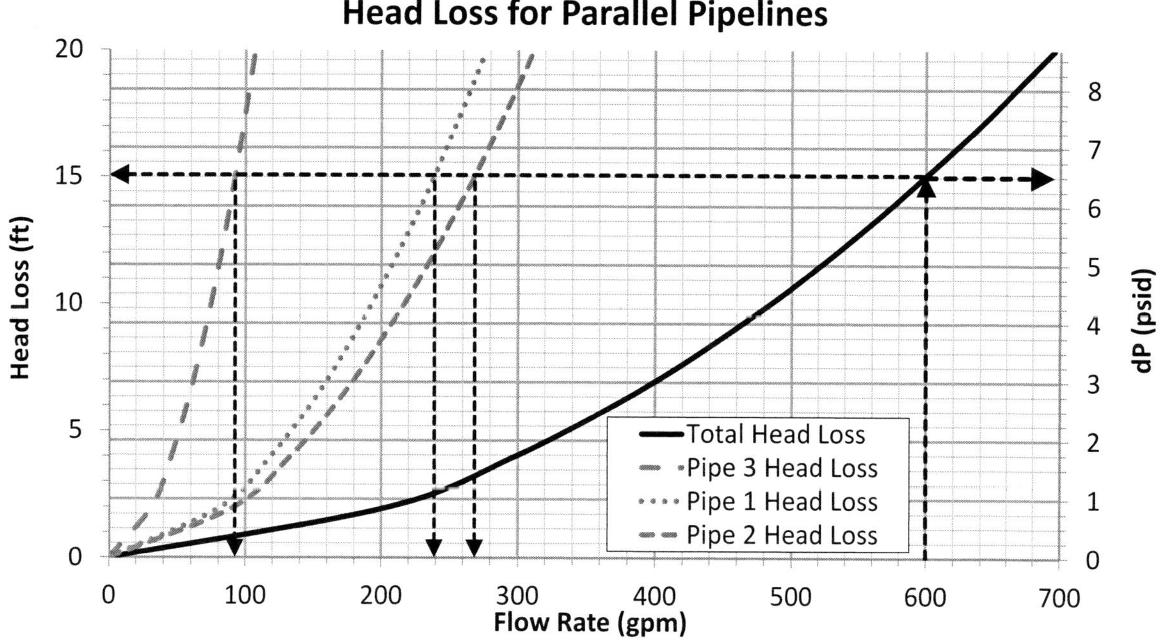

Figure 10-22. Graphically determining unknown flow rates in parallel piping.

Using the head loss and system resistance curves in Figure 10-22, at 600 gpm the head loss is about 15 feet with a corresponding pressure drop of about 6.5 psid. Since this head loss and pressure drop is the same for all three parallel pipelines, read off the flow rate for each pipeline that corresponds to 15 feet of head loss to determine the individual flow rates:

- Q_1, is about 240 gpm
- Q_2 is about 270 gpm
- Q_3 is about 90 gpm

To determine the unknown pressures, working backward from the known outlet pressure:

- $P_2 = 20 + 1.5 = 21.5$ psig
- $P_1 = 21.5 + 6.5 = 28$ psig
- $P_{inlet} = 28 + 1.5 = 29.5$ psig

This system could also be solved iteratively by assuming an initial flow rate for each pipeline and calculating the head loss. If the three head loss calculations were not equal, then an adjustment to each flow rate would need to be made by taking flow from the highest one and adding it to the others. The process would be repeated until all three head losses were equal.

Figure 10-23 shows the software solution for this system when modeled in Engineered Software's PIPE-FLO Professional® program. The software solution provides a higher level of accuracy for calculating the unknown flow rates and pressures.

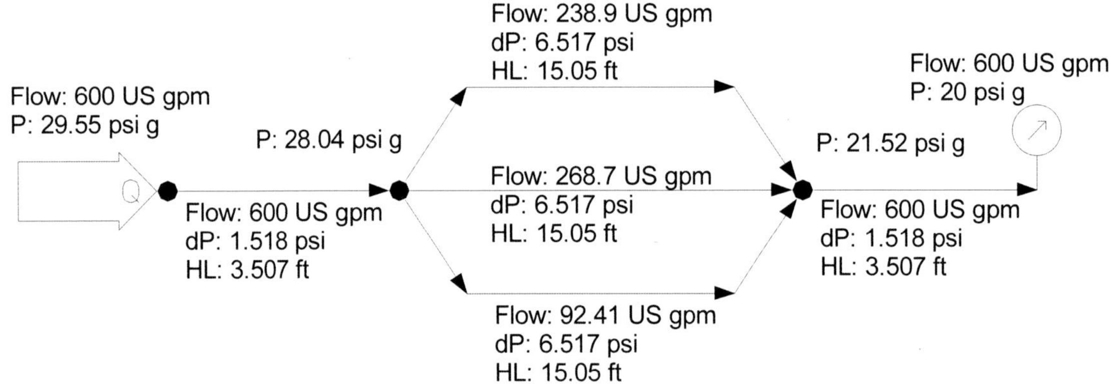

Figure 10-23. Software solution for determining unknown flow rates in parallel piping.

Head Loss for Pipelines in Branching Systems

A branching system has multiple users, one pressure source, and no parallel paths. In the system shown in Figure 10-24, a constant inlet pressure of 50 psig provides water to a 4-inch 400 foot long supply header. It tees off to three branches to shower nozzles spraying to atmosphere. Each line is a different pipe size or length and each has a control valve set to a desired flow rate. For this system, the outlet pressure of the control valves is atmospheric pressure.

Pipe 1 is 2.5-inch and 200 feet in length with a control valve that's 71% open to maintain a flow rate of 200 gpm. Pipe 2 is 2-inch and 150 feet long. Its control valve is 58% open at a flow rate of 75 gpm. Pipe 3 is 2-inch and 200 feet in length with a control valve that's 66% open at 100 gpm. There are no elevation changes in the system. The valve positions are determined by the size and flow coefficient profile for each valve.

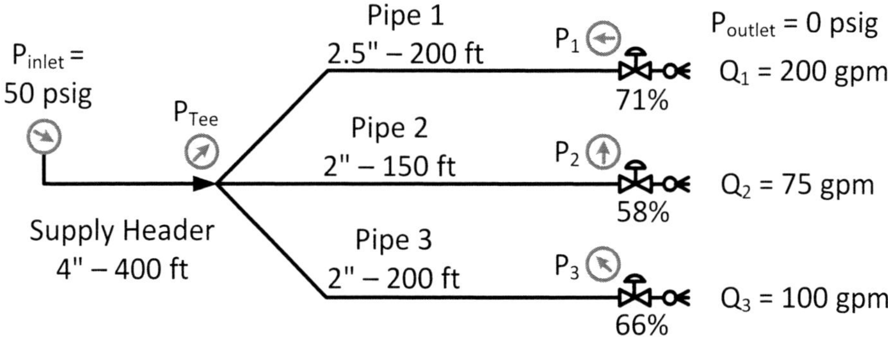

Figure 10-24. Evaluating head loss and pressure drops in a branching system.

Since the flow rates, pipe properties, and fluid properties are known, the head loss in each individual branch and the common supply header can be calculated. The head loss can be converted to pressure drop and the pressures at the tee and at the inlet of each control valve can be calcuated.

Figure 10-25 shows calculated results for the head loss and pressure drops in the branching system.

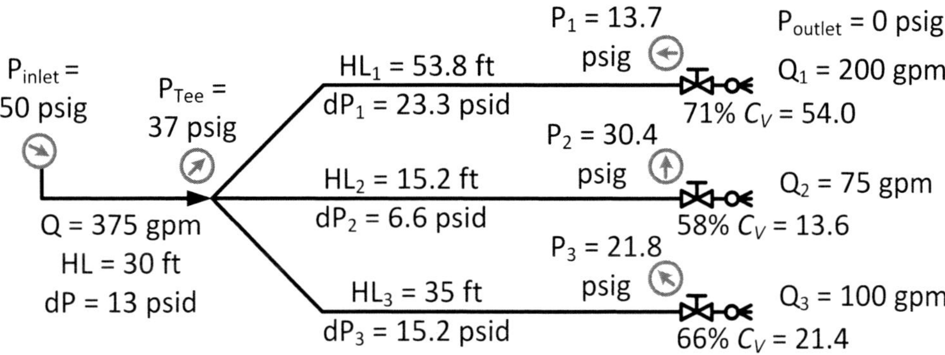

Figure 10-25. Head loss and pressure drops in a branching system.

Knowing the flow rate of 375 gpm, the head loss in the supply header can be calculated using the Darcy method and converted into pressure drop. For the given supply header, the head loss is 30 feet giving a corresponding pressure drop of 13 psid. Given the 50 psig supply header pressure, the pressure at the tee would be 37 psig.

The head loss in Pipe 1 is 53.8 feet with a pressure drop of 23.3 psid at a flow rate of 200 gpm, providing 13.7 psig at P_1, the inlet of the upper flow control valve. For Pipe 2 with a flow rate of 75 gpm, the head loss is 15.2 feet for a pressure drop of 6.6 psid, making P_2= 30.4 psig. Pipe 3 has a flow rate of 100 gpm which creates 35 feet of head loss and 15.2 psid of pressure drop, so P_3 = 21.8 psig.

Branching System Response to Changing Flow Rates with Automatic Control Valves

Because the end users in the branching system are hydraulically connected, what occurs in one branch will have an impact on the other end users. Consider a 30 gpm increase in the flow rate of Pipe 1, as shown in Figure 10-26 with the flow rates in the other two branches held constant with automatic flow control valves.

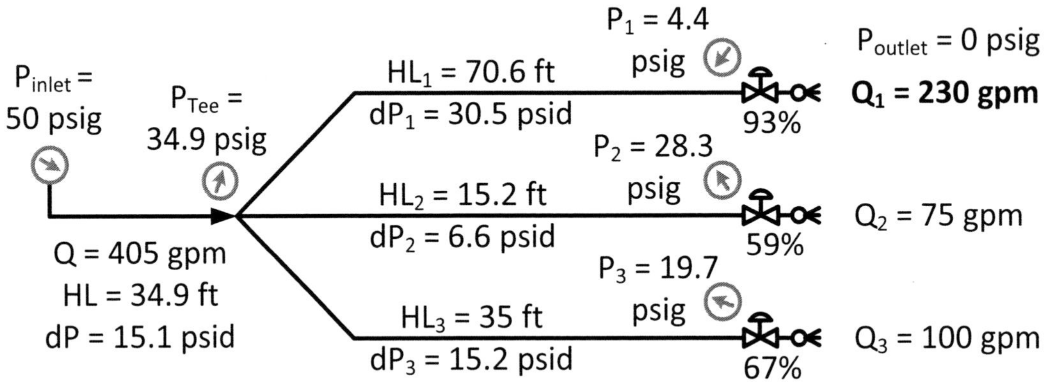

Figure 10-26. Branching system response to increased flow rate while other end user flow rates remain constant. **PF**

The increased flow rate is achieved by opening valve 1 from 71 to 93%. The amount it opens will depend on the size and flow characteristic of the valve.

The increased flow rate in Pipe 1 also increases the flow rate in the supply header. With a constant supply header pressure of 50 psig, the increased supply header flow rate increases its head loss and pressure drop, in this case to 34.9 feet of head loss and 15.1 psi of pressure drop, resulting in a lower pressure at the tee of 34.9 psig.

The increased flow rate in Pipe 1 increases its head loss and pressure drop, lowering the pressure at inlet of the #1 control valve from 13.7 psig to 4.4 psig.

In response, the lower pressure at the tee reduces the inlet pressures at control valves #2 and #3 causing them to open slightly to maintain their flow rates. Again, how much they open will depend on the characteristics of the valves. In this system they opened by about 1% to maintain their set flow rates.

Branching System Response to Changing Flow Rates with Manually Adjusted Valves

If the valves in the previous branching system are manually operated, their resistances and flow coefficients (C_V) will depend on their positions and will remain constant unless their positions are changed. If the valve in the upper branch is adjusted to increase the flow from 200 to 230 gpm, while the valves in the middle and lower branches remain fixed, the system response would be different, as shown in Figure 10-27.

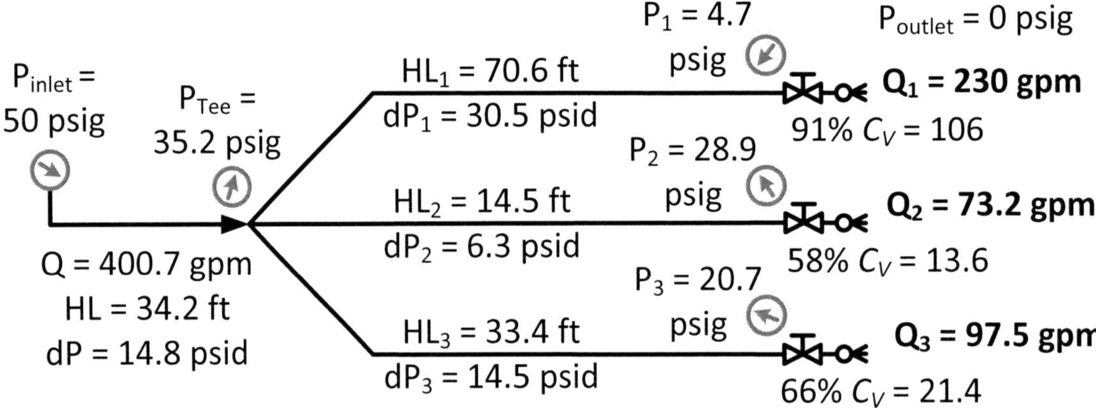

Figure 10-27. Branching system response to increased flow rate with manually operated valves. **PF**

The flow in the upper branch is increased by manually throttling open its valve from 71% to 91%, increasing its C_V from 54 to 106. Because the increased flow in the upper branch increases the flow in the supply header, the header has more head loss and a larger pressure drop, so the pressure at the tee decreases.

The reduced pressure at the tee causes a lower pressure at the inlet of the valves in the middle and lower branches. Since the valves in these branches are fixed, their flow coefficients don't change, and the reduced pressure drop across the valves causes the flow rates in the two branches to decrease.

The 30 gpm increase in the upper branch results in only 25.7 gpm increase in the supply header, the remaining 4.3 gpm comes from reducing the flow in middle and lower branches.

System Static and Dynamic Head

The resistance to the flow of fluid in a piping system is due to both static head and dynamic head in the system.

Static Head

Static head is the amount of energy that has to be added to the fluid to overcome elevation and pressure differences between the source and end users in the system, as shown in Equation 10-2.

$$Static\ Head = \Delta\ Elevation\ Head + \Delta\ Pressure\ Head$$

Equation 10-2

The elevation head is the difference in the elevation between the liquid surfaces in the product tank (or other end user) and the supply tank, as shown in Equation 10-3.

$$\Delta\ Elevation\ Head = \begin{pmatrix} Elevation\ of\ Discharge \\ Tank's\ Liquid\ Surface \end{pmatrix} - \begin{pmatrix} Elevation\ of\ Supply \\ Tank's\ Liquid\ Surface \end{pmatrix}$$

Equation 10-3

The pressure head is the difference in pressures between the two tanks converted to feet of fluid, as shown in Equation 10-4 which uses the units of psi for tank pressure. If a tank pressure is at a vacuum, convert to a negative value of psig to use this equation.

$$\Delta\ Pressure\ Head = \begin{pmatrix} Discharge\ Tank's & - & Supply\ Tank's \\ Surface\ Pressure & & Surface\ Pressure \end{pmatrix} \frac{144}{\rho}$$

Equation 10-4

Static head is the amount of energy that must be added by a pump before a single drop of fluid can move through the piping. It does not depend on the flow rate between the source and the end users, only the elevation and pressure differences. Static head can also be calculated between any two points in a system.

Dynamic Head

Dynamic head is the amount of energy needed to overcome the head loss caused by friction and changes in fluid momentum in the system. It can be calculated by adding the pipeline and component head losses together in series and parallel, or by subtracting the static head from the pump total head produced at the pump's flow rate, as shown in Equation 10-5.

$$Dynamic\ Head = Pump\ Total\ Head\ - Static\ Head \qquad \text{Equation 10-5}$$

Example 10-3: Calculating System Static and Dynamic Head

For the system shown in Figure 10-28, determine the amount of elevation head, pressure head, static head, the pump's total head, and the system dynamic head.

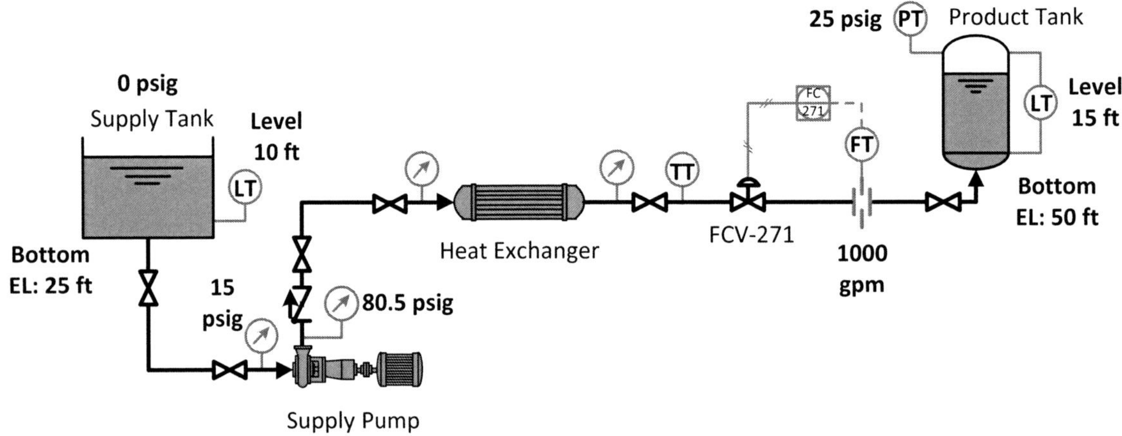

Figure 10-28. Calculating system static and dynamic head.

The bottom of the Supply Tank is at an elevation of 25 feet measured from the reference plane. The tank is open to atmosphere and has a level of 10 feet of 60 °F water with a fluid density of 62.4 lb/ft^3. The bottom elevation of the Product Tank is at 50 feet and the tank is pressurized to 25 psig and has a 15 foot liquid level in it. The pump has a suction pressure of 15 psig and a discharge pressure of 80.5 psig.

Using Equation 10-3 to calculate the elevation head:

$$\Delta\ Elevation\ Head = (50 + 15) - (25 + 10) = 30\ ft$$

Using Equation 10-4 to calculate the pressure head:

$$\Delta\ Pressure\ Head = \frac{144}{62.4}(25 - 0)psi = 57.7\ ft$$

Using Equation 10-2 to calculate the static head:

$$Static\ Head = 30\ ft + 57.7\ ft = 87.7\ ft$$

Equation 4-2 in the pump chapter can be used to estimate the total head the pump is producing:

$$TH = dP_{pump}\left(\frac{144}{\rho}\right) = (80.5 - 15)\left(\frac{144}{62.4}\right) = 151.2\ ft$$

The pump's total head can also be obtained from the pump curve at the measured flow rate.

The system dynamic head can now be calculated using Equation 10-5:

$$Dynamic\ Head = (Pump\ Total\ Head\ - Static\ Head) = (151.2\ - 87.7) = 63.5\ ft$$

The dynamic head could also be calculated by adding together the head loss across all the pipelines, valves, fitting, components, and controls.

Static and Dynamic Head in Various Systems

The amount of static and dynamic head in a piping system will depend on the configuration and the components in the system. For example, closed loop systems only have dynamic head, but no static head. This is because all the energy needed to raise the fluid to a higher elevation in the system is recovered as the fluid drops back to the pump suction in the return header in a closed loop system.

Open and branching systems can have a varying amount of static and dynamic head. They may be static head or dynamic head dominated or have a combination of both.

One thing to note is that the pump does not know how much of its total head is allocated to static or dynamic head in the system. The only thing the pump knows is that at a given flow rate the system on the suction side provides a certain amount of pressure to the pump inlet and the system on the discharge side presents a resistance to flow that determines the amount of pressure at the pump's outlet. The pump's differential pressure gain, or total head, exactly matches the hydraulic requirements of the piping system.

Visualizing Energy Addition and Losses in a Piping System

Pumps, tanks, and vessels provide energy to a fluid to cause it to flow in a piping system. Pipelines, valves, fittings, controls, instruments, and other components dissipate some of this energy in the form of head loss due to friction and changes in fluid momentum. The final fluid energy state at the end users will depend on the fluid's elevation, pressure, and veloctiy. There are a couple of ways to visualize these energy additions and losses in the system.

A system resistance curve graphed on the pump curve is the traditional way to view energy addition and losses and the interaction between the pump and system. The system resistance curve is a graph of the static and dynamic head of the system as a function of flow rate through the piping. This method is very useful for single path open systems and single loop closed systems, but has limitations for multi-path systems.

The Total Fluid Energy graph is another method to visualize the hydraulic energy in the system. This graph plots the amount of total hydraulic energy (elevation, pressure, and velocity head) along a flow path in the system and is more useful for multi-loop closed systems and branching systems.

The System Reslstance Curve and Pump Curve

The system resistance curve can be used to visualize the energy picture in a single path open or closed system. It is generated by adding the individual curves for the pipelines, valves, fittings, and components using the series and parallel path graphical method described earlier in this chapter.

Figure 10-29 shows a typical pump curve along with three system resistance curves, one with dynamic head only, one with 30 feet of static head, and one with 60 feet of static head. Each system requires 70 feet of head at 400 gpm.

The bottom system resistance curve could represent the resistance of a closed loop system or an open system with no static head. The middle curve shows the resistance for an open system with a combination of static and dynamic head, and the top curve is for a system that is static head dominated.

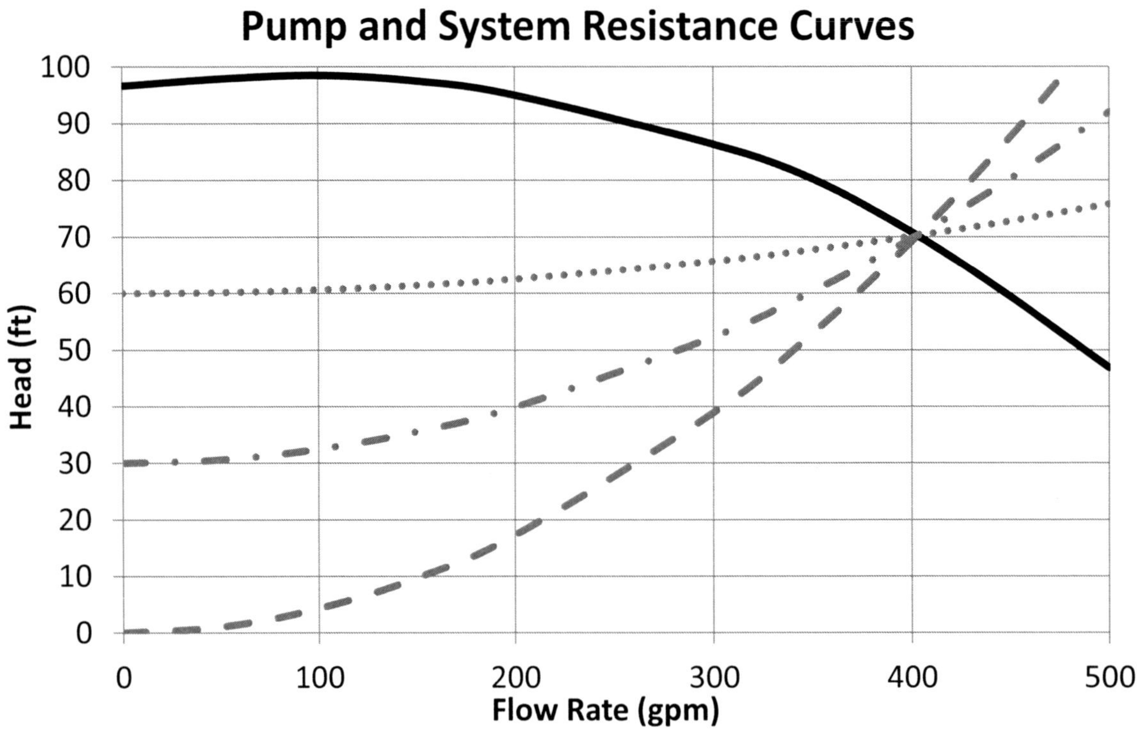

Figure 10-29. System resistance curves with various amounts of static and dynamic head.

The System Resistance Curve and the Effect of Throttling

The system resistance curve can include the resistance of all devices in the piping system, including the head loss across the control valves. In this case, the pump will operate at the intersection of the pump and system resistance curves. When the control valve is throttled to reduce the flow rate, the system resistance curve pivots and becomes steeper, as shown in Figure 10-30 as flow is reduced from 400 gpm to 300 gpm.

The disadvantage to this approach is that it is easy to lose sight of how much head loss and pressure drop occurs across the control valve at any given flow rate.

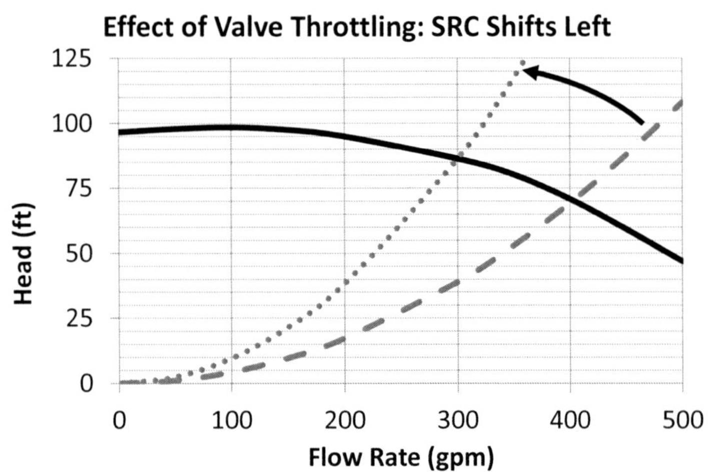

Figure 10-30. System resistance curve shifts with a change in valve position that causes a change in flow rate.

The system resistance curve can also be calculated by including only the resistance of fully open control valves. The curve can then be considered a base line reference curve that shows the maximum obtainable flow rate in the system, as shown in Figure 10-31.

The curve will not shift with a change in flow rate. Instead it remains fixed and the difference between the pump and system curves at a given flow rate represents the amount of head loss, or energy dissipated, across the control valve.

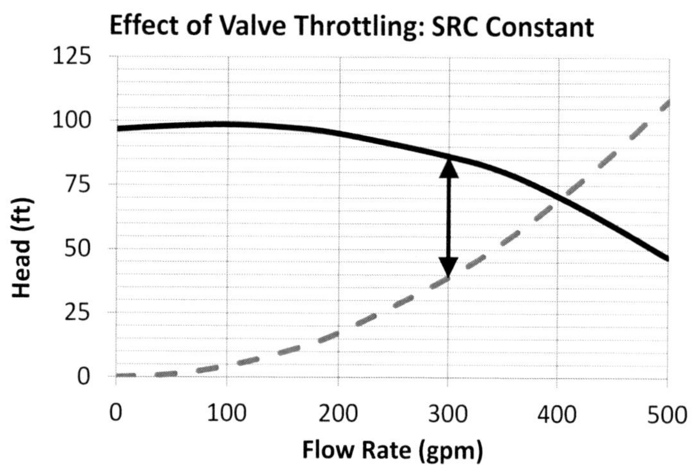

Figure 10-31. System resistance curve viewed as a fixed base line reference with all valves fully open.

For the case where the control valve is throttled to obtain 300 gpm, the pump produces about 85 feet of total head and the system (minus the control valve) requires about 40 feet, so the control valve will have to have about 45 feet of head loss across it, over 50% of the pump's total head.

Limitations of the System Resistance Curve

The system resistance curve is very useful for visualizing energy addition and losses in certain types of piping systems, particularly for single path open systems and single loop closed systems. But for some systems the curve is not as clearly defined because it is impossible to develop a single curve that represents the hydraulic performance of the entire system over a range of flow rates.

Branching systems, such as the one shown in Figure 10-32, show the limitations of the system resistance curve. The Supply Pump produces 181.9 feet of total head at 1,950 gpm, but the pump doesn't know how much of its total head is allocated to static head and dynamic head in the system.

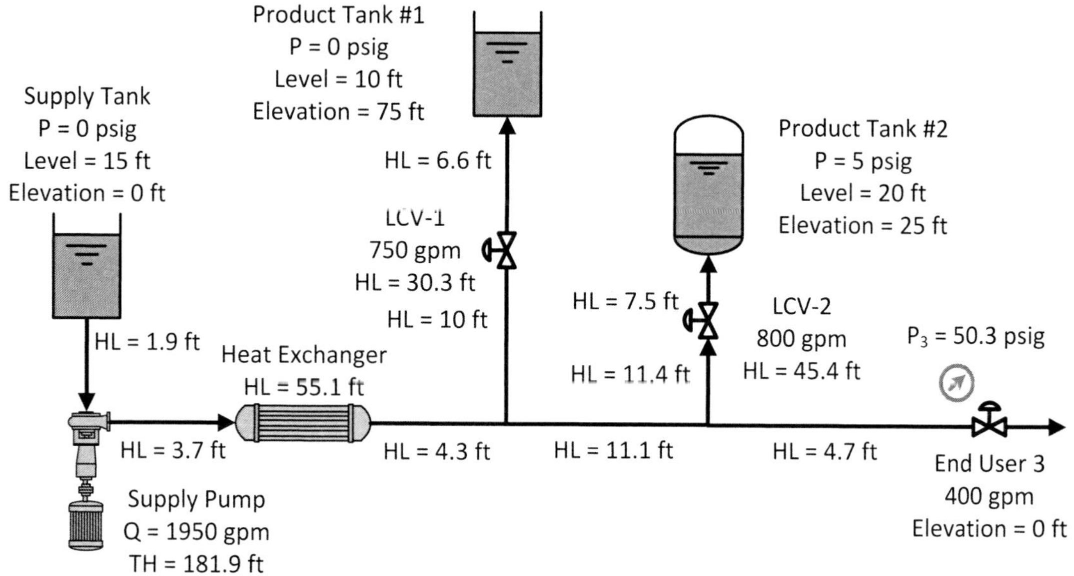

Figure 10-32. Limitations of the system resistance curve for branching systems.

In the branching system, a different amount of the pump's total head is allocated to the static and dynamic head of each branch depending on the elevations, pressures, and flow rates in the branch. But what must hold true is that the total energy added by the pump must equal the static head plus the dynamic head in each branch.

For example, for each branch the static head can be calculated between the Supply Tank and end user using Equation 10-2 to 10-4, and the dynamic head can be calculated by adding together the head losses for the pipelines, valves, fittings, and components from the Supply Tank to each end user.

For Branch #1:

Dynamic Head = (1.9 + 3.7 + 55.1 + 4.3 + 10 + 30.3 + 6.6) = 111.9 feet

Static Head = (85 - 15) + (0 - 0) x 144/62.4 = 70 feet

Total Head = 111.9 + 70 = 181.9 feet, which equals the total head of the pump

For Branch #2:

Dynamic Head = (1.9 + 3.7 + 55.1 + 4.3 + 11.1 + 11.4 + 45.4 + 7.5) = 140.4 feet

Static Head = (45 - 15) + (5 - 0) x 144/62.4 = 41.5 feet

Total Head = 140.4 + 41.5 = 181.9 feet, which equals the total head of the pump

For Branch #3:

Dynamic Head = (1.9 + 3.7 + 55.1 + 4.3 + 11.1 + 4.7) = 80.8 feet

Static Head = (0 - 15) + (50.3 - 0) x 144/62.4 = 101.1 feet

Total Head = 80.8 + 101.1 = 181.9 feet, which equals the total head of the pump

For each branch, the static head plus the dynamic head equals the total head of the pump, but there are different amounts allocated to each. This shows the limitation of the system resistance curve: there is no single curve that can be drawn to represent the performance of the entire system.

In addition, the system resistance will depend on the combination of the flows and resistances in all the branches. For example, if the flows are distributed differently to the branches, but the total is still 1,950 gpm, the pump will still produce 181.9 feet of total head. The static head will not change if the tank levels and pressures stay the same, but the dynamic head will shift from the throttled valves to the pipelines and other components in the branch. If the pressure or tank levels at the end users change, the static head in that branch will change.

The Total Energy Graph

The Total Energy Graph of the fluid's total energy as a function of the distance from the pump is a better way to visualize the energy added at the pump, the energy losses of the components in the system, and the final energy state at each end user for a branching system.

Total Energy Graph for Branching Systems

The Total Energy Graph of the branching system in the previous example is shown in Figure 10-33. With the pump suction at the zero distance mark, the beginning of the graph is the total energy provided by the liquid level in the tank, or 15 feet of fluid. There is a 1.9 feet drop in head due to the head loss in

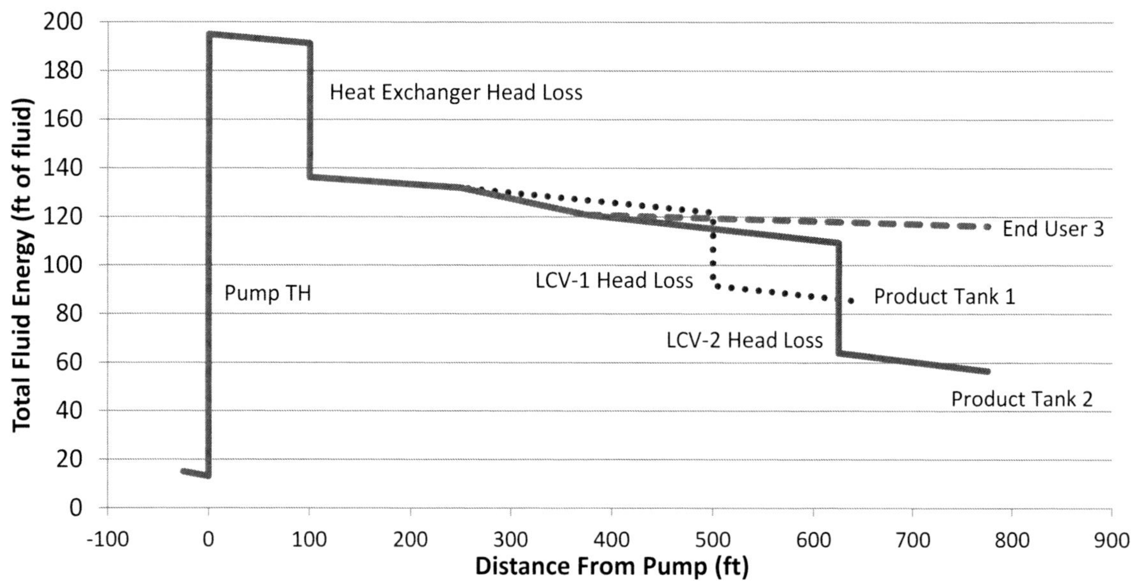

Figure 10-33. Total Energy Graph as a function of distance from the pump for a branching system.

the suction piping, then the pump adds 181.9 feet of head to the fluid.

Another 3.7 feet of head loss in the discharge piping from the pump to the heat exchanger occurs, then a large drop in the total energy due to the 55.1 feet of head loss across the heat exchanger, followed by another drop of 4.3 feet drop in the heat exchanger outlet piping to the first tee, which is about 250 feet distance from the pump.

At this point, some flow branches off to the first user to Product Tank #1, indicated by the dotted line representing the 10 feet of head loss in the LCV-1 inlet pipeline. Another 30.3 feet of head loss occurs across LCV-1, followed by 6.6 feet of head loss in the pipe between LCV-1 and Product Tank #1. The liquid in Product Tank #1 has 85 feet of energy at the surface of the tank.

From the first tee to the second tee there is 11.1 feet of head loss, which is common for Product Tank #2 and End User #3. The second tee is located 375 feet from the pump. The solid line represents the energy path to Product Tank #2 with the head loss for the inlet pipeline to LCV-2 (11.4 feet), the head loss across LCV-2 (45.4 feet), and the pipeline to Product Tank #2 (7.5 feet). The liquid in Product Tank #2 has 45 feet of elevation head plus another 11.5 feet of pressure head due to the 5 psig of pressure in the tank, for a total fluid energy state of 56.5 feet of head.

The End User #3 has 50.3 psig of hydraulic energy, or 116 feet of pressure head, measured at the inlet of the valve.

If the flow rate to each user is increased, the pump total head will decrease, each pipeline head loss will increase so the slope of their energy lines will become steeper, there will be more head loss in the heat exchanger, and less head loss across the level control valves. The final total energy state at Product Tank #1 and #2 will remain the same if their levels and pressures are constant. The total energy at End User #3 goes down because the pressure at the inlet of the valve decreases.

Total Energy Graph for Mult-Loop Closed Systems

Multi-loop closed systems pose a similar problem that a branching system does when trying to visualize the energy picture with a system resistance curve. There is no single curve that represents the hydraulic performance of the entire system because in a multi-loop closed system, a change in flow rate in any of the loops will affect the pressures and/or flow rates in all of the other loops. The Total Energy Graph is a more useful way to visualize the energy addition and losses in the system.

For a multi-loop closed system, one of the loops will be the Most Hydraulically Remote Loop (MHRL). This is the loop with the least amount of hydraulic energy, or differential pressure, available for control of the flow through the loop. Typically it is the loop physically farthest from the pump, but not necessarily. Higher head loss in pipelines or components in a loop closer to the pump can make it the MHRL. For a system with a MHRL close to the pump, an opportunity may exist to optimize the system.

Figure 10-34 shows a typical multi-loop closed chilled water system. The Supply Pump provides chilled water to three identical heat exchangers at 600 gpm each. The pump produces 241 feet of total head at 1,800 gpm. The Surge Tank level provides 10 feet of total hydraulic energy at the connection close to the pump suction.

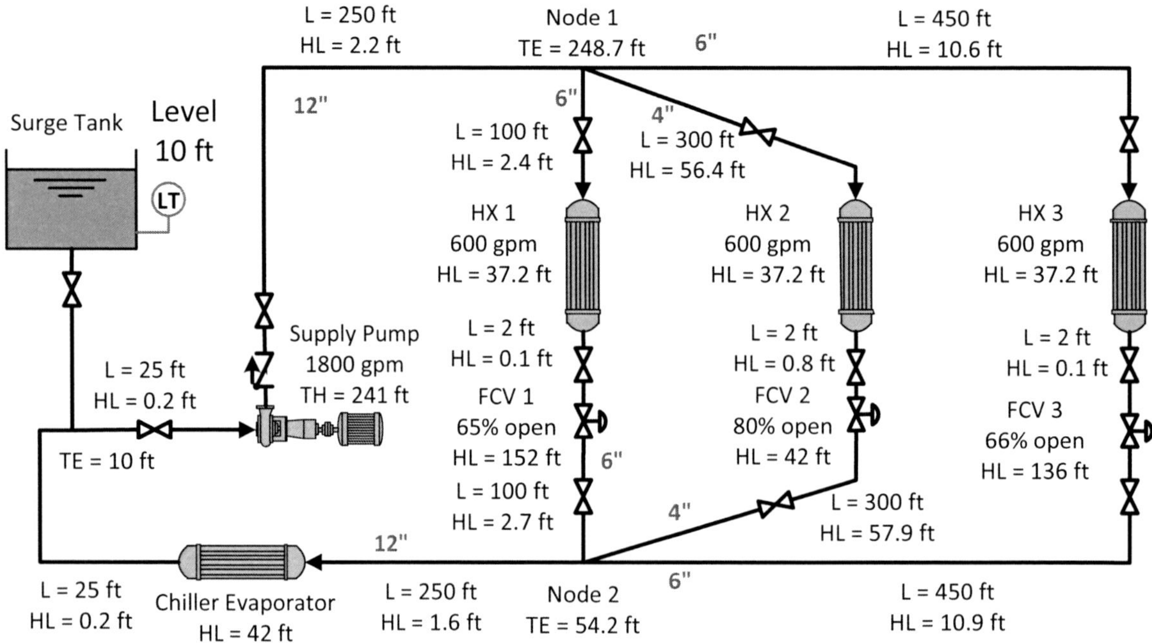

Figure 10-34. Multi-loop closed chilled water system.

Pipeline lengths and head losses are shown on the figure, along with the head loss across the heat exchangers and flow control valves. The losses around each loop must equal 241 feet according to Kirchhoff's Second Law and the Law of Conservation of Energy.

In this system, the pipelines going to and from HX-2 are 4-inch, whereas HX-1 and HX-3 have 6-inch lines. The smaller pipeline creates higher head loss per foot compared to the larger lines for the same 600 gpm flow rate. Because of the increased head loss in the middle loop, FCV-2 has less energy available for control so it has to be farther open compared to the other control valves with the same flow rate. FCV-1 is 65% open, FCV-2 is 80% open, and FCV-3 is 66% open. The middle loop is the most hydraulically remote loop, even though it is physically closer to the pump than the third loop.

Figure 10-35 shows the Total Energy Graph for this multi-loop closed system as a function of the distance from the pump. The total energy at the pump suction is 9.8 feet, which is the 10 feet of energy due to the liquid level in the surge tank minus the 0.2 feet of head loss in the suction piping. The pump's total

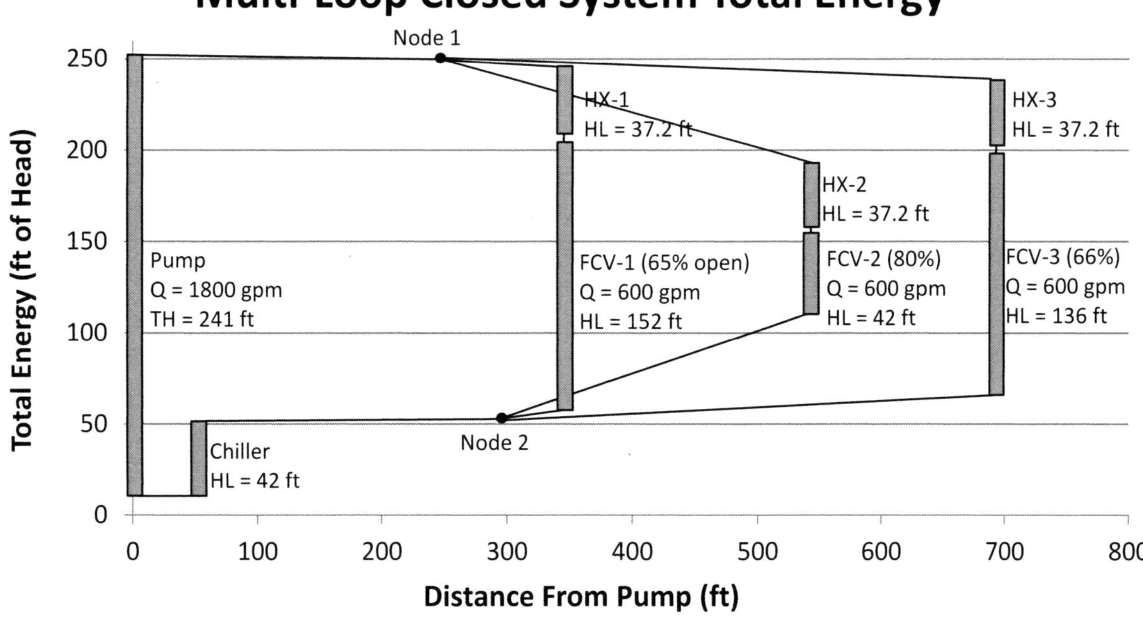

Figure 10-35. Total energy graph for the multi-loop closed system.

head of 241 feet at 1800 gpm makes the total energy at the discharge just over 250 feet.

The energy line for each pipeline has a slope that represents the amount of head loss per foot. The pipelines to and from HX-2 are steeper because the 4-inch pipelines have a higher velocity compared to the 6-inch lines to the other heat exchangers.

At 600 gpm, each heat exchanger has 37.2 feet of head loss across it. The chiller has 42 feet of head loss.

FCV-1 is 65% open with 152 feet of head loss (or 66 psid pressure drop), FCV-2 is 80% open and has 42 feet of head loss (18 psid), and FCV-3 is 66% open with 136 feet of head loss (59 psid). There is less head loss across FCV-2 and it is farther open because of the greater head loss occurring in the inlet pipeline to HX-1 and the outlet pipeline from FCV-2. Again, this indicates that the middle loop is the most hydraulically remote loop (MHRL), even though it is physically closer to the pump than the third loop. The center loop of this system is a bottleneck that may hamper expansion of the system.

The end users (the heat exchangers) may be satisfied with the performance of this system because their control valves can regulate the flow rates up to 600 gpm, but what if they need more than 600 gpm? As the flow rate in one loop increases as its control valve opens, the pump total head decreases according to its pump curve. The other control valves must open farther to maintain their flow rates, otherwise there will be a decrease in the flow rate in those loops.

Consider the system response when the end users require an increased flow rate to 750 gpm to each heat exchanger, as shown in Figure 10-36. At some point as the flow is increased to the first and third heat exchangers, FCV-2 becomes fully open, preventing an increase of the flow to the center loop.

With 750 gpm in the first and third loops and 600 gpm in the center loop, the pump produces 231 feet of total head at a combined flow of 2,100 gpm. Increased flow rates result in higher head losses in HX-1, HX-3, and the Chiller Evaporator, as well as increased head loss in the piping (some values don't

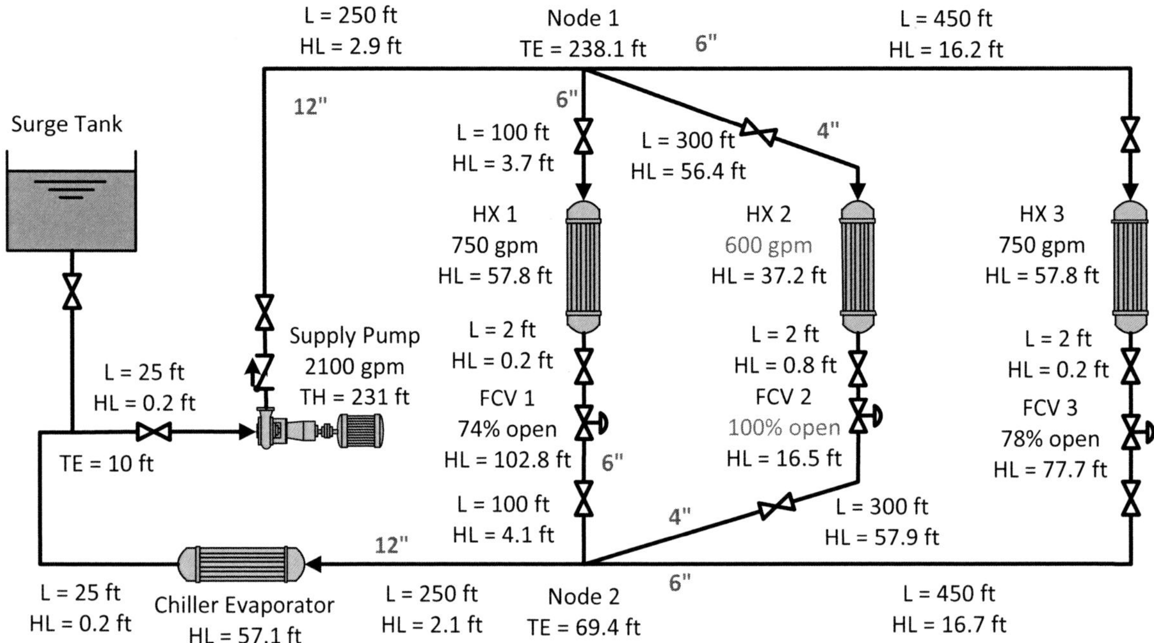

Figure 10-36. Evaluating increased flow rates in a bottlenecked multi-loop closed chilled water system. PF

reflect an increase because of rounding). There is less head loss across the control valves because they are farther open.

Figure 10-37 shows the Total Energy Graph for the multi-loop closed system at increased flow rates. The total energy available at the pump suction is still around 10 feet based on the liquid level in the Surge Tank minus the head loss in the suction piping. The reduced energy added by the pump combined

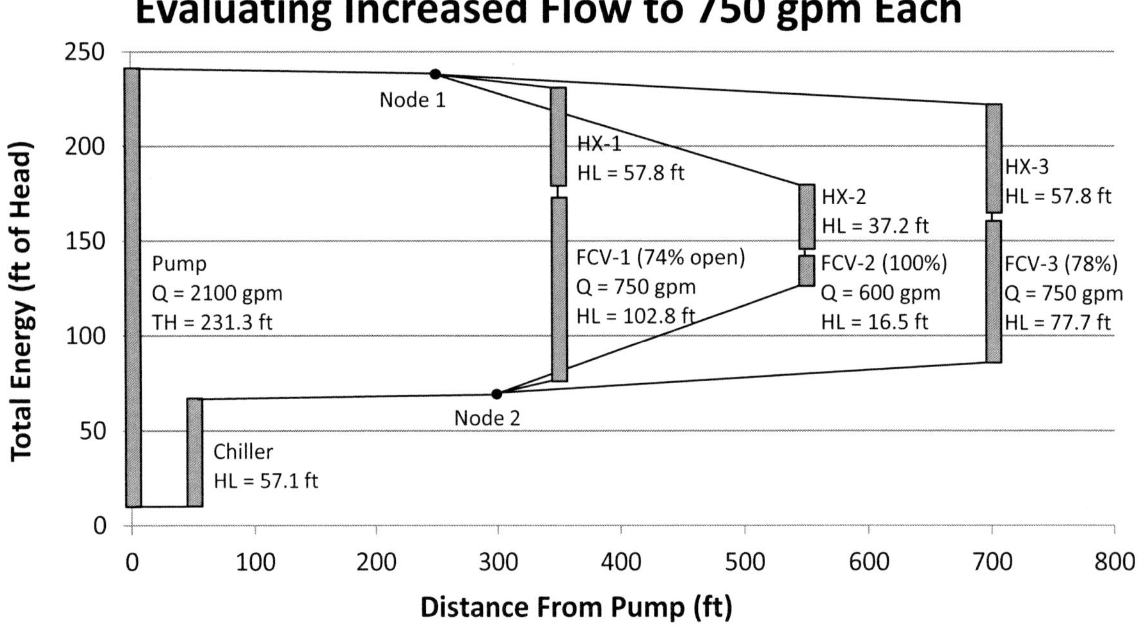

Figure 10-37. Total energy graph for the multi-loop closed system with increased flow rates.

with the increased head loss in the pump discharge header provides less total hydraulic energy available at Node 1. Because of the increased head loss in the Chiller Evaporator and the return header, Node 2 must be at a higher total energy state compared to the previous case at 1,800 gpm. This higher energy state is achieved because all of the flow control valves are farther open and have less head loss across them, thereby providing more energy to Node 2.

Having a loop physically closer to the pump than other loops that has less differential pressure (head loss) available for control is an indication that its end user may not get sufficient flow to meet its needs. It is also an indication that the system can be optimized for better performance. The center loop in this system is clearly the bottleneck because it is unable to achieve an increased flow rate to 750 gpm. In addition, if the flows to the first or third heat exchanger are increased above 750 gpm, because FCV-2 is already fully open, there will be a drop in the flow to HX-2.

De-bottlenecking Systems

What can be done to the system if each heat exchanger absolutely needed to have 750 gpm to meet the cooling requirements of the processes? One solution is to increase the amount of total head that the pump produces at the desired flow rates. This can potentially be done by increasing the pump impeller size, speeding up the pump with a variable speed drive, installing a larger pump, or placing a second pump in parallel.

Another solution is to de-bottleneck the system by replacing the 4-inch lines in the middle loop with 6-inch lines. This would reduce the fluid velocity and the head loss in the piping and provide more hydraulic energy to the control valve. This solution is shown in Figure 10-38 with the corresponding Total Energy Graph shown in Figure 10-39.

With the larger pipelines in the center loop, the pipelines have less resistance to flow and less head loss, which provides more fluid energy for the control valve to regulate flow. The most hydraulically remote

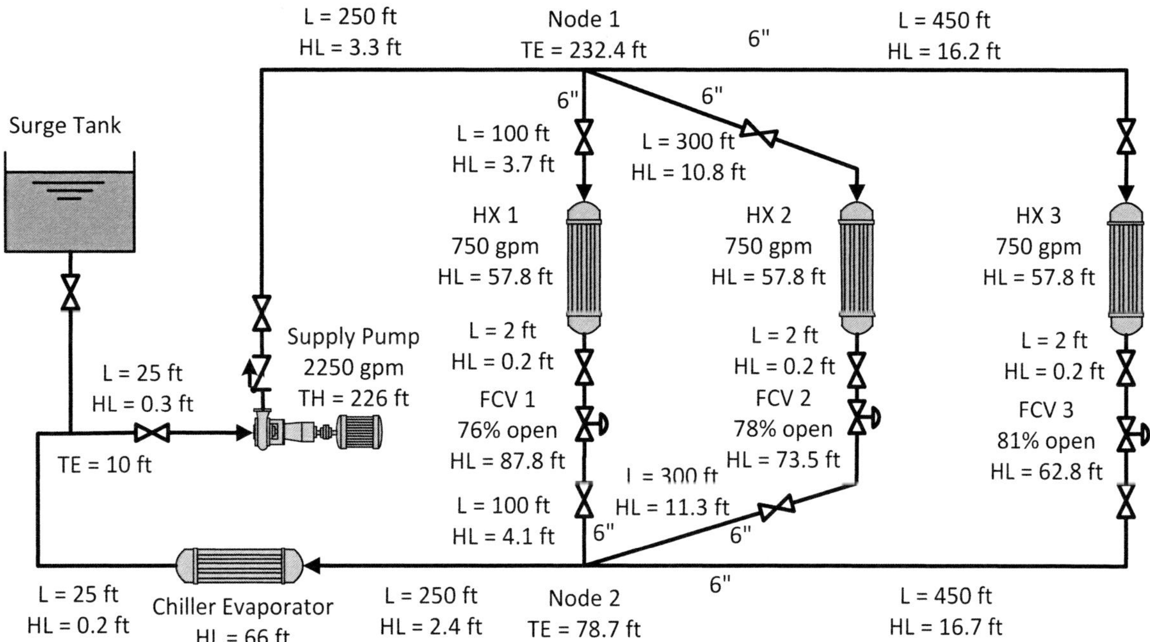

Figure 10-38. Removing the bottleneck and evaluating increased flow rates in the multi-loop closed chilled water system. PF

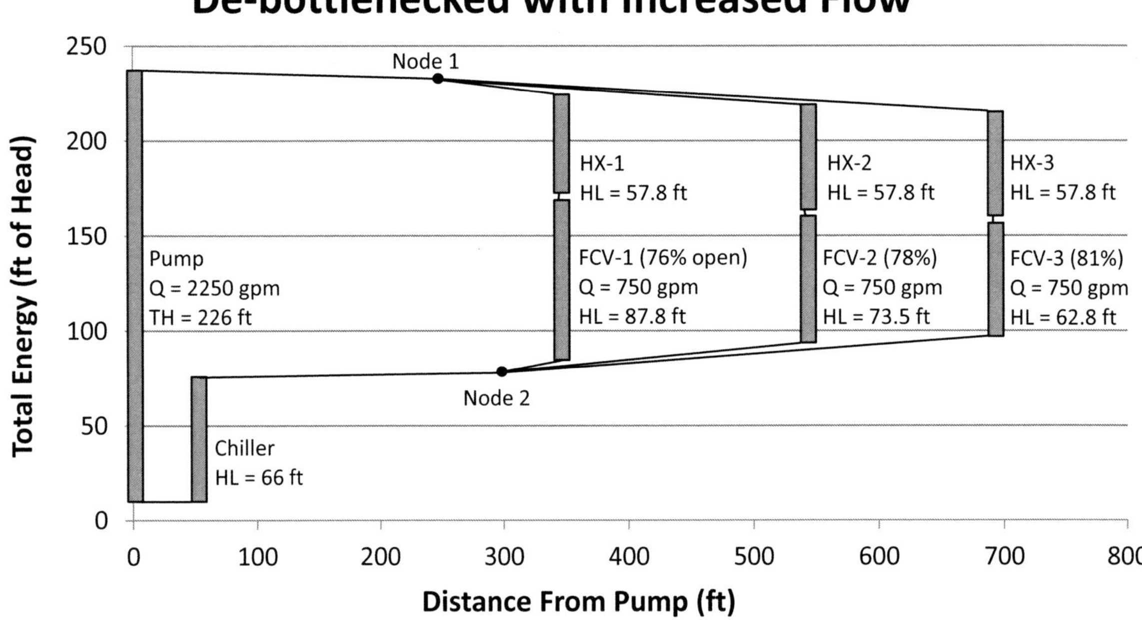

Figure 10-39. Total energy graph for the de-bottlenecked multi-loop closed system with increased flow rates.

loop has now shifted to the third loop, which is the one that is physically farthest from the pump and has the least amount of energy available for control, as shown by the position of the control valves.

The control valves have to be farther open the greater the distance the valve is from the pump: FCV-1 is 76% open, FCV-2 is 78% open, and FCV-3 is 81% open at 750 gpm each.

By removing the bottleneck in the system, not only can the higher desired flow rate to all the heat exchangers be achieved, but it is easy to see that the control valve in the most hydraulically remote loop has excess head available for control. This indicates that the system can be optimized to reduce the total energy consumption. This can be done by slowing the pump down with a variable speed drive or trimming the impeller to reduce the pump's total head. For example, if the impeller is trimmed to reduce total head by 30 feet, the head loss across all the control valves would be reduced by 30 feet.

Troubleshooting Abnormal Operating Conditions in a Piping System

Because the components of a piping system are hydraulically connected, a problem with one component will affect the performance of the devices in the rest of the system. For example, the root cause of a problem may be with a pump, but the symptoms of the problem may manifest itself at a control valve.

A key part of effectively troubleshooting any piping system is knowing what is "normal". If normal operating conditions are not known, it will be difficult to identify when abnormal conditions occur. Part of knowing what is normal is understanding the expected hydraulic performance of all the components in the system, what processes are occuring in the system, and how the performance of one device will affect the rest of the system.

Knowing the normal operating conditions requires monitoring key system parameters such as tank levels and pressures, pump suction and discharge pressures and flow rates, fluid temperatures, differential pressures across devices, control valve positions, and flow rates and pressures throughout the system.

The troubleshooter must have the right information available to identify normal and abnormal operating conditions and he/she must have confidence in the values that are observed. Unfortunately, many piping systems are not instrumented sufficiently to quickly identify problems as they occur, so it may take a long period of operation before symptoms are identified and the root cause corrected. In addition, instrumentation is susceptible to drift over time, so a calibration program that verifies the accuracy of process measurements is crucial for effective troubleshooting.

Normal Operating Conditions

The piping system in Figure 10-40 shows the normal operating conditions for a simple single path open system. The normal operating conditions shown are based on the Supply and Product Tank liquid levels and pressures, the Supply Pump's performance curve, and the hydraulic performances of the heat exchanger, flow control valve, and orifice plate flow meter. In addition, the size, length, and material of construction of the pipelines, the size and type of valves and fittings, and the fluid properties (water at 60 °F) determine the head loss and pressure drops throughout the system.

The Supply Tank is open to atmosphere and its level is maintained at 10 feet. The Supply Pump suction pressure is 15 psig and discharge pressure is 80.5 psig. The Heat Exchanger has an inlet pressure of 67 psig and an outlet pressure of 57 psig, for a total pressure drop of 10 psid at 1,000 gpm. The flow control valve FCV-271 is 85% open with 1,000 gpm flowing through it. The Product Tank is pressurized to 25 psig and has a liquid level of 15 feet.

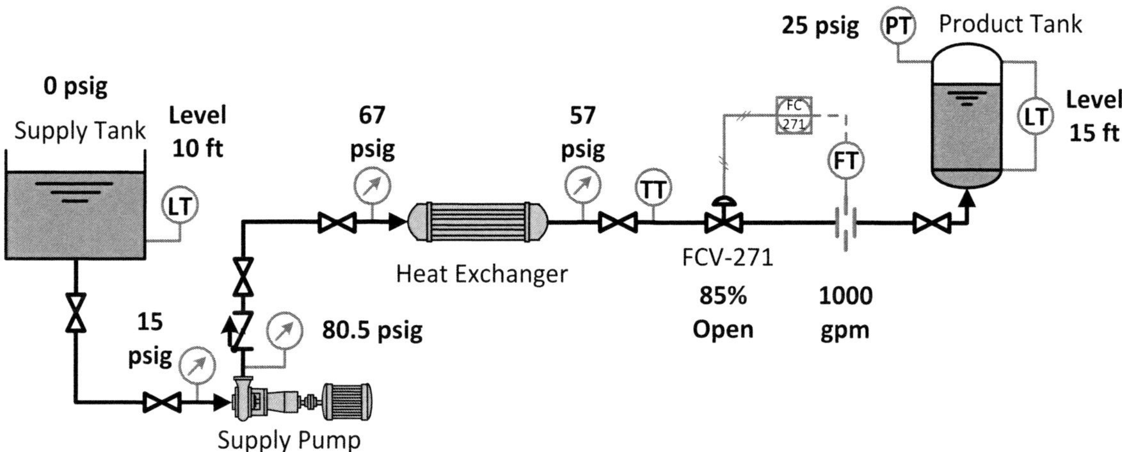

Figure 10-40. Normal operating conditions for a simple single path open system. PF

Troubleshooting Problem #1

Figure 10-41 shows a set of abnormal operating conditions for this piping system. In this case, FCV-271 is 100% open and can only obtain 940 gpm flow rate, so the flow rate from the Product Tank has to be reduced. This problem is limiting the overall plant production rate.

Table 10-2 summarizes the normal and abnormal operating conditions side-by-side and shows whether the measured value increased, decreased, or stayed the same. The table can be evaluated to determine potential causes that may explain why the given parameter changed and whether that change is expected knowing the normal operating performance of the equipment.

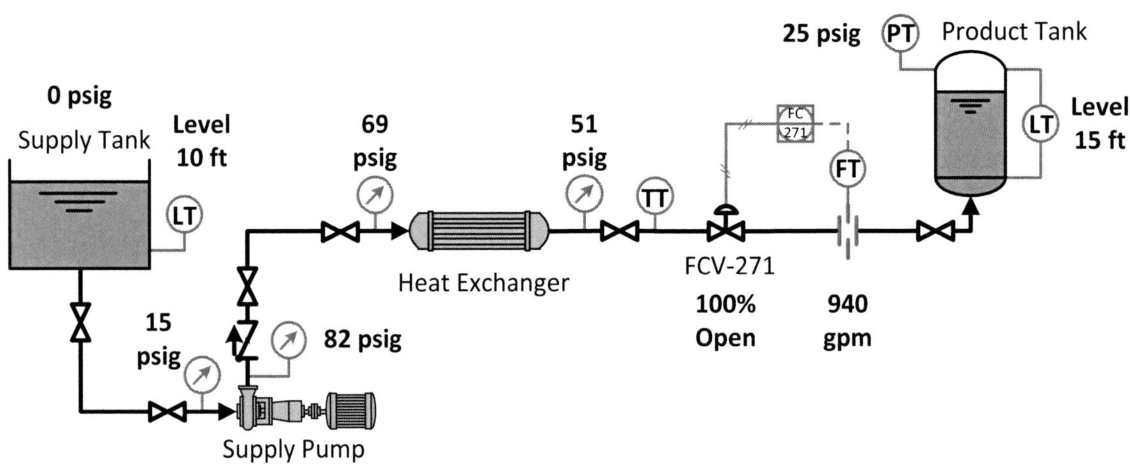

Figure 10-41. Abnormal operating conditions that limit plant production rate.

Table 10-2: Summary of Abnormal Operating Conditions

Device / Measurement	***Normal Conditions***	***Abnormal Conditions***	***Change***
Supply Tank			
Pressure (psig)	0	0	Same
Level (feet)	10	10	Same
Supply Pump			
Suction Pressure (psig)	15	15	Same
Discharge Pressure (psig)	80.5	**82**	**Increased**
Differential Pressure (psid)	65.5	**67**	**Increased**
Heat Exchanger			
Inlet Pressure (psig)	67	**69**	**Increased**
Outlet Pressure (psig)	57	**51**	**Decreased**
Differential Pressure (psid)	10	**18**	**Increased**
Flow Control Valve			
Position (%)	85	**100**	**Increased**
Flow Transmitter			
Flow Rate (gpm)	1000	**940**	**Decreased**
Product Tank			
Pressure (psig)	25	25	Same
Level (feet)	15	15	Same

The Supply and Product Tank levels and pressures are normal, along with the pump suction pressure. The Supply Pump discharge pressure is higher than normal as well as the overall differential pressure across the pump. This indicates that the pump's total head is greater than normal, but given the reduced flow rate through the pump, this may be expected performance since the pump is running further back on its pump curve. A check of the performance against the pump curve will show if this change is expected.

The flow control valve is open farther than normal and the flow rate is less than normal.

The Heat Exchanger inlet pressure is higher than normal, but this is expected because of the higher pump discharge pressure, as well as to the reduced head loss and pressure drop in the discharge line of the pump. The Heat Exchanger outlet pressure is lower than normal and the differential pressure across the Heat Exchanger is greater. The differential pressure is 18 psid at 940 gpm compared to 10 psid at 1000 gpm, indicating that the Heat Exchanger is partially plugged.

Troubleshooting Problem #2

Figure 10-42 shows another set of abnormal operating conditions that could occur in this piping system. In this scenario, plant expansion is being considered and will require this system to deliver 1,200 gpm to the Product Tank. The system is currently operating at its designed flow rate of 1,000 gpm with FCV-271 at 95% open. An operational test of the system showed that it could only deliver a maximum of 1,015 gpm. This problem is preventing the planned expansion of the plant.

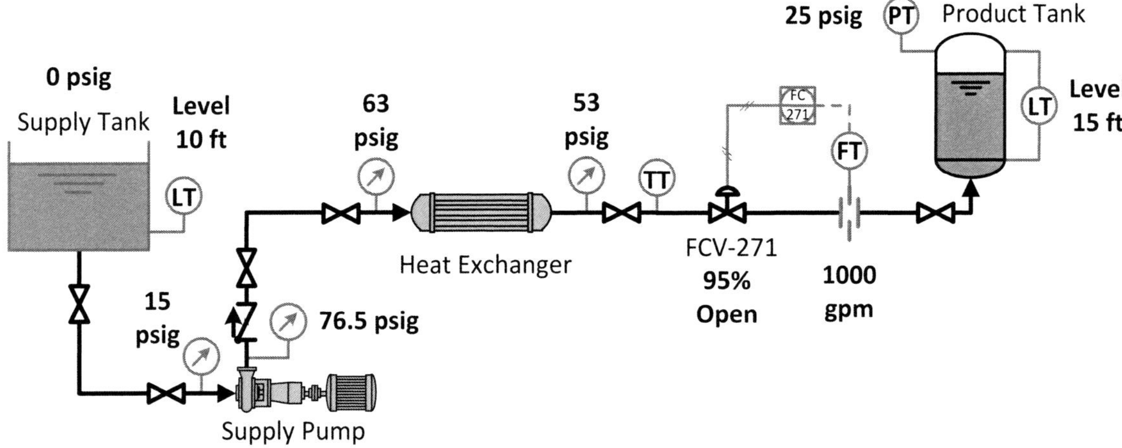

Figure 10-42. Abnormal operating conditions that are preventing plant expansion.

Table 10-3 summarizes the normal and abnormal operating conditions side-by-side and shows whether the measured value increased, decreased, or stayed the same. The table can be methodically evaluated to determine potential causes that may explain the changes and whether the change is expected given the expected performance of the equipment.

The Supply and Product Tank levels and pressures are normal, along with the pump suction pressure. The pump discharge pressure and the heat exchanger inlet and outlet pressures are lower than normal. The overall system flow rate is normal, but the control valve is operating farther open than normal in order to maintain this flow rate.

Although the Heat Exchanger inlet and outlet pressures are low, the differential pressure across the heat exchanger is normal at the measured flow rate of 1,000 gpm.

The low pump discharge pressure combined with the normal suction pressure indicates that the differential pressure across the pump is lower than normal, which means the pump is producing less total head at 1,000 gpm than it should be. The pump is operating below its designed pump curve, indicating that there is a potential problem with the pump, possibly a worn pump impeller, excessive clearance between the wear ring and the impeller, or cavitation occuring at the pump.

The lower pump discharge pressure explains why all the downstream pressures are lower than normal. The flow control valve has to be throttled farther open because its inlet pressure is lower.

Table 10-3: Summary of Abnormal Operating Conditions

Device / Measurement	Normal Conditions	Abnormal Conditions	Change
Supply Tank			
Pressure (psig)	0	0	Same
Level (feet)	10	10	Same
Supply Pump			
Suction Pressure (psig)	15	15	Same
Discharge Pressure (psig)	80.5	**76.5**	**Decreased**
Differential Pressure (psid)	65.5	**61.5**	**Decreased**
Heat Exchanger			
Inlet Pressure (psig)	67	**63**	**Decreased**
Outlet Pressure (psig)	57	**53**	**Decreased**
Differential Pressure (psid)	10	10	Same
Flow Control Valve			
Position (%)	85	**95**	**Increased**
Flow Transmitter			
Flow Rate (gpm)	1000	1000	Same
Product Tank			
Pressure (psig)	25	25	Same
Level (feet)	15	15	Same

Troubleshooting Problem #3

Figure 10-43 shows abnormal operating conditions that are causing temperature control problems on the secondary side of the Heat Exchanger. In this scenario, there are pressure oscillations on the pump supply and discharge pressure gages and poor temperature control that requires frequent venting of air from the Heat Exchanger to remedy.

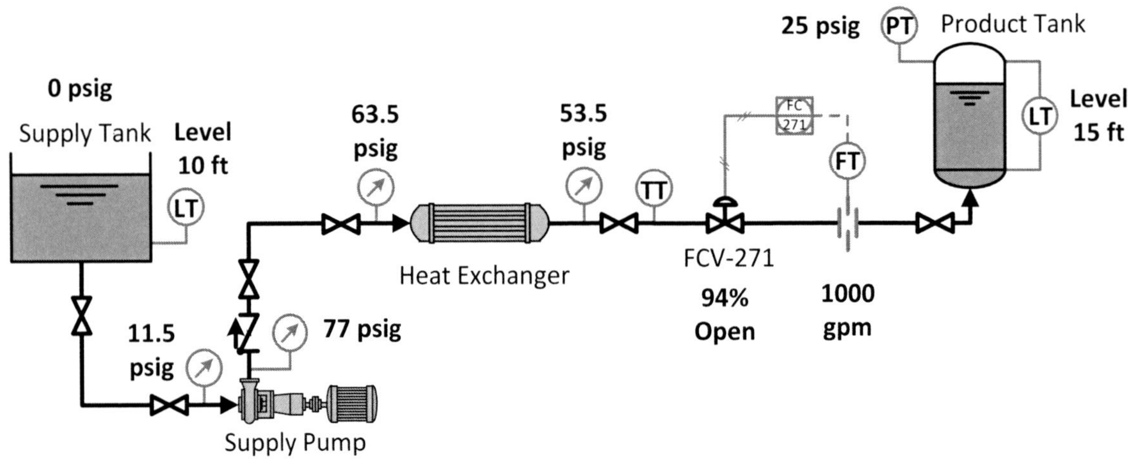

Figure 10-43. Abnormal operating conditions affecting temperature control. **PF**

Table 10-4 summarizes the normal and abnormal operating conditions side-by-side and shows whether the measured value increased, decreased, or stayed the same.

Table 10-4: Summary of Abnormal Operating Conditions

Device / Measurement	Normal Conditions	Abnormal Conditions	Change
Supply Tank			
Pressure (psig)	0	0	Same
Level (feet)	10	10	Same
Supply Pump			
Suction Pressure (psig)	15	**11.5**	**Decreased**
Discharge Pressure (psig)	80.5	**77**	**Decreased**
Differential Pressure (psid)	65.5	65.5	Same
Heat Exchanger			
Inlet Pressure (psig)	67	**63.5**	**Decreased**
Outlet Pressure (psig)	57	**53.5**	**Decreased**
Differential Pressure (psid)	10	10	Same
Flow Control Valve			
Position (%)	85	**94**	**Increased**
Flow Transmitter			
Flow Rate (gpm)	1000	1000	Same
Product Tank			
Pressure (psig)	25	25	Same
Level (feet)	15	15	Same

The Supply and Product Tank levels and pressures are normal, but the pump suction and discharge pressures are lower than normal. The pump differential pressure is normal, indicating that the pump is producing the right amount of total head at the measured flow rate.

The heat exchanger inlet and outlet pressures have decreased, but the differential pressure across the heat exchanger is normal. The system flow rate is normal but the control valve is operating farther open than normal in order to maintain this flow rate. This is probably due to a lower control valve inlet pressure, which is not measured directly but is indicated because of all the low system pressures.

The pressure gage oscillations on the pump indicate either cavitation or air entrainment is occuring. Because the pump differential pressure and total head are normal, cavitation may be eliminated as a problem.

Frequent air venting of the heat exchanger means air is getting into the system somewhere. The most likely source is at the supply tank, and although the level transmitter is indicating a normal level of 10 feet, the low pressure at the pump suction indicates that the actual level is lower than what is being indicated.

The suction pressure is 3.5 psig less than normal, which corresponds to about 8 feet of liquid. This indicates that the actual level is about 2 feet, which may be low enough to allow a vortex to form at the pump suction and allow air to be entrained into the fluid and into the pump.

Troubleshooting Problem #4

Figure 10-44 shows abnormal operating conditions that are also causing temperature control problems on the secondary side of the heat exchanger, and the operators are struggling with poor flow control on the primary side as well. Table 10-5 summarizes the normal and abnormal operating conditions.

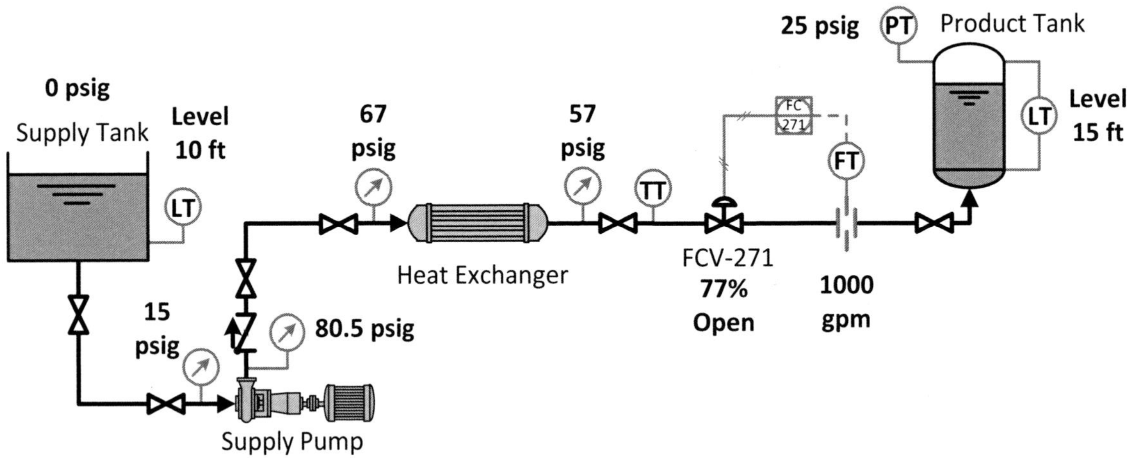

Figure 10-44. Abnormal operating conditions may not appear to be a problem.

Table 10-5: Summary of Abnormal Operating Conditions

Device / Measurement	Normal Conditions	Abnormal Conditions	Change
Supply Tank			
Pressure (psig)	0	0	Same
Level (feet)	10	10	Same
Supply Pump			
Suction Pressure (psig)	15	15	Same
Discharge Pressure (psig)	80.5	80.5	Same
Differential Pressure (psid)	65.5	65.5	Same
Heat Exchanger			
Inlet Pressure (psig)	67	67	Same
Outlet Pressure (psig)	57	57	Same
Differential Pressure (psid)	10	10	Same
Flow Control Valve			
Position (%)	85	**77**	**Decreased**
Flow Transmitter			
Flow Rate (gpm)	1000	1000	Same
Product Tank			
Pressure (psig)	25	25	Same
Level (feet)	15	15	Same

The Supply and Product Tank levels and pressures are normal, as well as the pump suction, discharge, and differential pressures. The heat exchanger inlet, outlet, and differential pressures are all normal.

The system flow rate is normal but the control valve is throttled more than normal in order to maintain this flow rate. Since the valve is maintaining flow with a smaller opening, this indicates that its flow coefficient is now the same as it was originally at the larger opening. It's acting like a larger valve. A worn flow control valve, either with excessive seat or disc wear, is indicated.

Another possibility is that since the control valve is more highly throttled, there is more head loss across it, so the outlet pressure of the control valve will be less. This could be the case if the hydraulic resistance offered by the Product Tank was lower, either due to a lower level or pressure than indicated. The level transmitter and pressure transmitter should be checked for calibration. It's also possible the orifice plate is excessively worn, creating less head loss across the orifice plate so more head loss has to be dissipated across the control valve by throttling more.

Becoming a Better Piping System Troubleshooter

The previous examples show the importance of several key concepts when troubleshooting operating problems in a piping system.

First, it is critical to have a clear picture of the entire piping system to understand the normal operating conditions of the system. This includes knowing the boundary conditions of the system, which can be a known flow rate through the system and known pressure boundaries. In this regard, tanks and vessels make good locations to divide complex systems into more manageable sub-systems for evaluation.

It's also important to understand the expected performance of the various devices that are found in a piping system. Knowing the differential pressure versus flow rate relationship of each component is key to identifying when the component is not operating as expected. This relationship is often established by manufacturers when they test their equipment in a test rig, so it is important to obtain this information from them. Pump curves, component curves, and flow coefficient data for control valves or other devices are good examples.

The general mathematics and physical laws that describe the performance of devices and processes should also be understood. Being able to calculate the head loss and pressure drop for piping, valves, fittings, and other devices will allow the troubleshooter to determine the pressure at any given point in the system by applying the Bernoulli equation from a known upstream or downsteam point.

It's also critical to measure pressures, flow rates, tank levels, and other parameters at the right locations in the system. These measurements should be taken with calibrated, reliable instruments to ensure confidence in the calculations. It becomes much more difficult to get to the root cause of the operating problems in the previous examples if pressures are not measured at the inlet and outlet of the pump and heat exchanger. Without critical measurements, troubleshooting efforts often boil down to a guessing game that ends up wasting a lot of time taking equipment apart to replace suspected causes, only to start back up again and discover that the problem is still there.

Finally, knowing that the devices in a piping system are hydraulically connected, a problem may manifest in one component but the root cause of the problem may be with a component located upstream or downstream of that device. Troubleshooting is often a team approach, requiring the skills and knowledge of many people familiar with different aspects of the piping system. The operators, maintenance technicians, process engineers, supervisors, and other plant support personnel may be called upon to provide their insight to resolve problems in complex piping systems.

Chapter Eleven

Case Studies and Piping System Examples

With a better understanding of the interaction of different components in a piping system, readers of this chapter will look at several case studies and other examples of how to use the knowledge from the previous chapters to analyze and evaluate various piping systems. The goal of any piping system is to meet the requirements of the end user, but with a minimum capital, maintenance, and operating cost.

Case Study #1: Evaluating an Increase in the System Capacity

The piping system shown in Figure 11-1 is an auxiliary cooling water system at a chemical plant used to provide cooling water to various end users in different buildings in the plant. The system supplies cooling water to operating equipment, heat exchangers, fan coolers, air compressor after coolers, and a variety of other heat generating equipment required for continued plant operation.

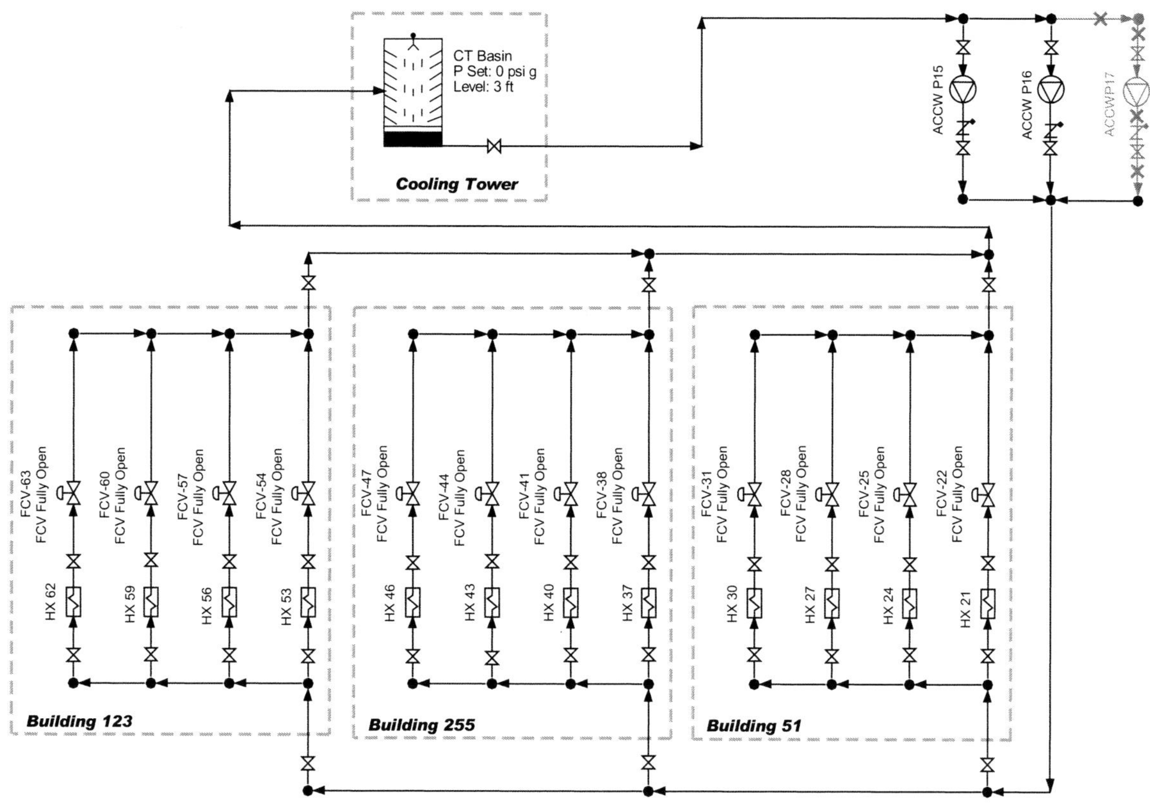

Figure 11-1. Auxiliary cooling water system at a chemical plant.

When the plant was first designed, the auxiliary cooling water requirements for the various heat loads were determined and the system was designed to meet those loads. Additional capacity for future loads was also factored into the original design. During the design process, each pipeline was sized to achieve the desired flow rate. The pumps were selected to meet the system flow requirements for both present and future loads. Manually operated throttling valves were installed for use in balancing the flow rate to each load.

After the system was built, the final step was to balance the system loads by adjusting the throttling valves so that each load received its specified flow rate of cooling water. When the system was put into commission, the auxiliary cooling water system provided sufficient cooling water to meet the full plant operation with two pumps running.

Over the life of the plant, new equipment was added as the capacity was increased and the processes changed. The additional cooling requirements for the new equipment were added to the existing auxiliary cooling water system loads. Plant service systems are often mistakenly considered to be infinite resources. As a result, the new loads were added without much regard to their effect on the existing loads.

In addition, equipment was beginning to wear out, and the heat exchangers had become fouled or partially plugged. This caused some of the equipment to overheat. Since the cooling water system must meet the system requirements, the plant operators adjusted the balancing valves to increase the flow rate to specific loads. This is often done without regard to what effect it will have on the other loads in the system.

One summer afternoon, the motor for one of the two operating auxiliary cooling pumps tripped on an over-current condition. The plant operators immediately started the standby auxiliary cooling water pump in order to return the system to normal operation. After investigating the problem with the auxiliary cooling water pump, it was determined that the two running pumps were operating off the end of their curves. This caused a high power draw from the motors, causing one to run into its service factor, which resulted in the motor trip on over-current. After it was determined that the pump and motor were operational, the third cooling water pump was started. Now, all three cooling water pumps were running within their manufacturers' supplied limits, and the cooling water system was operating satisfactorily and providing sufficient cooling water to all the end users.

The plant's operating procedure required a stand-by pump for all critical piping systems. Plant personnel felt that the system had been expanded over the years and now was the time to operate continuously with three pumps, so a work order was written requesting a design change to install a fourth auxiliary cooling water pump as the new standby.

Since this modification to the auxiliary cooling water system was required to increase plant reliability, the project was fast tracked. The scope of work involved specifying the new auxiliary cooling water pump, motor, and switchgear. In addition, design changes would be made to connect the new pump to the existing suction and discharge manifold and design the pump foundation, instrumentation, pipe supports, and the electrical cabling and conduit.

The first step involved specifying the new pump since it had the longest lead-time. The original idea was to install a fourth auxiliary cooling water pump identical to the existing three pumps. Since additional cooling loads had been added to the auxiliary cooling water system over the years, engineering wanted to ensure the existing three pumps could still meet the current plant cooling loads.

A system audit was conducted on all the heat loads being cooled by the auxiliary cooling water system. It was discovered that even with the newly added loads, the two existing pumps still had sufficient capacity to meet the heat transfer requirements. From that finding, it was determined that a full hydraulic analysis of the total piping system was needed to see why the existing system was unable to meet the current cooling needs.

Modeling the System with Commericially Available Software

The first step required modeling the piping system because of its size and complexity. It was decided that commercially available fluid piping software would be used. The software simulated the operation of the piping system by calculating the balanced flow rates and pressures in a network of pipelines. The results of the simulation software provided a clear picture of how the pipelines, pumps, components, and control valves operated together as a total system.

The majority of commercially available fluid piping software uses a drawing interface that shows how the items in the piping system are connected. Figure 11-1 shows an example output of a piping system model created using the PIPE-FLO® program by Engineered Software, Inc.

Although there are differences among the individual features found in the available programs, the creation of the piping system model involves the following steps:

- The piping system model is drawn in schematic form within the programs using their built-in drawing tools.
- The operating data for the various tanks, pumps, components, and controls is entered into the model.
- The details for the individual pipelines are entered, including pipe inside diameter, pipe length, and roughness, along with fluid properties, valves and fittings.

Many of the programs include engineering data tables so that the software can look up physical properties for the fluids, pipe material, valves, and fittings. This streamlines the creation of the piping system model.

Evaluating the Model Results

After the model was created, a full hydraulic network simulation was performed assuming that the end users received the flow rate required according to the calculated heat transfer requirements. While reviewing the results, it was confirmed that two auxiliary cooling water pumps should have provided sufficient flow while operating close to their Best Efficiency Point, and well within the manufacturer's allowable range of pump operation.

An additional system hydraulic analysis was performed of the auxiliary cooling system based on the way the system was currently operating with three pumps running. The flow rate through these pumps was well to the left of each of the pumps' Best Efficiency Point. When these calculated results were reviewed, it was discovered that there would have to be large pressure drops across the throttle valves if all three pumps were in operation.

Inspecting the Actual Piping System

With those results, it was time to look at the physical piping system. With the three pumps running in the auxiliary cooling water system, each pump had a discharge pressure approximately 10 to 15 psi lower than the discharge pressure calculated in the hydraulic analysis. This suggested that the pumps might be running further out on their pump curves, indicating greater flow through the pumps and system. This correlated to the way the system was actually operating.

After looking at the position of all the throttle valves serving the auxiliary cooling loads, it was discovered that the majority of the valves were fully open. In talking to the plant operators, it was discovered that over time the throttle valves needed to be opened from their initial balanced position to prevent overheating on various loads. Upon further investigation, it was determined that after each new load was added to the auxiliary cooling water system, there was no requirement to re-balance the system.

By not re-balancing the system after adding the new loads, the flow rates going to the new loads caused a reduction of the flow rate to the existing loads in the system. This increased the outlet temperatures of the existing loads, causing the operators to open the throttle valves to return the heat exchanger outlet temperatures to the required value. This went on for a long period of time until all the throttle valves in the auxiliary cooling water system were fully opened.

Re-visiting the Computer Model with Actual Operating Conditions

A hydraulic analysis of the system was performed with all throttle valves fully open, reflecting the current operation of the auxiliary cooling water system. It was discovered that with all throttle valves fully opened and two auxiliary cooling water pumps in operation, the pumps would run off the end of the pump curve, causing a large draw on the motors driving the auxiliary cooling water pumps. This is the reason that the pump tripped on over-current, requiring the third pump to be placed into operation.

Another analysis of the auxiliary cooling water system was performed, this time with three pumps in operation with all the throttling valves fully open. The calculated discharge pressure for the auxiliary cooling water pumps closely matched the observed discharge pressure in the plant. In addition, the pressures through the remainder of the system closely matched the calculated values of the hydraulic analysis, indicating that the hydraulic model of the auxiliary cooling water system closely matched the operation of the actual system.

Table 11-1 summarizes the flow rates calculated through each circuit in the hydraulic model with the throttling valves fully open, along with the throttle valve positions and pressure drops. The design flow rate column is based on heat transfer calculations.

Table 11-1: Calculated Flow Rates, Valve Pressure Drops, and Valve Positions

Throttling Valve	Flow Rate at 100% Open (gpm)	Calculated Heat Transfer Design Flow Rate (gpm)	Pressure Drop Across Throttling Valves at Design Flow Rate (psid)	Valve Position at Design Flow Rate (% Open)
FCV-22	417	300	30	67%
FCV-25	254	150	36	72%
FCV-28	171	150	30	70%
FCV-31	234	130	39	69%
FCV-38	973	700	37	57%
FCV-41	462	300	34	65%
FCV-44	287	175	37	73%
FCV-47	245	150	39	41%
FCV-54	327	175	42	73%
FCV-57	242	140	40	70%
FCV-60	245	150	40	72%
FCV-63	205	130	40	53%

The flow rates to all the loads in the auxiliary cooling water system with all throttle valves in their fully open position far exceed the required flows determined in the heat transfer audit, shown in the third column of Table 11-1.

Realizing That There Must be Some Other Problem

From this analysis, it was determined that there had to be a problem in the physical piping system. The engineers decided to approach the troubleshooting efforts by first balancing the auxiliary cooling water system by adjusting the balancing valves to the positions determined by the software with only two pump running.

The hydraulic analysis software was used to calculate the differential pressure across each control valve needed to balance the system to the design flow rate with only two pumps in operation. In addition, the program calculated the valve positions after the valve manufacturer's C_v values for each of the balancing valves was entered into the piping system model.

Each of the balancing valves in the actual system was set to the position calculated by the program. A portable ultrasonic flow meter was then used to check the actual flow rates to each load. After the measured flow rates were reviewed, it was determined that two of the loads in the auxiliary cooling water were not receiving their design flow rates, while the others had more flow than required.

A test of the two heat exchangers was then conducted at operating conditions. Pressure gages were placed across the heat exchangers in question, and it was discovered that the differential pressure was higher than indicated in the piping system model. The heat exchanger manufacturer was contacted and was able to supply a curve showing the differential pressure across the heat exchangers for a range of flow rates. The manufacturer's supplied head loss data was compared to the information in the model, and it was determined that the heat exchanger performance was modeled correctly.

Focus on Two Heat Exchangers

The manufacturer suggested a heat balance be conducted for the heat exchangers with high differential pressures to determine if there was fouling in the auxiliary cooling water side of the heat exchangers.

The inlet and outlet temperatures for both the load side and auxiliary cooling water system were gathered along with the observed flow rates, and it was determined that the heat transfer rates in the heat exchangers were below their design values. This information, along with the abnormally high differential pressure across the auxiliary cooling water tube sheets, was clear indication of fouling in the heat exchangers in question.

Using this information, the heat exchanger tube sheets were cleaned, and the auxiliary cooling water system was returned to normal operation with only two pumps in operation.

Case Study #1 Conclusion

After determining how the piping system was actually operating, the company was able to balance the system and meet the required flow rates for each load without the expense of running three pumps continuously and adding a forth auxiliary cooling water pump as a stand-by pump.

There are three costs associated with any piping system: the capital cost, the annual operating cost, and the maintenance cost.

The capital cost of adding the forth auxiliary cooling water pump includes:

- The engineering needed to design, install, and test the additional pump.
- The cost of the forth auxiliary cooling water pump and motor.
- The cost of pump/motor foundation, along with the cost to modify and tie in the suction and discharge piping into the auxiliary cooling water system.
- The cost of the motor control center, wiring, and instrumentation needed to supply power to the pump and control its operation.

There is no capital cost for balancing the existing auxiliary cooling water system. There were some costs associated with performing the hydraulic analysis needed to calculate the positions of the throttling valves, but that information was readily available once the piping system model was created.

The maintenance cost of adding the fourth auxiliary cooling water pump can be determined by assuming the new pump has the same maintenance requirements as the existing pumps. This assumption can be made because the flow rate through each of the three pumps operating with all valves open is very close to the flow rate through each of the two pumps operating with the balanced valves set for the required flow rate.

The capital and maintenance cost can vary widely based on the size of the pumps, the availability of support system within the plant, and the local labor rate, among others.

The operating cost can be calculated using Equation 4-20. Table 11-2 shows the annual power consumption and operating cost for two pump operation versus three pump operation using a utility rate of $0.10/kWh, 8,000 hours of operation per year, and motor efficiency of 95%.

Table 11-2: Annual Power Consumption and Operating Costs of Two Pump Operation Versus Three Pump Operation

Operating Mode	Flow per Pump (gpm)	Pump Total Head (ft)	Pump Efficiency (%)	Annual Power Consumption (kWh)	Annual Energy Costs ($)
Two Pumps	1,325	153	71.9	888,183	$88,818
Three Pumps	1,354	150	71.5	1,344,332	$134,433
Savings/year				456,149	$45,615

Resolving the problem with the fouled heat exchangers provided additional capacity for future cooling loads by more effectively utilizing the existing auxiliary cooling water. In addition, substantial energy savings were realized by balancing the system.

Another consideration when making any change to an operating plant is convincing management that recommendations are logical and valid. By modeling the piping system and accurately simulating its operation under expected operating conditions, how the proposed changes will affect the existing system can be demonstrated.

Often, when a problem is encountered in a piping system (the auxiliary cooling water pump motor tripping on high load), the first response is to add an additional pump. This results in the problem "going away" instead of being corrected. In this example, the plant staff was able to use a powerful piping system analysis tool to gain a clear picture of what was really happening in the piping system. With that clear picture, the plant staff was able to discover the root cause of the problem, try a variety of solutions, and correct the problem without having to resort to purchasing and installing additional equipment in the plant.

Once the accuracy of the hydraulic model of the auxiliary cooling system was demonstrated, recommendations could be simulated using the model. This eliminated the need to take the auxiliary cooling water system off line (along with the entire plant) to test the proposed changes. As it turned out, the entire balancing of the system could be performed without affecting the operation of the plant in any way. The only time any operational changes were required was when the two fouled heat exchangers were removed from service for cleaning, and this was accomplished during a scheduled plant outage.

This effort allowed the plant to correct the problem without the large expenditure of capital cost and increased maintenance and operating cost.

Case Study #2: Reducing Pumping Costs

Many of the piping systems currently in operation were designed when power costs were much less than they are today. With the upward pressure on energy cost, and the presence of the Demand Side Management programs in which the electrical utility will pay for part of their customers' power reduction modifications, many companies have active energy conservation programs.

In this case study, the engineers at a paper mill performed energy audits on a variety of pumped systems. Figure 11-2 shows the system in which they focused their efforts to reduce the energy consumption and costs. The system pumped water from a supply tank, through a filter, and into a spray header in a pressure vessel. Flow was regulated by a control valve. Various isolation valves were located in the piping as well.

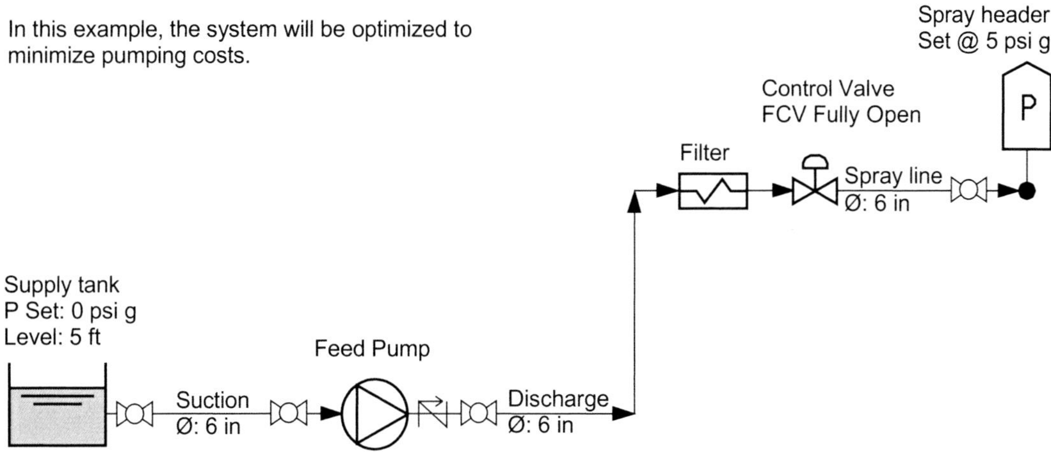

Figure 11-2. Water injection system evaluated for energy savings at a paper mill.

Their first step in performing the energy analysis was to evaluate the operation of the system under its current condition. In looking at the process measurements, they were able to determine that the differential pressure across the control valve was between 35 to 40 psid during normal operation. Based on the large differential pressure across the flow control valve, this system appears to be an excellent candidate for system optimization.

The next step was to determine how the system was normally operated: was the flow rate through the system constant or did the flow rate vary over a time? In addition, it was important to determine how the process was controlled: did the flow rate have to be maintained within a tight tolerance or could the flow vary without adversely affecting the process? Once this information was determined they ccould start considering the various design options for system optimization.

Based on the system's operational needs, three possible modifications were considered:

- Option 1 maintained the flow control with the flow control valve, but the pump impeller would be trimmed to reduce the differential pressure across the valve at 600 gpm.
- Option 2 maintained flow control with the flow control valve, but the impeller would be trimmed so that the system could support flow rates up to 800 gpm for future operation.
- Option 3 consisted of eliminating the flow control valve and installing a variable frequency drive to vary the speed of the feed pump in order to maintain the flow rate through the system.

Evaluating the System Operation with the Pump Curve

The pump was originally sized to develop 150 feet of total head at 800 gpm. Figure 11-3 shows the pump curve for the Feed Pump which had an impeller diameter of 13.25 inches.

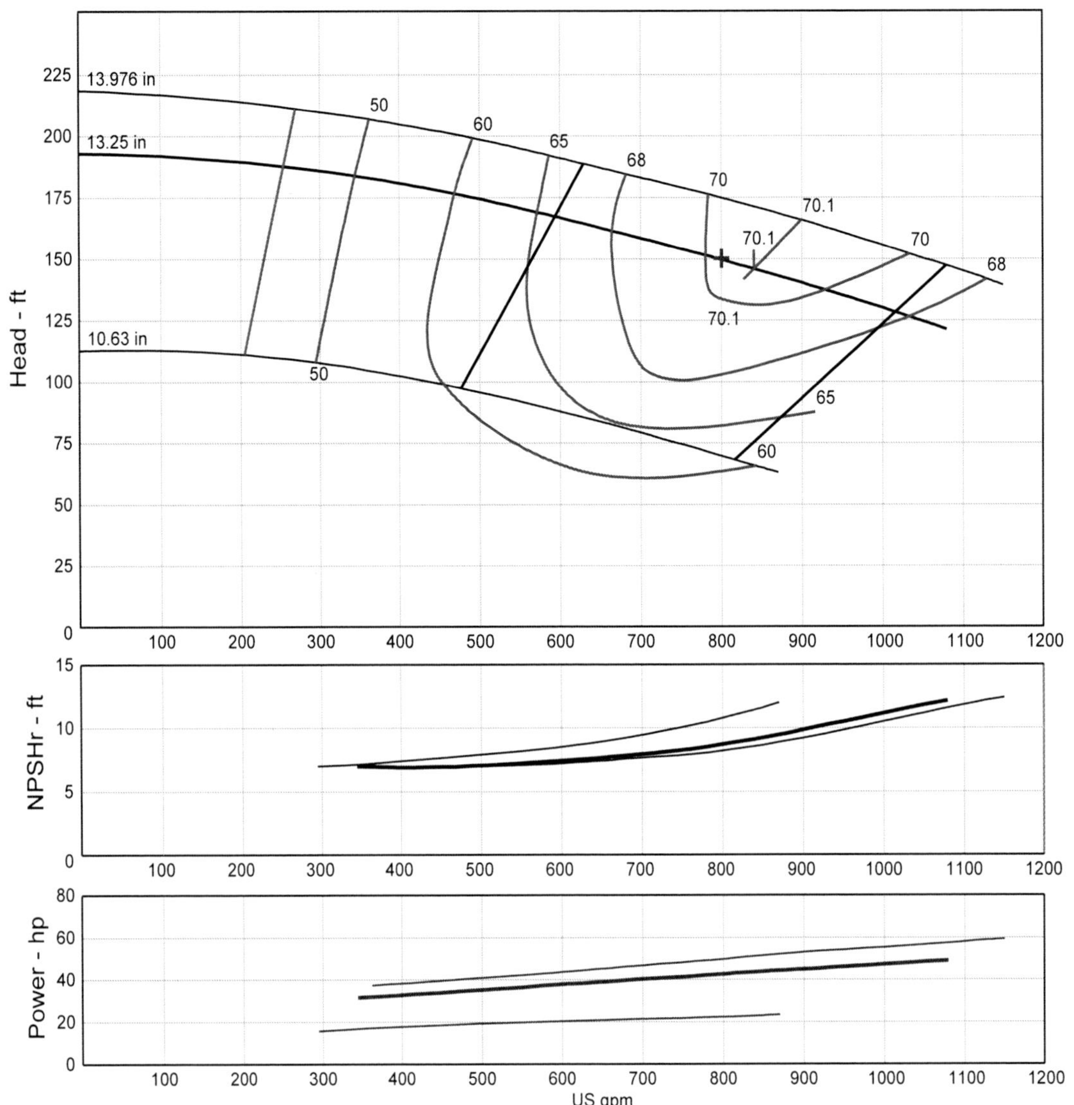

Figure 11-3. Pump curve for the centrifugal pump in the energy reduction audit.

At the time of the analysis, the system operated for 8,500 hours per year at a constant flow rate of 600 gpm. At this flow rate, the pump developed 167 feet of total head at a pump efficiency of 66%. With a motor efficiency of 93.5% and a power cost of $0.10 per kWh, the pump consumed about 259,150 kWh per year at a cost of $25,915.

Option 1

With the piping system operating at 600 gpm, the differential pressure across the control valve was between 35 to 40 psid. Based on the needs of the system and to ensure proper operation of the control valve, they evaluated trimming the impeller on the feed pump to achieve a 10 psi pressure drop across the control valve.

Trimming the pump impeller to 11.375 inches would reduce the pump head to 107 feet at 600 gpm. The resulting differential pressure across the control valve would be 10.9 psid. With the smaller diameter impeller pump operating for 8,500 hrs per year at a flow rate of 600 gpm, the pump efficiency would be 65%, and with a motor efficiency of 93.5% and a power cost of $.10 per kWh, the pump would consume 167,056 kWh at a cost of $16,705. This would result in an annual savings of $9,210 for this option.

Option 2

The system was originally designed to deliver 800 gpm and the pump was selected to produce 150 feet of head at this flow rate with an impeller diameter of 13.25 inches. When the system was placed into operation it was assumed that the process would run at 600 gpm for the first two to three years of operation, but run at an increased capacity of 800 gpm after an anticipated plant expansion. After five years the plant expansion hadn't occurred and was not expected in the foreseeable future, so the process was expected to continue operation at a fixed 600 gpm. However, plant management still considered the possibility of plant expansion and this system would have to increase the flow rate to 800 gpm at that time.

Trimming the impeller diameter to 13.125 inches would allow the control valve to operate at 80% open with a 10 psi pressure drop across the valve at 800 gpm. This option would reduce the current energy consumption by trimming 1/8 of an inch off the impeller diameter but still allow for expansion to 800 gpm if needed.

Since the system would still operate at 600 gpm for the foreseeable future, the energy savings would have to be calculated for this option based on current flow rates. With an impeller diameter of 13.125 inches, the feed pump would develop 163 feet of total head at 600 gpm at an efficiency of 66%. With power cost of $0.10 per kWh and a motor efficiency of 93.5%, the pump would consume 252,350 kWh and cost $25,235 per year to operate. This would result in an annual savings of only $680.

Option 3

The third option evaluated was to install a variable frequency drive on the feed pump. Instead of using the control valve to regulate the flow, the signal from the flow controller would be sent to the variable frequency drive, which would adjust the rotational speed of the centrifugal pump in order to achieve the desired flow rate.

If the pump was operated with a VFD, the pump impeller diameter remains 13.25 inches. The pump would operate at 1,375 rpm to develop the 89.8 feet of total head needed to achieve 600 gpm. At this lower speed and head, the pump would operate at 70% efficiency. With a utility rate of $0.10 per kWh and a motor drive efficiency of 93.5%, the pump would consume 131,925 kWh per year at an annual operating cost of $13,195. This would result in an annual savings of $12,720.

Another advantage of this option was that the system could immediately meet the increased flow rate of 800 gpm by increasing the pump speed.

These calculations were based on keeping the flow control valve in the system and placing the valve in its fully open position. Additional savings would be achieved by removing the valve to further reduce the head loss of the system and the total head required by the pump. The control valve may have been used in another system at the plant, thereby reducing capital costs in another project in the future.

Summarizing the Options

Table 11-3 summarizes the three options that were considered by the plant to reduce the energy costs of this system.

Table 11-3: Comparison of Options for Energy Conservation Analysis

Options	Pump Total Head (feet)	Annual Energy Consumption (kWh)	Annual Operating Costs ($)	Savings ($)	Simple Payback
Current Operation	167	259,150	$25,915		
Option 1	107	167,056	$16,705	$9,210	2.5 months
Option 2	163	252,350	$25,235	$680	18 months
Option 3	90	131,925	$13,195	$12,720	6 months

In Option 1, trimming the pump impeller in order to reduce the differential pressure across the control valve offers significant savings in operating cost. But, in order to make the changes, the feed pump must be disassembled, and the impeller must be removed, trimmed to its new impeller diameter, and then reassembled. The cost to make these changes is based on the size of the pump, hourly labor rates, and if the work will be done by plant maintenance staff or a repair shop. The plant engineers evaluating the system estimated the total cost of the modification at $2,000, resulting in a simple payback of 2.5 months. If this option was selected, a new impeller would have to be purchased and installed in order to return the system capacity to 800 gpm in the future.

Option 2 involved the same scope of work as Option 1, but provided the ability to run the current system up to 800 gpm while still obtaining a modest savings in operating cost. Based on the cost to make the modification, this option has a simple payback of 18 months.

In Option 3, a variable frequency drive would have to be purchased and integrated into the flow control loop for the feed pump. This would allow the pump to meet the current 600 gpm process conditions and still meet the future 800 gpm flow requirement. The disadvantage of this option was the additional cost of the variable frequency drive, and the fact that the system was continually operated at a constant flow rate of 600 gpm. The estimated cost to complete this modification was approximately $6,000, resulting in a simple payback of 6 months.

Because of the constant flow rate through the process and the low cost of trimming the impeller, Option 1 appeared to be the best solution.

Case Study #2 Conclusion

Often, decisions for energy conservation projects are made based on how much effort is involved in implementing a project rather than on the potential cost savings. Also, at an industrial facility there are pressures to keep the plant running and the maintenance department is overwhelmed with fixing breakdowns rather than implementing energy conservation projects. In this analysis, the mill management was presented with the option of reducing the impeller trim to save $9,210 annually in operating cost with a simple payback of 2.5 months.

However, the maintenance manager was reluctant to tackle the project, citing a full maintenance schedule. During additional discussions with the maintenance manager, it was discovered that he did not want to perform the modification because there was no benefit for his department. If any problems were encountered, it would affect his outage schedule and reflect poorly upon his department. Since his group was not judged on the amount of energy saved, he did not see this as a good use of his department's resources.

He did mention, in passing, that the control valve in the same piping system was a continual problem and had to be repaired every 18 to 24 months. This was a cost out of his budget of around $1,500 every time the valve had to be repaired. If he didn't have to repeatedly fix the control valve, which added to his heavy maintenance work load, he would have more time to implement energy savings projects.

Case Study #3: Minimizing Maintenance Cost

The control valve in the process system at a paper mill shown in Figure 11-2 needed to be overhauled every 18 to 24 months.

In looking at the normal operating conditions of the system, the valve position was between 55 and 60% open. The operators stated that the valve had always operated with the symptoms of cavitation so they assumed the valve was designed to cavitate. The mechanics mentioned that the valve experienced cavitation damage, along with excessive wear on the valve disk. Based on the comments from the operators and maintenance staff, the engineers decided to approach their energy conservation project from a maintenance reduction effort.

The control valve in question was a 4-inch butterfly type valve located in a 6-inch diameter pipeline. The differential pressure across the control valve ranged between 35 and 40 psi. After performing a control valve capacity calculation per the ISA-S75.01 Standard Flow Equations for Sizing Control Valves, it was determined that the valve was indeed operating under cavitation conditions. This was caused by high differential pressure across the control valve, the flow rate through the valve, and relatively low downstream pressure of 5 psig. The cavitation, turbulence, vibration, and noise caused the control valve to fail prematurely.

The control valve representative suggested replacing the valve with one that could better withstand the high differential pressure occurring in this application.

This system was originally designed to pass 800 gpm and the lower flow rate was supposed to be temporary. The differential pressure across the control valve at the design flow rate of 800 gpm was specified at 10 psid in the operating system. After the pump was selected and the system was built, the differential pressure was actually about 13 psid with the valve controlling at 800 gpm. Both of these differential pressure values are well within the capability of the selected butterfly control valve.

The problem with the valve that was originally selected was that the mill did not state that the system would be running at a reduced flow rate and higher differential pressure for a prolonged period.

Based on these findings, two options were considered. Option 1 involved trimming the impeller on the Feed Pump to reduce the differential pressure across the control valve. Option 2 involved replacing the 4-inch butterfly valve with a globe valve that could better handle the higher differential pressure across the flow control valve at the reduced flow rates.

Option 1

With the piping system operating at 600 gpm, the differential pressure across the control valve was between 35 and 40 psid. Based on the needs of the system and to ensure proper operation of the control valve, the engineers considered trimming the impeller on the feed pump to achieve a 10 psi pressure drop across the control valve at 600 gpm, which was well within the controlling range of the valve.

Trimming the pump impeller to 11.375 inches reduces the pump head at 600 gpm to 107 feet. The resulting differential pressure across the control valve would be 10.9 psid. Based on the local labor rate, it was assumed that the changes to the pump could be made for about $2,000.

Option 2

The other option required purchasing a new control valve, specifically a globe valve with cage trim. This valve design allowed for a higher differential pressure with less noise and vibration, and was less susceptible to cavitation at high differential pressures. The cost to purchase and install the new control valve was estimated at $3,500.

Case Study #3 Conclusion

Option 1 was selected because all of the work could be done by the maintenance department and did not require the purchase of any new capital equipment. In addition, it was the least expensive option with the quickest simple payback period.

Trimming the impeller on the Feed Pump to 11.375 inches not only reduced the differential pressure across the control valve, but also met the objectives of the energy reduction effort to use less power. With the pump operated with the smaller impeller for 8,500 hours per year at a flow rate of 600 gpm, pump efficiency of 65%, motor efficiency of 93.5%, and a power cost of $0.10 per kWh, the pump consumed 167,056 kWh at a cost of $16,705. This created a savings of $9,209 for this pump in operating cost.

When the maintenance manager realized that trimming the impeller on the Feed Pump would eliminate one of his major problems, he had no objection to allocating his resources and scheduling the work to get the job done.

References

Chapter 1: Introduction

Pump Life Cycle Cost: A Guide to LCC Analysis for Pumping Systems. © 2001 Hydraulic Institute, Europump. Published Hydraulic Institute, 9 Sylvan Way, Parsippany NJ 07054 ©2001

Chapter 2: Terminology, Units, and Physical Laws

Chemical Engineering Fluid Mechanics, Second Edition, Ron Darby © 2001 by Marcel Dekker, Inc. 270 Madison Avenue, NY, NY, 10016

Flow of Fluids Through Valves, Fittings, and Pipe, Technical Paper 410. © 2011 Crane Co., 100 First Stamford Place, Stamford, Connecticut 06902

Fluid Mechanics, Eight Edition, Victor L. Streeter, E. Benjamin Wylie © 1985 McGraw-Hill Inc.

Chapter 3: Tanks and Vessels

Level Measurement Guide for Complete Level Solutions, © 2011 Siemens AG Industry Sector Sensors and Communication, 76181 Karlsruhe, Germany

Chapter 4: Pumps

American National Standard for Centrifugal Pumps for Nomenclature and Definitions, ANSI/HI 1.1-1.2-2000, © 2000 Hydraulic Institute, 9 Sylvan Way, Parsippany, NJ 07054

American National Standard for Centrifugal and Vertical Pumps for Allowable Operating Range, ANSI/HI 9.6.3-1997© 1997 Institute, 9 Sylvan Way, Parsippany, NJ 07054

Pump Characteristics and Applications, Second Edition, Michael W. Volk © 2004 CRC Press

Pump Practices & Life, Paul Darringer, P.E., © 2004 Barringer & Associates, P.O. Box 3985, Humble, TX 77347-3985

Chapter 5: Pipelines

Flow of Fluids Through Valves, Fittings, and Pipe, Technical Paper 410. © 2011 Crane Co., 100 First Stamford Place, Stamford, Connecticut 06902

Chapter 6: Valves and Fittings

Flow of Fluids Through Valves, Fittings, and Pipe, Technical Paper 410. © 2011 Crane Co., 100 First Stamford Place, Stamford, Connecticut 06902

Valve Selection Handbook, Third Edition, R.W. Zappe, © 1991 Gulf Publishing Company, Houston, TX

Valve Handbook, Second Edition, Philip L. Skousen, © 2004 McGraw-Hill, Two Penn Plaza, New York, NY 10121

Chapter 7: Control Valves

Control Valve Handbook, fourth edition Fisher Controls International LLC © 2005 Emerson Process Management, 301 S. 1st Avenue, Marshalltown, IA 50158

Control Valve Primer, A Users Guide Third Edition Hans D. Baumann © 1998 Instrument Society of America, 67 Alexander Drive, Research Triangle Park, NC 27709

Control-Valve Selection and Sizing, Les Driskell © 1983 Instrument Society of America, 67 Alexander Drive, Research Triangle Park, NC 27709

ANSI/ISA-75.01.01-2007 Flow Equations for Sizing Control Valves © 2007 Instrument Society of America, 67 Alexander Drive, Research Triangle Park, NC 27709

Chapter 8: Process Measurement and Controls

ASME MFC-3M Measurement of Fluid Flow in Pipes Using Orifice, Nozzle, and Venturi © 1990 The American Society of Mechanical Engineers, 345 East 47th Street, New York, NY 10017

Flow Measurement Engineering Handbook Third Edition, Richard W. Miller, © 1996 McGraw-Hill, A Division of the McGraw-Hill Companies

Instrumentation & Control Process Control Fundamentals, © 2006 www.PAControl.com

Rosemount Level Instrumentation, 00803-0100-4161 Rev CB, © 2011 Emerson Process Management, 8200 Market Boulevard, Chanhassen, MN 55317

Temperature Measurement, Siemens FI01, © 2011 Siemens Industry, Inc., 3333 Old Milton Parkway, Alpharetta, GA 30005

The Steam and Condensate Loop, An Engineer's Best Practice Guide for Saving Energy, First Edition, © 2007 Spirax-Sarco Limited, Charlton House, Cheltenham, Gloucestershire, GL53 8ER, UK

Type 500X Electropneumatic Transducer (I/P, E/P), P/N 441-625-005, Control Air Inc., 8 Columbia Drive, Amherst, NH 03031

WIKA Handbook Pressure & Temperature Measurement, U.S. Edition, © 1998 WIKA Instrument Corporation, 1000 Wiegand Boulevard, Lawrenceville, GA 30043

Chapter 9: Processes and Process Equipment

Transport Processes and Unit Operations, Third Edition, Christie J. Geankoplis, © 1993 Prentice-Hall, Inc., A Simon & Schsuter Company, 113 Sylvan Avenue, Englewood Cliffs, NJ 07632

Nomenclature

Unless otherwise stated, frequently used symbols used in this book are defined below. Infrequently used symbols are defined in the text.

A = cross sectional flow area, in square feet (ft^2)

BEP = Best Efficiency Point

bhp = brake (shaft) horsepower (hp)

C_V = flow coefficient for valves or piping components

D = internal diameter (ft)

d = internal diameter (in)

dP = differential pressure, in lb/in^2 (psid)

ehp = electrical input power in horsepower (hp)

f = Darcy friction factor (unitless)

F_P = piping geometry factor (unitless)

f_T = Darcy friction factor in zone of complete turbulence (unitless)

g = gravitational acceleration = 32.2 ft/sec^2

g_c = gravitational constant = 32.2 lbm• ft/lbf•sec^2

H = fluid energy or head, in feet of fluid (ft)

h_L = head loss due to fluid flow, in feet of fluid (ft)

K = resistance coefficient for valves and fittings (unitless)

kWh = amount of power consumed, in kilowatt hours

L = length of pipe (ft)

L/D = equivalent length of a resistance to flow, in pipe diameters (unitless)

m = fluid mass, in pounds mass (lbm)

N = rotational speed, in revolutions per minute (rpm)

N_1 = numerical constant in control valve flow coefficient equation (=1.0 if using gpm and psi)

N_2 = numerical constant in piping geometry factor equation (= 890 if using units of inches)

$NPSHa$ = net positive suction head available, in feet (ft)

$NPSHr$ = net positive suction head required, in feet (ft)

OC = Operating cost, in U.S. dollars ($)

P = gauge pressure, in lb/in^2 (psig)

P_{atm} = local atmospheric pressure, in lb/in2 absolute (psia)

$P_{electrical}$ = motor or drive input power (kilowatts)

P_{tank} = tank surface pressure (psig)

P_{vp} = fluid vapor pressure, in lb/in^2 absolute (psia)

Q = volumetric flow rate, in gallons per minute (gpm)

q = volumetric flow rate, in cubic feet per second (cfs)

R_e = Reynolds number (unitless)

R_r = relative roughness (unitless)

SG = specific gravity of liquid at specified temperature relative to water at 60°F (unitless)

TH = pump total head, in feet of fluid (ft)

v = average fluid velocity, in ft/sec (fps)

W = mass flow rate, in pounds mass per hour (lb/hr)

w = mass flow rate, in pounds mass per second (lb/sec)

whp = water horse power, or pump output power (hp)

Z = elevation above or below a reference plane (ft)

Z_{Level} = height of the liquid surface in a tank measured from the bottom of the tank (ft)

Z_{pump} = elevation of pump suction measured from a reference plane (ft)

Z_{Tank} = elevation of the bottom of a tank measured from a reference plane (ft)

Greek Letters

Delta

Δ = differential between two points

Epsilon

ε = absolute roughness or effective height of pipe wall irregularities, in inches (in)

Eta

η_m = motor efficiency (unitless or percentage)

η_p = pump efficiency (unitless or percentage)

η_{vsd} = variable speed drive (vsd) efficiency (unitless or percentage)

Mu

μ= absolute (dynamic) viscosity, in centipoise (cP)

Rho

ρ = weight density of fluid (lb/ft^3)

Numerical Subscripts

(1) … inlet or upstream side

(2) … outlet or downstream side

PF ⓢ PIPE-FLO model found on accompanying CD

Glossary

Absolute Pressure Value of pressure measured from an absolute zero pressure state which would exist if all the atoms and molecules of substance is removed from a given volume.

Absolute Roughness The average height that material irregularities on the inside surface of a pipe wall protrude into the flow stream. The absolute roughness varies with the pipe material and manufacturing process.

Absolute Viscosity The measurement of the fluids resistance to internal deformation or shear, under an applied force. Viscosity is typically measured in poise or centipoise.

Affinity Rules See Pump Affinity Rules

Allowable Operating Region Range of operating flow rates recommended by a pump manufacturer to ensure the service life of the pump is not seriously reduced by continued operation

Atmospheric Pressure Force exerted on a surface due to the weight of a column of air above the surface. The local atmospheric pressure varies with elevation and slightly with weather conditions.

Barringer Curve Graph showing the results of a statistical study done on the mean time between failure of pump seals as a function of operating flow rate in relation to BEP.

Bernoulli Equation Mathematical equation that expresses the total energy of a fluid in a pipe as the sum of the fluid's elevation, pressure, and velocity head.

Best Efficiency Point (BEP) Point at which a pump is the most efficient at transforming mechanical energy into hydraulic energy.

Brake Horse Power (BHP) The amount of power applied to the shaft of a pump. Also called the pump input power or the shaft horse power.

Cavitation The formation and subsequent collapse of vapor bubbles as the fluid static pressure drops below then rises above the vapor pressure.

Centipoise Unit of viscosity, centimeter per gram per second. Abbreviation is cP.

Centrifugal Pump Type of pump that converts mechanical energy of a rotating shaft into hydraulic energy in the form of increased fluid head.

Characteristic Trim Method of classifying the hydraulic performance of a control valve based on how its flow coefficient changes with valve position. The design of the valve trim determines the valve's characteristic. Common characteristic trims include equal percentage, linear, and quick opening.

Closed Tank Tank that is sealed and is either completely filled with a liquid or a gas, or contains both a vapor space and a liquid. The vapor space can be either pressurized above atmospheric pressure or at a vacuum below atmospheric pressure.

Component A major item placed in the piping system that has a pressure drop that varies with the flow rate. Components can include items such as strainers, filters, heat exchangers, air handlers, and static mixers.

Conservation of Energy Physical law that states that the sum of a fluid's energy entering a pipeline equals the sum of a fluid's energy leaving the pipeline plus the amount of work done on or by the fluid, heat transfered into or out of the fluid, and energy loss between the two points.

Conservation of Mass Physical law that states that the sum of the mass flow rates entering a system equals the sum of the mass flow rates leaving the system plus the amount of mass accumulated in the system over a given period of time.

Conservation of Momentum Physical law that states that a force is exerted on the pipe wall as fluid flows through the piping system and its momentum changes.

Controller Component in a process control loop that compares the measured value from the primary element to a user-entered set point, then generates an output signal that is used to adjust the final control element.

Controller Action Mathematical functions that a process controller performs, including proportional action, integral action, and derivative action.

Controller Tuning Process by which mathematical constants are determined for use in the P-I-D equation to ensure the controller properly responds to a disturbance and quickly brings the measured value back to set point.

Control Valve Valve designed to allow changes to the size and shape of the flow passage in order to control the pressure, flow rate, tank level, fluid temperature, or some other parameter in a piping system.

Darcy-Weisbach Method Formula used to calculate head loss due to friction in ducts, pipes, and tubes. This formula is an analytical method that is valid for Newtonian fluids flowing in a fully charged pipe.

Demand Side Management (DSM) Programs that look at expanding the opportunities to increase the efficiency of energy service delivery. Also known as energy demand management, DSM programs offer solutions to problems such as load management, energy efficiency, strategic conservation, and related activities.

Density Ratio of the mass or weight of a substance to its volume, expressed in units of pounds per cubic foot. Also see *weight density.*

Diametre Nominal (DN) European equivalent of nominal pipe size (NPS)

Differential Pressure The magnitude of pressure difference between two points in a piping system. The differential pressure can be positive, indicating a drop in the pressure going from an upstream point to a point farther downstream. It can also be negative, indicating a pressure gain across the two points being measured.

Dynamic Head Amount of fluid energy (head loss) dissipated in a pipe, valve, fitting, or other component due to friction and changes in fluid momentum as fluid flows through the device.

Dynamic Pressure The fluid's kinetic energy, or velocity head, expressed in units of pressure.

Efficiency Ratio of the amount of power output to the amount of power input.

Elevation Head Amount of energy a fluid has due to its vertical height in a gravitational field. When referred to as a differential, elevation head is the difference in elevation between two points in a system.

Energy Grade Line A line representing the total head available to the fluid in a piping system.

Equivalent Length (L/D) Method of characterizing the hydraulic performance of a valve, fitting, or other component. This method calculates the equivalent length of pipe that would develop the same pressure drop measured at a given flow rate.

Final Control Element Component in a process control loop that is adjusted to maintain a measured value in a process at a desired value. Common final control elements include control valves, variable speed drives, and automatically actuated air duct dampers.

Fittings Devices placed in a piping system to connect pipe or change the direction of flow in the pipeline. Fittings can cause either a change in the direction of flow or a change in the velocity of the fluid.

Flow Coefficient Method of characterizing the hydraulic performance of a valve, fitting, or other component. This method measures the flow rate through the device when it has a 1 psi pressure drop across it.

Flow Meter An instrument used to measure the rate of flow in a pipeline. May be linear flow meters or differential pressure flow meters.

Flow Rate Volumetric flow rate is the total volume passing through a plane per unit of time. The traditional unit of flow in the U.S. is gallons per minute (gpm).

Fluid Dynamics The branch of fluid mechanics dealing with the properties of fluids in motion.

Fluid Properties Characteristics that define a fluid such as pressure, temperature, viscosity, density, and vapor pressure.

Friction Factor Dimensionless value that accounts for the fluid properties and pipeline properties in the Darcy head loss calculation.

Gage Pressure Value of pressure measured using the local atmospheric pressure as the zero pressure datum reference.

Hazen-Williams Method Formula used to calculate the pressure loss in a length of pipe due to friction dependent on the flow. This equation is commonly used for pressure drop calculations in American fire sprinkler, water distribution, and irrigation systems since it is only valid for water.

Head The energy content of a liquid per unit weight as referenced from a datum. In the U.S., head is typically expressed as feet of liquid. Can be in the form of pressure, elevation, and velocity head

Head Loss Amount of fluid energy converted into a non-recoverable form of energy due to friction and changes in fluid momentum. Head loss is energy dissipated from the fluid in the form of heat, noise, and vibration.

Heat Transfer Transit of thermal energy from a point of higher temperature to a point of lower temperature by conduction, convection, or radiation heat transfer.

Hydraulic Grade The sum of the elevation head and the static pressure head of a fluid at any given point. It is the fluid's total energy minus the velocity head.

Hydraulic Head A specific measurement of water pressure or total energy of the fluid per unit weight above a datum. It is measured as a liquid surface elevation expressed in units of length above a standpipe.

Impeller Rotating component of a centrifugal pump that imparts kinetic energy to the fluid due to centrifugal forces

Inside Diameter Pipe diameter as measured on the inside surface of the pipe. Inside diameter is used in head loss calculations.

Isolation Valve A valve that is inserted into the system to isolate equipment or stop flow. Isolation valves are either placed in the fully open position or fully closed position.

Kinematic Viscosity The ratio of the absolute viscosity to the mass density. The unit for kinematic viscosity is the stoke and is measured in units of square centimeter per second.

Kirchhoff's Laws Essentially the law of conservation of mass and energy when applied to analyzing hydraulic piping systems.

Mass Flow Rate Measure of the amount of mass or fluid passing through a plane per unit time. Expressed in units of pounds per second (lb/sec) or pounds per hour (lb/hr).

Mass Transfer Type of process that occurs as a result of a difference between the mass concentrations of substances in a fluid. Molecules of one substance is physically separated from another substance.

Mechancial Seal Shaft sealing mechanism used in centrifugal pumps consisting of O-rings, gaskets, and a carbon ring riding on a highly polished surface to form the seal.

Momentum Transfer Transfer process that occurs in moving fluids due to a change in the fluid's velocity or direction, resulting in forces exerted on piping walls.

Most Hydraulically Remote Loop (MHRL) The loop or branch in a multi-path system with the least amount of hydraulic energy, or differential pressure, available for control.

Net Positive Suction Head (NPSH) The total amount of fluid energy at the pump's suction, as measured from absolute zero energy. NPSHr is the amountof fluid energy at the suction when cavitation begins. NPSHa is the amount of fluid energy the piping system provides to the pump suction.

Newtonian Fluid (Named for Isaac Newton) A fluid that flows like water— with a viscosity that does not change with rate of flow. In common terms, this means the fluid continues to flow, regardless of the forces acting on it. Examples include water, single-grade oils, and paint solvents.

Nominal Pipe Sizes (NPS) A set of standard pipe sizes used for pressure piping in North America. The same pipe dimensions are used in Europe with different names. Sizes are defined with two non-dimensional numbers; a Nominal Pipe Size (NPS) and a schedule (SCH). The values of NPS from 1/8 to 12 roughly equate to the inside pipe diameter, but from NPS 14 and larger the NPS equals the outside diameter (OD).

Non-Newtonian Fluid A fluid with a viscosity that changes with the applied strain rate or rate of flow. Non-Newtonian fluids may not have a well-defined viscosity. When stirred, non-Newtonian fluids can leave a "hole" behind (that gradually fills up over time - this behavior is seen in materials such as pudding, ketchup, or, to a less rigorous extent, sand), or cause the fluid to become thinner, the drop in viscosity causing it to flow more (this is seen in non-drip paints, which brush on easily but become more viscous when on walls).

Open Tank Tank in which the space above the surface of the liquid is exposed to atmospheric pressure and the tank is neither pressurized or under a vacuum.

Outside Diameter Pipe diameter as measured on the outside surface of the pipe.

Packing Gland Shaft sealing mechanism used in centrifugal pumps and valves that consists of graphite impregnated rings of braided packing compressed in a stuffing box to seal the shaft and the casing.

Pascal's Law Physical law that states that the pressure applied to the surface of an enclosed fluid is transmitted equally and undiminished in all directions throughout the fluid and to the walls of its container.

Pipe A conduit with circular cross section used to convey a working fluid (either a gas or a liquid).

Pipe Diameter A term that describes the size of a pipe. When refering to pipe there are three diameters that are used; the nominal size, the outside diameter, and the inside diameter. The inside diameter is the dimension needed for hydraulic calculations.

Pipe Schedules Numbering system that defines the pipe wall thickness.

Pipe Standard Specification The standard specification is created by a standards organization, such as ASTM International, ISO, ANSI, ASME, or DIN. The primary hydraulic information found in a pipe standard is the available pipe sizes, schedules, and the inside diameter for the pipe material. When using proprietary pipe, the manufacturer of the pipe must provide the appropriate dimensions to perform pressure drop calculations.

Piping Geometry Factor Dimensionless value less than or equal to 1.0. It is used in the control valve sizing equations to adjust the flow coefficient to take into account any valves or fittings installed 2D upstream or 6D downstream of the control valve.

Positioner Device mounted on a control valve that measures the valve stem position and ajusts air pressure to the actuator to position the valve at a desired position.

Primary Element Component in a process control loop that measures a property of a process such as flow rate, tank level, fluid temperature, etc. The orifice plate, level sensor, or thermocouple would be the primary element.

Proportional - Integral - Derivative (P-I-D) Controller Type of controller that uses the proportional, integral, and derivative mathematical relationship in determining the controller output in response to a deviation between the set point and measured value.

Pump An energy conversion device that transforms mechanical energy into hydraulic energy to increase the energy state of the fluid. The pressure, elevation, and/or velocity of the fluid will be increased. Centrifugal pumps use a rotating impeller and volute to achieve the energy conversion, positive displacement pumps use a fixed volume of fluid and linear or rotary motion to increase the energy state of the working fluid.

Pump Affinity Rules Mathematical relationship that describes how a pump's head, flow, and power performance is effected by a change in pump speed or impeller diameter.

Pump Curve Graph of the hydraulic performance of a pump over an expected range of flow rates. Displays the total head, efficiency, pump input power, and NPSHr for the pump as a function of flow rate.

Pump Input Power Amount of power applied to the shaft of the pump by the driver. Also called brake horse power (bhp) and shaft horse power (shp).

Pump Output Power Amount of power added to the liquid flowing through the pump. Also called the water horse power (whp).

Preferred Operating Region Range of operating flow rates established by the pump user to increase the pump reliability

Pressure Measurement of the value of force per area, traditionally based on one of two datum-referenced values, absolute pressure or gage pressure.

Pressure Head Amount of energy a fluid has due to its static pressure, expressed in units of feet of fluid. When referred to as a differential, pressure head is the difference in pressures between two points in a system, converted to units of feet.

Process Mechanism by which the properties of a fluid are changed. All processes fall into three categories: momentum transfer, heat transfer, or mass transfer.

Process Equipment Unique devices installed in a piping system designed to carry out a process. A heat exchanger is used for heat transfer, a nozzle involves momentum transfer, and a strainer involves mass transfer.

Process Measurement and Control Infrastructure implemented at a facility with piping systems to measure and control key process parameters such as flow rate, pressure, fluid temperature, tank level, or some other fluid property.

Relative Roughness A dimensionless ratio of the absolute roughness to the inside diameter of the pipe.

Resistant Coefficient Method of characterizing the hydraulic performance of a valve, fitting, or other component. This method combines the equivalent lenght with the turbulent friction factor to determine how much resistance to flow the fitting provides.

Reynolds Number A dimensionless ratio that characterizes the flow regime in a pipeline. Used to determine the Darcy friction factor when calculating pipeline head loss.

Shear The lateral deformation produced in a body by an external force, expressed as the ratio of the lateral displacement between two points lying in parallel planes to the vertical distance between the planes.

Shutoff Head Amount of energy added to the fluid with no flow through the pump

Siphon Hydraulic driving force between two points that causes fluid to flow when there is an elevation increase and subsequent drop.

Specific Gravity The ratio of the density of any substance to the density of a standard, water being the standard for liquids and solids, and air being the standard for gases.

Specific Volume Amount of volume occupied by a given weight of fluid, units of ft^3/lb; the reciprocal of density.

Standard Atmospheric Pressure Defined as 14.696 pounds per square inch absolute (psia). The local atmospheric pressure varies with elevation. For example, the local atmospheric pressure in Denver, CO (5200 ft above sea level) is approximately 12.1 psia.

Static Head Amount of fluid energy needed to overcome elevation and pressure differences between two points in a piping system.

Static Pressure Force exerted on a surface per unit area. The static pressure is what is felt if moving along the flow stream.

Stoke A unit of kinematic viscosity, equal to the viscosity of a fluid in poises divided by the density of the fluid in grams per cubic centimeter.

System Resistance Curve Graphical representation of the amount of static and dynamic head in a system as a function of flow rate.

Tank Enclosed vessel used in a piping system to provided short- or long-term storage of a fluid, either a liquid or a gas. Tanks can be open to atmosphere, pressurized by internal pressure, or under a vacuum due to external pressure.

Total Energy Graph Graphical representation of the amount of total fluid energy as a function of distance travelled through the system.

Total Head Total amount of energy added to the fluid by a pump. Previously called Total Developed Head.

Total Pressure Sum of the fluid's static pressure and dynamic pressure (which is the velocity head expressed in units of pressure).

Transducer Component of a process control loop that converts a signal from one form of energy to another. An I/P converts a 4-20 mA electrical signal from a controller into a 3-15 psig pneumatic air signal that can be used at a control valve actuator.

Trim Components of a control valve that have a surface in contact with the fluid flowing through the valve. The valve seat, plug, cage, stem, and guide are all considered part of the valve trim.

Troubleshooting Process by which operating parameters are observed and compared to previous conditions or expected performance in order to methodically identify the root cause of a problem in a piping system.

Vacuum An enclosed volume with a static pressure below the local atmospheric pressure. A vacuum is usually expressed in inches of mercury or inches of water column.

Valve Device installed in a pipeline to start or stop flow, redirect flow, prevent reverse flow, or to connect pipelines together.

Vapor Pressure Pressure at which a liquid at a given temperature changes phase to a gas by evaporation.

Variable Speed Drive (VSD) Mechanism that varies the rotational speed of a shaft by electrical or mechanical means. A variable frequency drive (VFD) changes the frequency of the electrical power to change a motor speed.

Velocity Average velocity of all the molecules of fluid flowing through a pipeline at a given location.

Vessel A type of closed tank used in a piping system that is either pressurized by internal pressure or under a vacuum because its internal pressure is less than the local atmospheric external pressure.

Viscosity Measure of a fluid's ability to flow, or it's resistance to internal deformation when acted upon by a force. Can be expressed as absolute or kinematic viscosity.

Volumetric Flow Rate Volume of fluid passing through a plane per unit time. Expressed in units of gallons per minute (gpm), cubic feet per second (ft^3/sec), or other units.

Volute Part of a centrifugal part that converts velocity head into pressure head due to an increasing cross-sectional flow area as the fluid passes through the volute. Its shape is determined by the pump casing.

Water Horse Power (whp) The amount of power added to the fluid by the pump. Also called the pump output power.

Weight Density The weight per unit volume of a substance or object.

Topic

Index

H

I

K

L

M

N

O

P

R

Customer Note

IF THIS BOOK IS ACCOMPANIED BY SOFTWARE, PLEASE READ THE FOLLOWING BEFORE OPENING THE PACKAGE.

This CD contains software and computer models of some of the piping systems and calculations done in this book as designated by the symbols PF ®. By opening the package, you are agreeing to be bound by the following agreement:

The software product is protected by copyright and all rights are reserved by the author and Engineered Software, Inc. You are licensed to use the demo software and the models included as examples and case studies only.

This software product is included with this book and sold without warranty of any kind, expressed or implied, including but not limited to the implied warranty of merchantability and fitness for a particular purpose. Engineered Software, Inc. assumes no liability of any alleged or actual damages arising from the use of or the inability to use this software.

ABOUT THE PIPE-FLO DEMO

PIPE-FLO Professional Demo version allows a non time limited software access with the following restrictions: Five (5) pipe segments or smaller systems ONLY will calculate, larger systems may be built but will not calculate in this Demo version, limited export functions, and saving of view only files. Projects saved in the trial version cannot be opened in a fully-licensed version of PIPE-FLO Professional or the PIPE-FLO Viewer program.

When prompted select save instead of run and save it to your Desktop. The PIPE-FLO Demo consists of a single file that does not require installation on your computer. To start the demo, click on the PIPE-FLO Demo icon. This program is for use on Windows® operating system only.

This demo may be downloaded from the Engineered Software, Inc. website at: www.eng-software.com/demo.